ORIGINAL SINS

ORIGINAL SINS

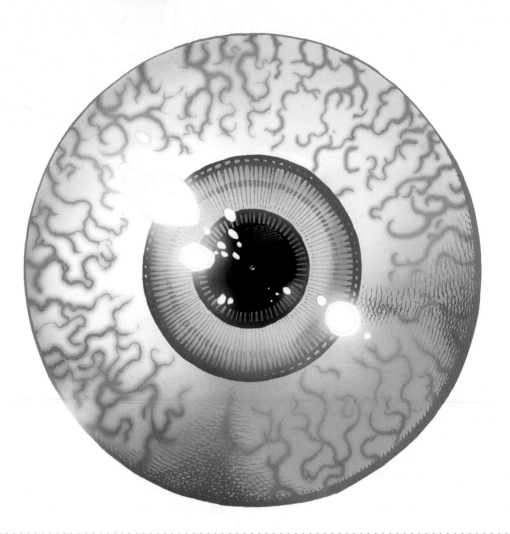

Collection Editor: Jennifer Grünwald • Assistant Editor: Sarah Brunstad • Associate Managing Editor: Alex Starbuck • Editor, Special Projects: Mark D. Beazley
Senior Editor, Special Projects: Jeff Youngquist • SVP Print, Sales & Marketing: David Gabriel • Book Design: Jeff Powell

Editor in Chief: Axel Alonso • Chief Creative Officer: Joe Quesada • Publisher: Dan Buckley Executive • Producer: Alan Fine

ORIGINAL SINS. Contains material originally published in magazine form as ORIGINAL SINS #1-5 and ORIGINAL SIN ANNUAL #1. First printing 2015. ISBN# 978-0-7851-9151-3. Published by MARVEL WORLDWIDE, INC., a subsidiary of MARVEL ENTERTAINMENT, LLC. OFFICE OF PUBLICATION: 135 West 50th Street, New York, NY 10020. Copyright © 2015 MARVEL No similarity between any of the names, characters, persons, and/or institutions in this magazine with those of any living or dead person or institution is intended, and any such similarity which may exist is purely coincidental. **Printed in the U.S.A.** ALAN FINE, President, Marvel Entertainment; DAN BUCKLEY, President, TV, Publishing and Brand Management; JOE QUESADA, Chief Creative Officer; TOM BREVOORT, SVP of Publishing; DAVID BOGART, SVP of Operations & Procurement, Publishing; C.B. CEBULSKI, SVP of Creator & Content Development; DAVID GABRIEL, SVP Print, Sales & Marketing; JIM O'KEEFE, VP of Operations & Logistics; DAN CARR, Executive Director of Publishing Technology; SUSAN CRESPI, Editorial Operations Manager; ALEX MORALES, Publishing Operations Manager; STAN LEE, Chairman Emeritus. For information regarding advertising in Marvel Comics or on Marvel.com, please contact Niza Disla, Director of Marvel Partnerships, at ndisla@marvel.com. For Marvel subscription inquiries, please call 800-217-9158. **Manufactured between 3/6/2015 and 4/13/2015 by R.R. DONNELLEY, INC., SALEM, VA, USA.**

10 9 8 7 6 5 4 3 2 1

ORIGINAL SINS #1-5

Writers: Ryan North, Nathan Edmondson,
Stuart Moore, Frank Tieri, Ty Templeton,
Charles Soule, Dan Slott, James Robinson,
David Abadta & Pablo Durá, Al Ewing
and Chip Zdarsky

Artists: Ramon Villalobos, Mike Perkins, Rick
Geary, Raffaele Ienco, Ty Templeton, Ryan Brown,
Mark Bagley & Joe Rubinstein, Alex Maleev, Erica
Henderson, Butch Guice & Scott Hanna
and Chip Zdarsky

Color Artists: Jordan Gibson, Andy Troy,
Ive Svorcina, Brad Anderson, Paul Mounts,
Edgar Delgado, Cris Peter, Erica Henderson,
Matthew Wilson and Chip Zdarsky

Letterer: VC's Clayton Cowles

Cover Art: Mark Brooks

Assistant Editors: Jake Thomas & Devin Lewis

Editors: Tom Brevoort, Wil Moss & Nick Lowe

ORIGINAL SIN ANNUAL

Writer: Jason Latour

Artist: Enis Cisic

Color Artist: Chris Chuckry

Letterers: Chris Eliopoulos & Clayton Cowles

Cover Art: Julian Totino Tedesco

Assistant Editor: Jake Thomas

Editors: Tom Brevoort with Wil Moss

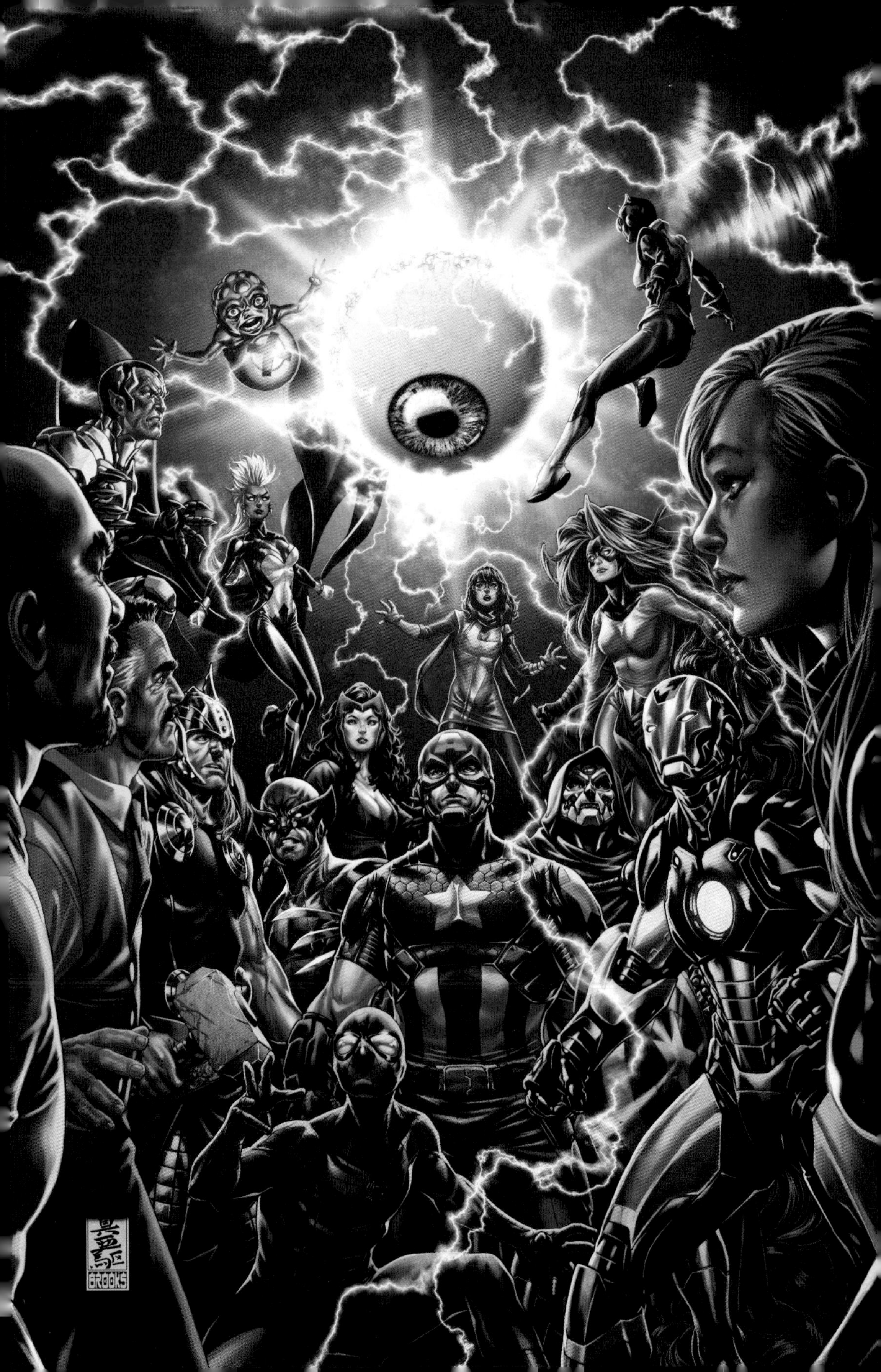
BROOKS

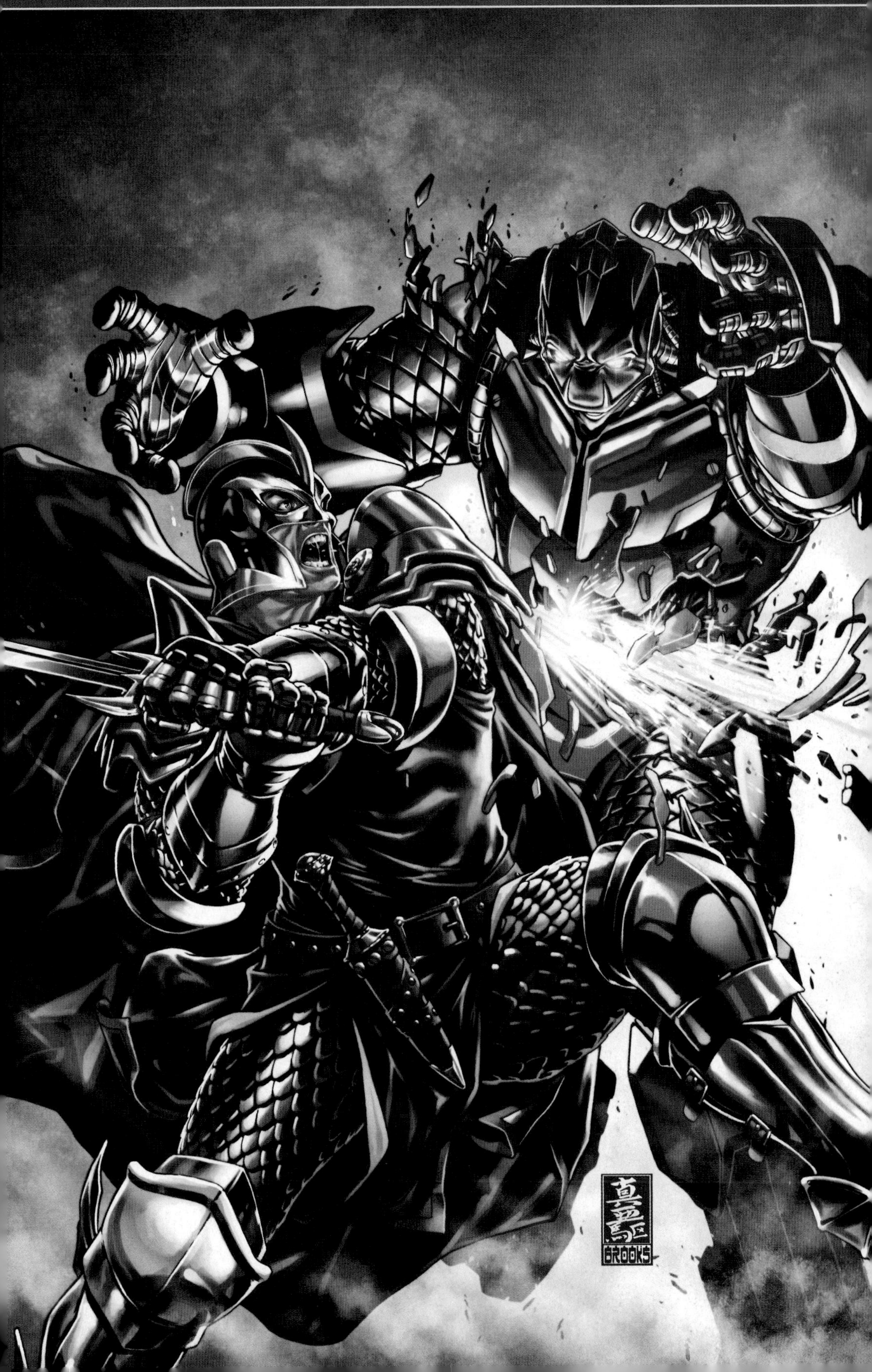
BROOKS

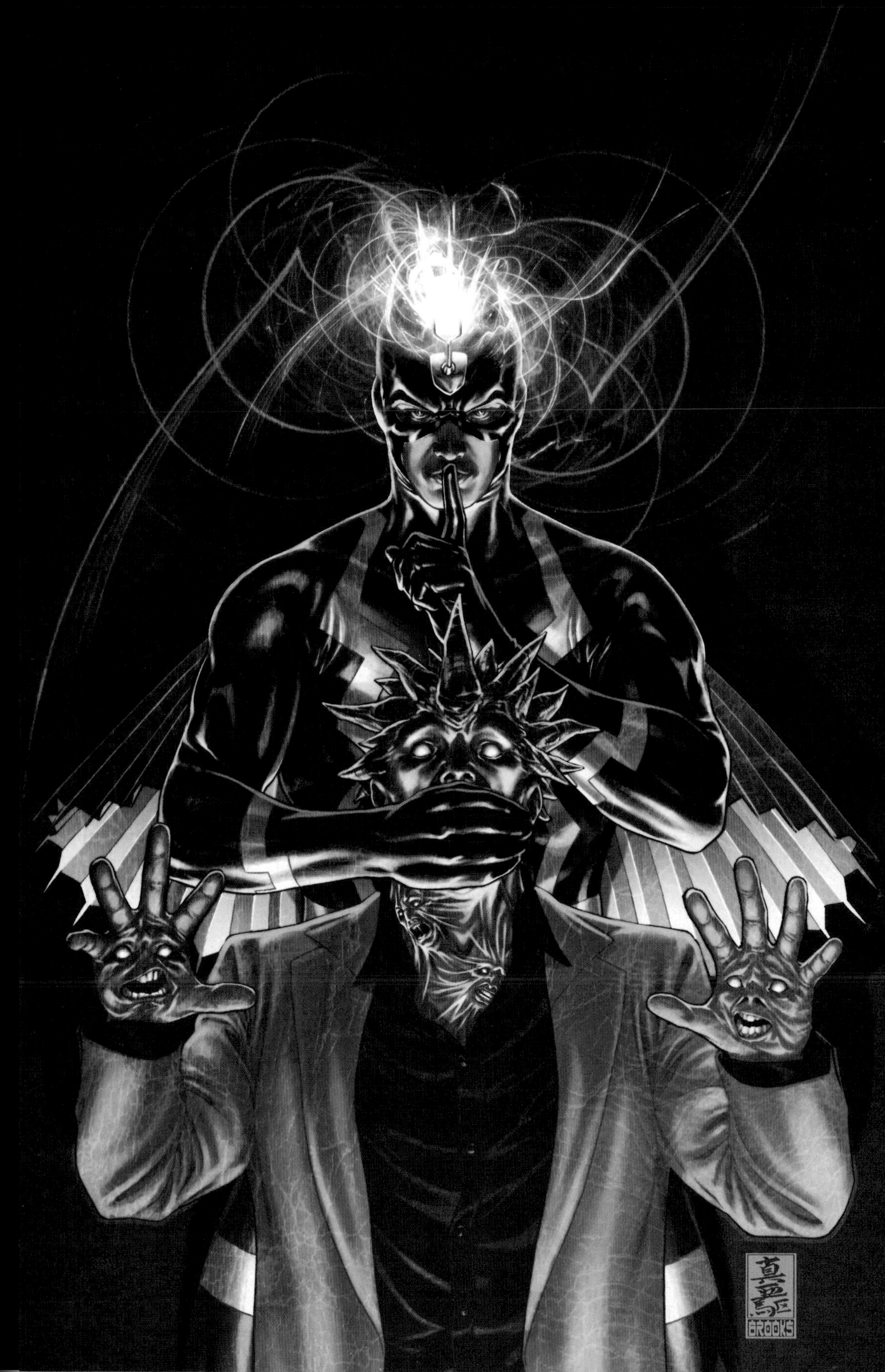
BROOKS

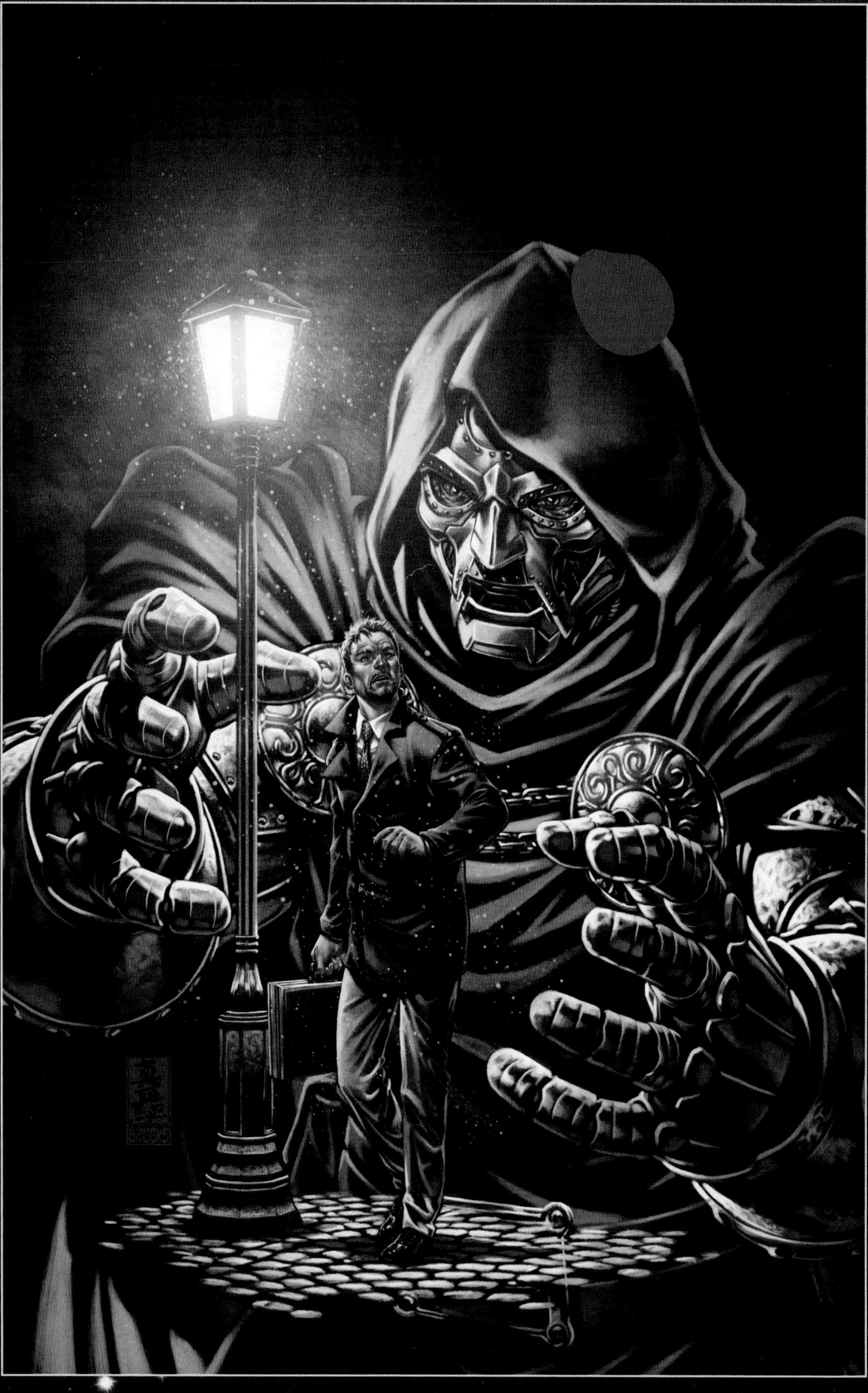

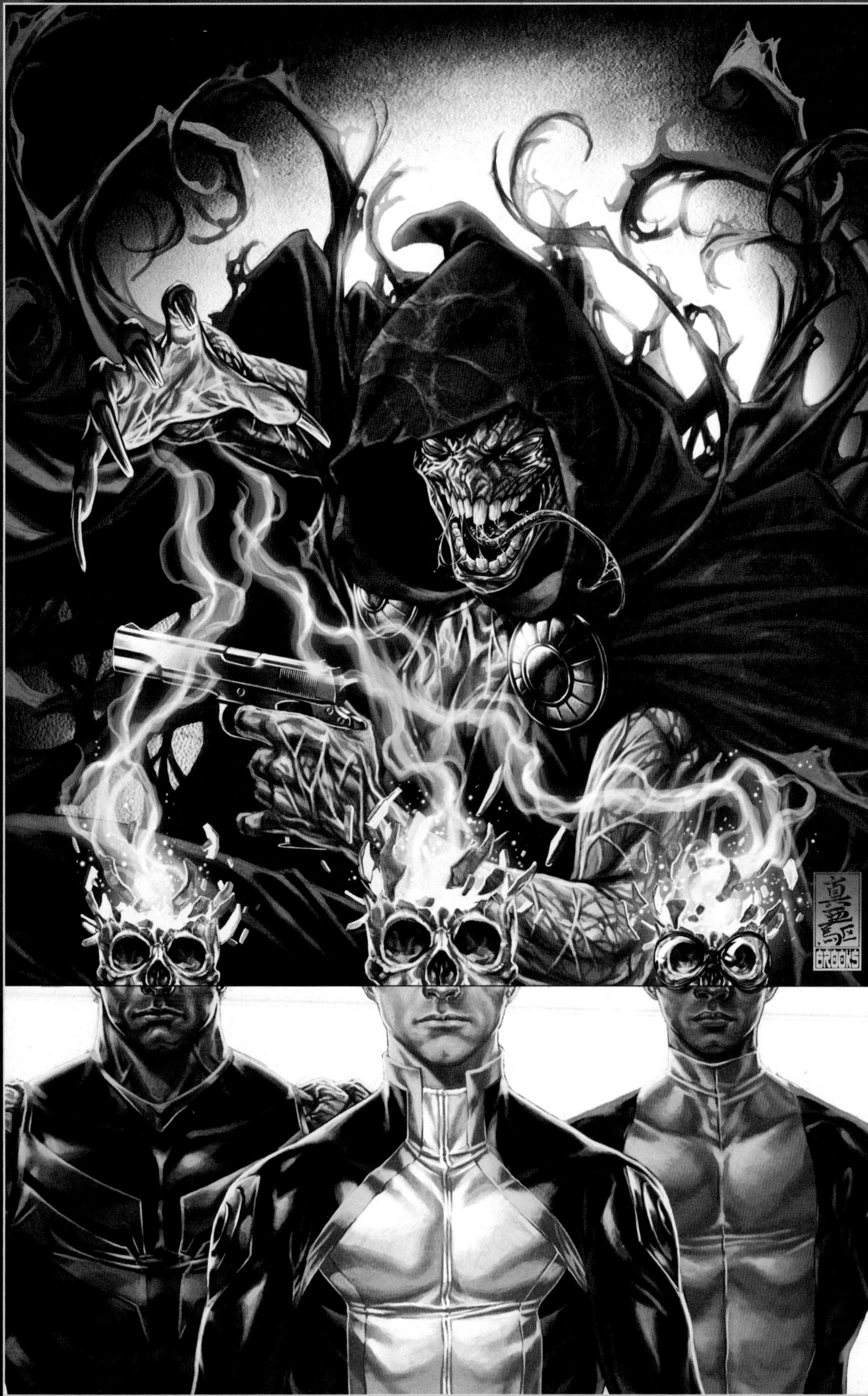
BROOKS

ORIGINAL SINS

THE WATCHER
HAS BEEN MURDERED!

HIS EYES WERE STOLEN.

DURING A CONFLICT WITH THE THIEVES,
ONE OF THE WATCHER'S
EYES DETONATED...

...IMPARTING SECRETS OF THE MARVEL
UNIVERSE ONTO ANYONE WITHIN THE
BLAST RANGE.

YOUNG AVENGERS

ARE A COLLECTIVE OF EARTH'S
MIGHTIEST HEROES WHO
ARE...WELL...YOUNGER THAN USUAL, I
SUPPOSE. PREVIOUSLY IN THE
ADVENTURES OF THE YOUNG
AVENGERS, THE TEAM SAVED THE
WORLD. YAY! AND THEN KATE BISHOP
AND MARVEL BOY BROKE UP. SAD!

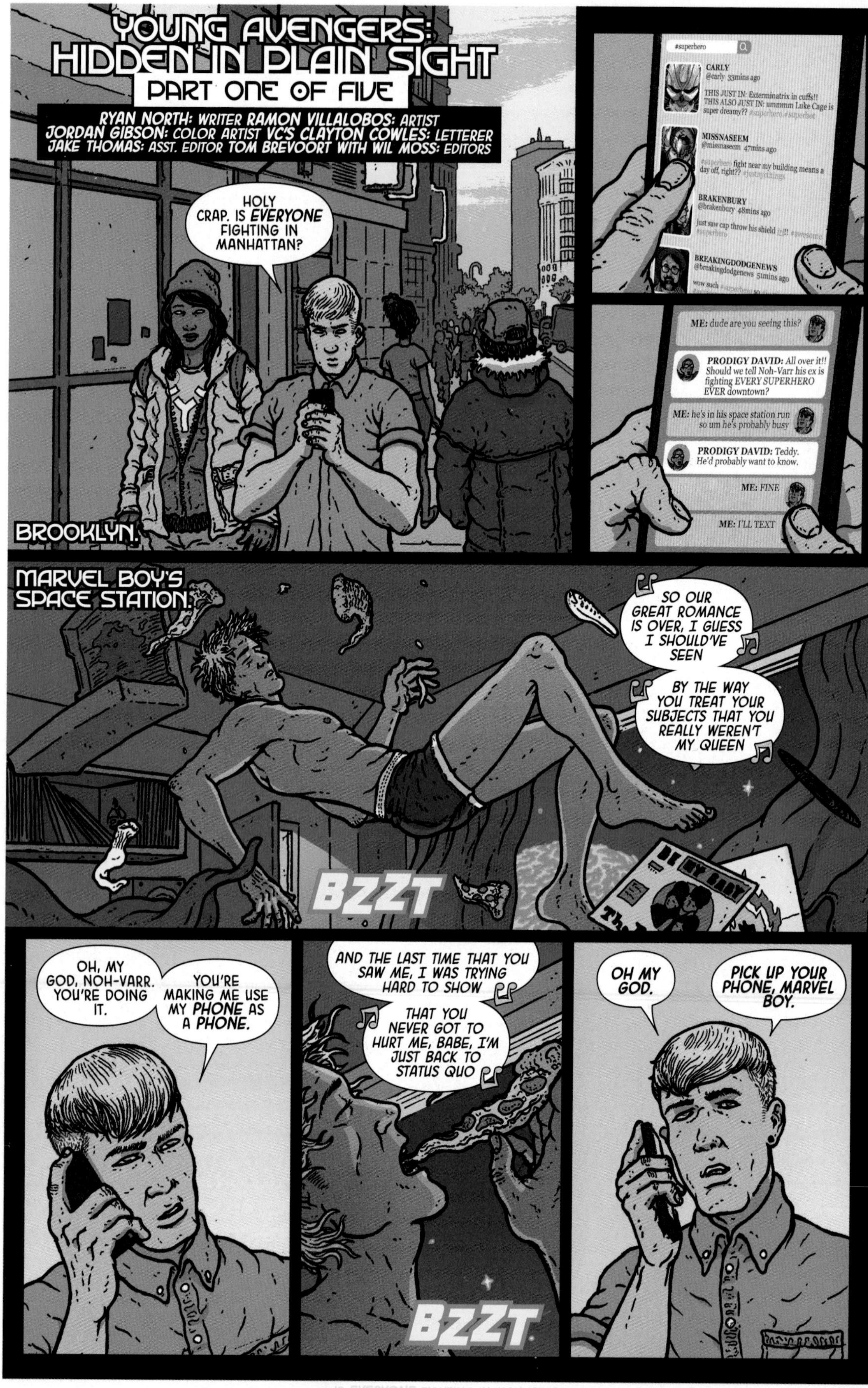

YOUNG AVENGERS: HIDDEN IN PLAIN SIGHT
PART ONE OF FIVE
RYAN NORTH: WRITER RAMON VILLALOBOS: ARTIST
JORDAN GIBSON: COLOR ARTIST VC'S CLAYTON COWLES: LETTERER
JAKE THOMAS: ASST. EDITOR TOM BREVOORT WITH WIL MOSS: EDITORS
HOLY CRAP. IS EVERYONE FIGHTING IN MANHATTAN?
BROOKLYN.
#superhero
CARLY
@carly 33mins ago
THIS JUST IN: Exterminatrix in cuffs!! THIS ALSO JUST IN: ummmm Luke Cage is super dreamy??
MISSNASEEM
@missnaseem 47mins ago
fight near my building means a day off, right??
BRAKENBURY
@brakenbury 48mins ago
just saw cap throw his shield
BREAKINGDODGENEWS
@breakingdodgenews 51mins ago
wow such
ME: dude are you seeing this?
PRODIGY DAVID: All over it!! Should we tell Noh-Varr his ex is fighting EVERY SUPERHERO EVER downtown?
ME: he's in his space station run so um he's probably busy
PRODIGY DAVID: Teddy. He'd probably want to know.
ME: FINE
ME: I'LL TEXT
MARVEL BOY'S SPACE STATION.
SO OUR GREAT ROMANCE IS OVER, I GUESS I SHOULD'VE SEEN
BY THE WAY YOU TREAT YOUR SUBJECTS THAT YOU REALLY WEREN'T MY QUEEN
BZZT
OH, MY GOD, NOH-VARR. YOU'RE DOING IT.
YOU'RE MAKING ME USE MY PHONE AS A PHONE.
AND THE LAST TIME THAT YOU SAW ME, I WAS TRYING HARD TO SHOW
THAT YOU NEVER GOT TO HURT ME, BABE, I'M JUST BACK TO STATUS QUO
BZZT
OH MY GOD.
PICK UP YOUR PHONE, MARVEL BOY.

IS *EVERYONE* FIGHTING IN MANHATTAN? SHOULD...SHOULD *I* BE FIGHTING IN MANHATTAN?

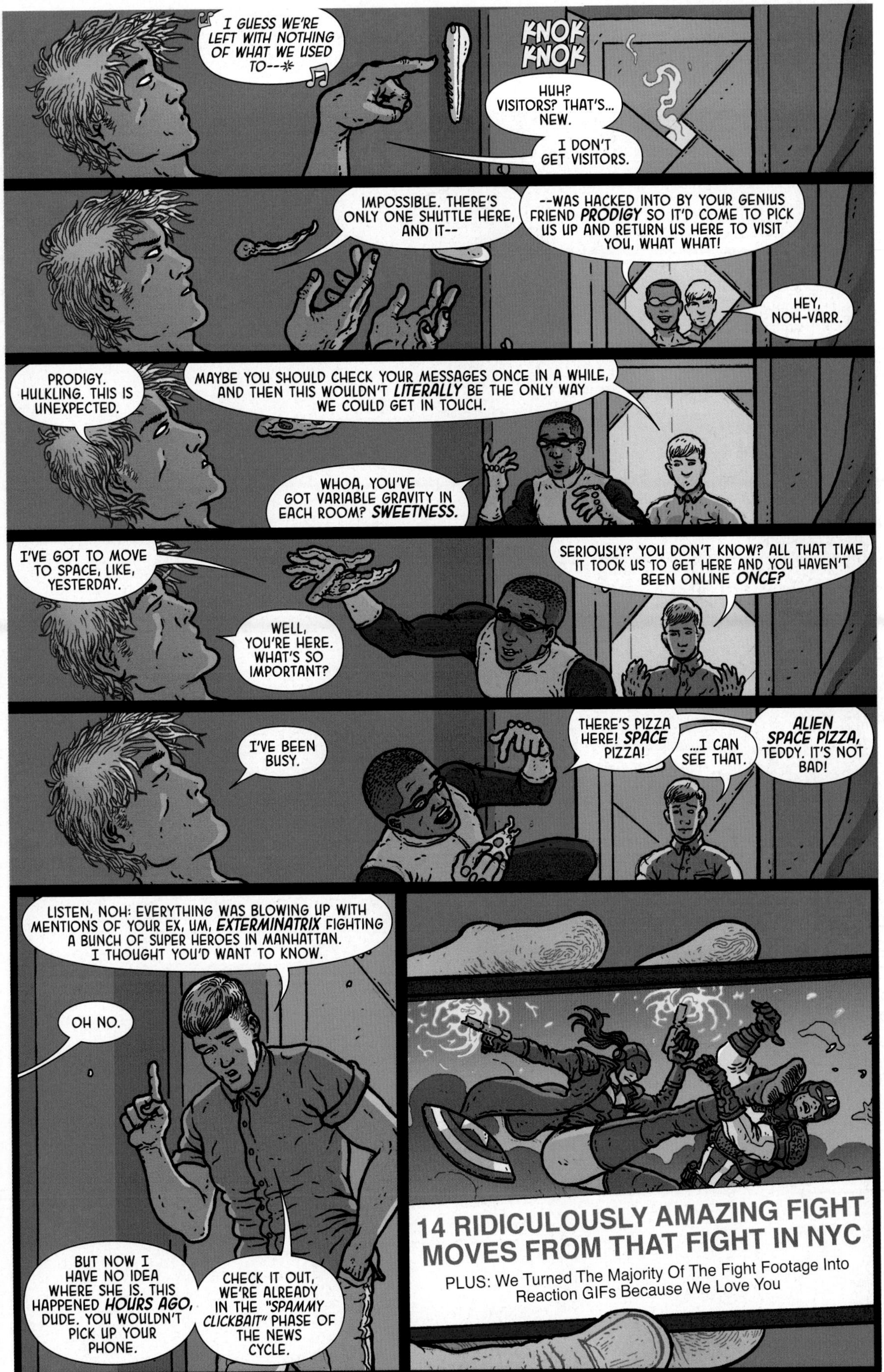
I GUESS WE'RE LEFT WITH NOTHING OF WHAT WE USED TO--
KNOK KNOK
HUH? VISITORS? THAT'S... NEW.
I DON'T GET VISITORS.
IMPOSSIBLE. THERE'S ONLY ONE SHUTTLE HERE, AND IT--
--WAS HACKED INTO BY YOUR GENIUS FRIEND PRODIGY SO IT'D COME TO PICK US UP AND RETURN US HERE TO VISIT YOU, WHAT WHAT!
HEY, NOH-VARR.
PRODIGY. HULKLING. THIS IS UNEXPECTED.
MAYBE YOU SHOULD CHECK YOUR MESSAGES ONCE IN A WHILE, AND THEN THIS WOULDN'T LITERALLY BE THE ONLY WAY WE COULD GET IN TOUCH.
WHOA, YOU'VE GOT VARIABLE GRAVITY IN EACH ROOM? SWEETNESS.
I'VE GOT TO MOVE TO SPACE, LIKE, YESTERDAY.
WELL, YOU'RE HERE. WHAT'S SO IMPORTANT?
SERIOUSLY? YOU DON'T KNOW? ALL THAT TIME IT TOOK US TO GET HERE AND YOU HAVEN'T BEEN ONLINE ONCE?
I'VE BEEN BUSY.
THERE'S PIZZA HERE! SPACE PIZZA!
...I CAN SEE THAT.
ALIEN SPACE PIZZA, TEDDY. IT'S NOT BAD!
LISTEN, NOH: EVERYTHING WAS BLOWING UP WITH MENTIONS OF YOUR EX, UM, EXTERMINATRIX FIGHTING A BUNCH OF SUPER HEROES IN MANHATTAN. I THOUGHT YOU'D WANT TO KNOW.
OH NO.
BUT NOW I HAVE NO IDEA WHERE SHE IS. THIS HAPPENED HOURS AGO, DUDE. YOU WOULDN'T PICK UP YOUR PHONE.
CHECK IT OUT, WE'RE ALREADY IN THE "SPAMMY CLICKBAIT" PHASE OF THE NEWS CYCLE.
14 RIDICULOUSLY AMAZING FIGHT MOVES FROM THAT FIGHT IN NYC
PLUS: We Turned The Majority Of The Fight Footage Into Reaction GIFs Because We Love You

EATING PIZZA IN SPACE = EVERYONE'S SECRET LIFE GOAL?? IT SEEMS LIKELY.

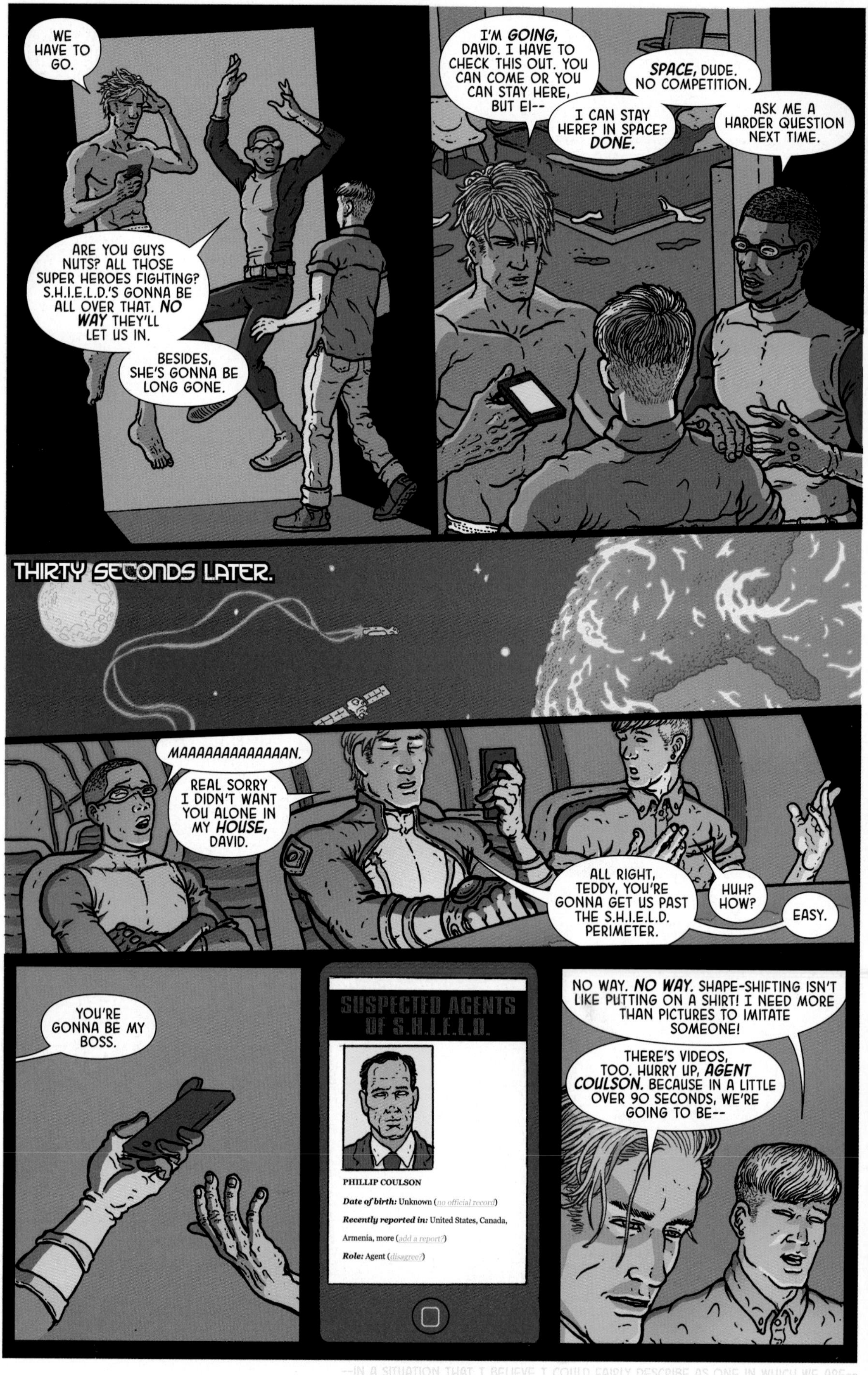

WE HAVE TO GO.
ARE YOU GUYS NUTS? ALL THOSE SUPER HEROES FIGHTING? S.H.I.E.L.D.'S GONNA BE ALL OVER THAT. NO WAY THEY'LL LET US IN.
BESIDES, SHE'S GONNA BE LONG GONE.
I'M GOING, DAVID. I HAVE TO CHECK THIS OUT. YOU CAN COME OR YOU CAN STAY HERE, BUT EI--
I CAN STAY HERE? IN SPACE? DONE.
SPACE, DUDE. NO COMPETITION.
ASK ME A HARDER QUESTION NEXT TIME.
THIRTY SECONDS LATER.
MAAAAAAAAAAAAAN.
REAL SORRY I DIDN'T WANT YOU ALONE IN MY HOUSE, DAVID.
ALL RIGHT, TEDDY, YOU'RE GONNA GET US PAST THE S.H.I.E.L.D. PERIMETER.
HUH? HOW?
EASY.
YOU'RE GONNA BE MY BOSS.
SUSPECTED AGENTS OF S.H.I.E.L.D.
PHILLIP COULSON
Date of birth: Unknown (no official record)
Recently reported in: United States, Canada, Armenia, more (add a report?)
Role: Agent (disagree?)
NO WAY. NO WAY. SHAPE-SHIFTING ISN'T LIKE PUTTING ON A SHIRT! I NEED MORE THAN PICTURES TO IMITATE SOMEONE!
THERE'S VIDEOS, TOO. HURRY UP, AGENT COULSON. BECAUSE IN A LITTLE OVER 90 SECONDS, WE'RE GOING TO BE--

--IN A SITUATION THAT I BELIEVE I COULD FAIRLY DESCRIBE AS ONE IN WHICH WE ARE--

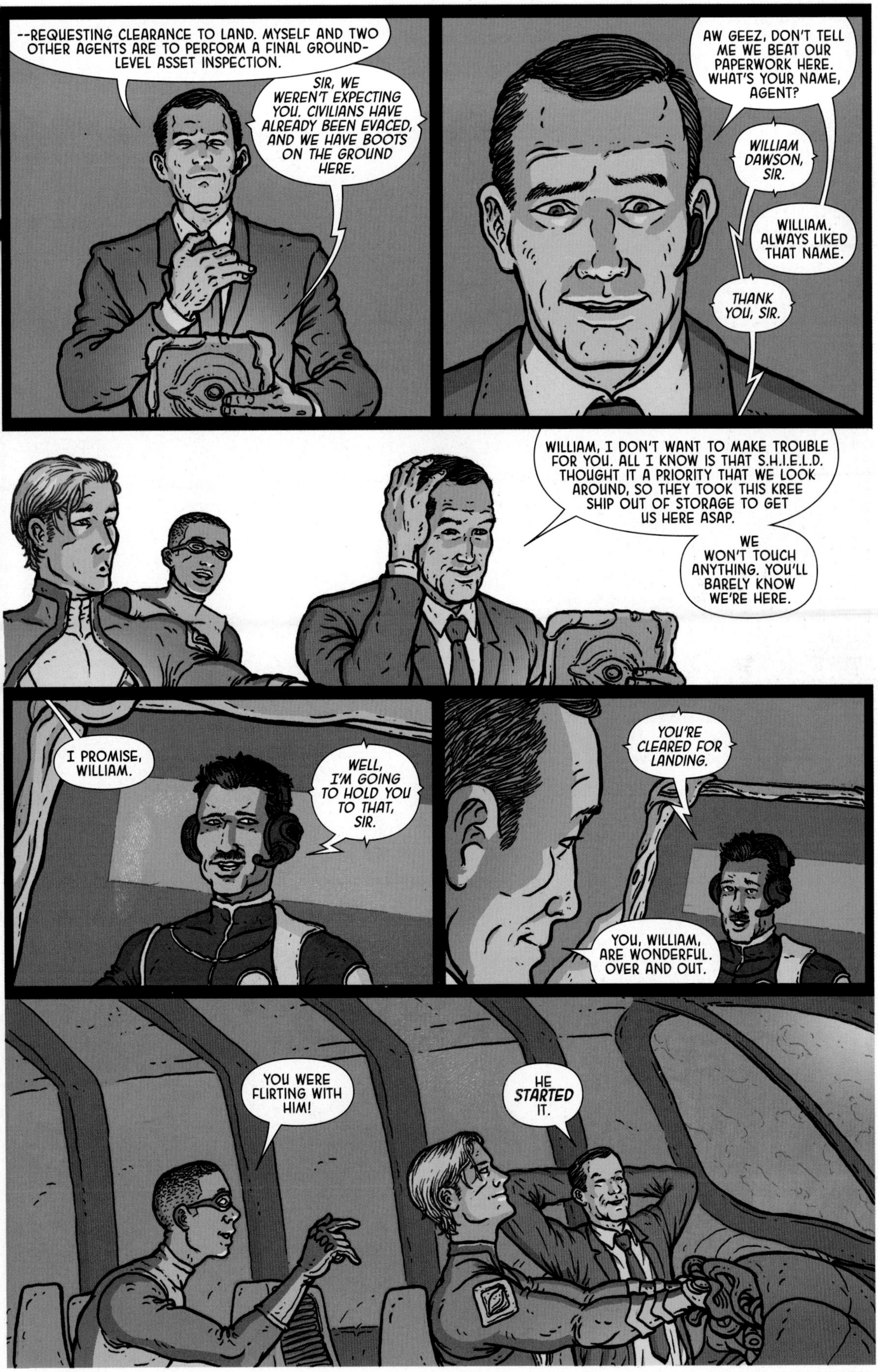
--REQUESTING CLEARANCE TO LAND. MYSELF AND TWO OTHER AGENTS ARE TO PERFORM A FINAL GROUND-LEVEL ASSET INSPECTION.
SIR, WE WEREN'T EXPECTING YOU. CIVILIANS HAVE ALREADY BEEN EVACED, AND WE HAVE BOOTS ON THE GROUND HERE.
AW GEEZ, DON'T TELL ME WE BEAT OUR PAPERWORK HERE. WHAT'S YOUR NAME, AGENT?
WILLIAM DAWSON, SIR.
WILLIAM. ALWAYS LIKED THAT NAME.
THANK YOU, SIR.
WILLIAM, I DON'T WANT TO MAKE TROUBLE FOR YOU. ALL I KNOW IS THAT S.H.I.E.L.D. THOUGHT IT A PRIORITY THAT WE LOOK AROUND, SO THEY TOOK THIS KREE SHIP OUT OF STORAGE TO GET US HERE ASAP.
WE WON'T TOUCH ANYTHING. YOU'LL BARELY KNOW WE'RE HERE.
I PROMISE, WILLIAM.
WELL, I'M GOING TO HOLD YOU TO THAT, SIR.
YOU'RE CLEARED FOR LANDING.
YOU, WILLIAM, ARE WONDERFUL. OVER AND OUT.
YOU WERE FLIRTING WITH HIM!
HE *STARTED* IT.

IT'LL BE AWKWARD WHEN THE REAL AGENT COULSON RUNS INTO AGENT DAWSON AT THE S.H.I.E.L.D. CHRISTMAS PARTY THIS YEAR. OR MAYBE...NOT AWKWARD AT ALL?

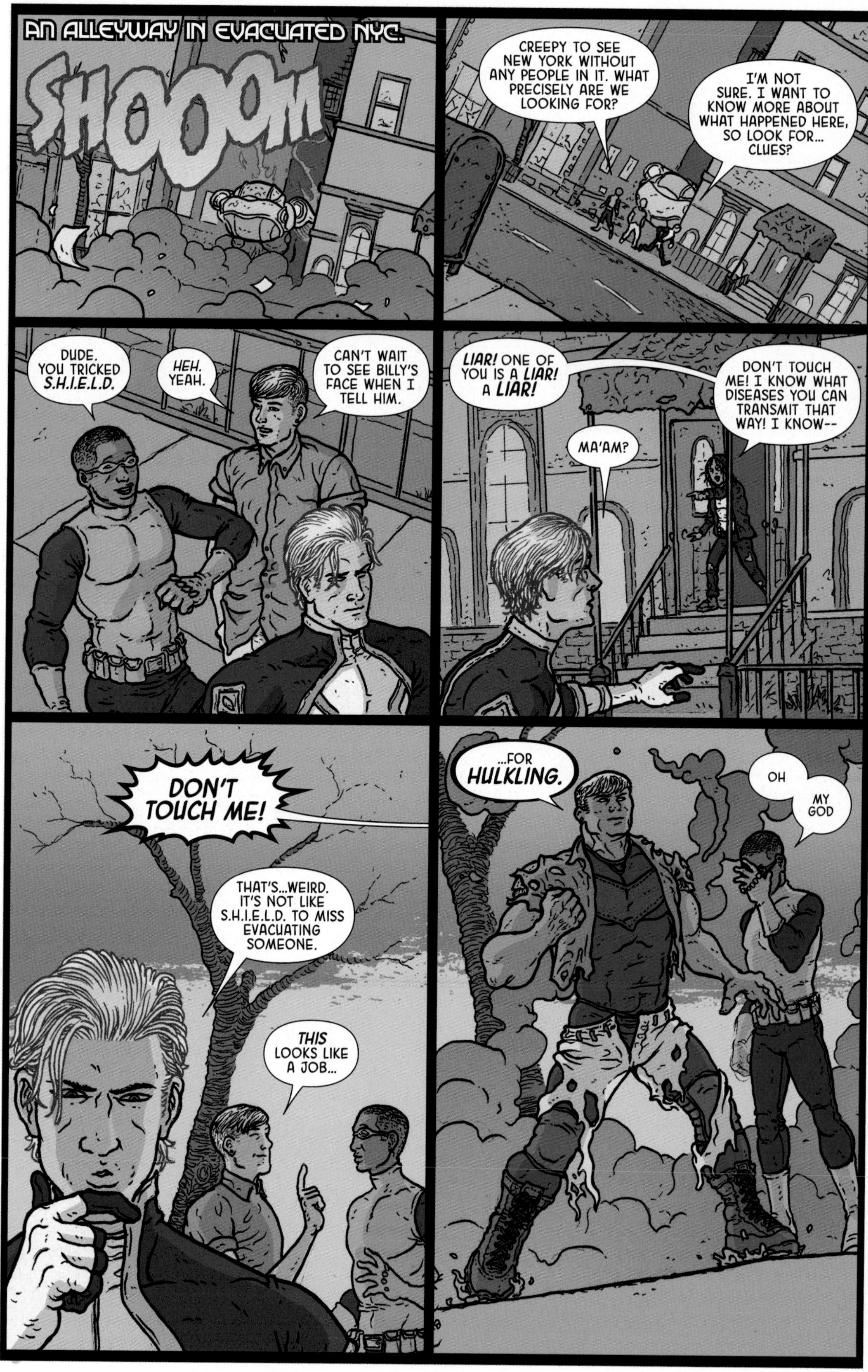
AN ALLEYWAY IN EVACUATED NYC.
SHOOOM
CREEPY TO SEE NEW YORK WITHOUT ANY PEOPLE IN IT. WHAT PRECISELY ARE WE LOOKING FOR?
I'M NOT SURE. I WANT TO KNOW MORE ABOUT WHAT HAPPENED HERE, SO LOOK FOR... CLUES?
DUDE. YOU TRICKED S.H.I.E.L.D.
HEH. YEAH.
CAN'T WAIT TO SEE BILLY'S FACE WHEN I TELL HIM.
LIAR! ONE OF YOU IS A LIAR! A LIAR!
DON'T TOUCH ME! I KNOW WHAT DISEASES YOU CAN TRANSMIT THAT WAY! I KNOW--
MA'AM?
DON'T TOUCH ME!
THAT'S...WEIRD. IT'S NOT LIKE S.H.I.E.L.D. TO MISS EVACUATING SOMEONE.
THIS LOOKS LIKE A JOB...
...FOR HULKLING.
OH
MY GOD

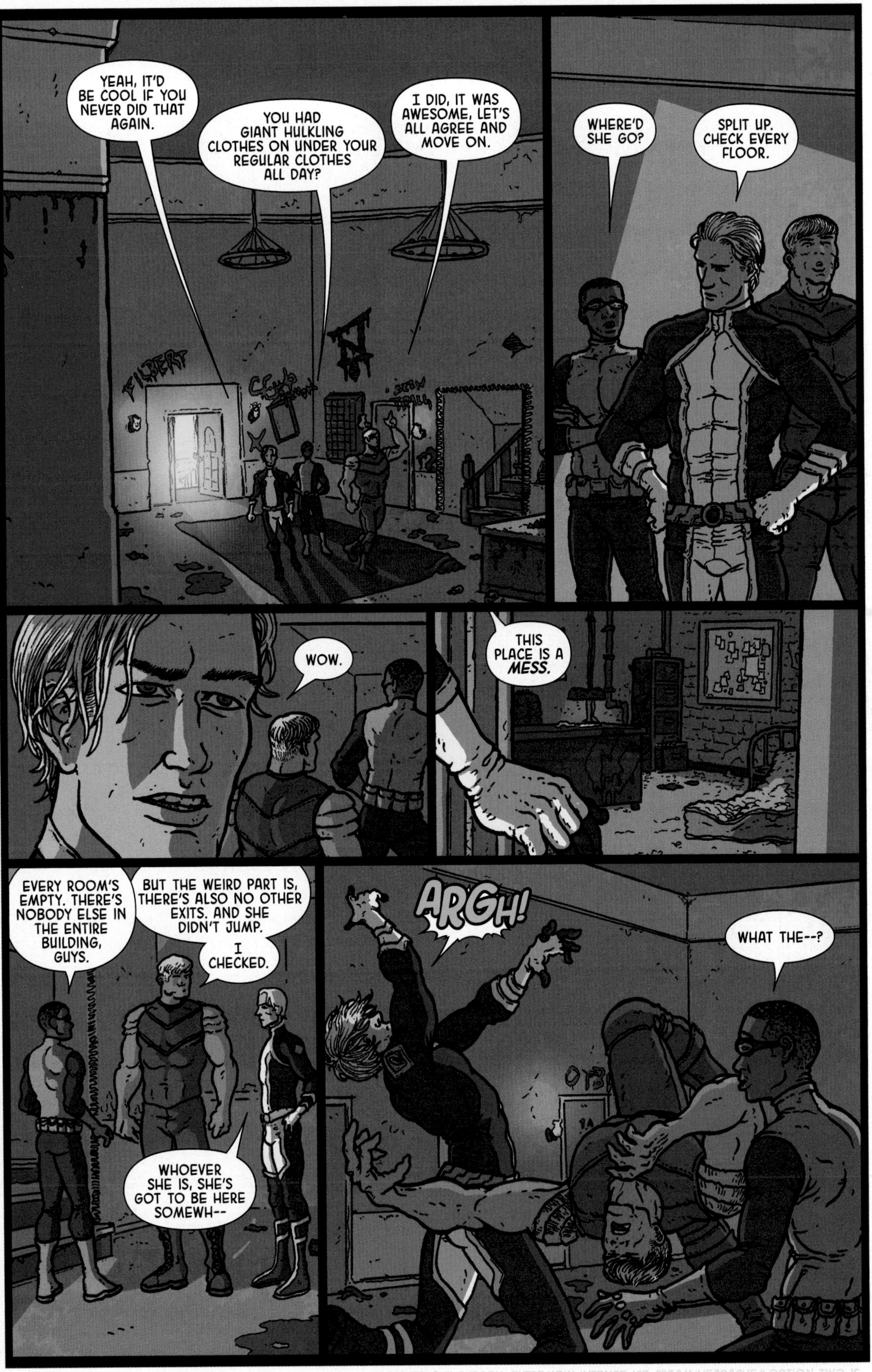

YEAH, IT'D BE COOL IF YOU NEVER DID THAT AGAIN.
YOU HAD GIANT HULKLING CLOTHES ON UNDER YOUR REGULAR CLOTHES ALL DAY?
I DID, IT WAS AWESOME, LET'S ALL AGREE AND MOVE ON.
WHERE'D SHE GO?
SPLIT UP. CHECK EVERY FLOOR.
WOW.
THIS PLACE IS A *MESS.*
EVERY ROOM'S EMPTY. THERE'S NOBODY ELSE IN THE ENTIRE BUILDING, GUYS.
BUT THE WEIRD PART IS, THERE'S ALSO NO OTHER EXITS. AND SHE DIDN'T JUMP.
I CHECKED.
WHOEVER SHE IS, SHE'S GOT TO BE HERE SOMEWH--
ARGH!
WHAT THE--?

THERE'S TWO OPTIONS HERE. OPTION ONE IS *"DELAYED BUT SUDDEN, EXTREMELY INTENSE ICE CREAM HEADACHE."* OPTION TWO IS...

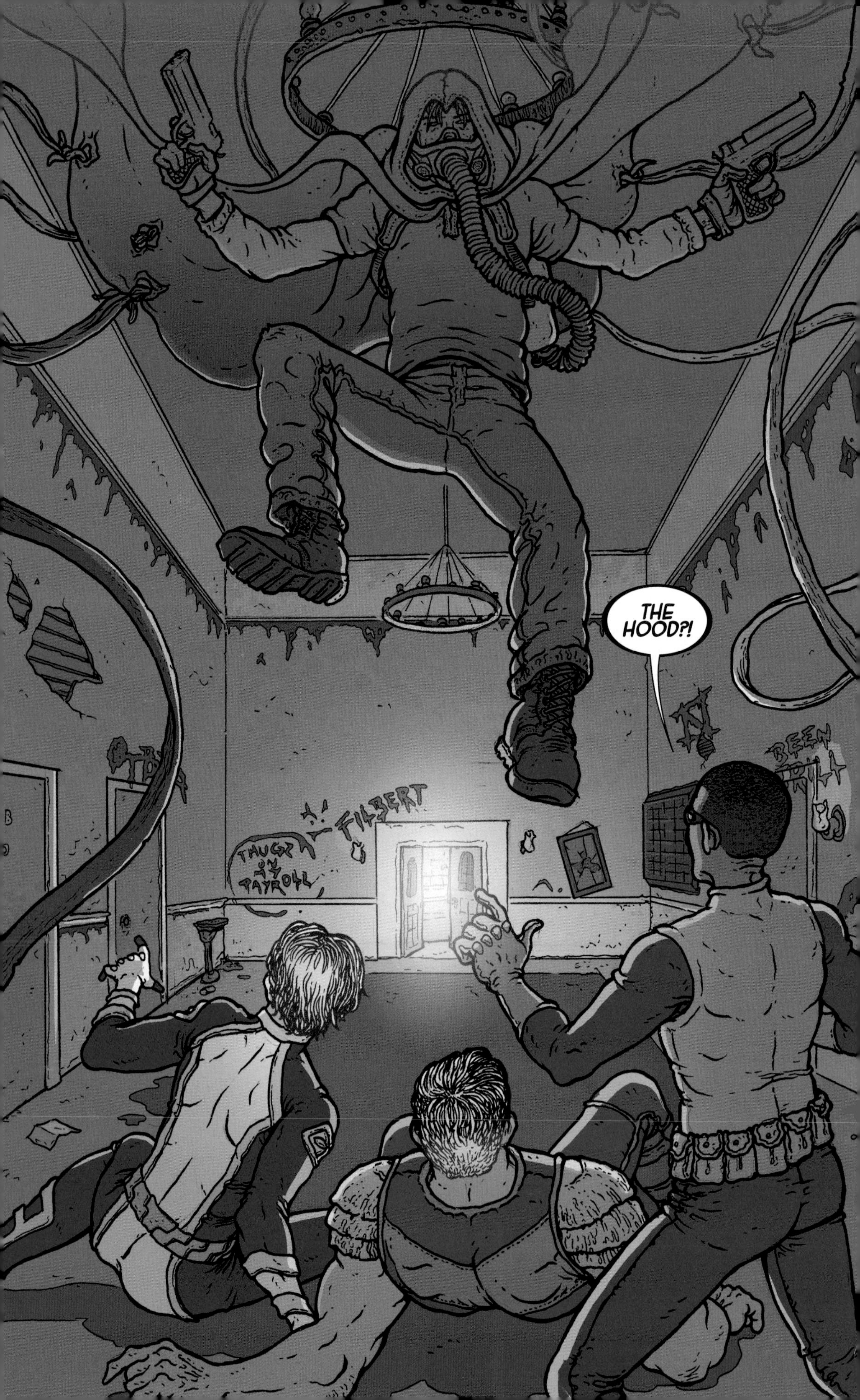
THE HOOD?!
FILBERT

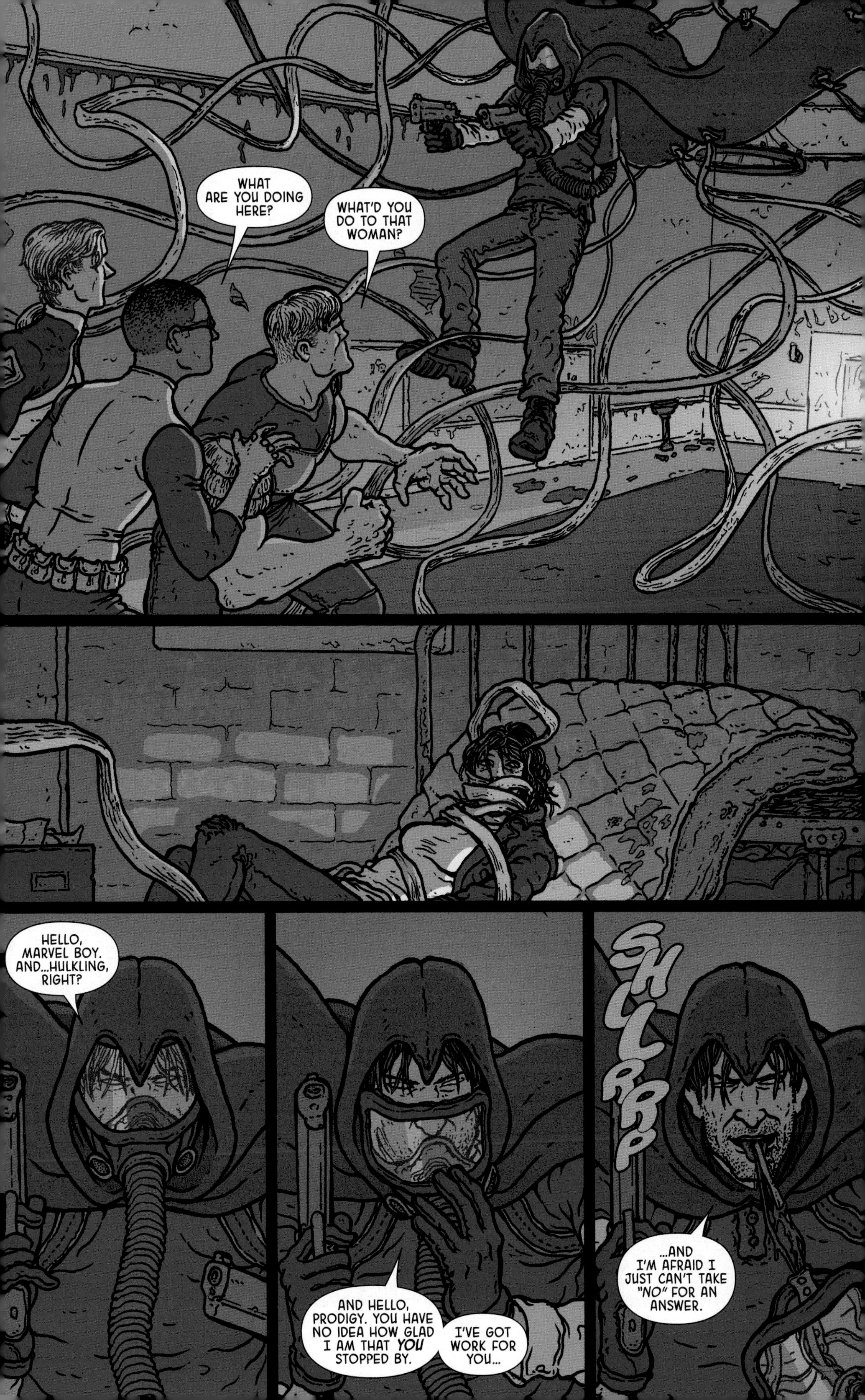
WHAT ARE YOU DOING HERE?
WHAT'D YOU DO TO THAT WOMAN?
HELLO, MARVEL BOY. AND...HULKLING, RIGHT?
AND HELLO, PRODIGY. YOU HAVE NO IDEA HOW GLAD I AM THAT YOU STOPPED BY.
I'VE GOT WORK FOR YOU...
SHLRRP
...AND I'M AFRAID I JUST CAN'T TAKE "NO" FOR AN ANSWER.

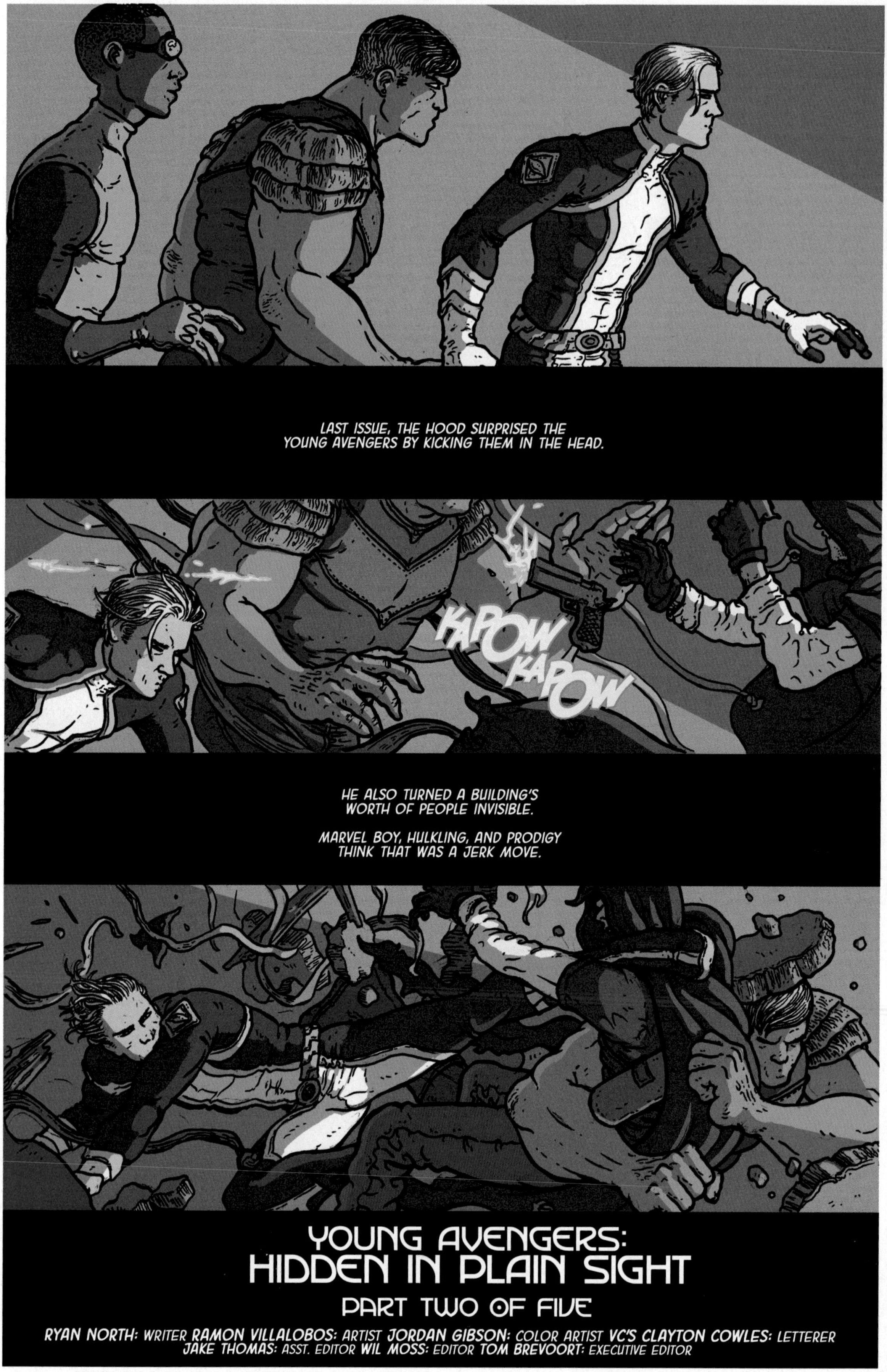
LAST ISSUE, THE HOOD SURPRISED THE YOUNG AVENGERS BY KICKING THEM IN THE HEAD.
KAPOW KAPOW
HE ALSO TURNED A BUILDING'S WORTH OF PEOPLE INVISIBLE.
MARVEL BOY, HULKLING, AND PRODIGY THINK THAT WAS A JERK MOVE.
YOUNG AVENGERS: HIDDEN IN PLAIN SIGHT
PART TWO OF FIVE
RYAN NORTH: WRITER RAMON VILLALOBOS: ARTIST JORDAN GIBSON: COLOR ARTIST VC'S CLAYTON COWLES: LETTERER
JAKE THOMAS: ASST. EDITOR WIL MOSS: EDITOR TOM BREVOORT: EXECUTIVE EDITOR

DURING THE BLACK PANELS, HULKLING AND MARVEL BOY ARE PUNCHING THE HOOD SO HARD THAT THE LIGHTS GO OUT IN THE BUILDING. IF YOU DON'T THINK THAT'S POSSIBLE, YOU OBVIOUSLY HAVEN'T PUNCHED HARD ENOUGH YET.

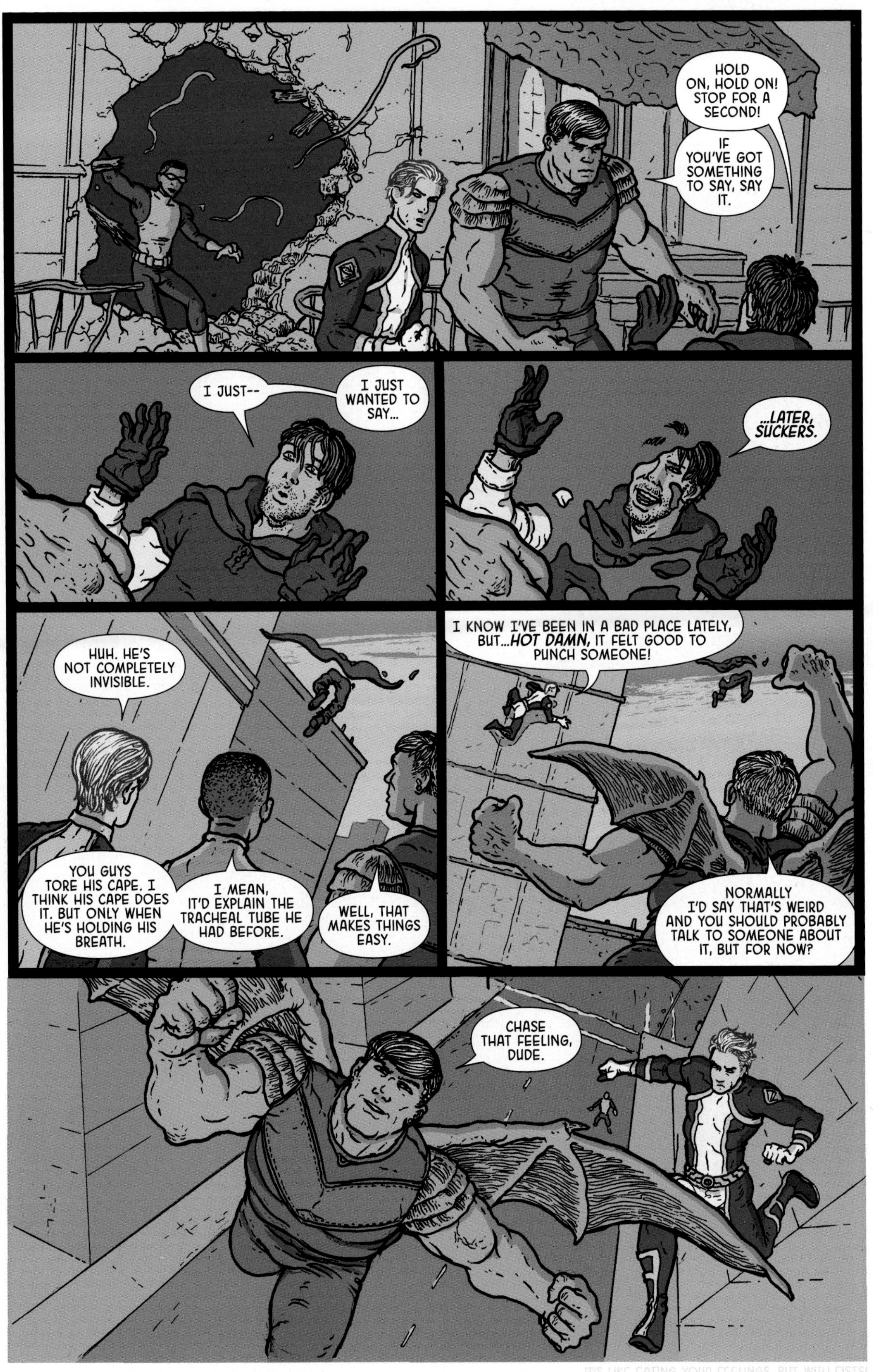
HOLD ON, HOLD ON! STOP FOR A SECOND!
IF YOU'VE GOT SOMETHING TO SAY, SAY IT.
I JUST--
I JUST WANTED TO SAY...
...LATER, SUCKERS.
HUH. HE'S NOT COMPLETELY INVISIBLE.
YOU GUYS TORE HIS CAPE. I THINK HIS CAPE DOES IT. BUT ONLY WHEN HE'S HOLDING HIS BREATH.
I MEAN, IT'D EXPLAIN THE TRACHEAL TUBE HE HAD BEFORE.
WELL, THAT MAKES THINGS EASY.
I KNOW I'VE BEEN IN A BAD PLACE LATELY, BUT...HOT DAMN, IT FELT GOOD TO PUNCH SOMEONE!
NORMALLY I'D SAY THAT'S WEIRD AND YOU SHOULD PROBABLY TALK TO SOMEONE ABOUT IT, BUT FOR NOW?
CHASE THAT FEELING, DUDE.

IT'S LIKE EATING YOUR FEELINGS, BUT WITH FISTS!

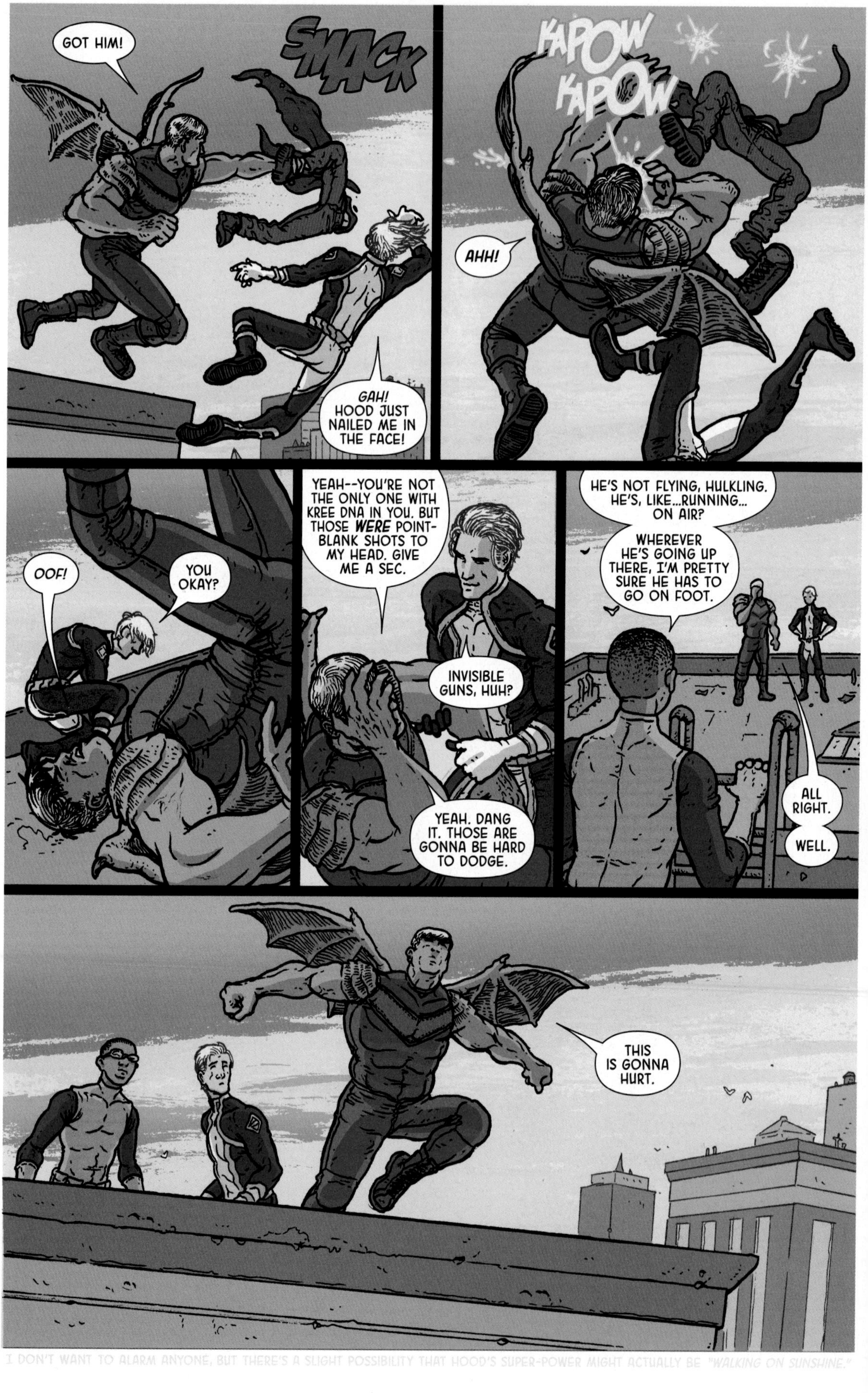
GOT HIM!
SMACK
GAH! HOOD JUST NAILED ME IN THE FACE!
KAPOW KAPOW
AHH!
OOF!
YOU OKAY?
YEAH--YOU'RE NOT THE ONLY ONE WITH KREE DNA IN YOU. BUT THOSE *WERE* POINT-BLANK SHOTS TO MY HEAD. GIVE ME A SEC.
INVISIBLE GUNS, HUH?
YEAH. DANG IT. THOSE ARE GONNA BE HARD TO DODGE.
HE'S NOT FLYING, HULKLING. HE'S, LIKE...RUNNING... ON AIR?
WHEREVER HE'S GOING UP THERE, I'M PRETTY SURE HE HAS TO GO ON FOOT.
ALL RIGHT.
WELL.
THIS IS GONNA HURT.

I DON'T WANT TO ALARM ANYONE, BUT THERE'S A SLIGHT POSSIBILITY THAT HOOD'S SUPER-POWER MIGHT ACTUALLY BE *"WALKING ON SUNSHINE."*

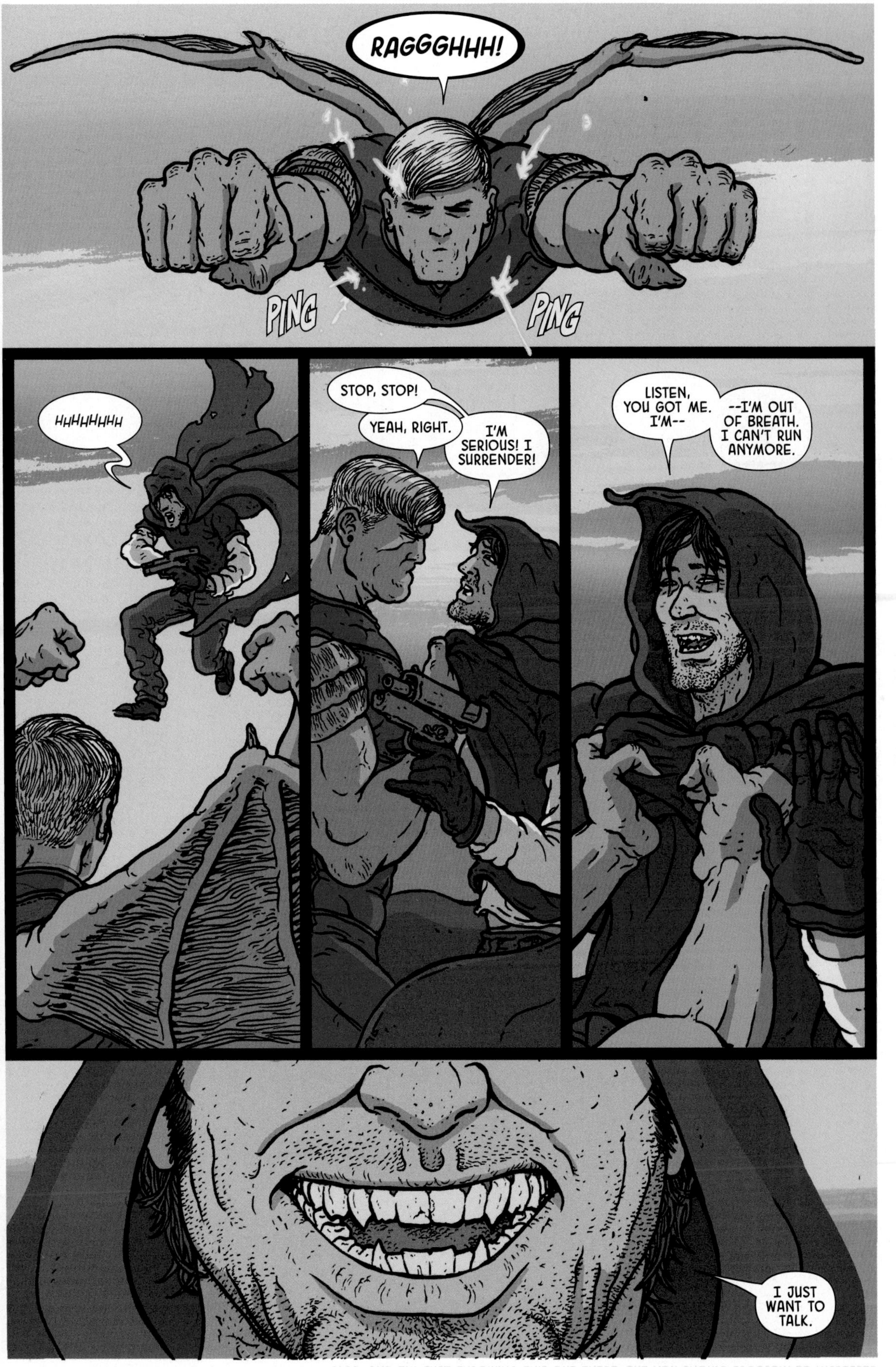
RAGGGHHH!
PING
PING
HHHHHHHH
STOP, STOP!
YEAH, RIGHT.
I'M SERIOUS! I SURRENDER!
LISTEN, YOU GOT ME. I'M--
--I'M OUT OF BREATH. I CAN'T RUN ANYMORE.
I JUST WANT TO TALK.

ALSO, AND I'M JUST THROWING THIS OUT THERE, BUT YOU SHOULD PROBABLY BE IMPRESSED
I COULD HOLD MY BREATH WHILE RUNNING FOR THAT LONG IN THE FIRST PLACE.

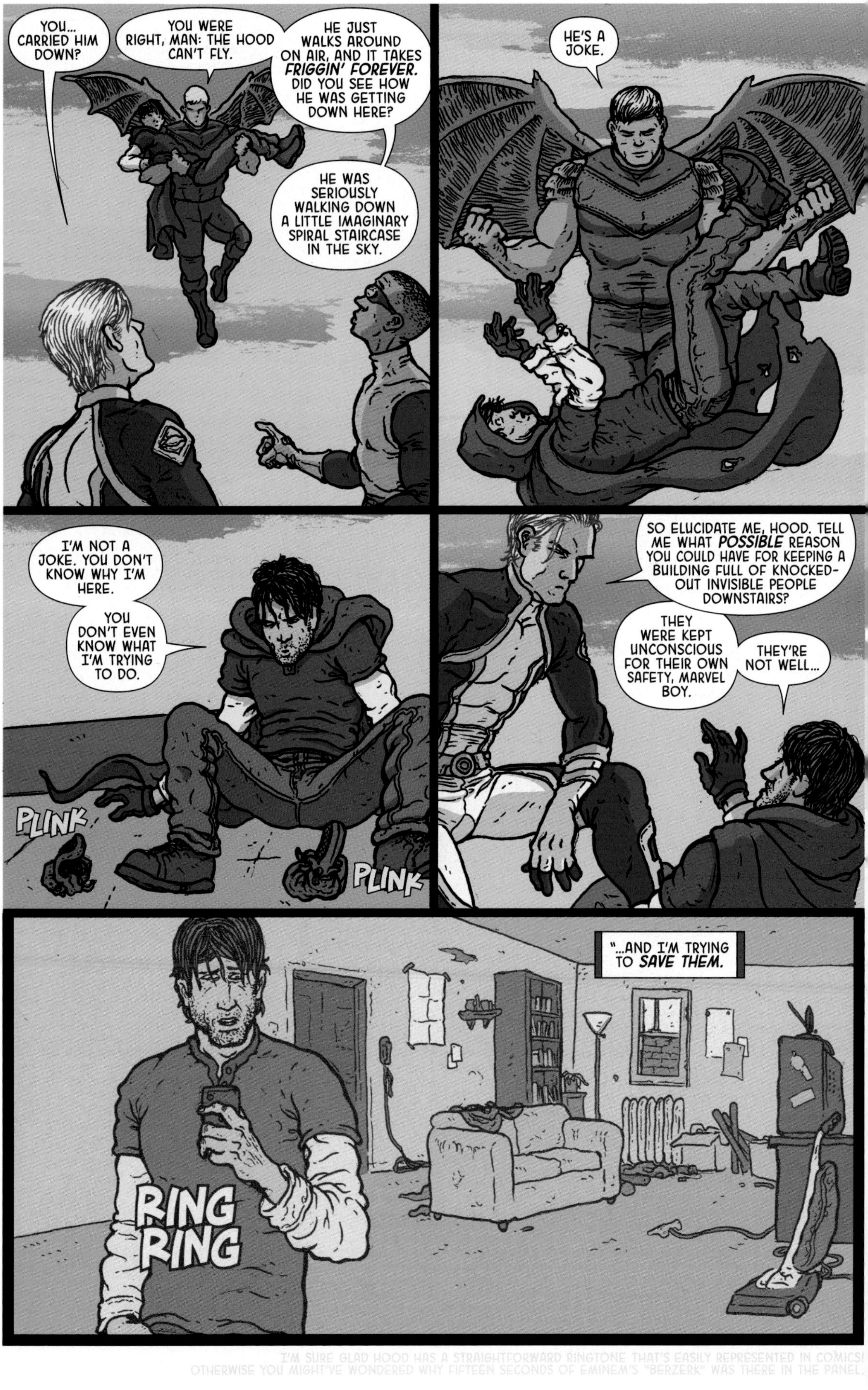
YOU... CARRIED HIM DOWN?
YOU WERE RIGHT, MAN: THE HOOD CAN'T FLY.
HE JUST WALKS AROUND ON AIR, AND IT TAKES FRIGGIN' FOREVER. DID YOU SEE HOW HE WAS GETTING DOWN HERE?
HE WAS SERIOUSLY WALKING DOWN A LITTLE IMAGINARY SPIRAL STAIRCASE IN THE SKY.
HE'S A JOKE.
I'M NOT A JOKE. YOU DON'T KNOW WHY I'M HERE.
YOU DON'T EVEN KNOW WHAT I'M TRYING TO DO.
PLINK
PLINK
SO ELUCIDATE ME, HOOD. TELL ME WHAT POSSIBLE REASON YOU COULD HAVE FOR KEEPING A BUILDING FULL OF KNOCKED-OUT INVISIBLE PEOPLE DOWNSTAIRS?
THEY WERE KEPT UNCONSCIOUS FOR THEIR OWN SAFETY, MARVEL BOY.
THEY'RE NOT WELL...
"...AND I'M TRYING TO SAVE THEM.
RING RING

I'M SURE GLAD HOOD HAS A STRAIGHTFORWARD RINGTONE THAT'S EASILY REPRESENTED IN COMICS! OTHERWISE YOU MIGHT'VE WONDERED WHY FIFTEEN SECONDS OF EMINEM'S "BERZERK" WAS THERE IN THE PANEL.

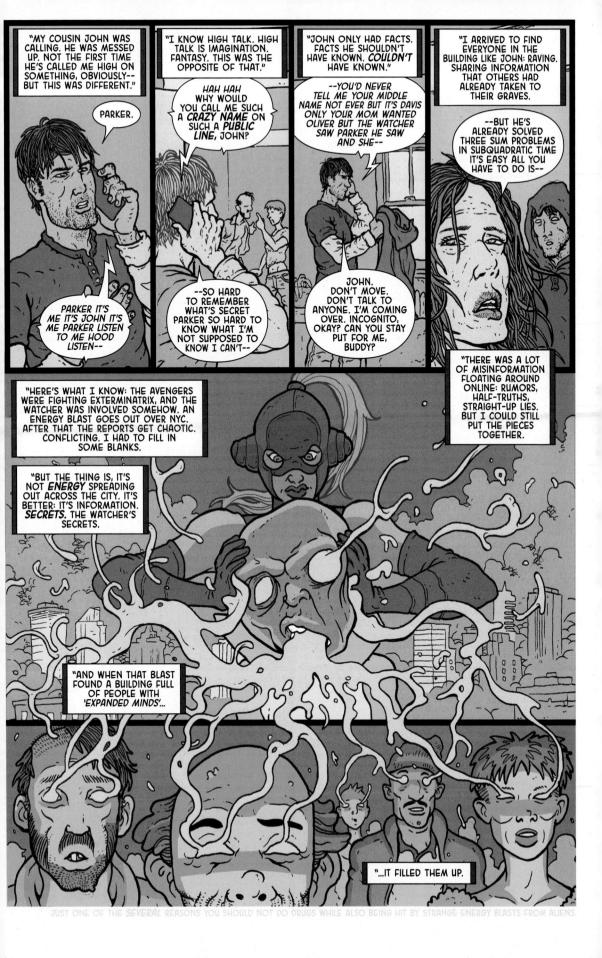

"MY COUSIN JOHN WAS CALLING. HE WAS MESSED UP. NOT THE FIRST TIME HE'S CALLED ME HIGH ON SOMETHING, OBVIOUSLY-- BUT THIS WAS DIFFERENT."

PARKER.

PARKER IT'S ME IT'S JOHN IT'S ME PARKER LISTEN TO ME HOOD LISTEN--

"I KNOW HIGH TALK. HIGH TALK IS IMAGINATION. FANTASY. THIS WAS THE OPPOSITE OF THAT."

HAH HAH WHY WOULD YOU CALL ME SUCH A *CRAZY NAME* ON SUCH A *PUBLIC LINE*, JOHN?

--SO HARD TO REMEMBER WHAT'S SECRET PARKER SO HARD TO KNOW WHAT I'M NOT SUPPOSED TO KNOW I CAN'T--

"JOHN ONLY HAD FACTS. FACTS HE SHOULDN'T HAVE KNOWN. *COULDN'T* HAVE KNOWN."

--YOU'D NEVER TELL ME YOUR MIDDLE NAME NOT EVER BUT IT'S DAVIS ONLY YOUR MOM WANTED OLIVER BUT THE WATCHER SAW PARKER HE SAW AND SHE--

JOHN. DON'T MOVE. DON'T TALK TO ANYONE. I'M COMING OVER. INCOGNITO, OKAY? CAN YOU STAY PUT FOR ME, BUDDY?

"I ARRIVED TO FIND EVERYONE IN THE BUILDING LIKE JOHN: RAVING. SHARING INFORMATION THAT OTHERS HAD ALREADY TAKEN TO THEIR GRAVES.

--BUT HE'S ALREADY SOLVED THREE SUM PROBLEMS IN SUBQUADRATIC TIME IT'S EASY ALL YOU HAVE TO DO IS--

"THERE WAS A LOT OF MISINFORMATION FLOATING AROUND ONLINE: RUMORS, HALF-TRUTHS, STRAIGHT-UP LIES. BUT I COULD STILL PUT THE PIECES TOGETHER.

"HERE'S WHAT I KNOW: THE AVENGERS WERE FIGHTING EXTERMINATRIX, AND THE WATCHER WAS INVOLVED SOMEHOW. AN ENERGY BLAST GOES OUT OVER NYC. AFTER THAT THE REPORTS GET CHAOTIC. CONFLICTING. I HAD TO FILL IN SOME BLANKS.

"BUT THE THING IS, IT'S NOT *ENERGY* SPREADING OUT ACROSS THE CITY. IT'S BETTER: IT'S INFORMATION. *SECRETS.* THE WATCHER'S SECRETS.

"AND WHEN THAT BLAST FOUND A BUILDING FULL OF PEOPLE WITH 'EXPANDED MINDS'...

"...IT FILLED THEM UP.

JUST ONE OF THE *SEVERAL* REASONS YOU SHOULD NOT DO DRUGS WHILE ALSO BEING HIT BY STRANGE ENERGY BLASTS FROM ALIENS.

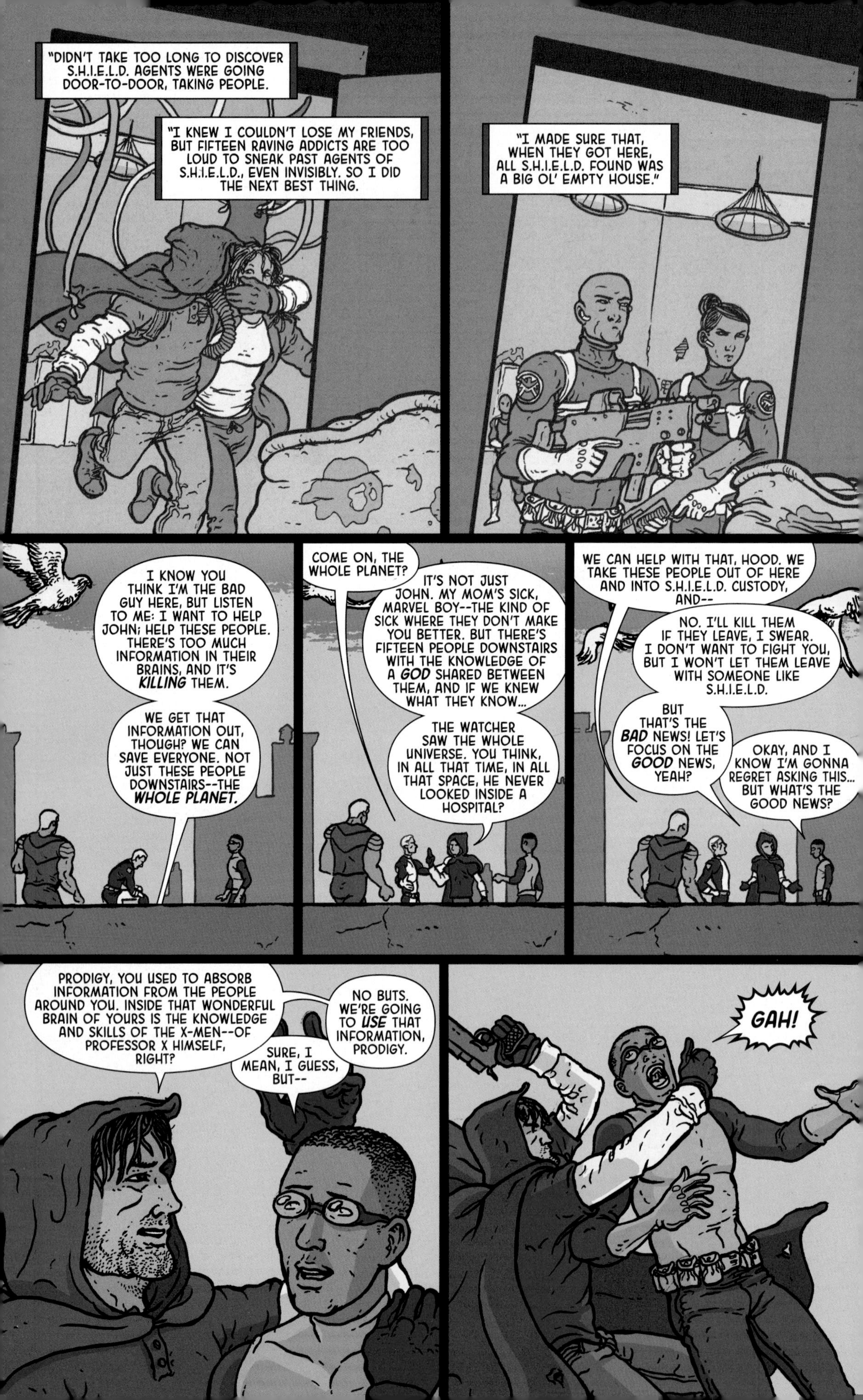
"DIDN'T TAKE TOO LONG TO DISCOVER S.H.I.E.L.D. AGENTS WERE GOING DOOR-TO-DOOR, TAKING PEOPLE.
"I KNEW I COULDN'T LOSE MY FRIENDS, BUT FIFTEEN RAVING ADDICTS ARE TOO LOUD TO SNEAK PAST AGENTS OF S.H.I.E.L.D., EVEN INVISIBLY. SO I DID THE NEXT BEST THING.
"I MADE SURE THAT, WHEN THEY GOT HERE, ALL S.H.I.E.L.D. FOUND WAS A BIG OL' EMPTY HOUSE."
I KNOW YOU THINK I'M THE BAD GUY HERE, BUT LISTEN TO ME: I WANT TO HELP JOHN; HELP THESE PEOPLE. THERE'S TOO MUCH INFORMATION IN THEIR BRAINS, AND IT'S KILLING THEM.
WE GET THAT INFORMATION OUT, THOUGH? WE CAN SAVE EVERYONE. NOT JUST THESE PEOPLE DOWNSTAIRS--THE WHOLE PLANET.
COME ON, THE WHOLE PLANET?
IT'S NOT JUST JOHN. MY MOM'S SICK, MARVEL BOY--THE KIND OF SICK WHERE THEY DON'T MAKE YOU BETTER. BUT THERE'S FIFTEEN PEOPLE DOWNSTAIRS WITH THE KNOWLEDGE OF A GOD SHARED BETWEEN THEM, AND IF WE KNEW WHAT THEY KNOW...
THE WATCHER SAW THE WHOLE UNIVERSE. YOU THINK, IN ALL THAT TIME, IN ALL THAT SPACE, HE NEVER LOOKED INSIDE A HOSPITAL?
WE CAN HELP WITH THAT, HOOD. WE TAKE THESE PEOPLE OUT OF HERE AND INTO S.H.I.E.L.D. CUSTODY, AND--
NO. I'LL KILL THEM IF THEY LEAVE, I SWEAR. I DON'T WANT TO FIGHT YOU, BUT I WON'T LET THEM LEAVE WITH SOMEONE LIKE S.H.I.E.L.D.
BUT THAT'S THE BAD NEWS! LET'S FOCUS ON THE GOOD NEWS, YEAH?
OKAY, AND I KNOW I'M GONNA REGRET ASKING THIS... BUT WHAT'S THE GOOD NEWS?
PRODIGY, YOU USED TO ABSORB INFORMATION FROM THE PEOPLE AROUND YOU. INSIDE THAT WONDERFUL BRAIN OF YOURS IS THE KNOWLEDGE AND SKILLS OF THE X-MEN--OF PROFESSOR X HIMSELF, RIGHT?
SURE, I MEAN, I GUESS, BUT--
NO BUTS. WE'RE GOING TO USE THAT INFORMATION, PRODIGY.
GAH!

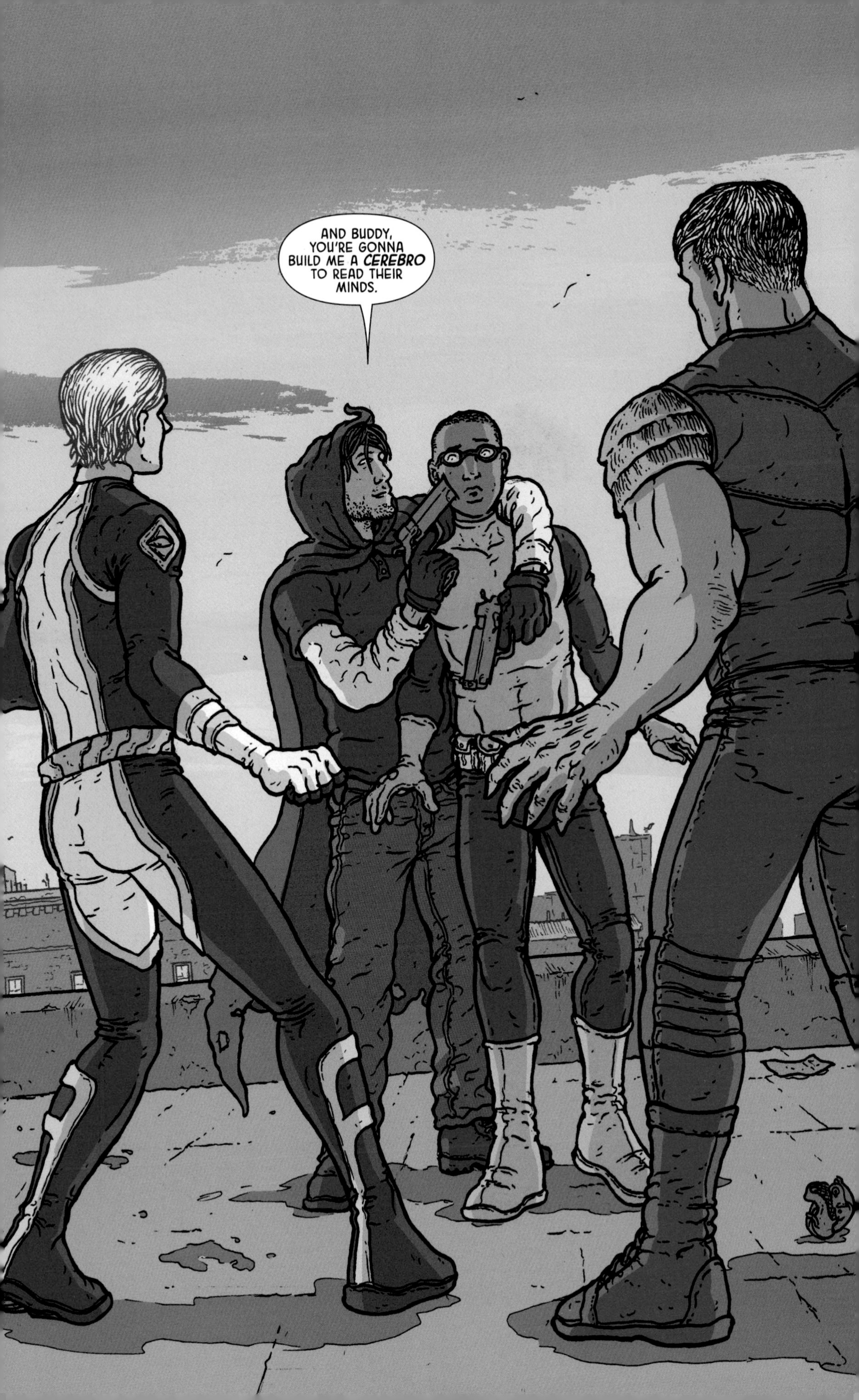
AND BUDDY, YOU'RE GONNA BUILD ME A *CEREBRO* TO READ THEIR MINDS.

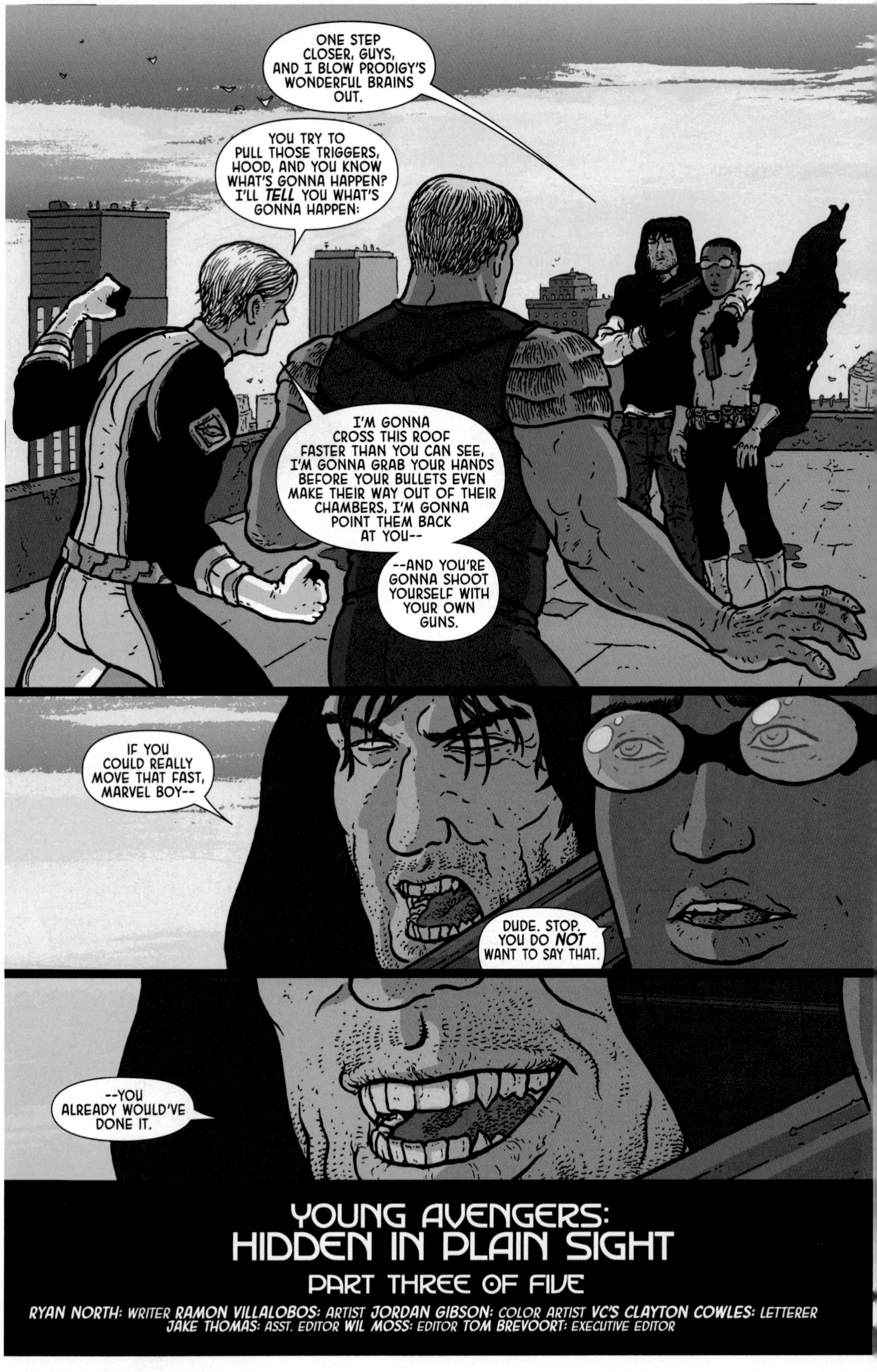
ONE STEP CLOSER, GUYS, AND I BLOW PRODIGY'S WONDERFUL BRAINS OUT.
YOU TRY TO PULL THOSE TRIGGERS, HOOD, AND YOU KNOW WHAT'S GONNA HAPPEN? I'LL *TELL* YOU WHAT'S GONNA HAPPEN:
I'M GONNA CROSS THIS ROOF FASTER THAN YOU CAN SEE, I'M GONNA GRAB YOUR HANDS BEFORE YOUR BULLETS EVEN MAKE THEIR WAY OUT OF THEIR CHAMBERS, I'M GONNA POINT THEM BACK AT YOU--
--AND YOU'RE GONNA SHOOT YOURSELF WITH YOUR OWN GUNS.
IF YOU COULD REALLY MOVE THAT FAST, MARVEL BOY--
DUDE. STOP. YOU DO ***NOT*** WANT TO SAY THAT.
--YOU ALREADY WOULD'VE DONE IT.

YOUNG AVENGERS: HIDDEN IN PLAIN SIGHT

PART THREE OF FIVE

RYAN NORTH: WRITER **RAMON VILLALOBOS:** ARTIST **JORDAN GIBSON:** COLOR ARTIST **VC'S CLAYTON COWLES:** LETTERER
JAKE THOMAS: ASST. EDITOR **WIL MOSS:** EDITOR **TOM BREVOORT:** EXECUTIVE EDITOR

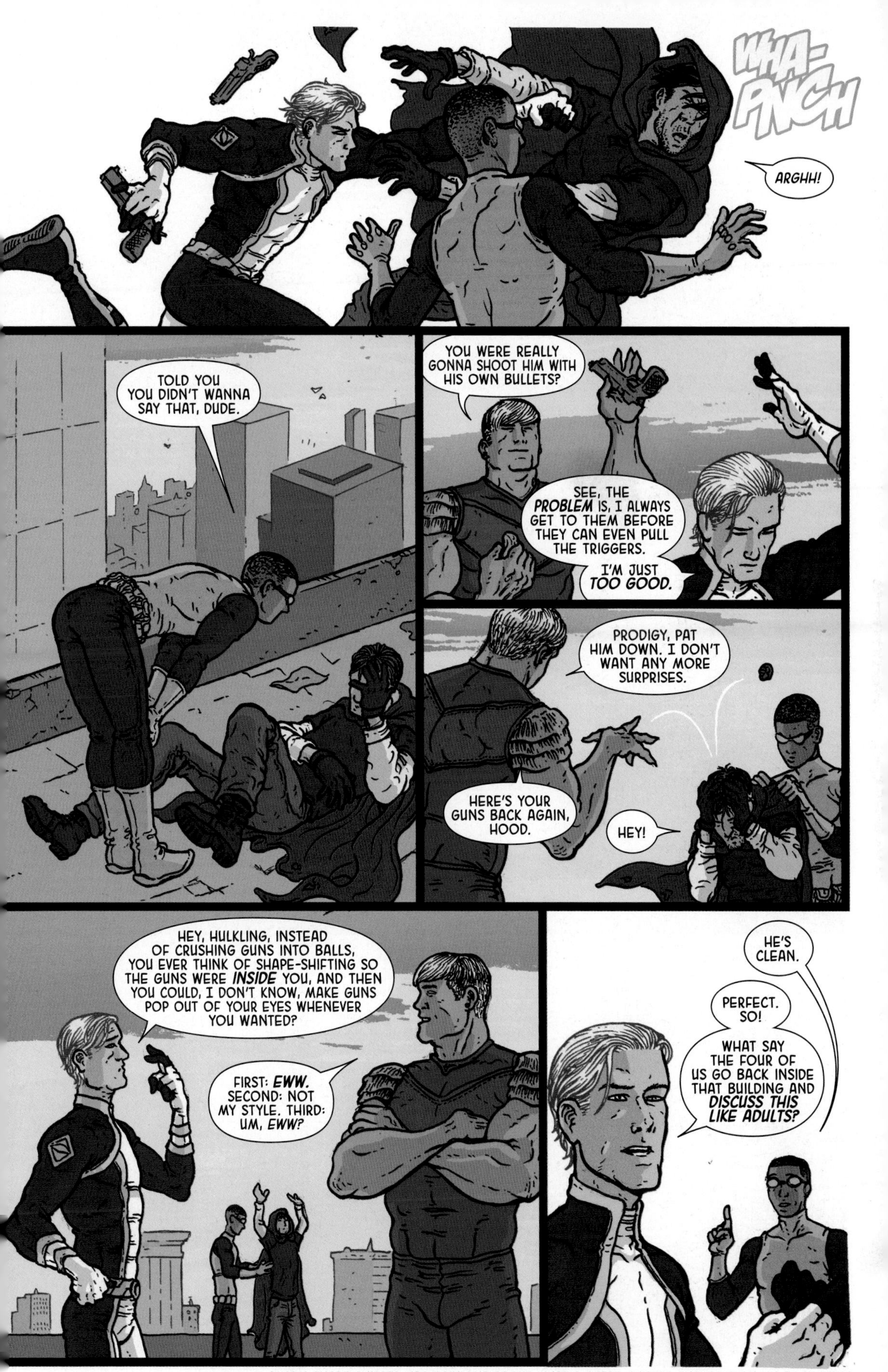
WHA-PNCH
ARGHH!
TOLD YOU YOU DIDN'T WANNA SAY THAT, DUDE.
YOU WERE REALLY GONNA SHOOT HIM WITH HIS OWN BULLETS?
SEE, THE PROBLEM IS, I ALWAYS GET TO THEM BEFORE THEY CAN EVEN PULL THE TRIGGERS.
I'M JUST TOO GOOD.
PRODIGY, PAT HIM DOWN. I DON'T WANT ANY MORE SURPRISES.
HERE'S YOUR GUNS BACK AGAIN, HOOD.
HEY!
HEY, HULKLING, INSTEAD OF CRUSHING GUNS INTO BALLS, YOU EVER THINK OF SHAPE-SHIFTING SO THE GUNS WERE INSIDE YOU, AND THEN YOU COULD, I DON'T KNOW, MAKE GUNS POP OUT OF YOUR EYES WHENEVER YOU WANTED?
FIRST: EWW. SECOND: NOT MY STYLE. THIRD: UM, EWW?
HE'S CLEAN.
PERFECT. SO!
WHAT SAY THE FOUR OF US GO BACK INSIDE THAT BUILDING AND DISCUSS THIS LIKE ADULTS?

A NON-SHAPE-SHIFTER HAS OPINIONS ABOUT WHAT A SHAPE-SHIFTER SHOULD TURN HIS BODY INTO! *WHAT A SURPRISE!*

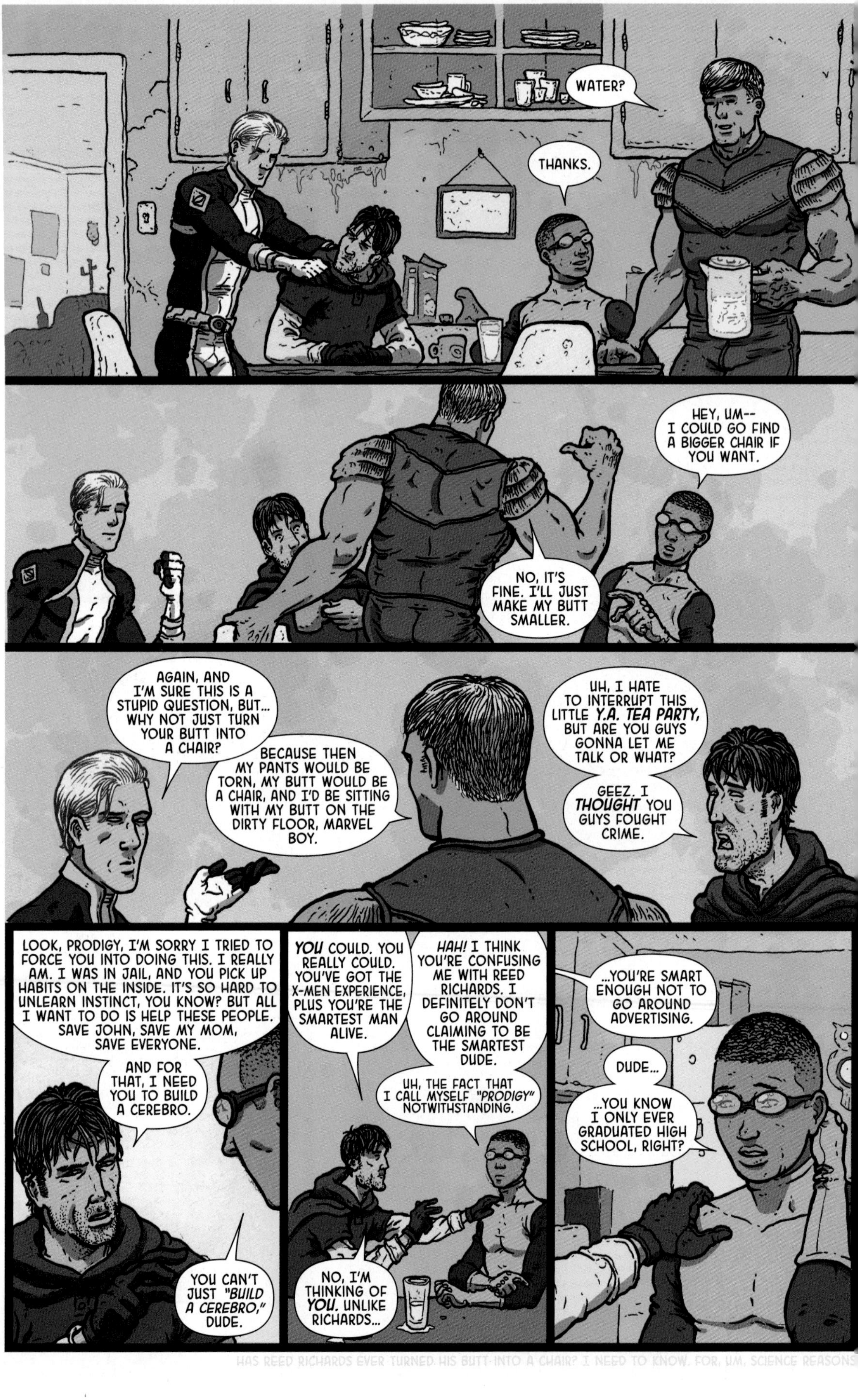
WATER?
THANKS.
HEY, UM-- I COULD GO FIND A BIGGER CHAIR IF YOU WANT.
NO, IT'S FINE. I'LL JUST MAKE MY BUTT SMALLER.
AGAIN, AND I'M SURE THIS IS A STUPID QUESTION, BUT... WHY NOT JUST TURN YOUR BUTT INTO A CHAIR?
BECAUSE THEN MY PANTS WOULD BE TORN, MY BUTT WOULD BE A CHAIR, AND I'D BE SITTING WITH MY BUTT ON THE DIRTY FLOOR, MARVEL BOY.
UH, I HATE TO INTERRUPT THIS LITTLE Y.A. TEA PARTY, BUT ARE YOU GUYS GONNA LET ME TALK OR WHAT?
GEEZ. I THOUGHT YOU GUYS FOUGHT CRIME.
LOOK, PRODIGY, I'M SORRY I TRIED TO FORCE YOU INTO DOING THIS. I REALLY AM. I WAS IN JAIL, AND YOU PICK UP HABITS ON THE INSIDE. IT'S SO HARD TO UNLEARN INSTINCT, YOU KNOW? BUT ALL I WANT TO DO IS HELP THESE PEOPLE. SAVE JOHN, SAVE MY MOM, SAVE EVERYONE.
AND FOR THAT, I NEED YOU TO BUILD A CEREBRO.
YOU CAN'T JUST "BUILD A CEREBRO," DUDE.
YOU COULD. YOU REALLY COULD. YOU'VE GOT THE X-MEN EXPERIENCE, PLUS YOU'RE THE SMARTEST MAN ALIVE.
HAH! I THINK YOU'RE CONFUSING ME WITH REED RICHARDS. I DEFINITELY DON'T GO AROUND CLAIMING TO BE THE SMARTEST DUDE.
UH, THE FACT THAT I CALL MYSELF "PRODIGY" NOTWITHSTANDING.
NO, I'M THINKING OF YOU. UNLIKE RICHARDS...
...YOU'RE SMART ENOUGH NOT TO GO AROUND ADVERTISING.
DUDE...
...YOU KNOW I ONLY EVER GRADUATED HIGH SCHOOL, RIGHT?

HAS REED RICHARDS EVER TURNED HIS BUTT INTO A CHAIR? I NEED TO KNOW. FOR, UM, SCIENCE REASONS.

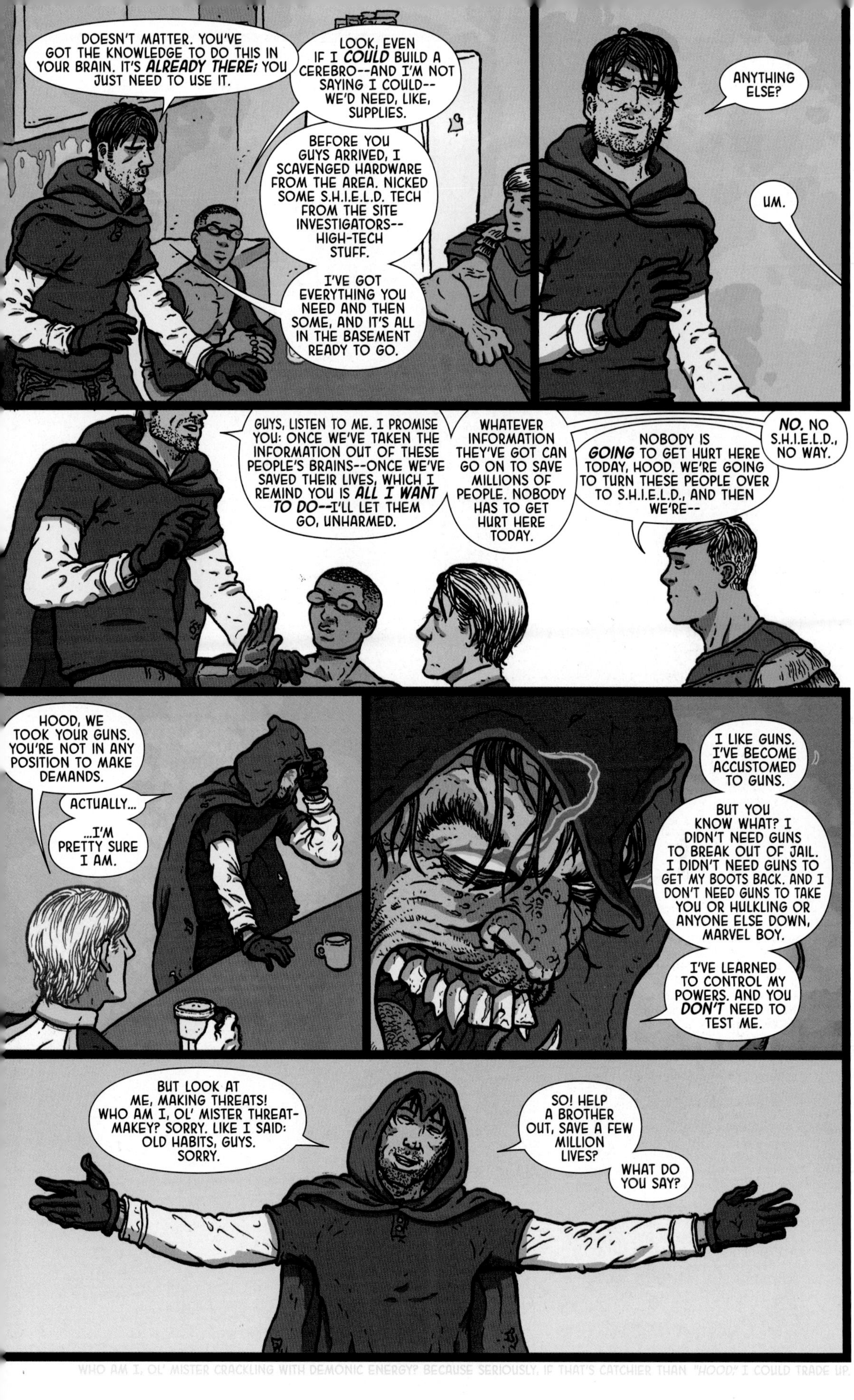
DOESN'T MATTER. YOU'VE GOT THE KNOWLEDGE TO DO THIS IN YOUR BRAIN. IT'S *ALREADY THERE;* YOU JUST NEED TO USE IT.
LOOK, EVEN IF I *COULD* BUILD A CEREBRO--AND I'M NOT SAYING I COULD--WE'D NEED, LIKE, SUPPLIES.
BEFORE YOU GUYS ARRIVED, I SCAVENGED HARDWARE FROM THE AREA. NICKED SOME S.H.I.E.L.D. TECH FROM THE SITE INVESTIGATORS--HIGH-TECH STUFF.
I'VE GOT EVERYTHING YOU NEED AND THEN SOME, AND IT'S ALL IN THE BASEMENT READY TO GO.
ANYTHING ELSE?
UM.
GUYS, LISTEN TO ME. I PROMISE YOU: ONCE WE'VE TAKEN THE INFORMATION OUT OF THESE PEOPLE'S BRAINS--ONCE WE'VE SAVED THEIR LIVES, WHICH I REMIND YOU IS *ALL I WANT TO DO*--I'LL LET THEM GO, UNHARMED.
WHATEVER INFORMATION THEY'VE GOT CAN GO ON TO SAVE MILLIONS OF PEOPLE. NOBODY HAS TO GET HURT HERE TODAY.
NOBODY IS *GOING* TO GET HURT HERE TODAY, HOOD. WE'RE GOING TO TURN THESE PEOPLE OVER TO S.H.I.E.L.D., AND THEN WE'RE--
NO. NO S.H.I.E.L.D., NO WAY.
HOOD, WE TOOK YOUR GUNS. YOU'RE NOT IN ANY POSITION TO MAKE DEMANDS.
ACTUALLY...
...I'M PRETTY SURE I AM.
I LIKE GUNS. I'VE BECOME ACCUSTOMED TO GUNS.
BUT YOU KNOW WHAT? I DIDN'T NEED GUNS TO BREAK OUT OF JAIL. I DIDN'T NEED GUNS TO GET MY BOOTS BACK. AND I DON'T NEED GUNS TO TAKE YOU OR HULKLING OR ANYONE ELSE DOWN, MARVEL BOY.
I'VE LEARNED TO CONTROL MY POWERS. AND YOU *DON'T* NEED TO TEST ME.
BUT LOOK AT ME, MAKING THREATS! WHO AM I, OL' MISTER THREAT-MAKEY? SORRY. LIKE I SAID: OLD HABITS, GUYS. SORRY.
SO! HELP A BROTHER OUT, SAVE A FEW MILLION LIVES?
WHAT DO YOU SAY?

WHO AM I, OL' MISTER CRACKLING WITH DEMONIC ENERGY? BECAUSE SERIOUSLY, IF THAT'S CATCHIER THAN *"HOOD,"* I COULD TRADE UP.

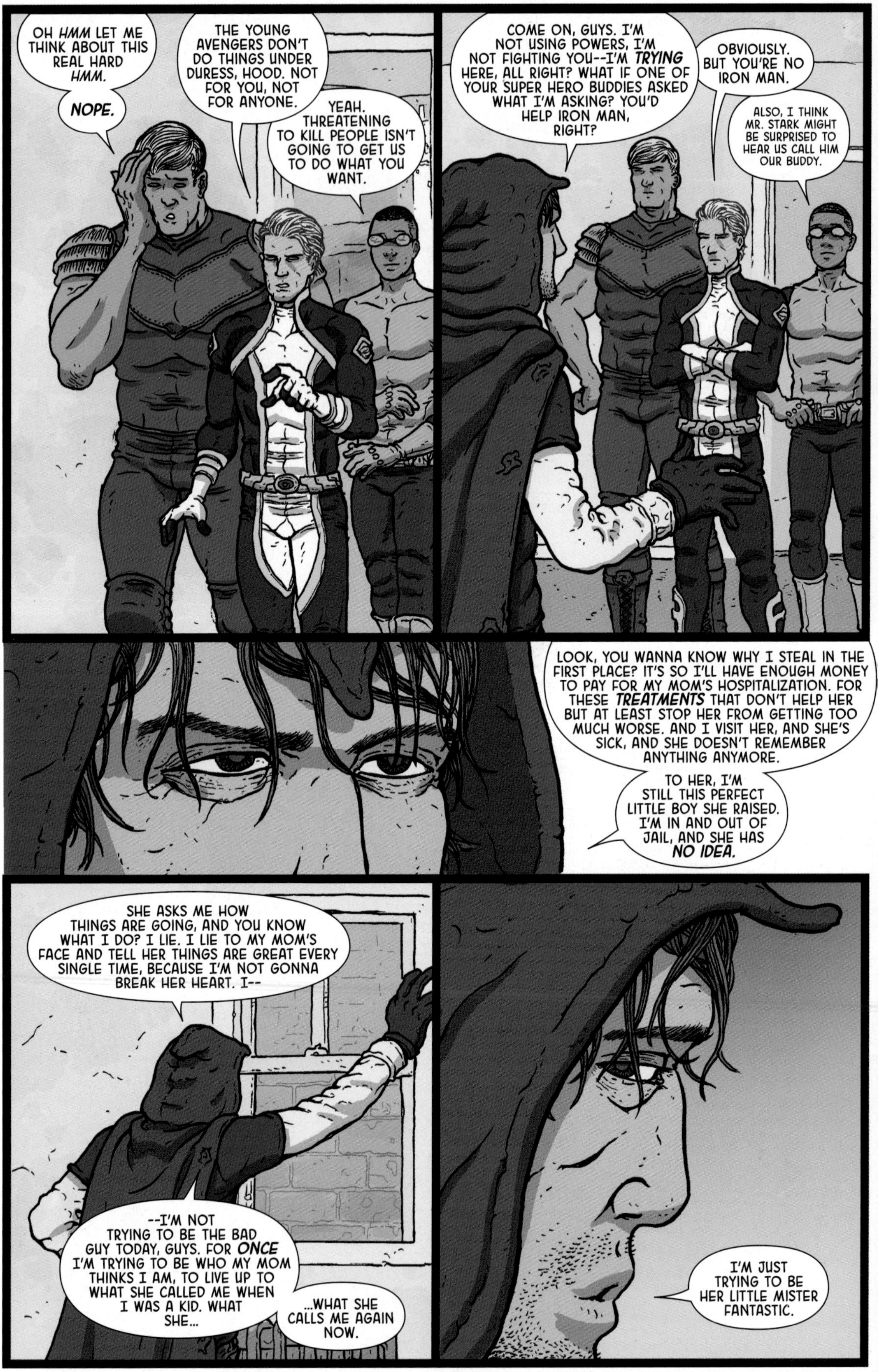
OH *HMM* LET ME THINK ABOUT THIS REAL HARD *HMM.*
NOPE.
THE YOUNG AVENGERS DON'T DO THINGS UNDER DURESS, HOOD. NOT FOR YOU, NOT FOR ANYONE.
YEAH. THREATENING TO KILL PEOPLE ISN'T GOING TO GET US TO DO WHAT YOU WANT.
COME ON, GUYS. I'M NOT USING POWERS, I'M NOT FIGHTING YOU--I'M ***TRYING*** HERE, ALL RIGHT? WHAT IF ONE OF YOUR SUPER HERO BUDDIES ASKED WHAT I'M ASKING? YOU'D HELP IRON MAN, RIGHT?
OBVIOUSLY. BUT YOU'RE NO IRON MAN.
ALSO, I THINK MR. STARK MIGHT BE SURPRISED TO HEAR US CALL HIM OUR BUDDY.
LOOK, YOU WANNA KNOW WHY I STEAL IN THE FIRST PLACE? IT'S SO I'LL HAVE ENOUGH MONEY TO PAY FOR MY MOM'S HOSPITALIZATION. FOR THESE ***TREATMENTS*** THAT DON'T HELP HER BUT AT LEAST STOP HER FROM GETTING TOO MUCH WORSE. AND I VISIT HER, AND SHE'S SICK, AND SHE DOESN'T REMEMBER ANYTHING ANYMORE.
TO HER, I'M STILL THIS PERFECT LITTLE BOY SHE RAISED. I'M IN AND OUT OF JAIL, AND SHE HAS ***NO IDEA.***
SHE ASKS ME HOW THINGS ARE GOING, AND YOU KNOW WHAT I DO? I LIE. I LIE TO MY MOM'S FACE AND TELL HER THINGS ARE GREAT EVERY SINGLE TIME, BECAUSE I'M NOT GONNA BREAK HER HEART. I--
--I'M NOT TRYING TO BE THE BAD GUY TODAY, GUYS. FOR ***ONCE*** I'M TRYING TO BE WHO MY MOM THINKS I AM, TO LIVE UP TO WHAT SHE CALLED ME WHEN I WAS A KID. WHAT SHE...
...WHAT SHE CALLS ME AGAIN NOW.
I'M JUST TRYING TO BE HER LITTLE MISTER FANTASTIC.

YOU CAN TELL THE YOUNG AVENGERS ARE GOOD GUYS HERE BECAUSE NONE OF THEM REPLY TO HOOD WITH *"WOW, MISTER FANTASTIC? THAT'S A STRETCH."*
THANK YOU, YOUNG AVENGERS.

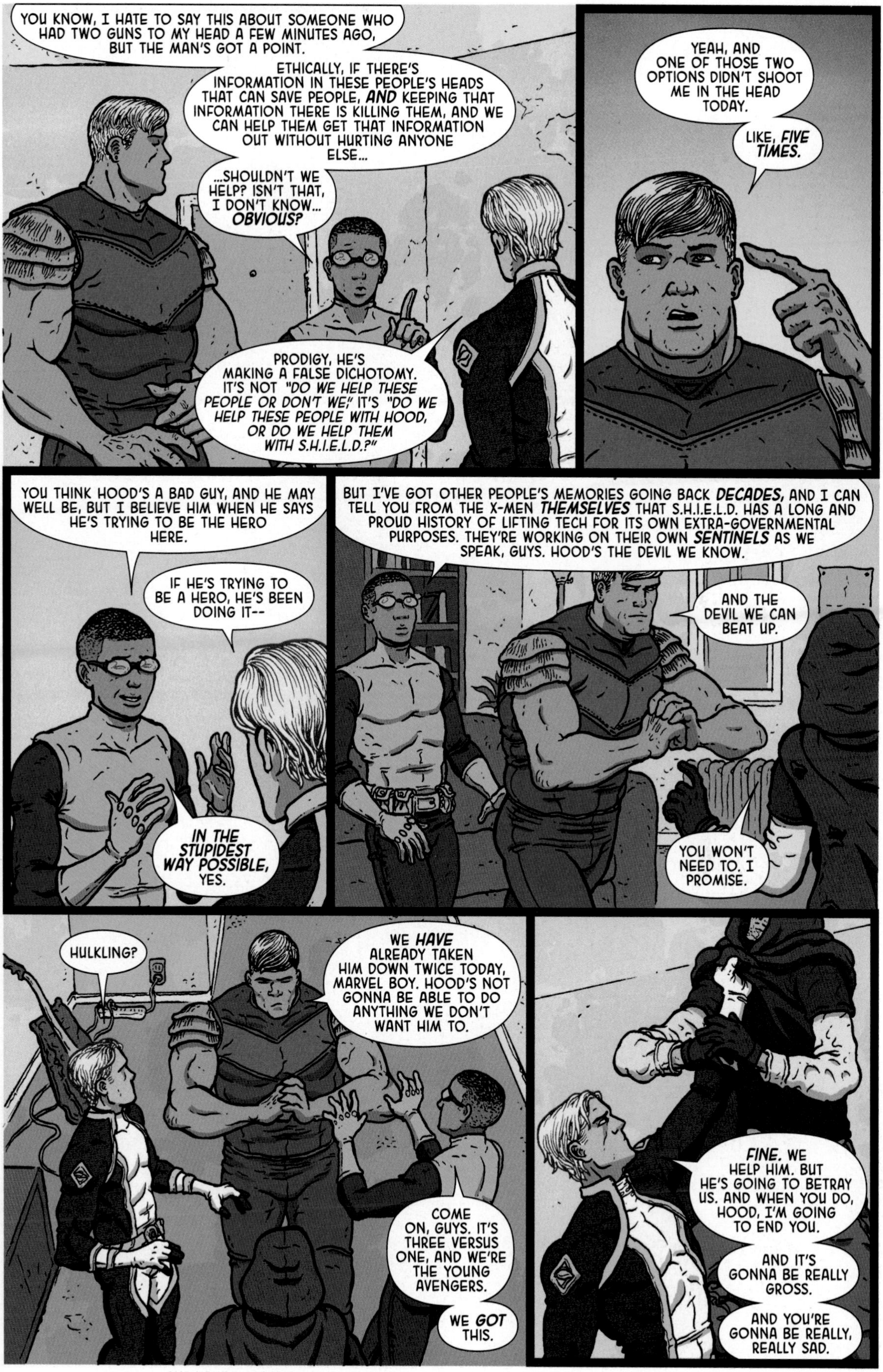

YOU KNOW, I HATE TO SAY THIS ABOUT SOMEONE WHO HAD TWO GUNS TO MY HEAD A FEW MINUTES AGO, BUT THE MAN'S GOT A POINT.
ETHICALLY, IF THERE'S INFORMATION IN THESE PEOPLE'S HEADS THAT CAN SAVE PEOPLE, ***AND*** KEEPING THAT INFORMATION THERE IS KILLING THEM, AND WE CAN HELP THEM GET THAT INFORMATION OUT WITHOUT HURTING ANYONE ELSE...
...SHOULDN'T WE HELP? ISN'T THAT, I DON'T KNOW... ***OBVIOUS?***
PRODIGY, HE'S MAKING A FALSE DICHOTOMY. IT'S NOT *"DO WE HELP THESE PEOPLE OR DON'T WE,"* IT'S *"DO WE HELP THESE PEOPLE WITH HOOD, OR DO WE HELP THEM WITH S.H.I.E.L.D.?"*
YEAH, AND ONE OF THOSE TWO OPTIONS DIDN'T SHOOT ME IN THE HEAD TODAY.
LIKE, ***FIVE TIMES.***
YOU THINK HOOD'S A BAD GUY, AND HE MAY WELL BE, BUT I BELIEVE HIM WHEN HE SAYS HE'S TRYING TO BE THE HERO HERE.
IF HE'S TRYING TO BE A HERO, HE'S BEEN DOING IT--
IN THE STUPIDEST WAY POSSIBLE, YES.
BUT I'VE GOT OTHER PEOPLE'S MEMORIES GOING BACK ***DECADES,*** AND I CAN TELL YOU FROM THE X-MEN ***THEMSELVES*** THAT S.H.I.E.L.D. HAS A LONG AND PROUD HISTORY OF LIFTING TECH FOR ITS OWN EXTRA-GOVERNMENTAL PURPOSES. THEY'RE WORKING ON THEIR OWN ***SENTINELS*** AS WE SPEAK, GUYS. HOOD'S THE DEVIL WE KNOW.
AND THE DEVIL WE CAN BEAT UP.
YOU WON'T NEED TO. I PROMISE.
HULKLING?
WE ***HAVE*** ALREADY TAKEN HIM DOWN TWICE TODAY, MARVEL BOY. HOOD'S NOT GONNA BE ABLE TO DO ANYTHING WE DON'T WANT HIM TO.
COME ON, GUYS. IT'S THREE VERSUS ONE, AND WE'RE THE YOUNG AVENGERS.
WE ***GOT*** THIS.
FINE. WE HELP HIM. BUT HE'S GOING TO BETRAY US. AND WHEN YOU DO, HOOD, I'M GOING TO END YOU.
AND IT'S GONNA BE REALLY GROSS.
AND YOU'RE GONNA BE REALLY, REALLY SAD.

AND YOU'RE GOING TO BE A CHUNKY RED SLURRY IN THE MIDDLE OF THE ROAD THAT PEOPLE WILL WALK PAST AND SAY
"OH WOW, LOOKS LIKE SOMONE SHOULD'VE LISTENED TO MARVEL BOY WHEN HE HAD THE CHANCE."

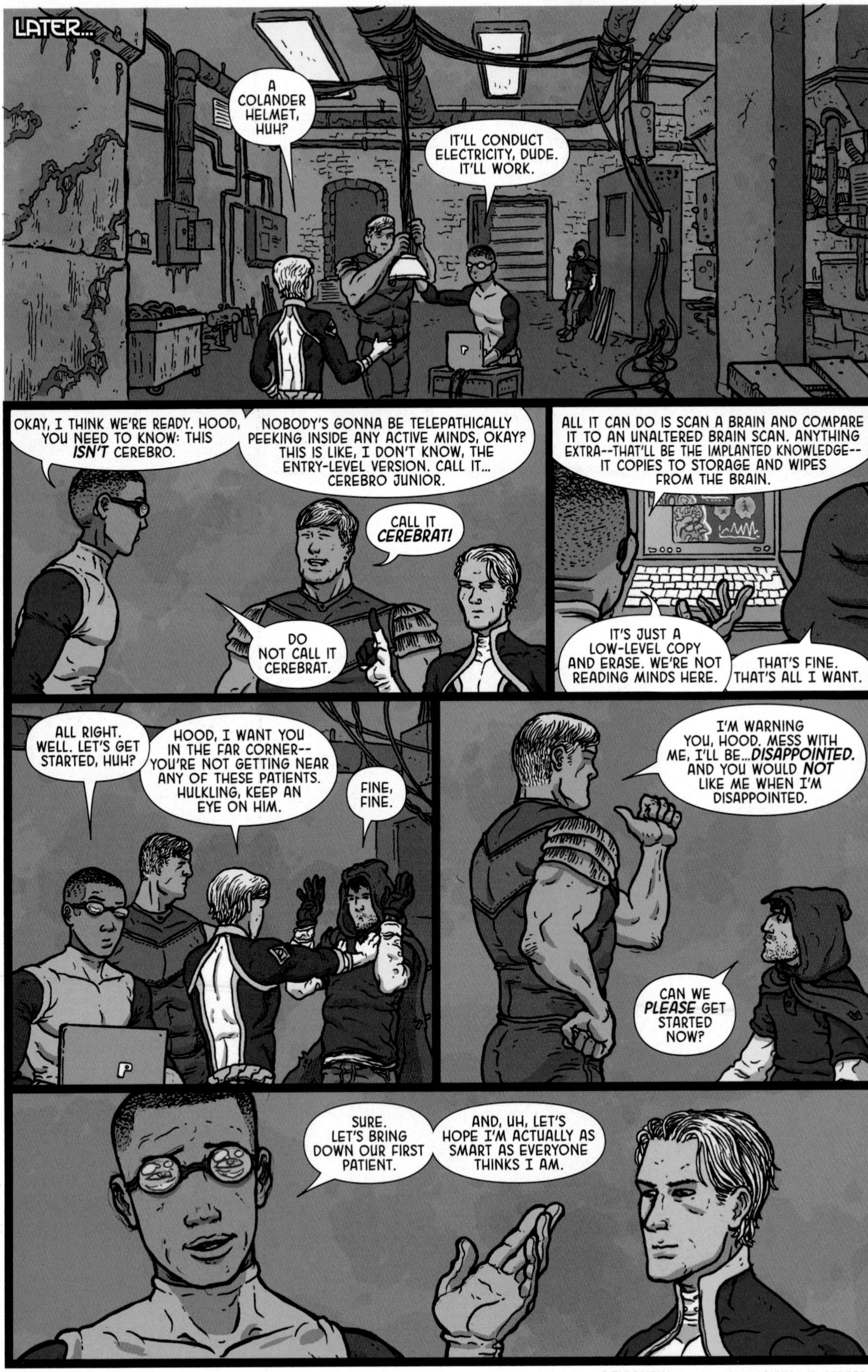
LATER...
A COLANDER HELMET, HUH?
IT'LL CONDUCT ELECTRICITY, DUDE. IT'LL WORK.
OKAY, I THINK WE'RE READY. HOOD, YOU NEED TO KNOW: THIS *ISN'T* CEREBRO.
NOBODY'S GONNA BE TELEPATHICALLY PEEKING INSIDE ANY ACTIVE MINDS, OKAY? THIS IS LIKE, I DON'T KNOW, THE ENTRY-LEVEL VERSION. CALL IT... CEREBRO JUNIOR.
CALL IT *CEREBRAT!*
DO NOT CALL IT CEREBRAT.
ALL IT CAN DO IS SCAN A BRAIN AND COMPARE IT TO AN UNALTERED BRAIN SCAN. ANYTHING EXTRA--THAT'LL BE THE IMPLANTED KNOWLEDGE--IT COPIES TO STORAGE AND WIPES FROM THE BRAIN.
IT'S JUST A LOW-LEVEL COPY AND ERASE. WE'RE NOT READING MINDS HERE.
THAT'S FINE. THAT'S ALL I WANT.
ALL RIGHT. WELL. LET'S GET STARTED, HUH?
HOOD, I WANT YOU IN THE FAR CORNER--YOU'RE NOT GETTING NEAR ANY OF THESE PATIENTS. HULKLING, KEEP AN EYE ON HIM.
FINE, FINE.
I'M WARNING YOU, HOOD. MESS WITH ME, I'LL BE...*DISAPPOINTED.* AND YOU WOULD *NOT* LIKE ME WHEN I'M DISAPPOINTED.
CAN WE *PLEASE* GET STARTED NOW?
SURE. LET'S BRING DOWN OUR FIRST PATIENT.
AND, UH, LET'S HOPE I'M ACTUALLY AS SMART AS EVERYONE THINKS I AM.
OBVIOUSLY I'M ALREADY CALLING IT CEREBRAT

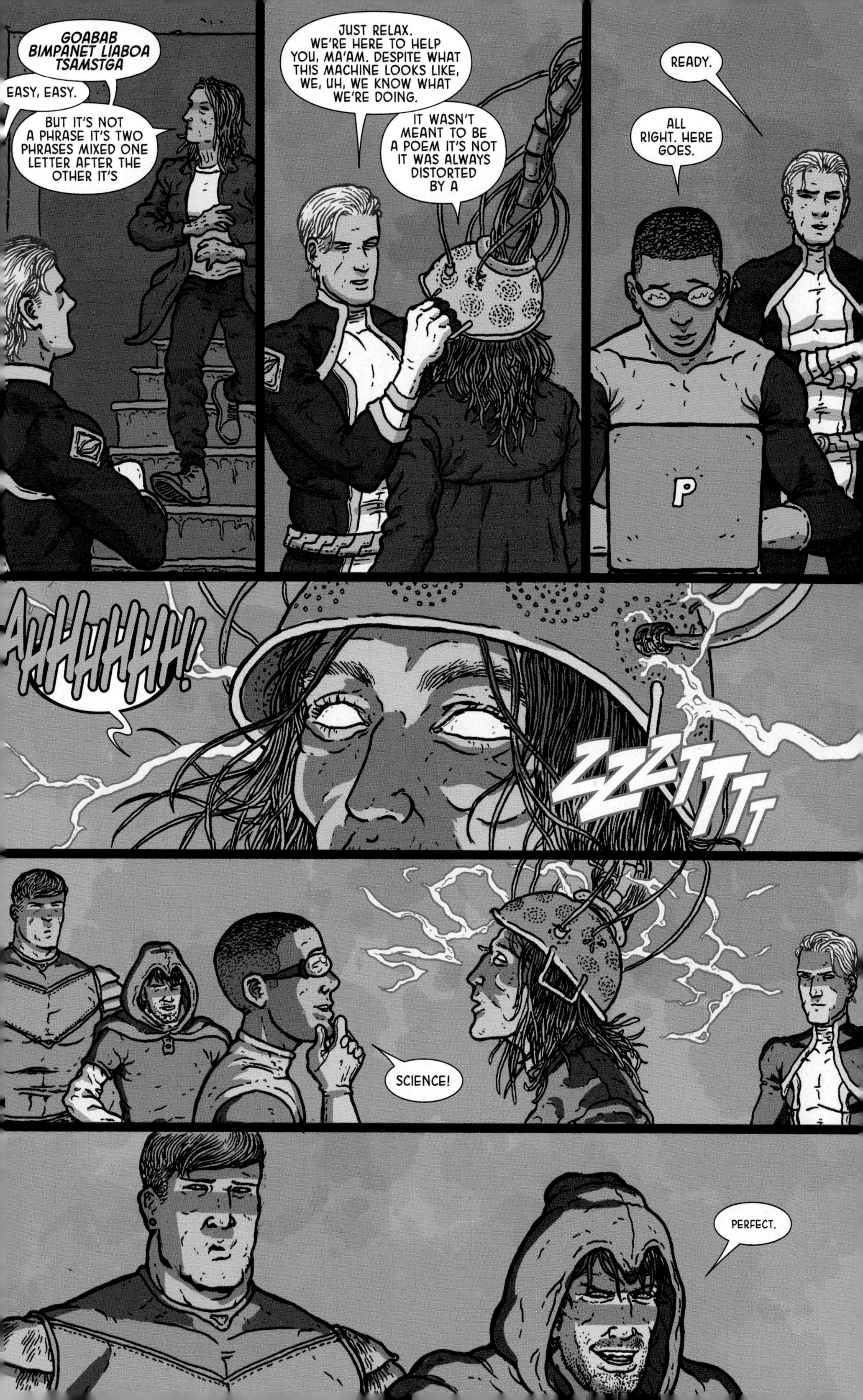
GOABAB BIMPANET LIABOA TSAMSTGA
EASY, EASY.
BUT IT'S NOT A PHRASE IT'S TWO PHRASES MIXED ONE LETTER AFTER THE OTHER IT'S
JUST RELAX. WE'RE HERE TO HELP YOU, MA'AM. DESPITE WHAT THIS MACHINE LOOKS LIKE, WE, UH, WE KNOW WHAT WE'RE DOING.
IT WASN'T MEANT TO BE A POEM IT'S NOT IT WAS ALWAYS DISTORTED BY A
READY.
ALL RIGHT. HERE GOES.
P
AHHHHHH!
ZZZTTTT
SCIENCE!
PERFECT.

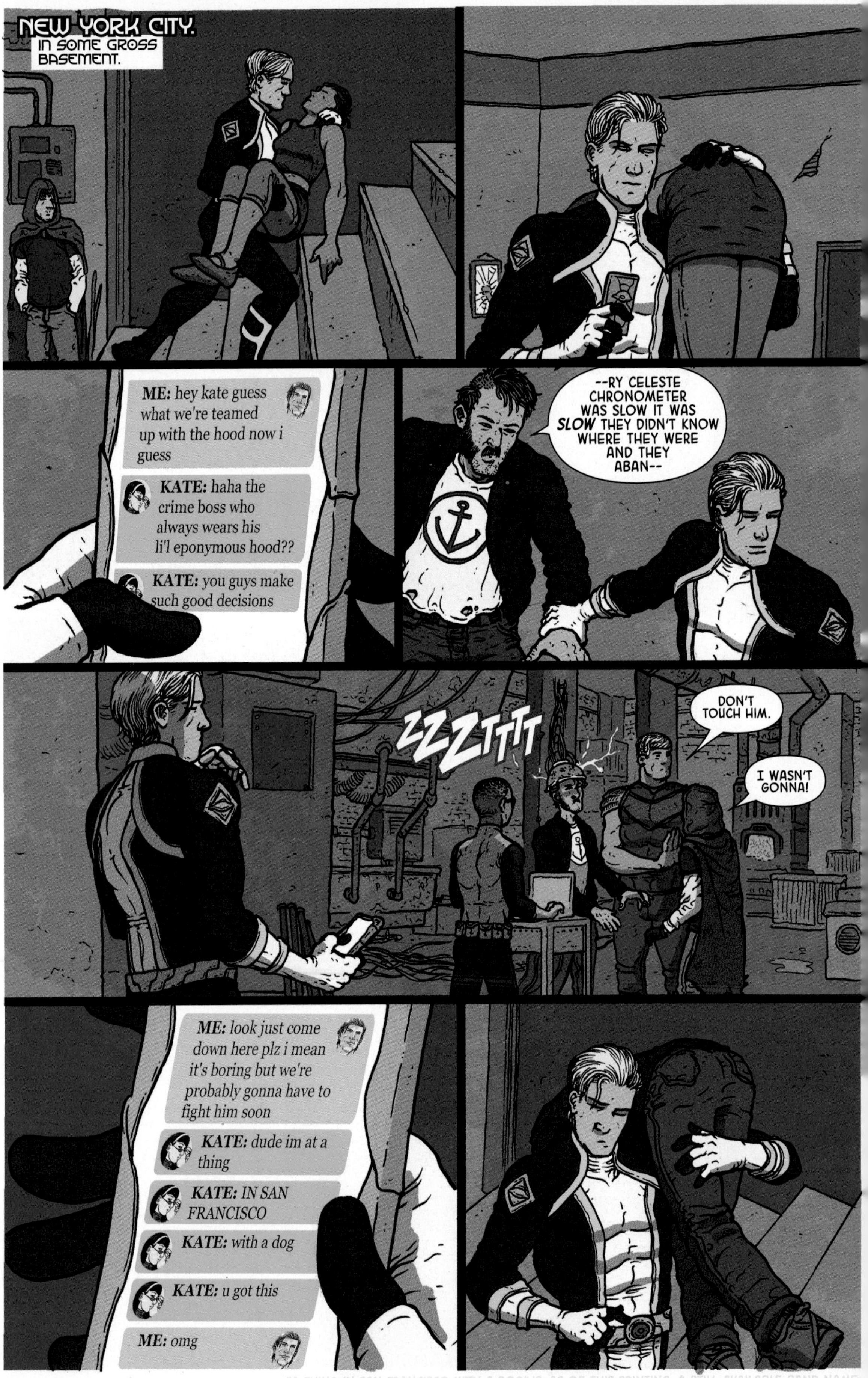
NEW YORK CITY.
IN SOME GROSS BASEMENT.
ME: hey kate guess what we're teamed up with the hood now i guess
KATE: haha the crime boss who always wears his li'l eponymous hood??
KATE: you guys make such good decisions
--RY CELESTE CHRONOMETER WAS SLOW IT WAS SLOW THEY DIDN'T KNOW WHERE THEY WERE AND THEY ABAN--
ZZZTTTT
DON'T TOUCH HIM.
I WASN'T GONNA!
ME: look just come down here plz i mean it's boring but we're probably gonna have to fight him soon
KATE: dude im at a thing
KATE: IN SAN FRANCISCO
KATE: with a dog
KATE: u got this
ME: omg

"A THING IN SAN FRANCISCO WITH A DOG" IS, AS OF THIS PRINTING, A STILL-AVAILABLE BAND NAME.

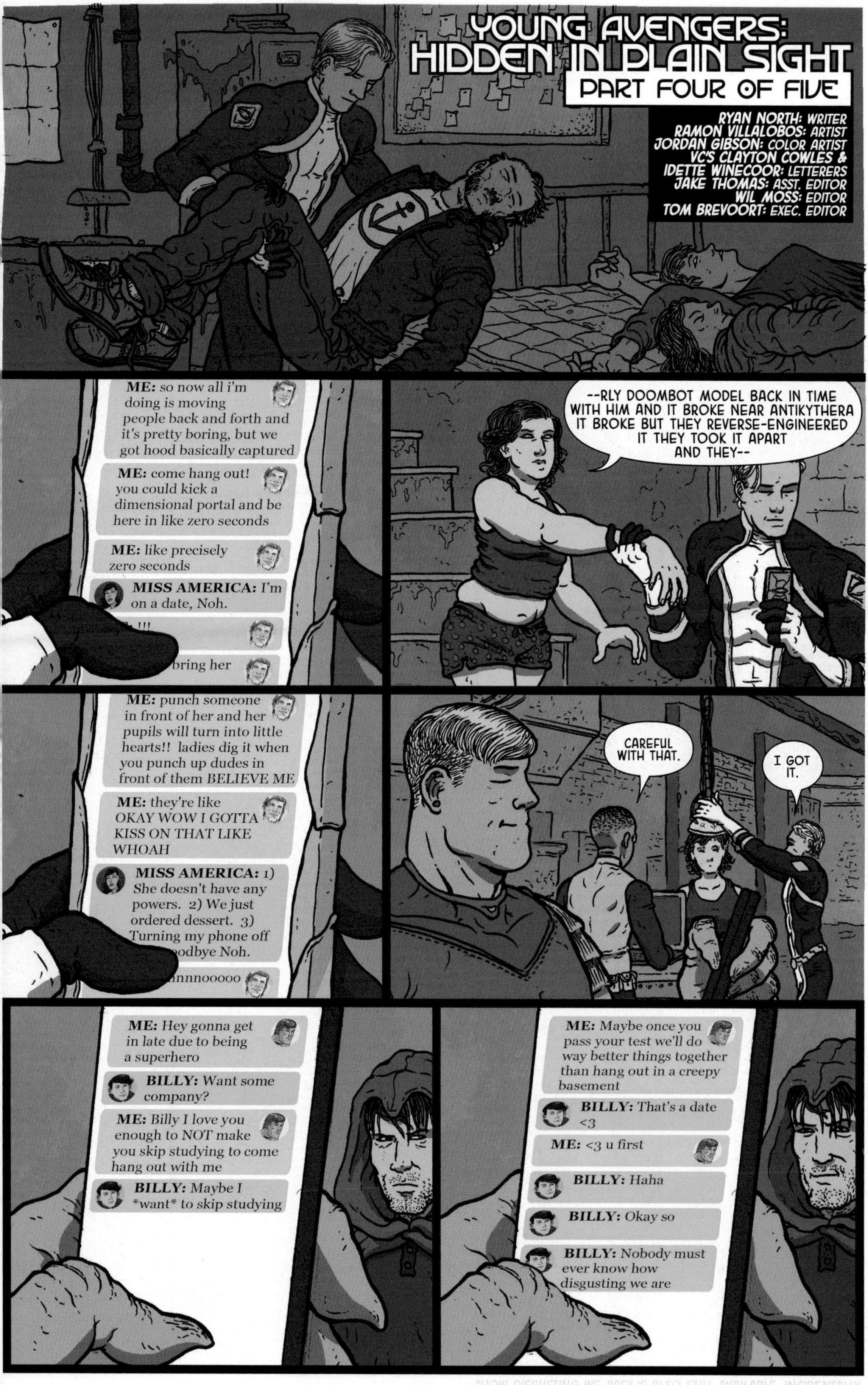
YOUNG AVENGERS: HIDDEN IN PLAIN SIGHT
PART FOUR OF FIVE
RYAN NORTH: WRITER
RAMON VILLALOBOS: ARTIST
JORDAN GIBSON: COLOR ARTIST
VC'S CLAYTON COWLES & IDETTE WINECOOR: LETTERERS
JAKE THOMAS: ASST. EDITOR
WIL MOSS: EDITOR
TOM BREVOORT: EXEC. EDITOR
ME: so now all i'm doing is moving people back and forth and it's pretty boring, but we got hood basically captured
ME: come hang out! you could kick a dimensional portal and be here in like zero seconds
ME: like precisely zero seconds
MISS AMERICA: I'm on a date, Noh.
bring her
--RLY DOOMBOT MODEL BACK IN TIME WITH HIM AND IT BROKE NEAR ANTIKYTHERA IT BROKE BUT THEY REVERSE-ENGINEERED IT THEY TOOK IT APART AND THEY--
ME: punch someone in front of her and her pupils will turn into little hearts!! ladies dig it when you punch up dudes in front of them BELIEVE ME
ME: they're like OKAY WOW I GOTTA KISS ON THAT LIKE WHOAH
MISS AMERICA: 1) She doesn't have any powers. 2) We just ordered dessert. 3) Turning my phone off
CAREFUL WITH THAT.
I GOT IT.
ME: Hey gonna get in late due to being a superhero
BILLY: Want some company?
ME: Billy I love you enough to NOT make you skip studying to come hang out with me
BILLY: Maybe I *want* to skip studying
ME: Maybe once you pass your test we'll do way better things together than hang out in a creepy basement
BILLY: That's a date <3
ME: <3 u first
BILLY: Haha
BILLY: Okay so
BILLY: Nobody must ever know how disgusting we are

"HOW DISGUSTING WE ARE" IS ALSO STILL AVAILABLE, INCIDENTALLY.

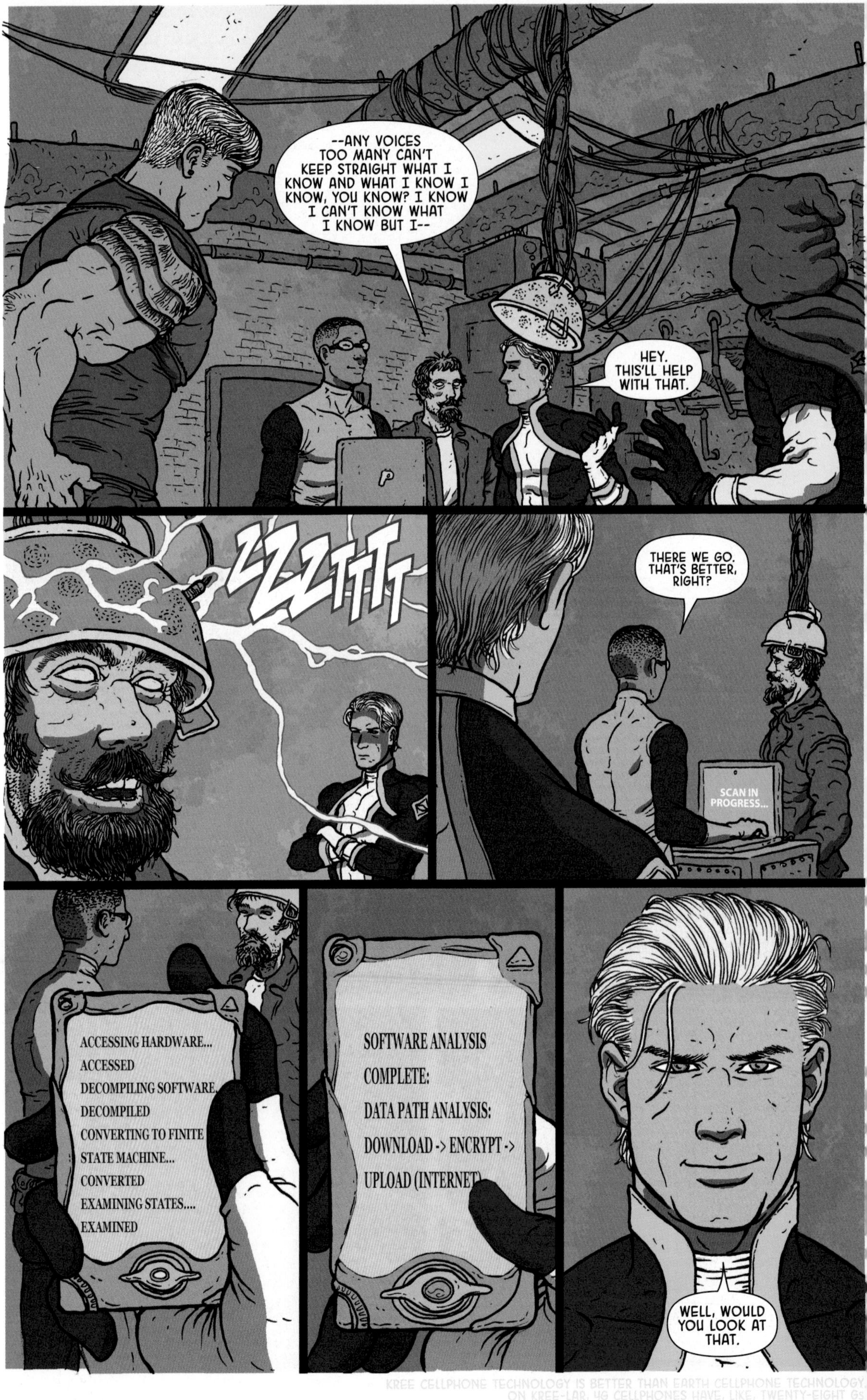
--ANY VOICES TOO MANY CAN'T KEEP STRAIGHT WHAT I KNOW AND WHAT I KNOW I KNOW, YOU KNOW? I KNOW I CAN'T KNOW WHAT I KNOW BUT I--
HEY. THIS'LL HELP WITH THAT.
ZZZTTTT
THERE WE GO. THAT'S BETTER, RIGHT?
SCAN IN PROGRESS...
ACCESSING HARDWARE...
ACCESSED
DECOMPILING SOFTWARE...
DECOMPILED
CONVERTING TO FINITE STATE MACHINE...
CONVERTED
EXAMINING STATES....
EXAMINED
SOFTWARE ANALYSIS COMPLETE:
DATA PATH ANALYSIS:
DOWNLOAD -> ENCRYPT ->
UPLOAD (INTERNET)
WELL, WOULD YOU LOOK AT THAT.

KREE CELLPHONE TECHNOLOGY IS BETTER THAN EARTH CELLPHONE TECHNOLOGY.
ON KREE-LAR, 4G CELLPHONES HAVE, LIKE, TWENTY-EIGHT Gs

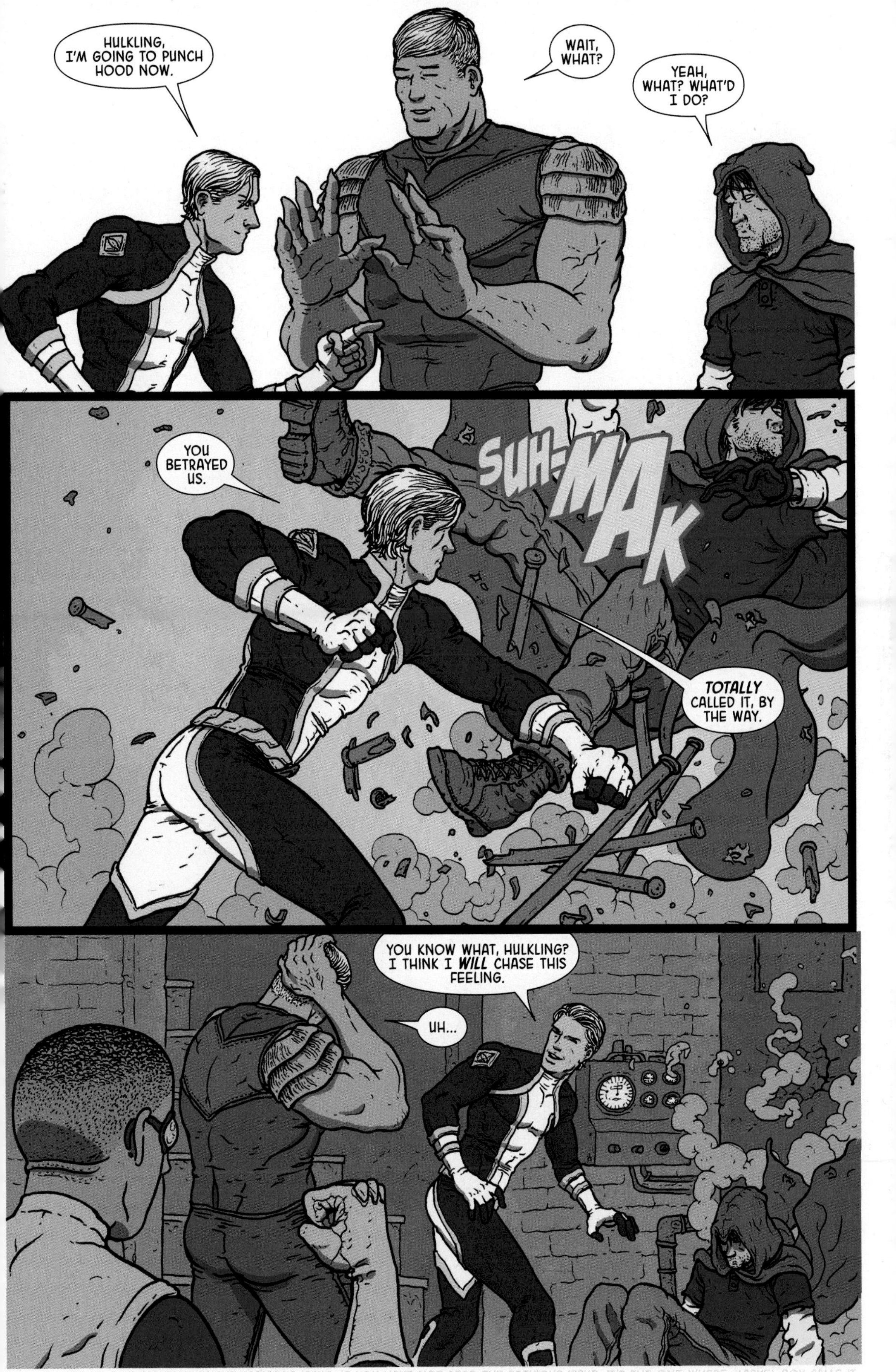
HULKLING, I'M GOING TO PUNCH HOOD NOW.
WAIT, WHAT?
YEAH, WHAT? WHAT'D I DO?
YOU BETRAYED US.
SUH-MAK
TOTALLY CALLED IT, BY THE WAY.
YOU KNOW WHAT, HULKLING? I THINK I WILL CHASE THIS FEELING.
UH...

MARVEL BOY CALLED IT IN THE PREVIOUS ISSUE. IF YOU HAVE NOT READ THE PREVIOUS ISSUE, IT'S THE ONE WHERE MARVEL BOY CALLS IT. THERE! NOW YOU CAN PASS AS SOMEONE WHO READ THE PREVIOUS ISSUE!

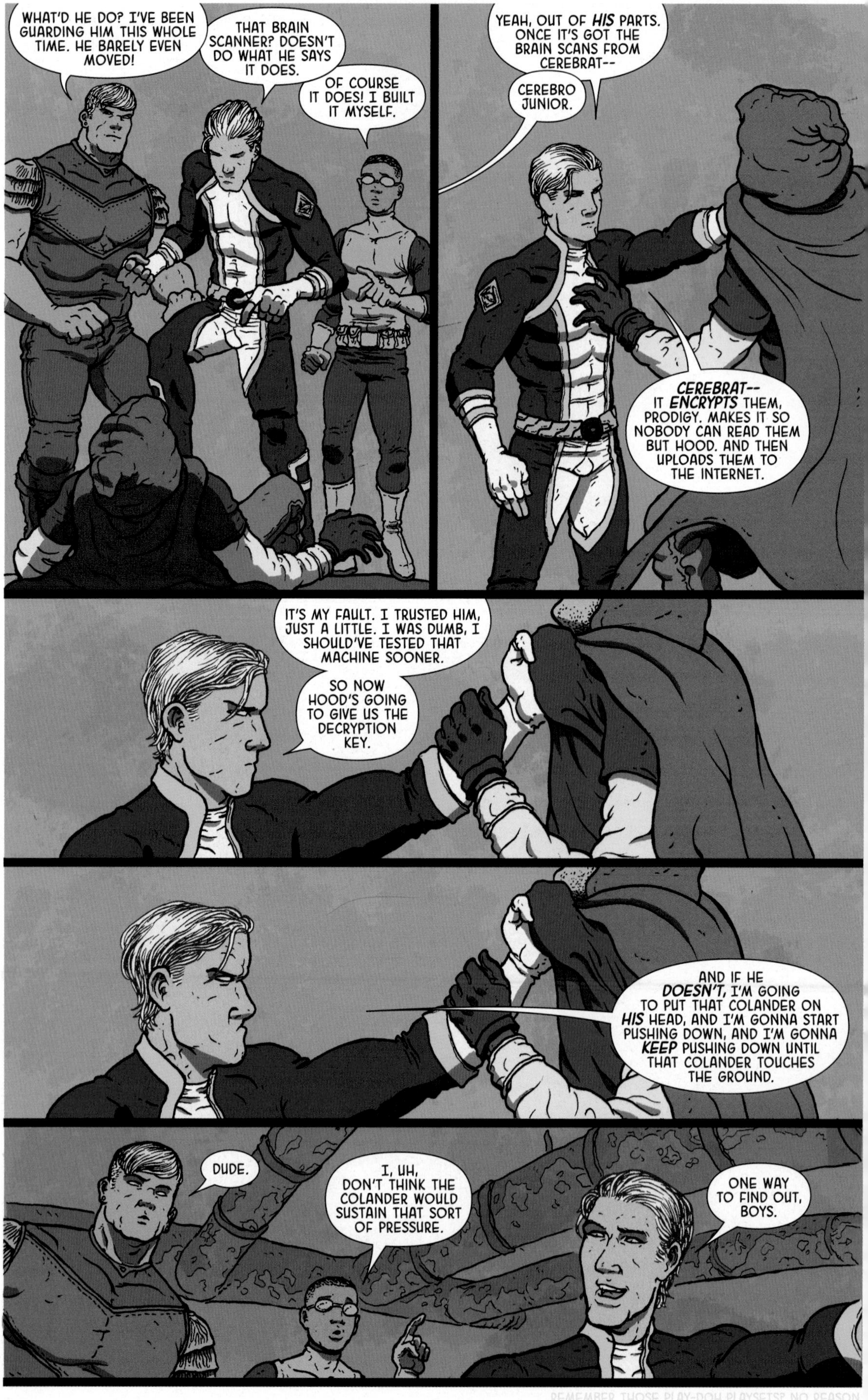
WHAT'D HE DO? I'VE BEEN GUARDING HIM THIS WHOLE TIME. HE BARELY EVEN MOVED!
THAT BRAIN SCANNER? DOESN'T DO WHAT HE SAYS IT DOES.
OF COURSE IT DOES! I BUILT IT MYSELF.
YEAH, OUT OF HIS PARTS. ONCE IT'S GOT THE BRAIN SCANS FROM CEREBRAT--
CEREBRO JUNIOR.
CEREBRAT-- IT ENCRYPTS THEM, PRODIGY. MAKES IT SO NOBODY CAN READ THEM BUT HOOD. AND THEN UPLOADS THEM TO THE INTERNET.
IT'S MY FAULT. I TRUSTED HIM, JUST A LITTLE. I WAS DUMB, I SHOULD'VE TESTED THAT MACHINE SOONER.
SO NOW HOOD'S GOING TO GIVE US THE DECRYPTION KEY.
AND IF HE DOESN'T, I'M GOING TO PUT THAT COLANDER ON HIS HEAD, AND I'M GONNA START PUSHING DOWN, AND I'M GONNA KEEP PUSHING DOWN UNTIL THAT COLANDER TOUCHES THE GROUND.
DUDE.
I, UH, DON'T THINK THE COLANDER WOULD SUSTAIN THAT SORT OF PRESSURE.
ONE WAY TO FIND OUT, BOYS.

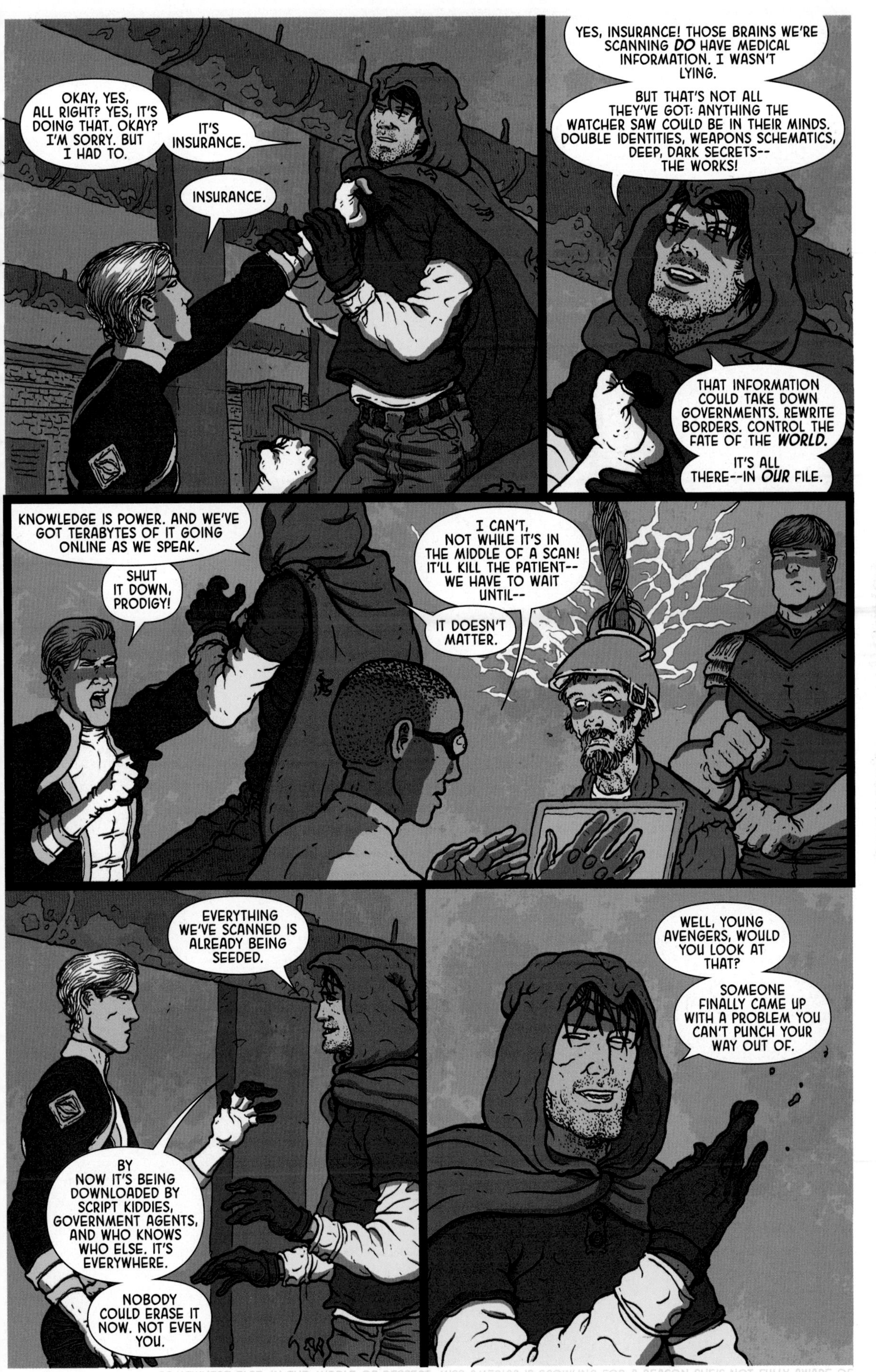
OKAY, YES, ALL RIGHT? YES, IT'S DOING THAT. OKAY? I'M SORRY. BUT I HAD TO.
IT'S INSURANCE.
INSURANCE.
YES, INSURANCE! THOSE BRAINS WE'RE SCANNING DO HAVE MEDICAL INFORMATION. I WASN'T LYING.
BUT THAT'S NOT ALL THEY'VE GOT: ANYTHING THE WATCHER SAW COULD BE IN THEIR MINDS. DOUBLE IDENTITIES, WEAPONS SCHEMATICS, DEEP, DARK SECRETS-- THE WORKS!
THAT INFORMATION COULD TAKE DOWN GOVERNMENTS. REWRITE BORDERS. CONTROL THE FATE OF THE WORLD.
IT'S ALL THERE--IN OUR FILE.
KNOWLEDGE IS POWER. AND WE'VE GOT TERABYTES OF IT GOING ONLINE AS WE SPEAK.
SHUT IT DOWN, PRODIGY!
I CAN'T, NOT WHILE IT'S IN THE MIDDLE OF A SCAN! IT'LL KILL THE PATIENT-- WE HAVE TO WAIT UNTIL--
IT DOESN'T MATTER.
EVERYTHING WE'VE SCANNED IS ALREADY BEING SEEDED.
BY NOW IT'S BEING DOWNLOADED BY SCRIPT KIDDIES, GOVERNMENT AGENTS, AND WHO KNOWS WHO ELSE. IT'S EVERYWHERE.
NOBODY COULD ERASE IT NOW. NOT EVEN YOU.
WELL, YOUNG AVENGERS, WOULD YOU LOOK AT THAT?
SOMEONE FINALLY CAME UP WITH A PROBLEM YOU CAN'T PUNCH YOUR WAY OUT OF.

SOMEWHERE ELSE, IN THE MIDDLE OF DESSERT, MISS AMERICA IS SCOWLING FOR A REASON SHE'S NOT FULLY AWARE OF

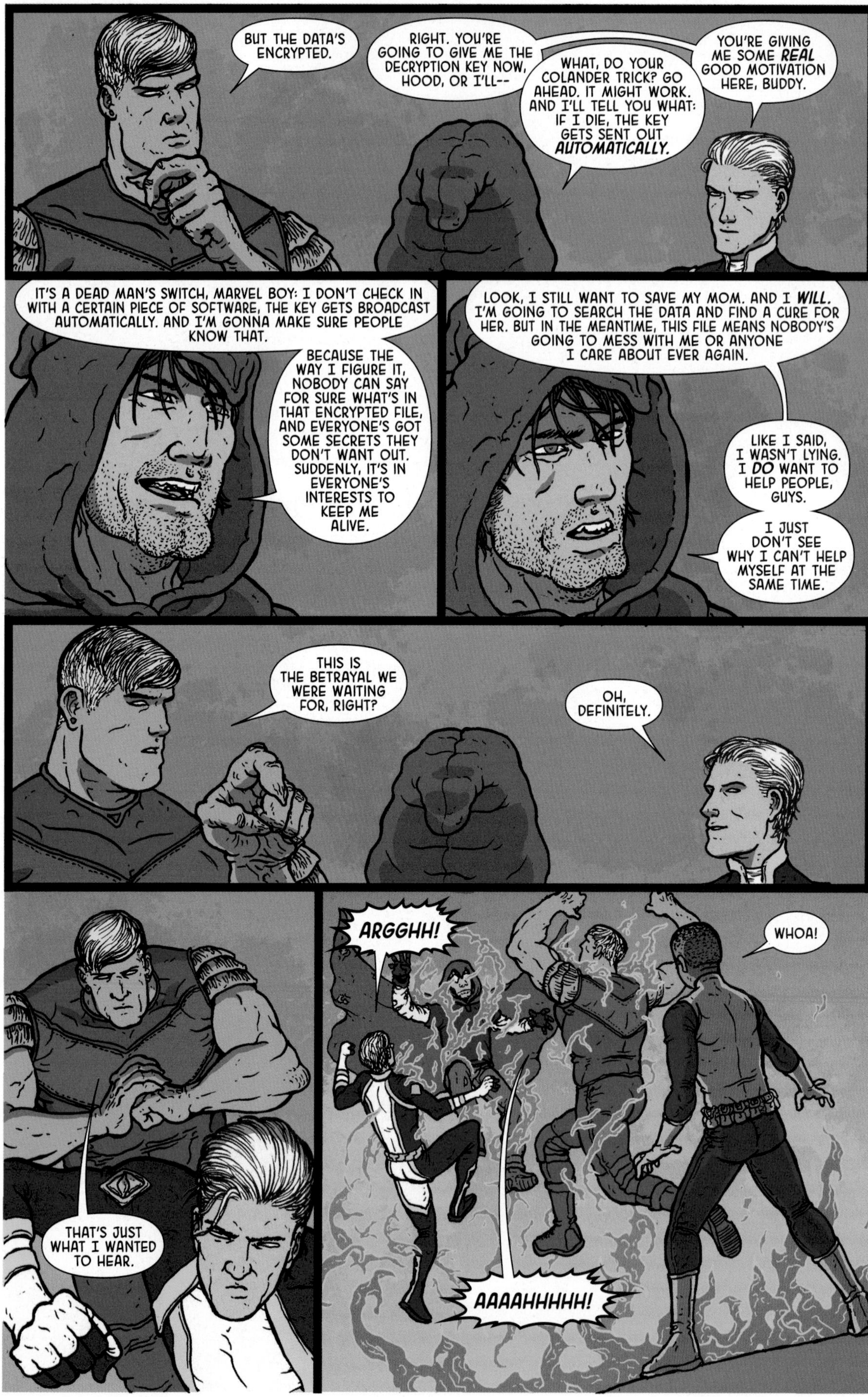
BUT THE DATA'S ENCRYPTED.
RIGHT. YOU'RE GOING TO GIVE ME THE DECRYPTION KEY NOW, HOOD, OR I'LL--
YOU'RE GIVING ME SOME REAL GOOD MOTIVATION HERE, BUDDY.
WHAT, DO YOUR COLANDER TRICK? GO AHEAD. IT MIGHT WORK. AND I'LL TELL YOU WHAT: IF I DIE, THE KEY GETS SENT OUT AUTOMATICALLY.
IT'S A DEAD MAN'S SWITCH, MARVEL BOY: I DON'T CHECK IN WITH A CERTAIN PIECE OF SOFTWARE, THE KEY GETS BROADCAST AUTOMATICALLY. AND I'M GONNA MAKE SURE PEOPLE KNOW THAT.
BECAUSE THE WAY I FIGURE IT, NOBODY CAN SAY FOR SURE WHAT'S IN THAT ENCRYPTED FILE, AND EVERYONE'S GOT SOME SECRETS THEY DON'T WANT OUT. SUDDENLY, IT'S IN EVERYONE'S INTERESTS TO KEEP ME ALIVE.
LOOK, I STILL WANT TO SAVE MY MOM. AND I WILL. I'M GOING TO SEARCH THE DATA AND FIND A CURE FOR HER. BUT IN THE MEANTIME, THIS FILE MEANS NOBODY'S GOING TO MESS WITH ME OR ANYONE I CARE ABOUT EVER AGAIN.
LIKE I SAID, I WASN'T LYING. I DO WANT TO HELP PEOPLE, GUYS.
I JUST DON'T SEE WHY I CAN'T HELP MYSELF AT THE SAME TIME.
THIS IS THE BETRAYAL WE WERE WAITING FOR, RIGHT?
OH, DEFINITELY.
THAT'S JUST WHAT I WANTED TO HEAR.
ARGGHH!
WHOA!
AAAAHHHHH!

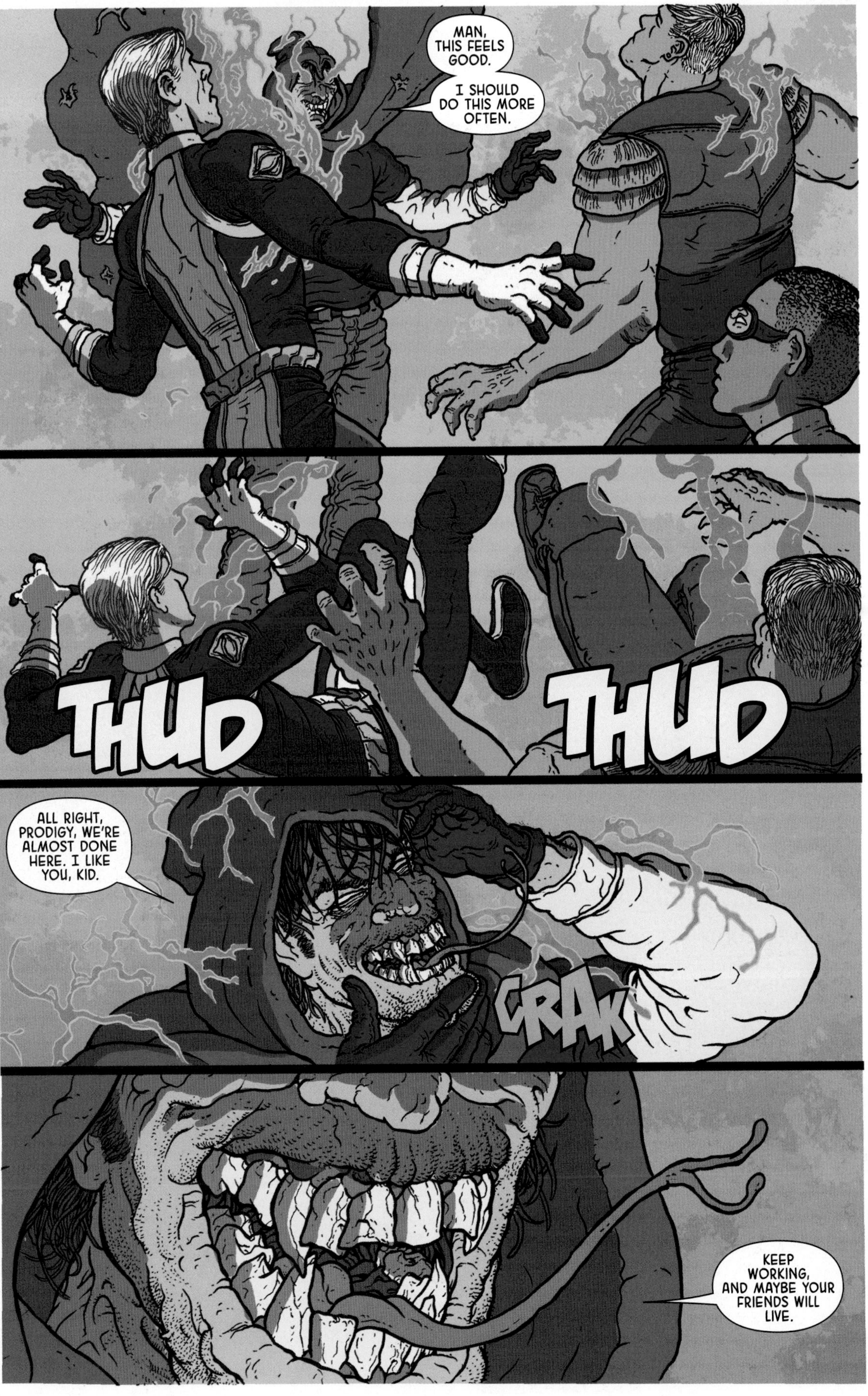
MAN, THIS FEELS GOOD.
I SHOULD DO THIS MORE OFTEN.
THUD
THUD
ALL RIGHT, PRODIGY, WE'RE ALMOST DONE HERE. I LIKE YOU, KID.
CRAK
KEEP WORKING, AND MAYBE YOUR FRIENDS WILL LIVE.

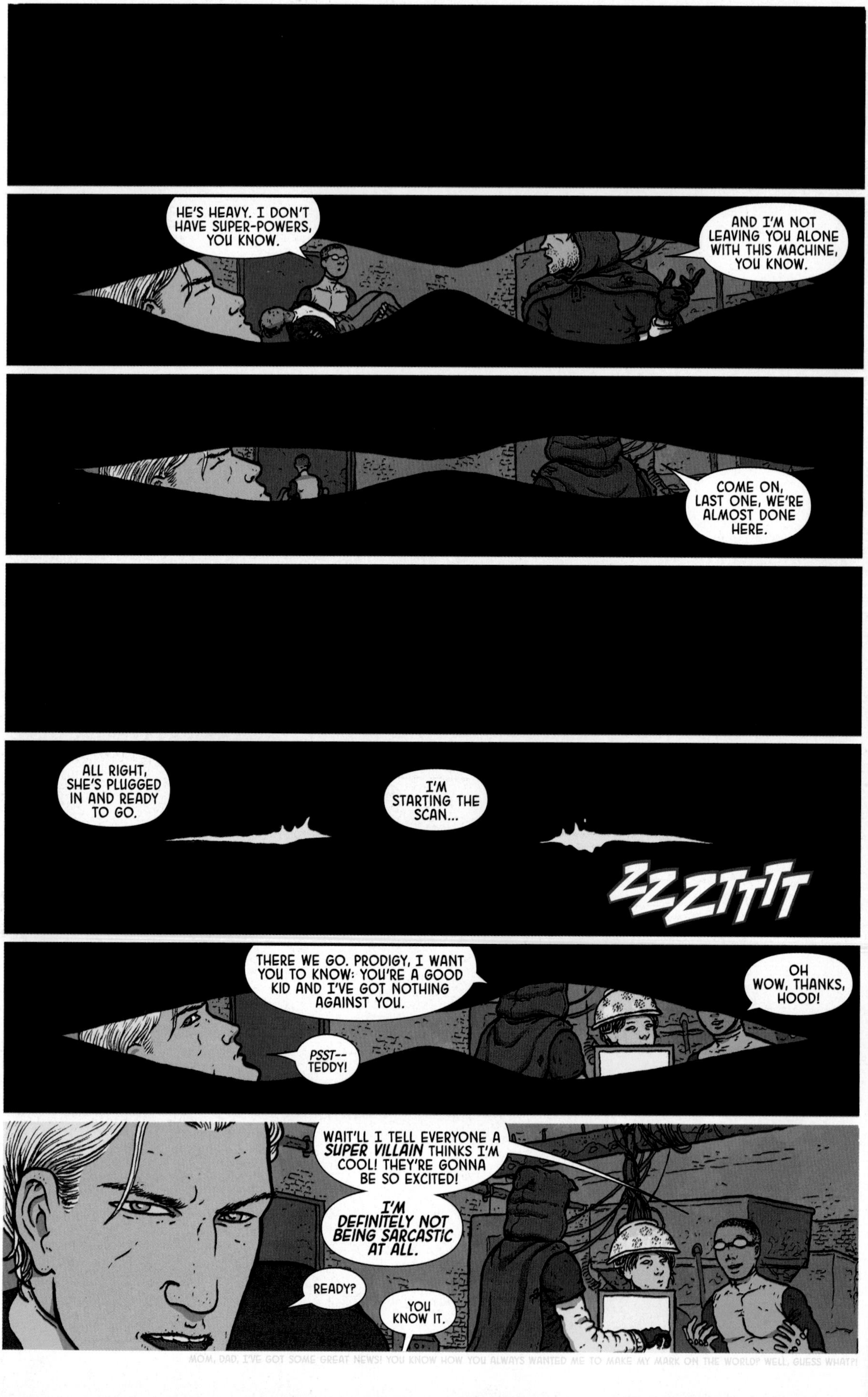
HE'S HEAVY. I DON'T HAVE SUPER-POWERS, YOU KNOW.
AND I'M NOT LEAVING YOU ALONE WITH THIS MACHINE, YOU KNOW.
COME ON, LAST ONE, WE'RE ALMOST DONE HERE.
ALL RIGHT, SHE'S PLUGGED IN AND READY TO GO.
I'M STARTING THE SCAN...
ZZZTTTT
THERE WE GO. PRODIGY, I WANT YOU TO KNOW: YOU'RE A GOOD KID AND I'VE GOT NOTHING AGAINST YOU.
OH WOW, THANKS, HOOD!
PSST-- TEDDY!
WAIT'LL I TELL EVERYONE A SUPER VILLAIN THINKS I'M COOL! THEY'RE GONNA BE SO EXCITED!
I'M DEFINITELY NOT BEING SARCASTIC AT ALL.
READY?
YOU KNOW IT.

MOM, DAD, I'VE GOT SOME GREAT NEWS! YOU KNOW HOW YOU ALWAYS WANTED ME TO MAKE MY MARK ON THE WORLD? WELL, GUESS WHAT?!

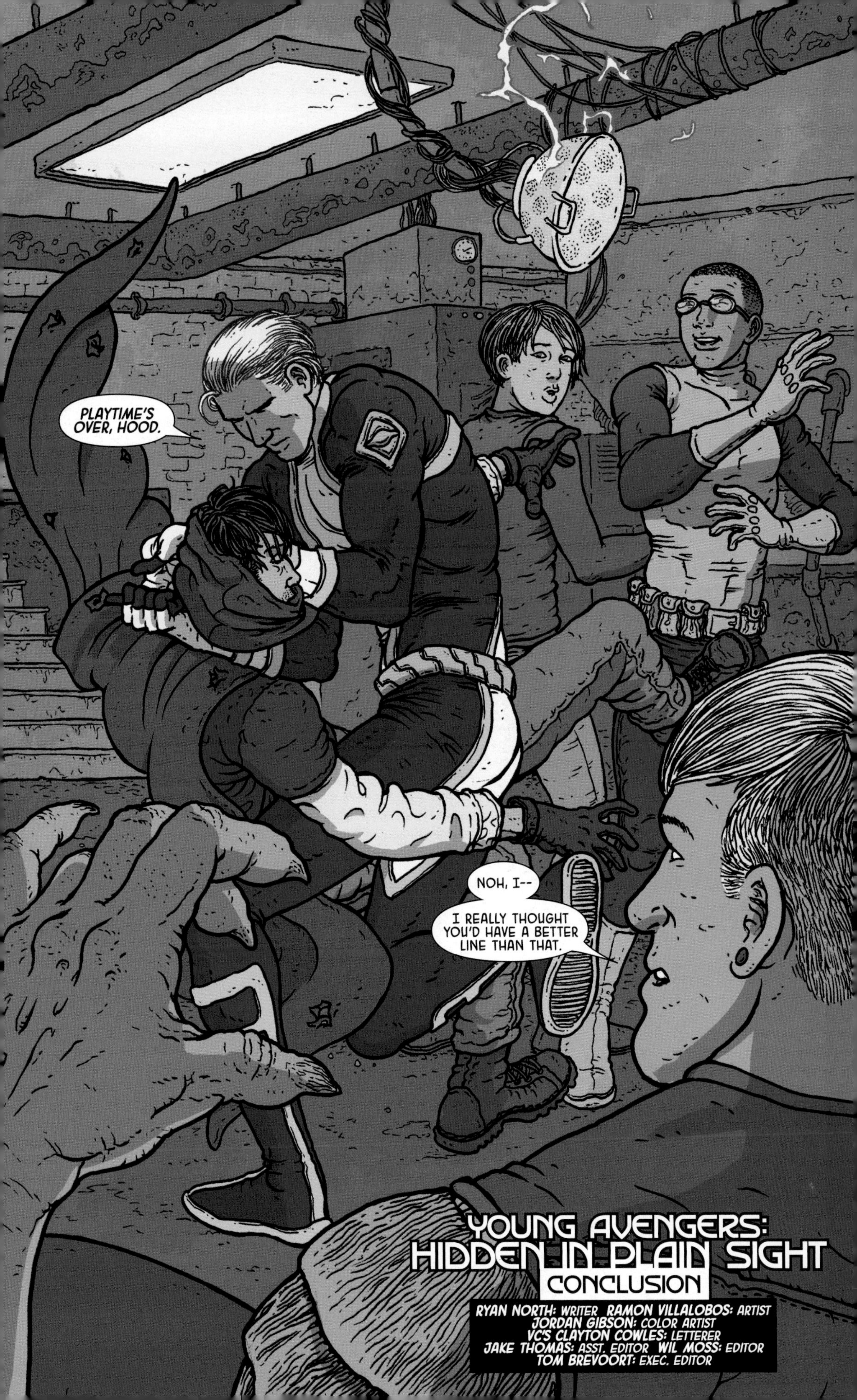
PLAYTIME'S OVER, HOOD.
NOH, I--
I REALLY THOUGHT YOU'D HAVE A BETTER LINE THAN THAT.
YOUNG AVENGERS: HIDDEN IN PLAIN SIGHT
CONCLUSION
RYAN NORTH: WRITER RAMON VILLALOBOS: ARTIST
JORDAN GIBSON: COLOR ARTIST
VC'S CLAYTON COWLES: LETTERER
JAKE THOMAS: ASST. EDITOR WIL MOSS: EDITOR
TOM BREVOORT: EXEC. EDITOR

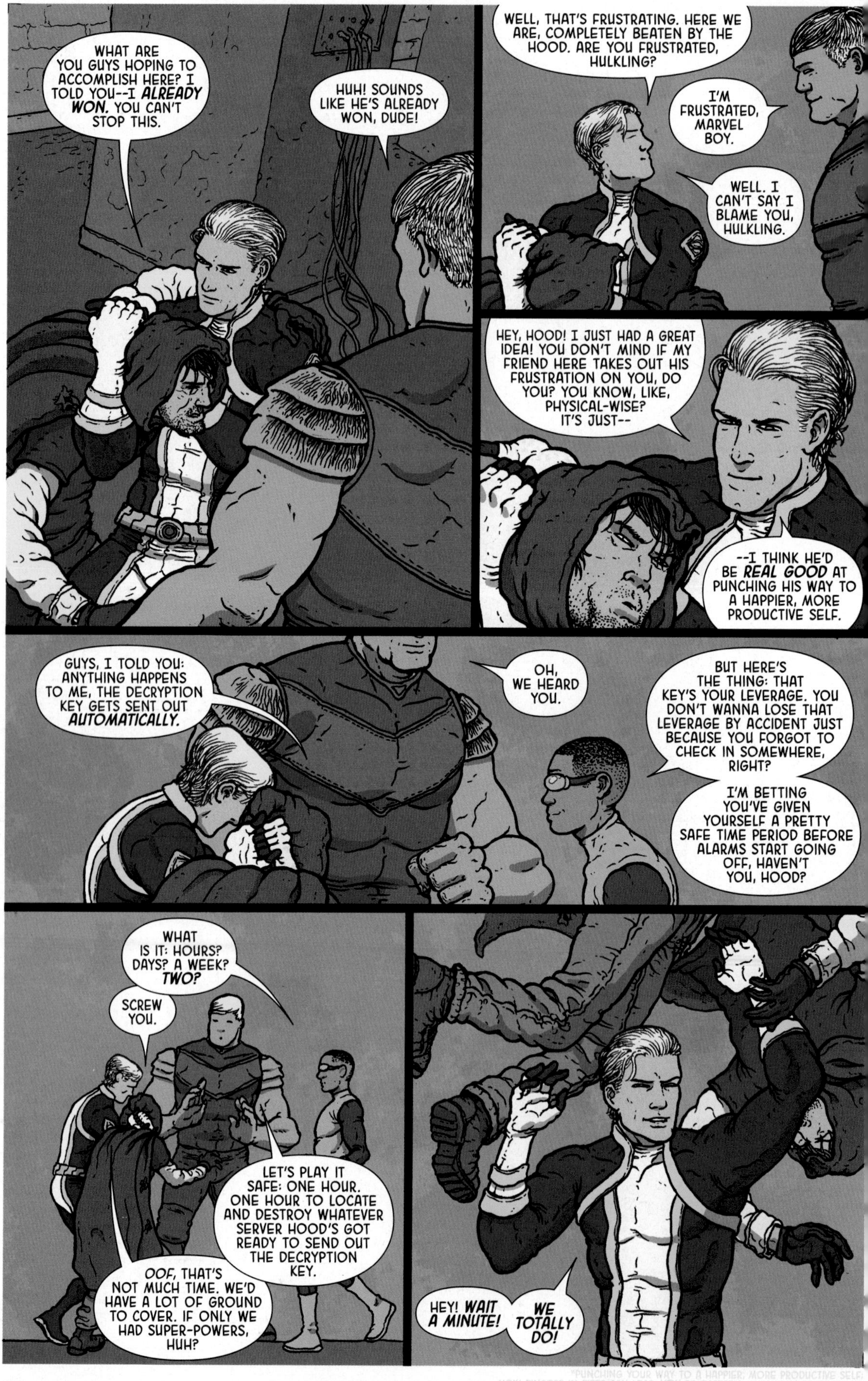

WHAT ARE YOU GUYS HOPING TO ACCOMPLISH HERE? I TOLD YOU--I ***ALREADY WON.*** YOU CAN'T STOP THIS.
HUH! SOUNDS LIKE HE'S ALREADY WON, DUDE!
WELL, THAT'S FRUSTRATING. HERE WE ARE, COMPLETELY BEATEN BY THE HOOD. ARE YOU FRUSTRATED, HULKLING?
I'M FRUSTRATED, MARVEL BOY.
WELL. I CAN'T SAY I BLAME YOU, HULKLING.
HEY, HOOD! I JUST HAD A GREAT IDEA! YOU DON'T MIND IF MY FRIEND HERE TAKES OUT HIS FRUSTRATION ON YOU, DO YOU? YOU KNOW, LIKE, PHYSICAL-WISE? IT'S JUST--
--I THINK HE'D BE ***REAL GOOD*** AT PUNCHING HIS WAY TO A HAPPIER, MORE PRODUCTIVE SELF.
GUYS, I TOLD YOU: ANYTHING HAPPENS TO ME, THE DECRYPTION KEY GETS SENT OUT ***AUTOMATICALLY.***
OH, WE HEARD YOU.
BUT HERE'S THE THING: THAT KEY'S YOUR LEVERAGE. YOU DON'T WANNA LOSE THAT LEVERAGE BY ACCIDENT JUST BECAUSE YOU FORGOT TO CHECK IN SOMEWHERE, RIGHT?
I'M BETTING YOU'VE GIVEN YOURSELF A PRETTY SAFE TIME PERIOD BEFORE ALARMS START GOING OFF, HAVEN'T YOU, HOOD?
WHAT IS IT: HOURS? DAYS? A WEEK? ***TWO?***
SCREW YOU.
LET'S PLAY IT SAFE: ONE HOUR. ONE HOUR TO LOCATE AND DESTROY WHATEVER SERVER HOOD'S GOT READY TO SEND OUT THE DECRYPTION KEY.
OOF, THAT'S NOT MUCH TIME. WE'D HAVE A LOT OF GROUND TO COVER. IF ONLY WE HAD SUPER-POWERS, HUH?
HEY! ***WAIT A MINUTE!***
WE TOTALLY DO!

"PUNCHING YOUR WAY TO A HAPPIER, MORE PRODUCTIVE SELF: HOW FINGERS IN FISTS CAN LEAD *YOU* TO ECSTATIC, ENERGETIC EFFECTIVITY."

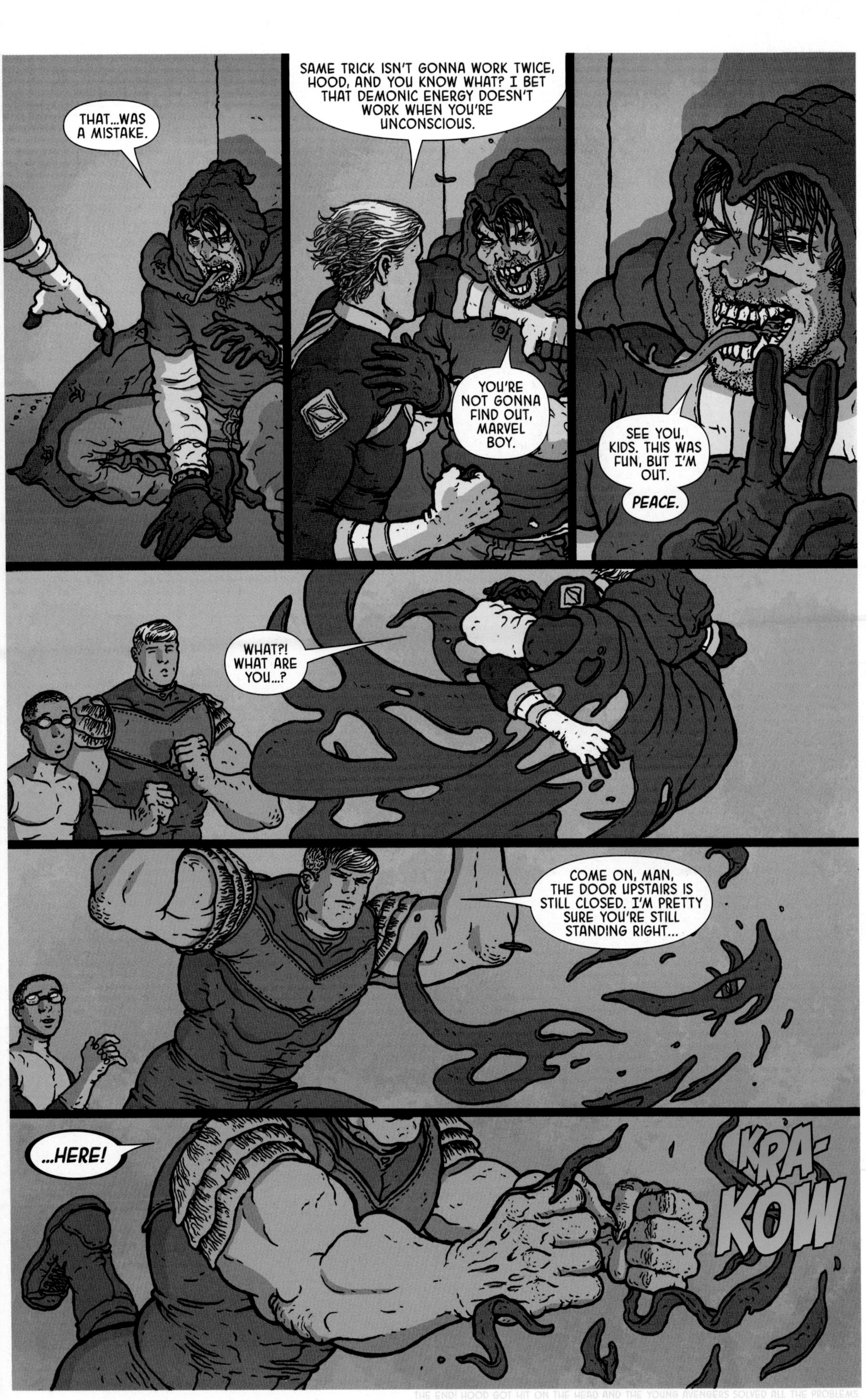
THAT...WAS A MISTAKE.
SAME TRICK ISN'T GONNA WORK TWICE, HOOD, AND YOU KNOW WHAT? I BET THAT DEMONIC ENERGY DOESN'T WORK WHEN YOU'RE UNCONSCIOUS.
YOU'RE NOT GONNA FIND OUT, MARVEL BOY.
SEE YOU, KIDS. THIS WAS FUN, BUT I'M OUT.
PEACE.
WHAT?! WHAT ARE YOU...?
COME ON, MAN, THE DOOR UPSTAIRS IS STILL CLOSED. I'M PRETTY SURE YOU'RE STILL STANDING RIGHT...
...HERE!
KRA-KOW

THE END! HOOD GOT HIT ON THE HEAD AND THE YOUNG AVENGERS SOLVED ALL THE PROBLEMS.
THANKS FOR READING!

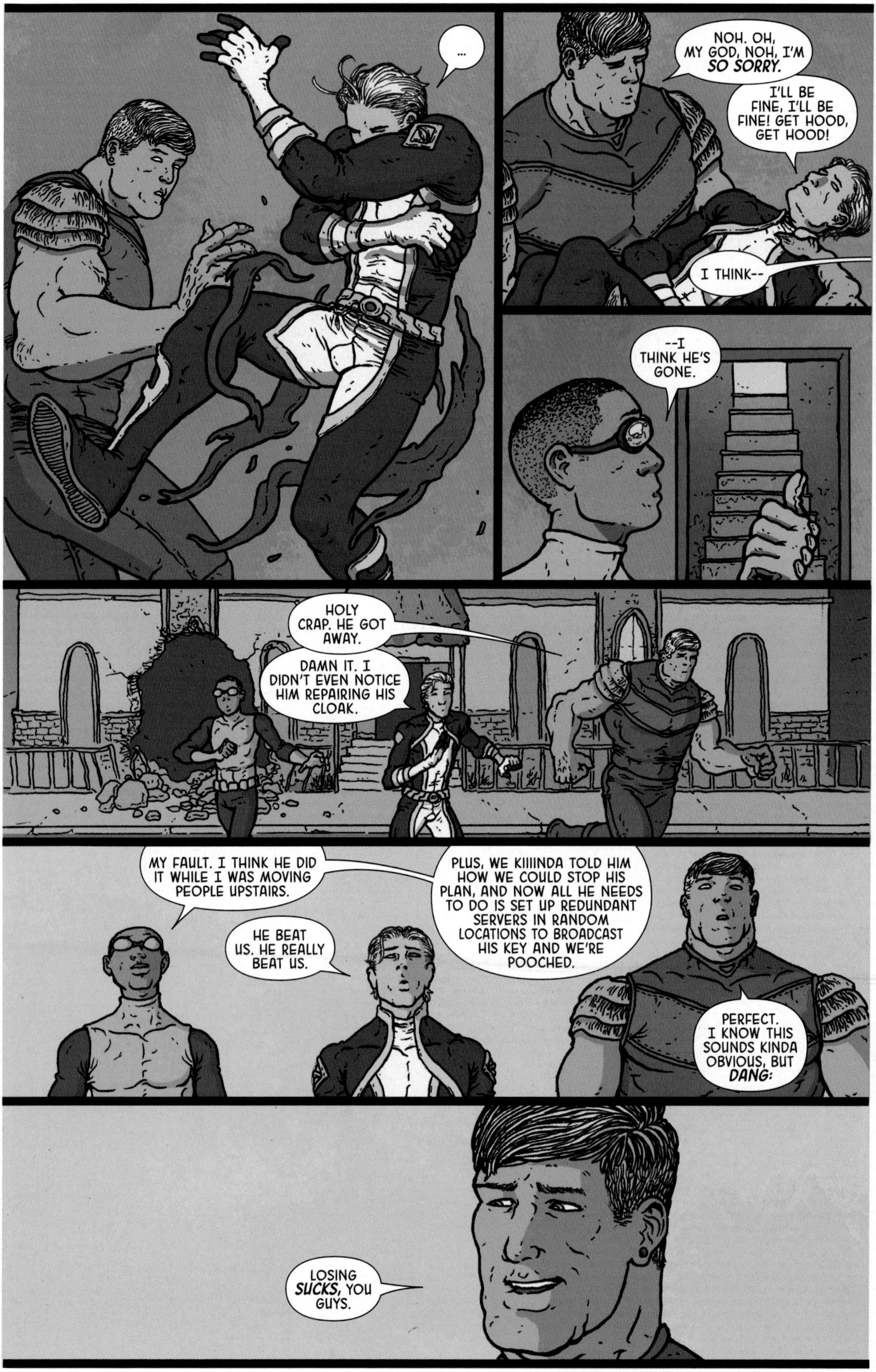
...
NOH. OH, MY GOD, NOH, I'M *SO SORRY.*
I'LL BE FINE, I'LL BE FINE! GET HOOD, GET HOOD!
I THINK--
--I THINK HE'S GONE.
HOLY CRAP. HE GOT AWAY.
DAMN IT. I DIDN'T EVEN NOTICE HIM REPAIRING HIS CLOAK.
MY FAULT. I THINK HE DID IT WHILE I WAS MOVING PEOPLE UPSTAIRS.
HE BEAT US. HE REALLY BEAT US.
PLUS, WE KIIIINDA TOLD HIM HOW WE COULD STOP HIS PLAN, AND NOW ALL HE NEEDS TO DO IS SET UP REDUNDANT SERVERS IN RANDOM LOCATIONS TO BROADCAST HIS KEY AND WE'RE POOCHED.
PERFECT. I KNOW THIS SOUNDS KINDA OBVIOUS, BUT *DANG:*
LOSING *SUCKS,* YOU GUYS.

OH WAIT, WHOOPS, IT WASN'T THE END AFTER ALL. OKAY, NEVER MIND!

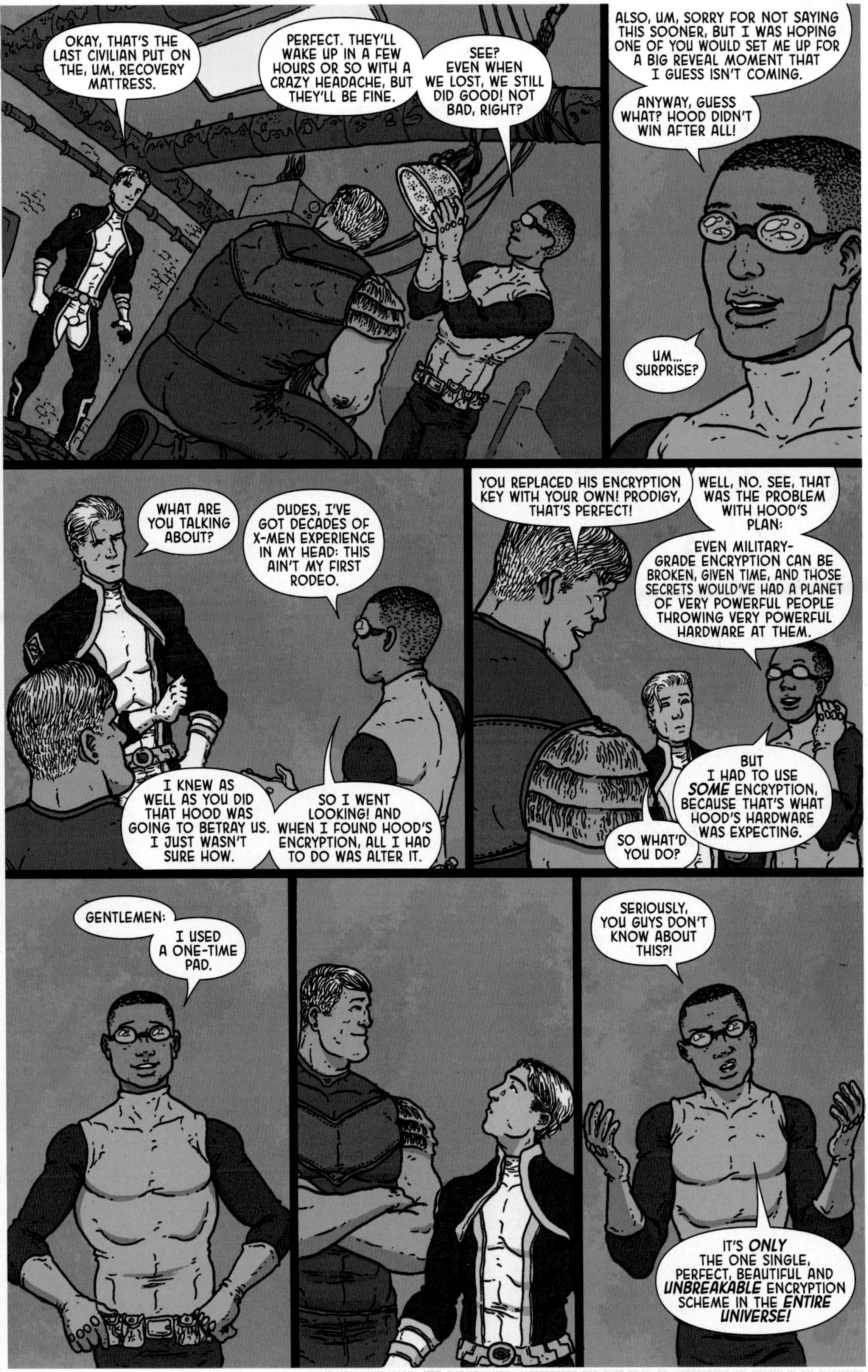
OKAY, THAT'S THE LAST CIVILIAN PUT ON THE, UM, RECOVERY MATTRESS.
PERFECT. THEY'LL WAKE UP IN A FEW HOURS OR SO WITH A CRAZY HEADACHE, BUT THEY'LL BE FINE.
SEE? EVEN WHEN WE LOST, WE STILL DID GOOD! NOT BAD, RIGHT?
ALSO, UM, SORRY FOR NOT SAYING THIS SOONER, BUT I WAS HOPING ONE OF YOU WOULD SET ME UP FOR A BIG REVEAL MOMENT THAT I GUESS ISN'T COMING.
ANYWAY, GUESS WHAT? HOOD DIDN'T WIN AFTER ALL!
UM... SURPRISE?
WHAT ARE YOU TALKING ABOUT?
DUDES, I'VE GOT DECADES OF X-MEN EXPERIENCE IN MY HEAD: THIS AIN'T MY FIRST RODEO.
I KNEW AS WELL AS YOU DID THAT HOOD WAS GOING TO BETRAY US. I JUST WASN'T SURE HOW.
SO I WENT LOOKING! AND WHEN I FOUND HOOD'S ENCRYPTION, ALL I HAD TO DO WAS ALTER IT.
YOU REPLACED HIS ENCRYPTION KEY WITH YOUR OWN! PRODIGY, THAT'S PERFECT!
WELL, NO. SEE, THAT WAS THE PROBLEM WITH HOOD'S PLAN:
EVEN MILITARY-GRADE ENCRYPTION CAN BE BROKEN, GIVEN TIME, AND THOSE SECRETS WOULD'VE HAD A PLANET OF VERY POWERFUL PEOPLE THROWING VERY POWERFUL HARDWARE AT THEM.
BUT I HAD TO USE *SOME* ENCRYPTION, BECAUSE THAT'S WHAT HOOD'S HARDWARE WAS EXPECTING.
SO WHAT'D YOU DO?
GENTLEMEN:
I USED A ONE-TIME PAD.
SERIOUSLY, YOU GUYS DON'T KNOW ABOUT THIS?!
IT'S *ONLY* THE ONE SINGLE, PERFECT, BEAUTIFUL AND *UNBREAKABLE* ENCRYPTION SCHEME IN THE *ENTIRE UNIVERSE!*

IF YOU MUST KNOW, *YES,* THE RECOVERY MATTRESSES ARE JUST REGULAR MATTRESSES WE FOUND IN AN ALLEYWAY. BUT THEY'RE STILL GOOD! THEY'RE *PERFECTLY FINE.*

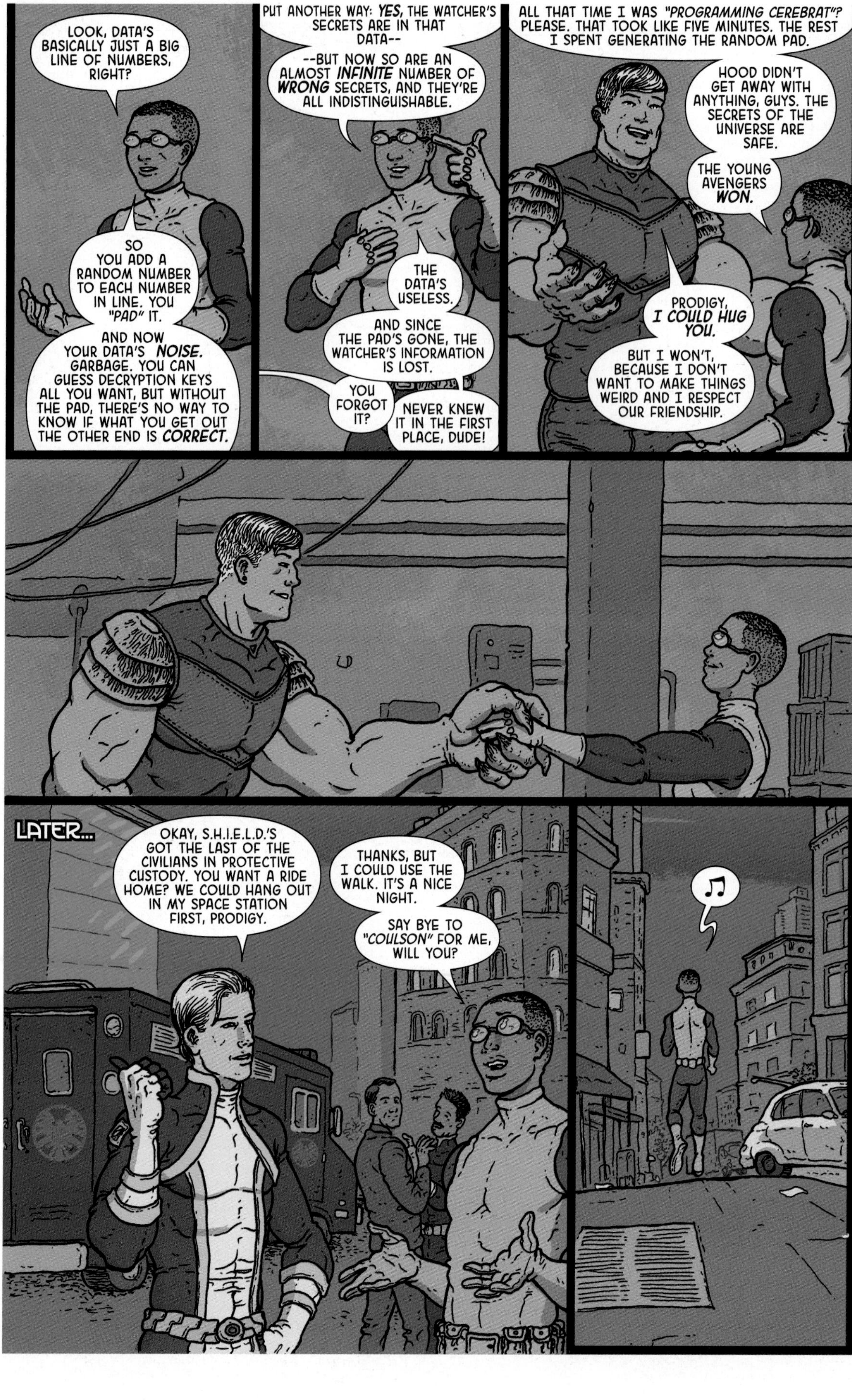
LOOK, DATA'S BASICALLY JUST A BIG LINE OF NUMBERS, RIGHT?
SO YOU ADD A RANDOM NUMBER TO EACH NUMBER IN LINE. YOU "PAD" IT.
AND NOW YOUR DATA'S NOISE. GARBAGE. YOU CAN GUESS DECRYPTION KEYS ALL YOU WANT, BUT WITHOUT THE PAD, THERE'S NO WAY TO KNOW IF WHAT YOU GET OUT THE OTHER END IS CORRECT.
PUT ANOTHER WAY: YES, THE WATCHER'S SECRETS ARE IN THAT DATA--
--BUT NOW SO ARE AN ALMOST INFINITE NUMBER OF WRONG SECRETS, AND THEY'RE ALL INDISTINGUISHABLE.
THE DATA'S USELESS.
AND SINCE THE PAD'S GONE, THE WATCHER'S INFORMATION IS LOST.
YOU FORGOT IT?
NEVER KNEW IT IN THE FIRST PLACE, DUDE!
ALL THAT TIME I WAS "PROGRAMMING CEREBRAT"? PLEASE. THAT TOOK LIKE FIVE MINUTES. THE REST I SPENT GENERATING THE RANDOM PAD.
HOOD DIDN'T GET AWAY WITH ANYTHING, GUYS. THE SECRETS OF THE UNIVERSE ARE SAFE.
THE YOUNG AVENGERS WON.
PRODIGY, I COULD HUG YOU.
BUT I WON'T, BECAUSE I DON'T WANT TO MAKE THINGS WEIRD AND I RESPECT OUR FRIENDSHIP.
LATER...
OKAY, S.H.I.E.L.D.'S GOT THE LAST OF THE CIVILIANS IN PROTECTIVE CUSTODY. YOU WANT A RIDE HOME? WE COULD HANG OUT IN MY SPACE STATION FIRST, PRODIGY.
THANKS, BUT I COULD USE THE WALK. IT'S A NICE NIGHT.
SAY BYE TO "COULSON" FOR ME, WILL YOU?
♫

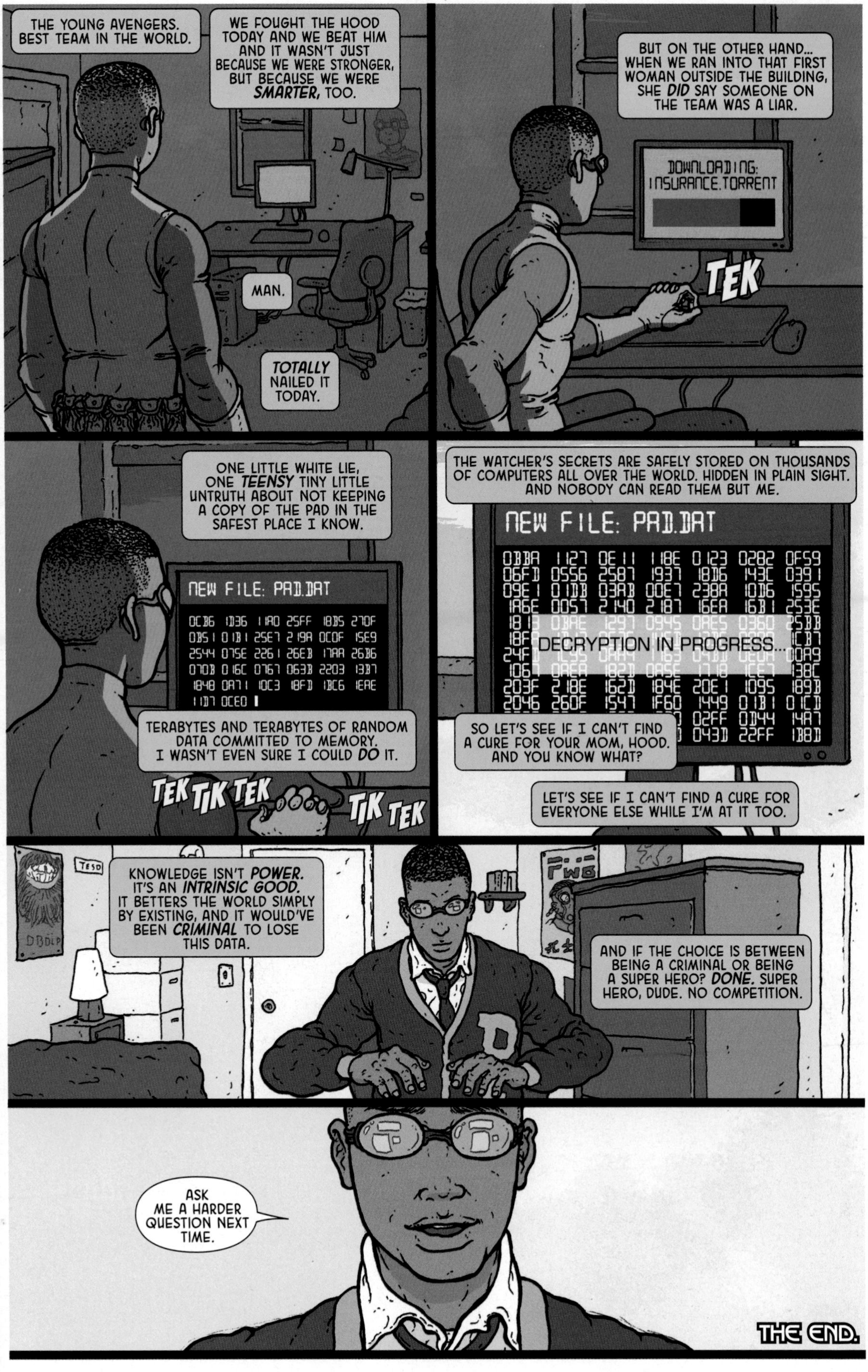
THE YOUNG AVENGERS. BEST TEAM IN THE WORLD.
WE FOUGHT THE HOOD TODAY AND WE BEAT HIM AND IT WASN'T JUST BECAUSE WE WERE STRONGER, BUT BECAUSE WE WERE SMARTER, TOO.
MAN.
TOTALLY NAILED IT TODAY.
BUT ON THE OTHER HAND... WHEN WE RAN INTO THAT FIRST WOMAN OUTSIDE THE BUILDING, SHE DID SAY SOMEONE ON THE TEAM WAS A LIAR.
DOWNLOADING: INSURANCE.TORRENT
TEK
ONE LITTLE WHITE LIE, ONE TEENSY TINY LITTLE UNTRUTH ABOUT NOT KEEPING A COPY OF THE PAD IN THE SAFEST PLACE I KNOW.
NEW FILE: PAD.DAT
TERABYTES AND TERABYTES OF RANDOM DATA COMMITTED TO MEMORY. I WASN'T EVEN SURE I COULD DO IT.
TEK TIK TEK
TIK TEK
THE WATCHER'S SECRETS ARE SAFELY STORED ON THOUSANDS OF COMPUTERS ALL OVER THE WORLD. HIDDEN IN PLAIN SIGHT. AND NOBODY CAN READ THEM BUT ME.
NEW FILE: PAD.DAT
DECRYPTION IN PROGRESS...
SO LET'S SEE IF I CAN'T FIND A CURE FOR YOUR MOM, HOOD. AND YOU KNOW WHAT?
LET'S SEE IF I CAN'T FIND A CURE FOR EVERYONE ELSE WHILE I'M AT IT TOO.
KNOWLEDGE ISN'T POWER. IT'S AN INTRINSIC GOOD. IT BETTERS THE WORLD SIMPLY BY EXISTING, AND IT WOULD'VE BEEN CRIMINAL TO LOSE THIS DATA.
AND IF THE CHOICE IS BETWEEN BEING A CRIMINAL OR BEING A SUPER HERO? DONE. SUPER HERO, DUDE. NO COMPETITION.
ASK ME A HARDER QUESTION NEXT TIME.
THE END.

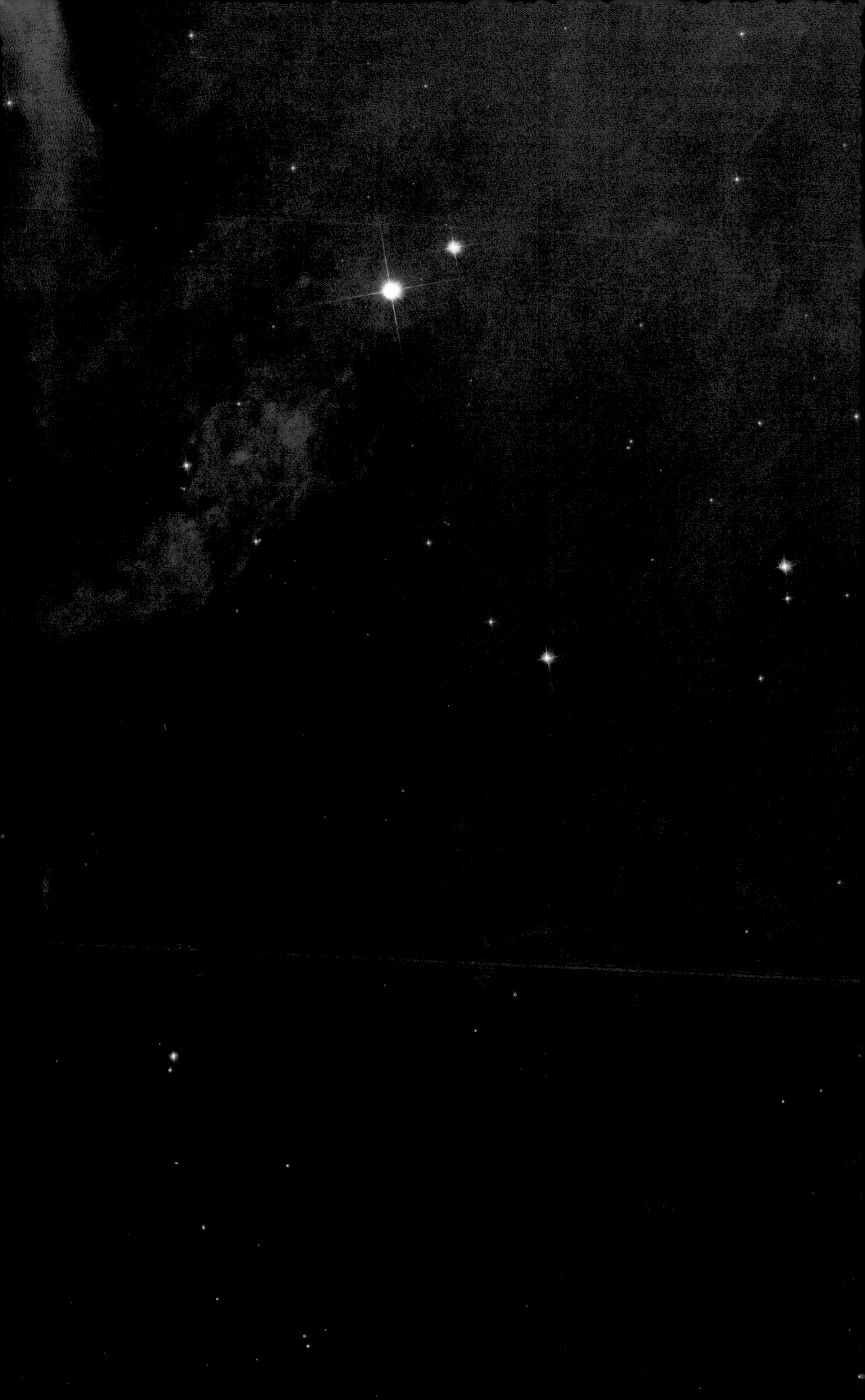

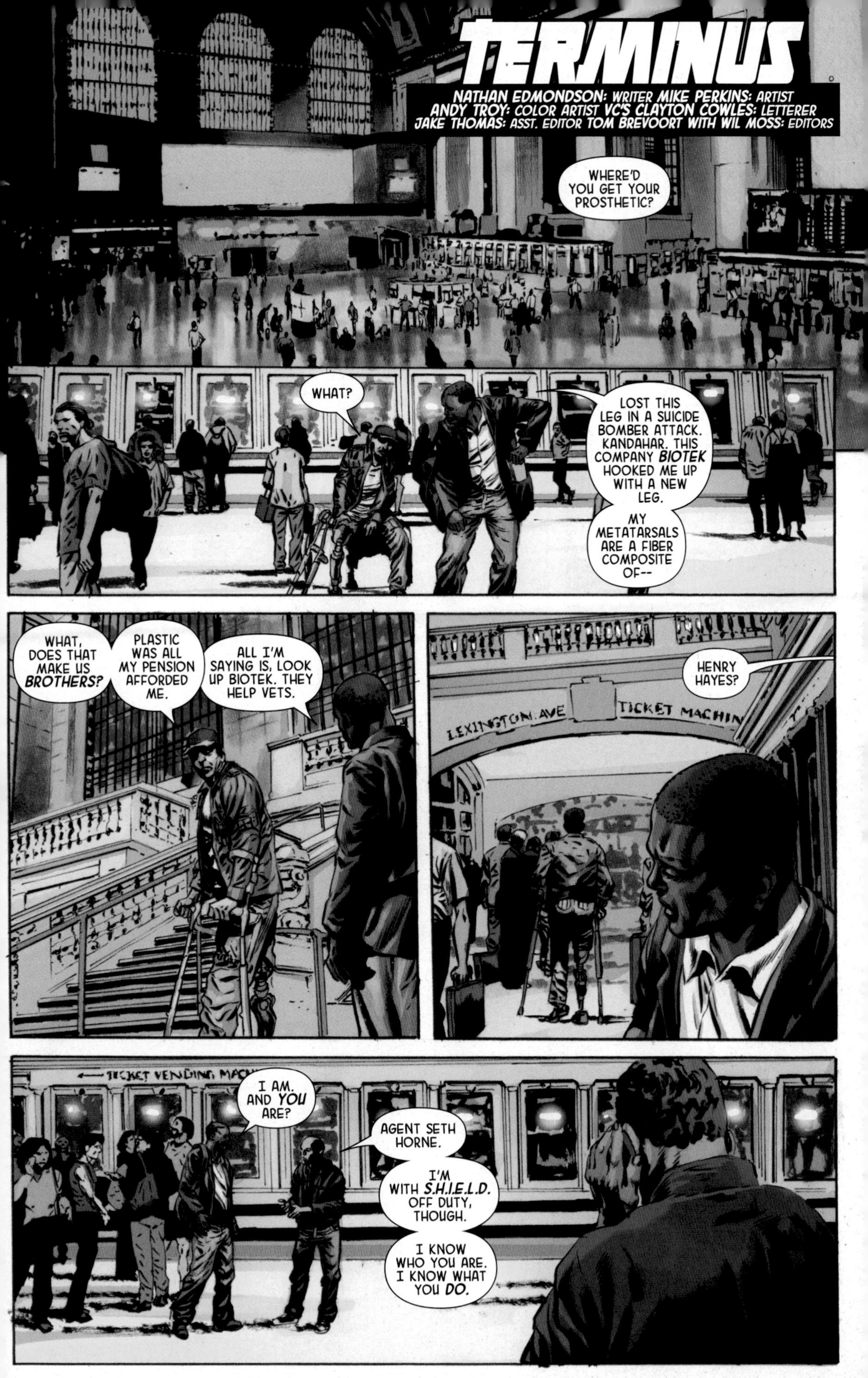
TERMINUS
NATHAN EDMONDSON: WRITER MIKE PERKINS: ARTIST
ANDY TROY: COLOR ARTIST VC'S CLAYTON COWLES: LETTERER
JAKE THOMAS: ASST. EDITOR TOM BREVOORT WITH WIL MOSS: EDITORS
WHERE'D YOU GET YOUR PROSTHETIC?
WHAT?
LOST THIS LEG IN A SUICIDE BOMBER ATTACK. KANDAHAR. THIS COMPANY BIOTEK HOOKED ME UP WITH A NEW LEG.
MY METATARSALS ARE A FIBER COMPOSITE OF--
WHAT, DOES THAT MAKE US BROTHERS?
PLASTIC WAS ALL MY PENSION AFFORDED ME.
ALL I'M SAYING IS, LOOK UP BIOTEK. THEY HELP VETS.
HENRY HAYES?
LEXINGTON AVE
TICKET MACHIN
TICKET VENDING MACH
I AM. AND YOU ARE?
AGENT SETH HORNE.
I'M WITH S.H.I.E.L.D. OFF DUTY, THOUGH.
I KNOW WHO YOU ARE. I KNOW WHAT YOU DO.

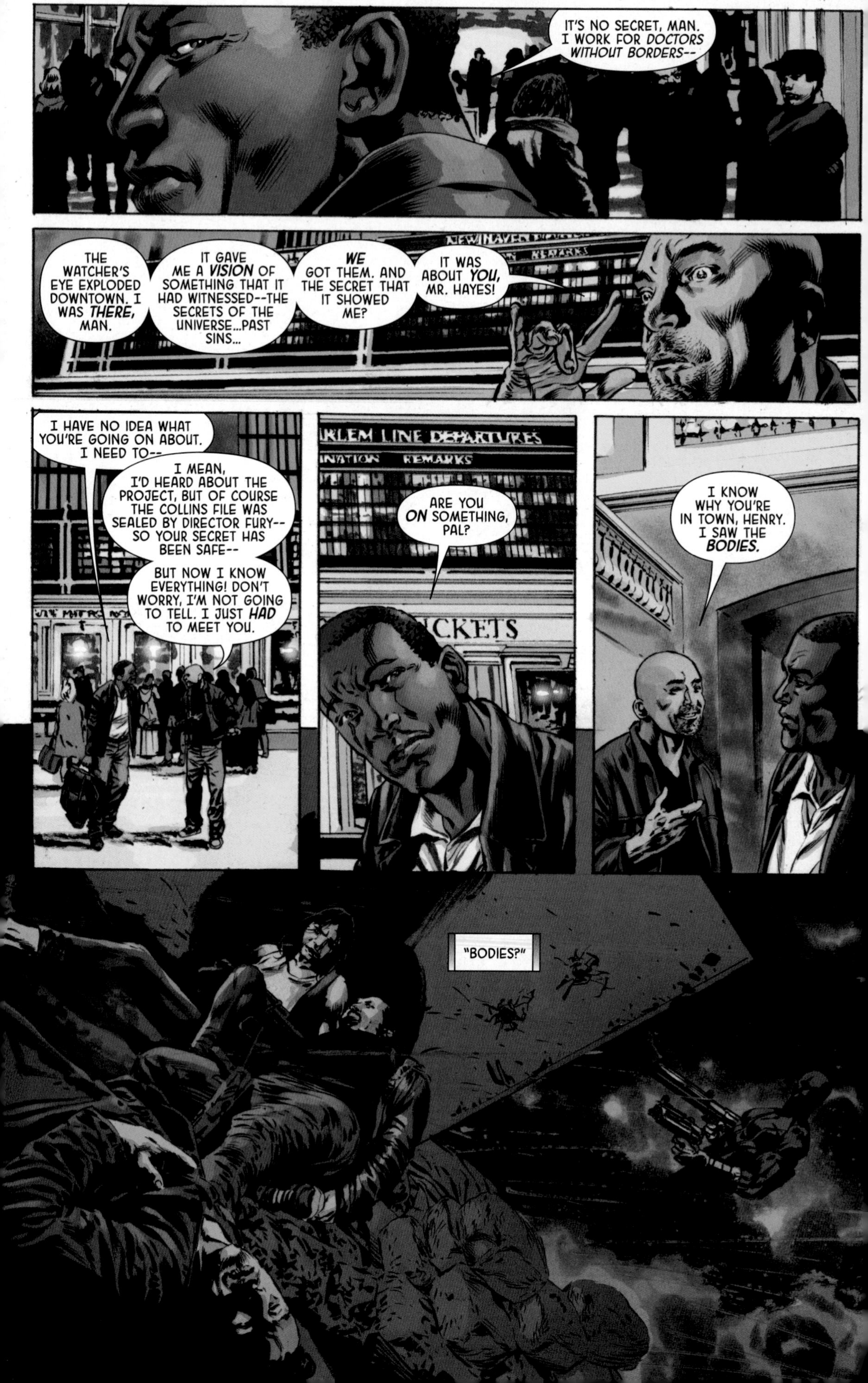
IT'S NO SECRET, MAN. I WORK FOR DOCTORS WITHOUT BORDERS--
THE WATCHER'S EYE EXPLODED DOWNTOWN. I WAS THERE, MAN.
IT GAVE ME A VISION OF SOMETHING THAT IT HAD WITNESSED--THE SECRETS OF THE UNIVERSE...PAST SINS...
WE GOT THEM. AND THE SECRET THAT IT SHOWED ME?
IT WAS ABOUT YOU, MR. HAYES!
I HAVE NO IDEA WHAT YOU'RE GOING ON ABOUT. I NEED TO--
I MEAN, I'D HEARD ABOUT THE PROJECT, BUT OF COURSE THE COLLINS FILE WAS SEALED BY DIRECTOR FURY--SO YOUR SECRET HAS BEEN SAFE--
BUT NOW I KNOW EVERYTHING! DON'T WORRY, I'M NOT GOING TO TELL. I JUST HAD TO MEET YOU.
ARLEM LINE DEPARTURES
INATION REMARKS
ARE YOU ON SOMETHING, PAL?
ICKETS
I KNOW WHY YOU'RE IN TOWN, HENRY. I SAW THE BODIES.
"BODIES?"

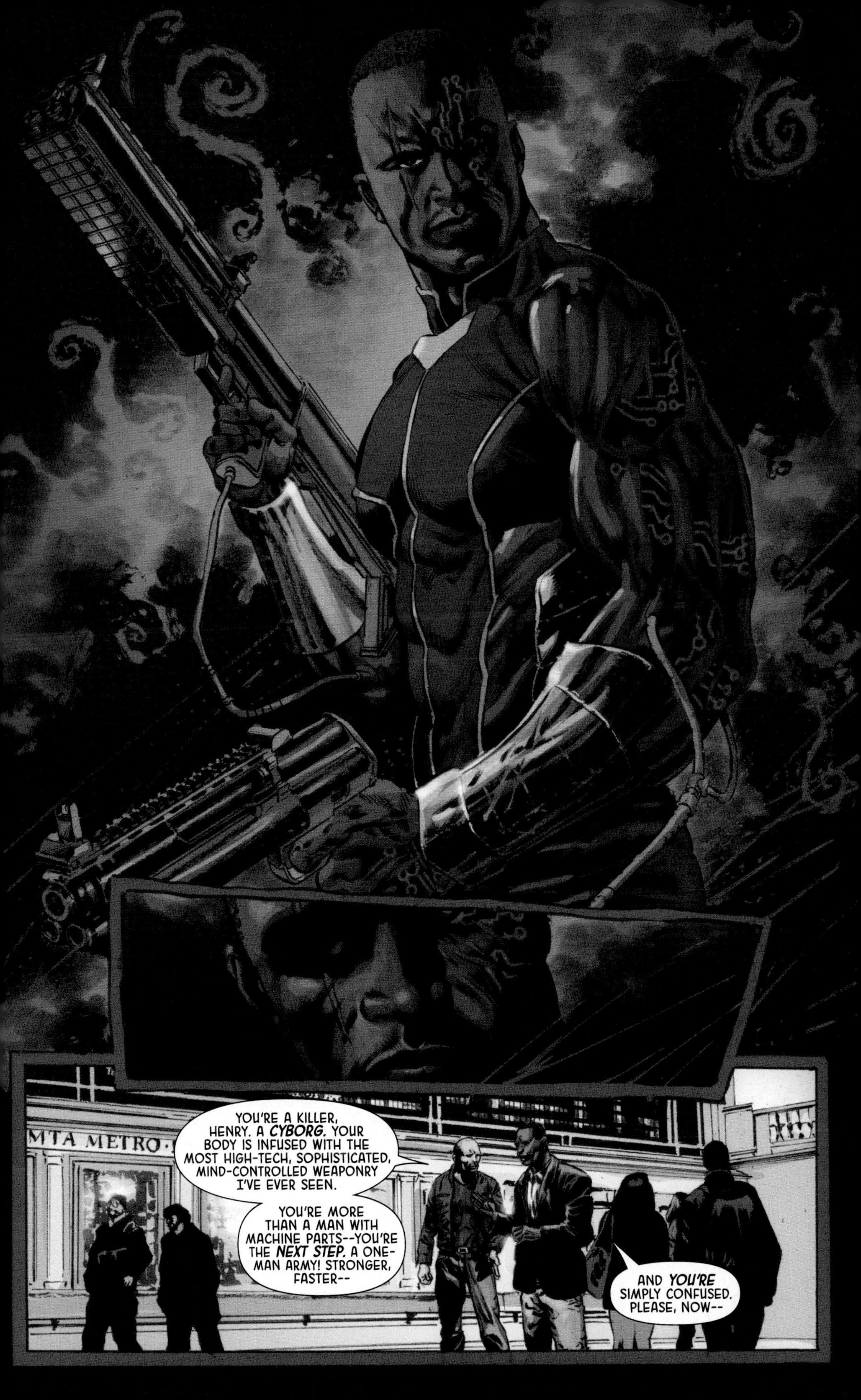
MTA METRO
YOU'RE A KILLER, HENRY. A *CYBORG.* YOUR BODY IS INFUSED WITH THE MOST HIGH-TECH, SOPHISTICATED, MIND-CONTROLLED WEAPONRY I'VE EVER SEEN.
YOU'RE MORE THAN A MAN WITH MACHINE PARTS--YOU'RE THE *NEXT STEP.* A ONE-MAN ARMY! STRONGER, FASTER--
AND *YOU'RE* SIMPLY CONFUSED. PLEASE, NOW--

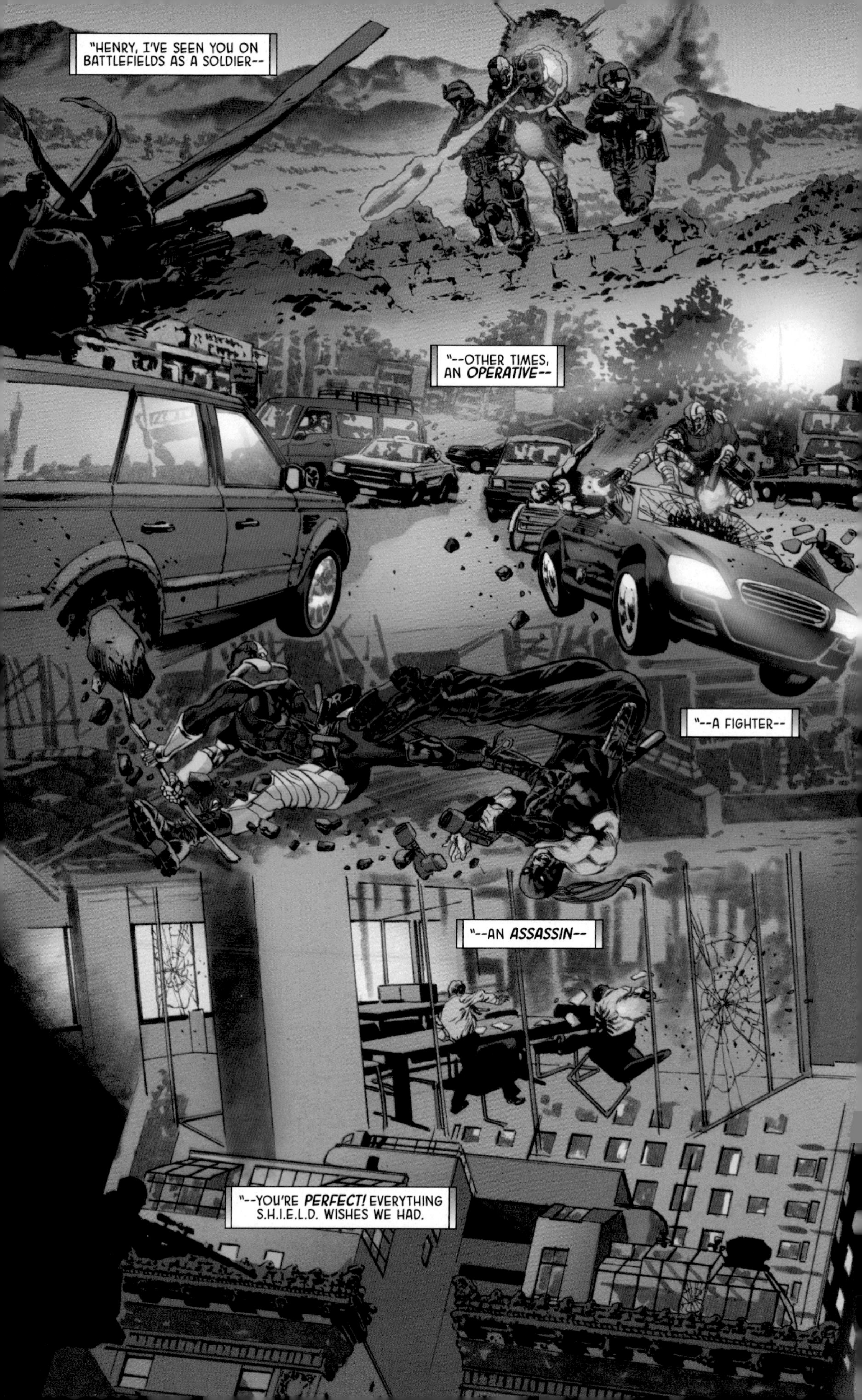
"HENRY, I'VE SEEN YOU ON BATTLEFIELDS AS A SOLDIER--
"--OTHER TIMES, AN *OPERATIVE*--
"--A FIGHTER--
"--AN **ASSASSIN**--
"--YOU'RE ***PERFECT!*** EVERYTHING S.H.I.E.L.D. WISHES WE HAD.

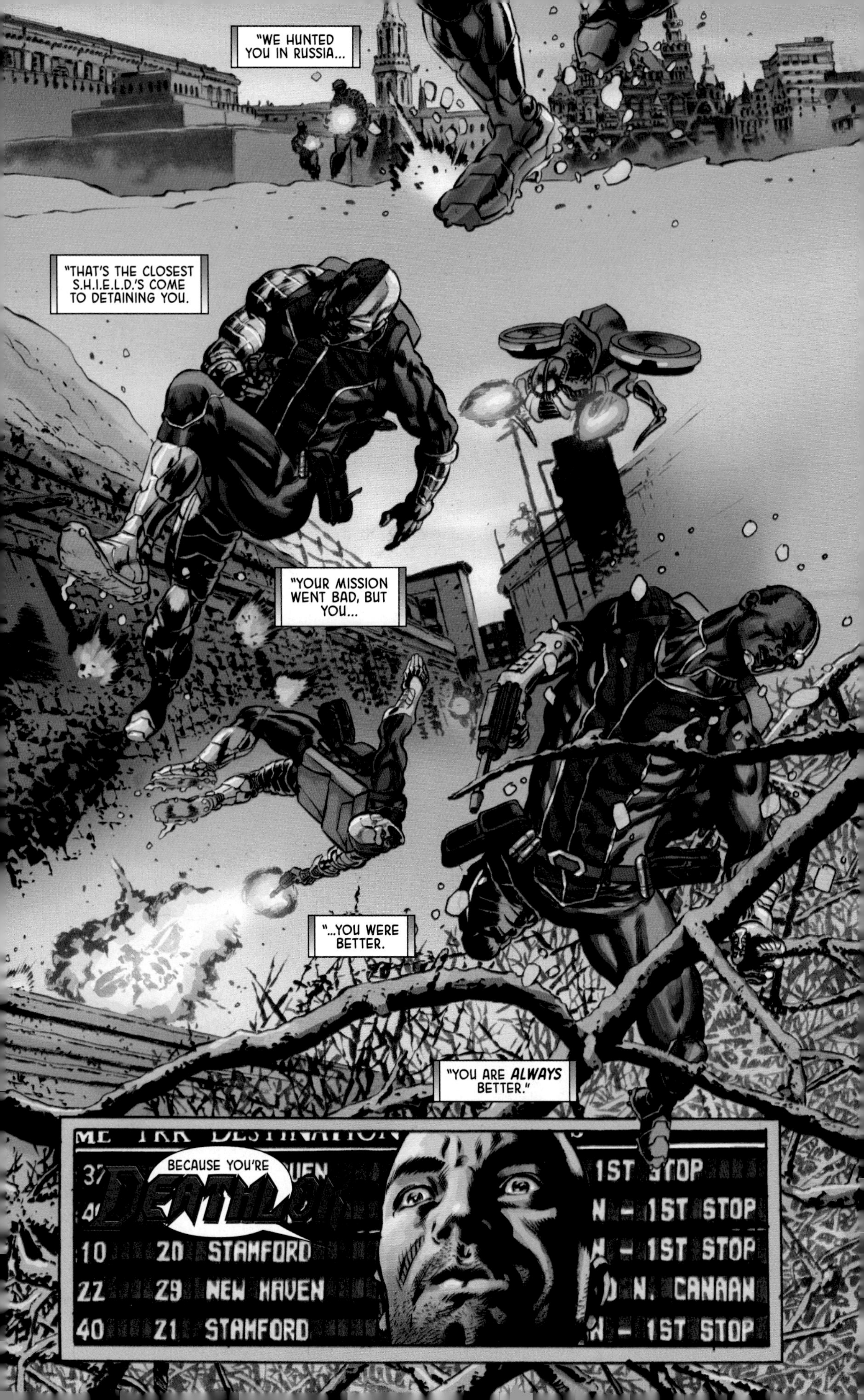
"WE HUNTED YOU IN RUSSIA...
"THAT'S THE CLOSEST S.H.I.E.L.D.'S COME TO DETAINING YOU.
"YOUR MISSION WENT BAD, BUT YOU...
"...YOU WERE BETTER.
"YOU ARE *ALWAYS* BETTER."
BECAUSE YOU'RE
1ST STOP
N - 1ST STOP
10 20 STAMFORD
N - 1ST STOP
22 29 NEW HAVEN
D N. CANAAN
40 21 STAMFORD
N - 1ST STOP

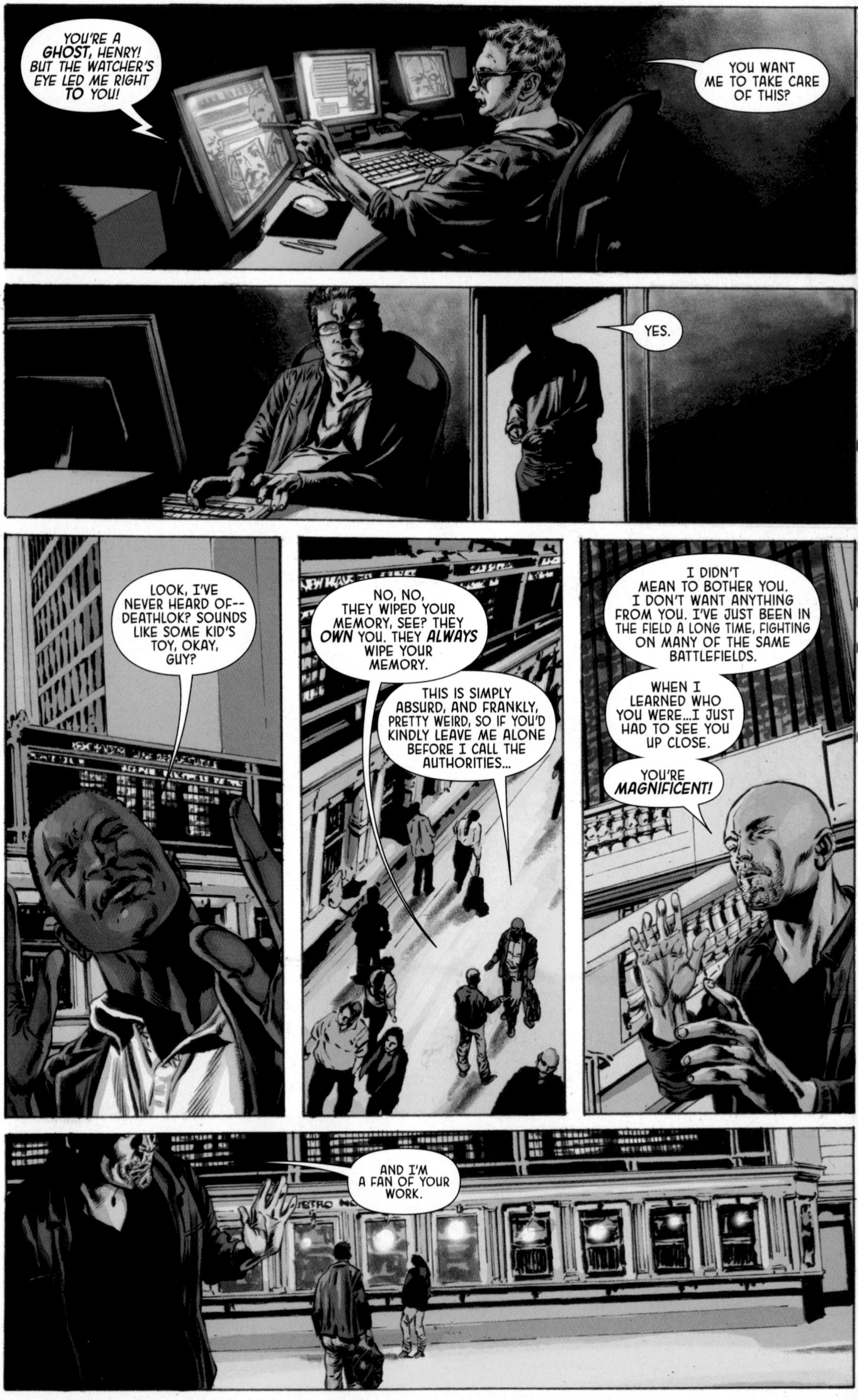
YOU'RE A GHOST, HENRY! BUT THE WATCHER'S EYE LED ME RIGHT TO YOU!
YOU WANT ME TO TAKE CARE OF THIS?
YES.
LOOK, I'VE NEVER HEARD OF-- DEATHLOK? SOUNDS LIKE SOME KID'S TOY, OKAY, GUY?
NO, NO, THEY WIPED YOUR MEMORY, SEE? THEY OWN YOU. THEY ALWAYS WIPE YOUR MEMORY.
THIS IS SIMPLY ABSURD, AND FRANKLY, PRETTY WEIRD, SO IF YOU'D KINDLY LEAVE ME ALONE BEFORE I CALL THE AUTHORITIES...
I DIDN'T MEAN TO BOTHER YOU. I DON'T WANT ANYTHING FROM YOU. I'VE JUST BEEN IN THE FIELD A LONG TIME, FIGHTING ON MANY OF THE SAME BATTLEFIELDS.
WHEN I LEARNED WHO YOU WERE...I JUST HAD TO SEE YOU UP CLOSE.
YOU'RE MAGNIFICENT!
AND I'M A FAN OF YOUR WORK.

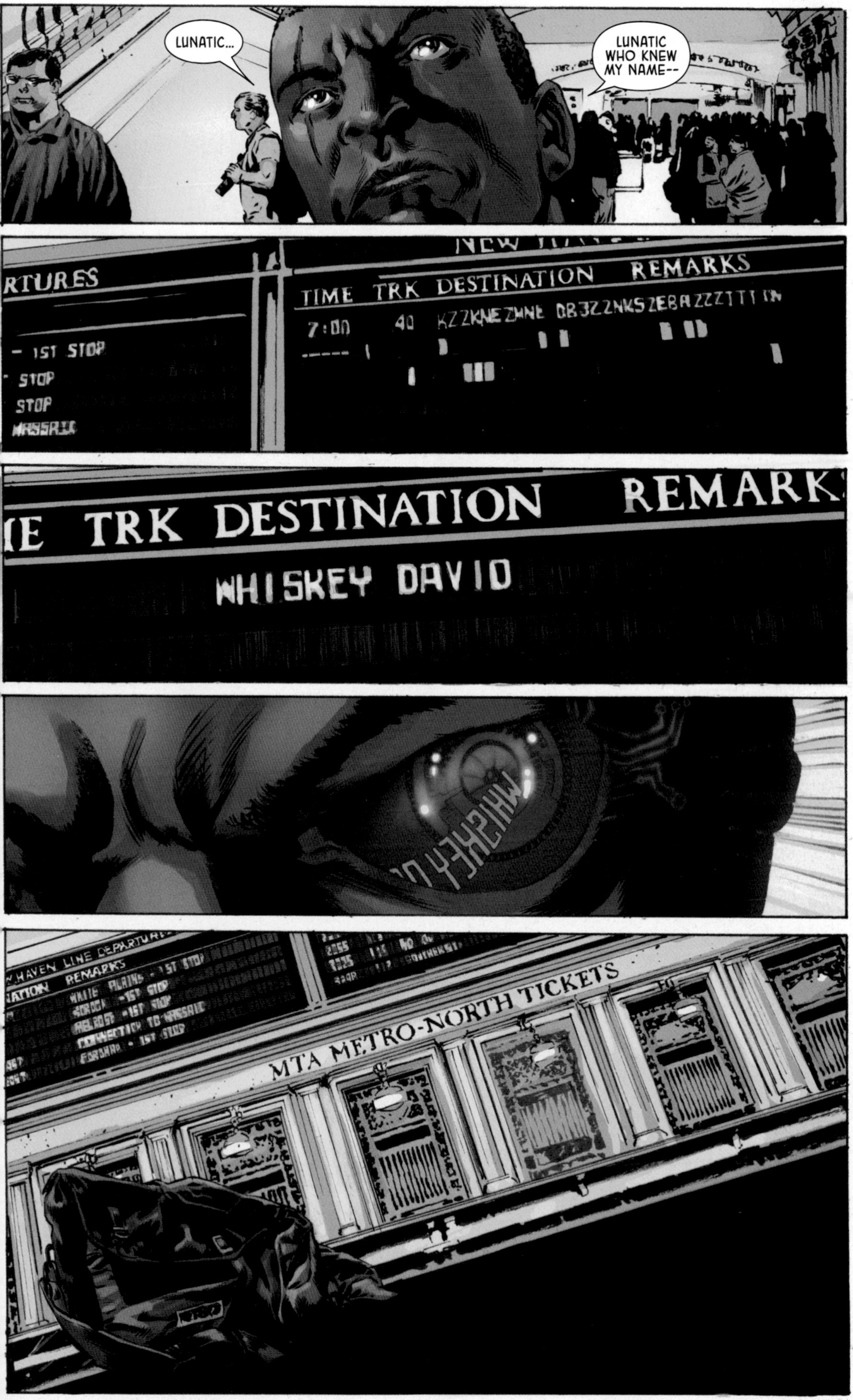
LUNATIC...
LUNATIC WHO KNEW MY NAME--
TIME TRK DESTINATION REMARKS
7:00 40
TRK DESTINATION REMARKS
WHISKEY DAVID
MTA METRO-NORTH TICKETS

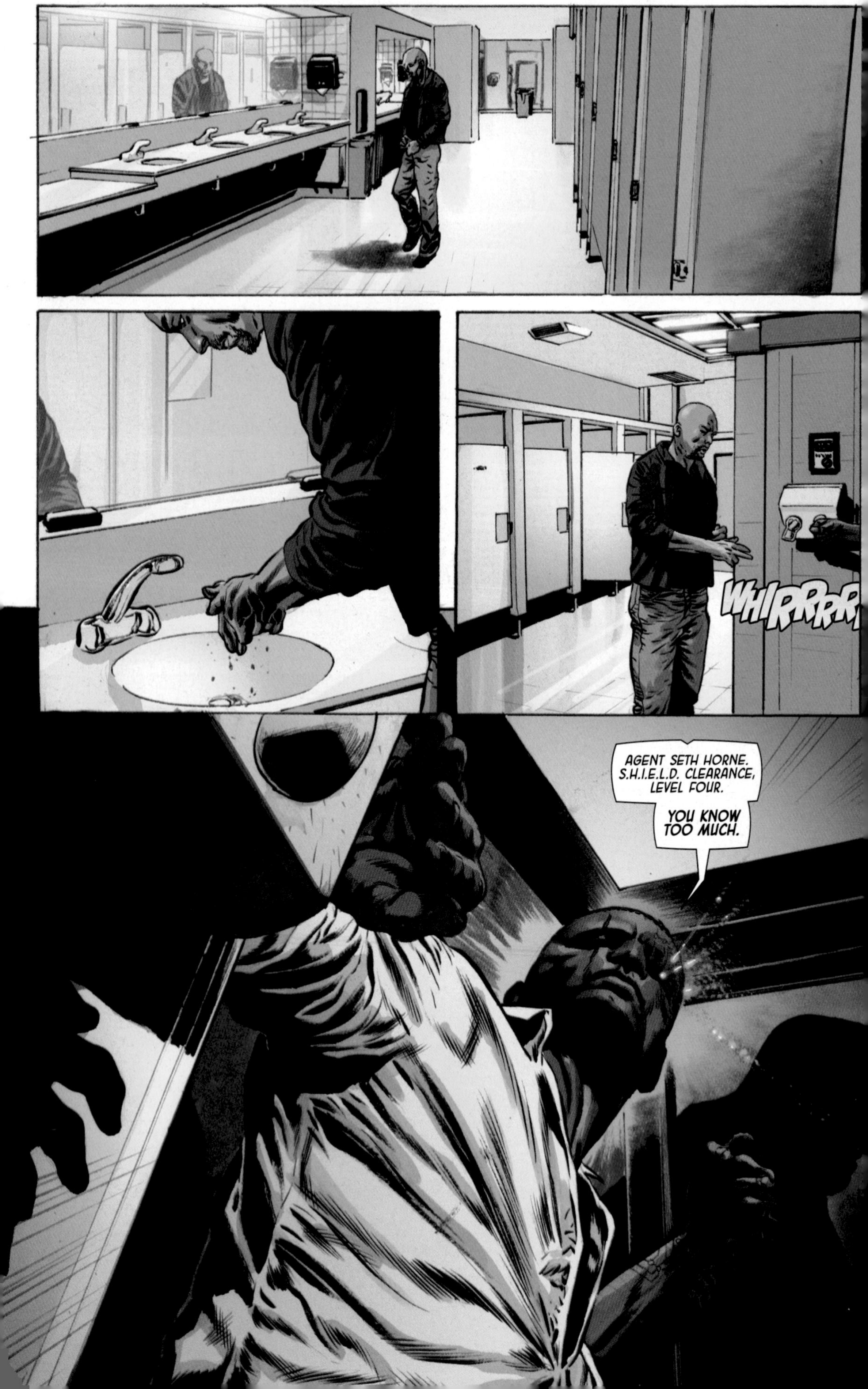
WHIRRRRR
AGENT SETH HORNE. S.H.I.E.L.D. CLEARANCE, LEVEL FOUR.
YOU KNOW TOO MUCH.

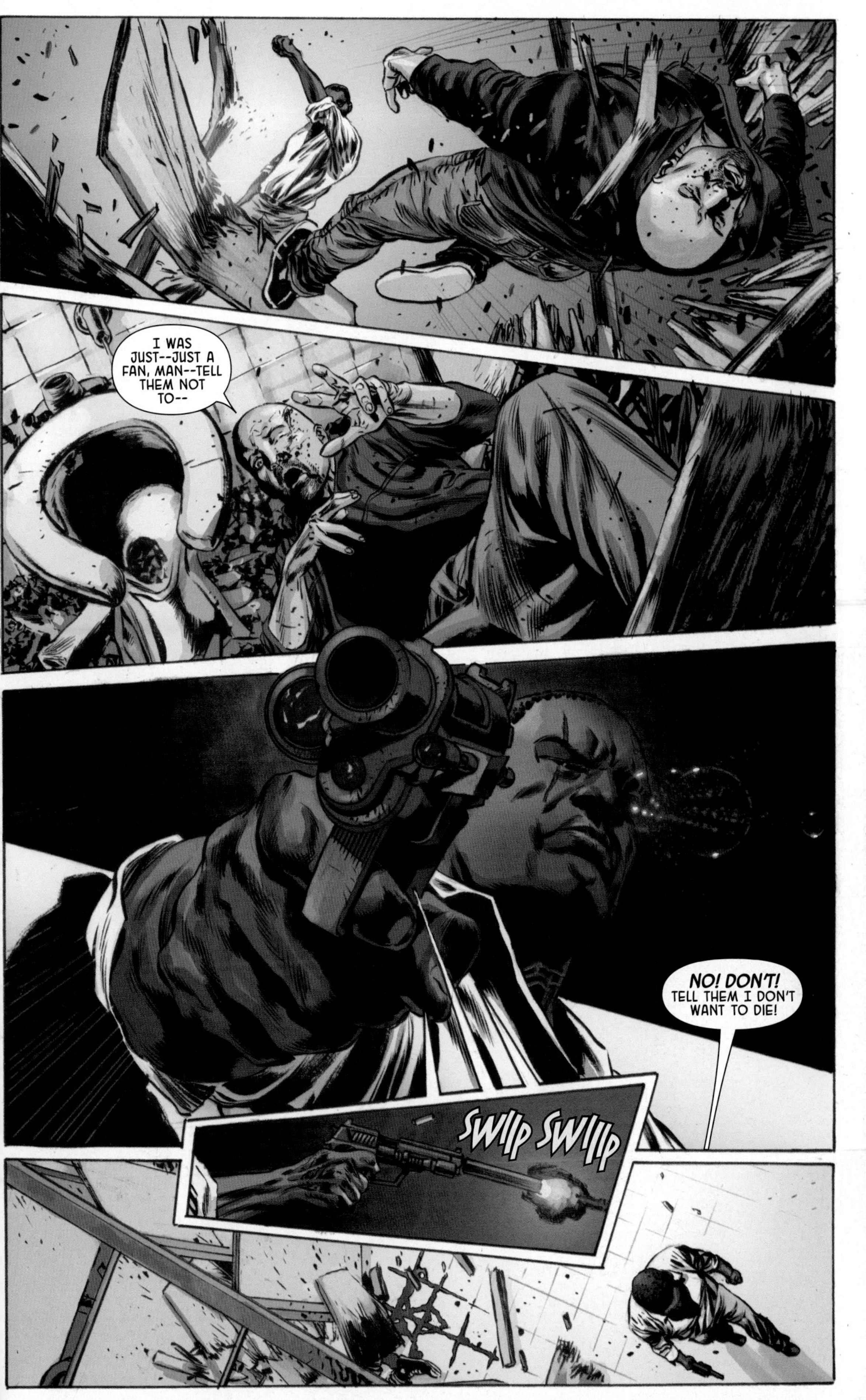

I WAS JUST--JUST A FAN, MAN--TELL THEM NOT TO--
NO! DON'T! TELL THEM I DON'T WANT TO DIE!
SWIIP SWIIP

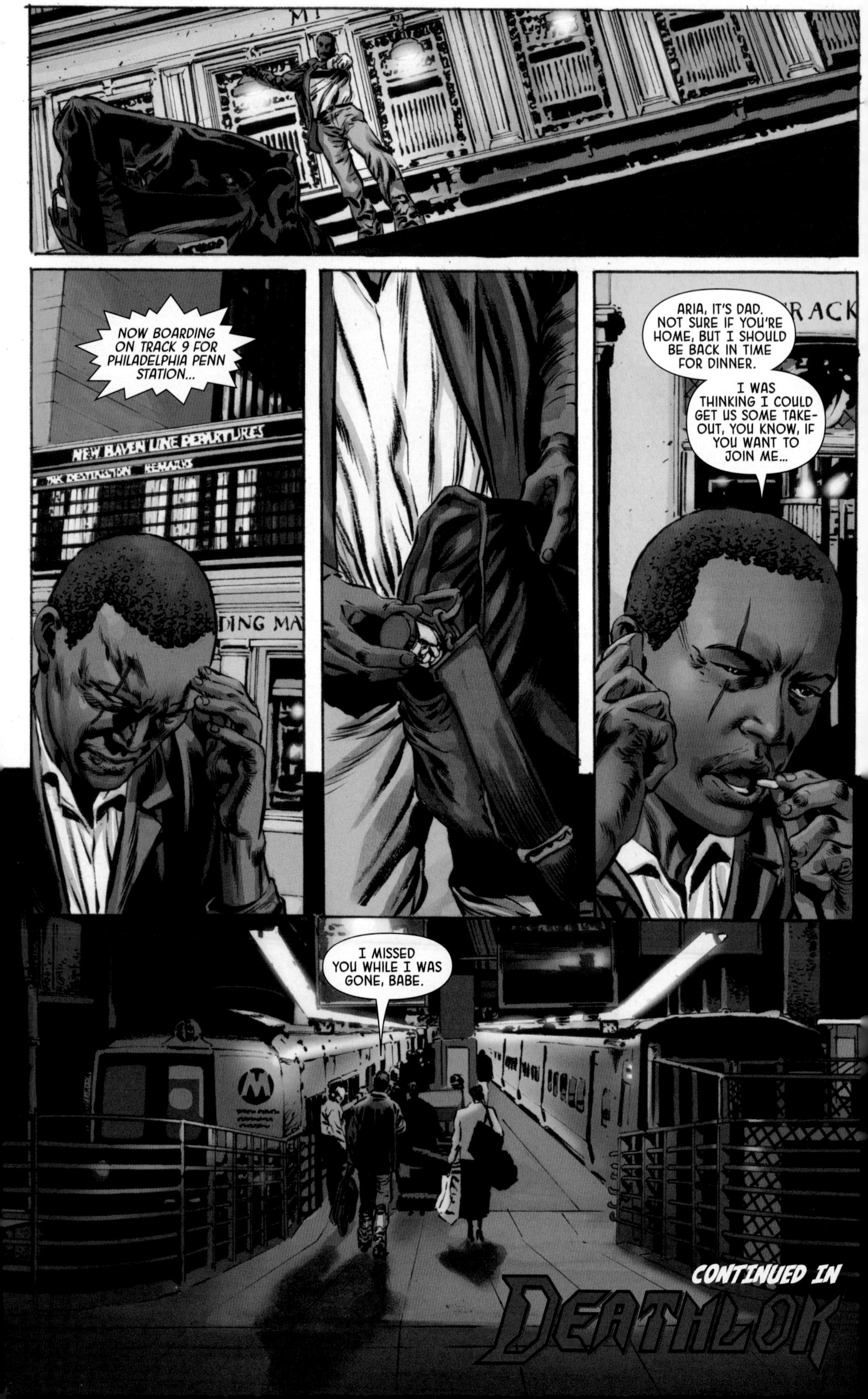
NOW BOARDING ON TRACK 9 FOR PHILADELPHIA PENN STATION...
NEW HAVEN LINE DEPARTURES
ARIA, IT'S DAD. NOT SURE IF YOU'RE HOME, BUT I SHOULD BE BACK IN TIME FOR DINNER.
I WAS THINKING I COULD GET US SOME TAKE-OUT, YOU KNOW, IF YOU WANT TO JOIN ME...
I MISSED YOU WHILE I WAS GONE, BABE.
CONTINUED IN
DEATHLOK

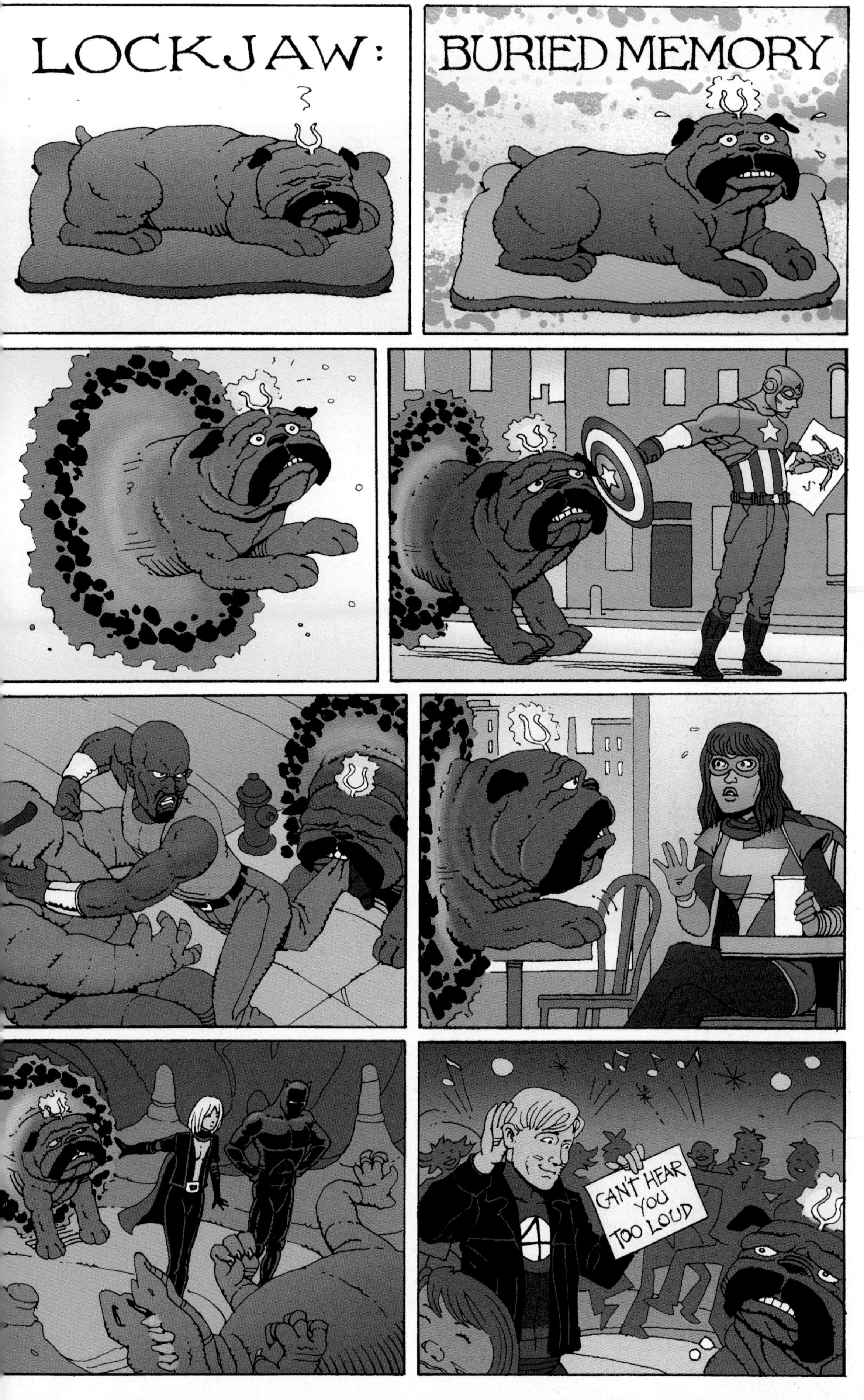
LOCKJAW: BURIED MEMORY
CAN'T HEAR YOU TOO LOUD

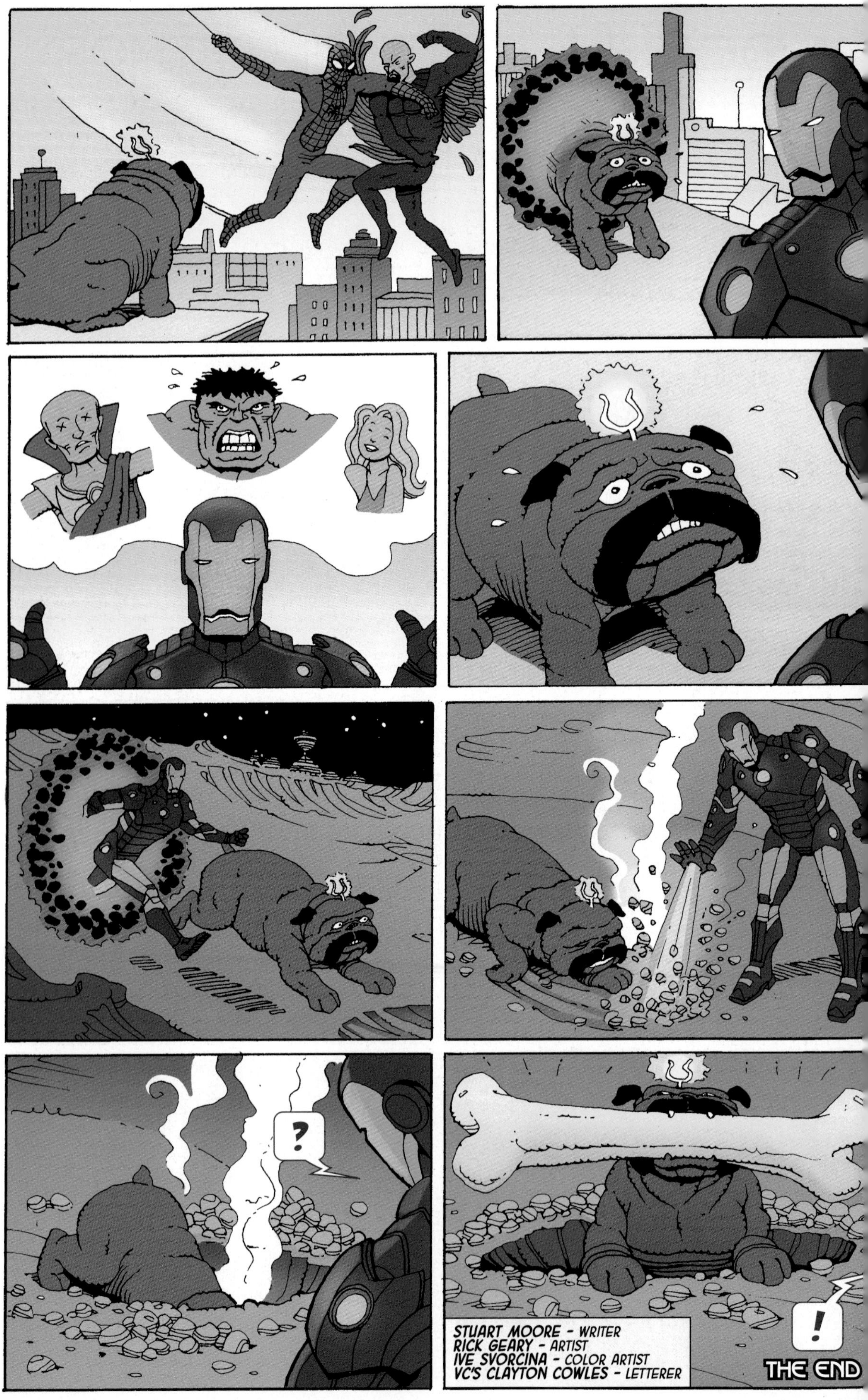
?
STUART MOORE - WRITER
RICK GEARY - ARTIST
IVE SVORCINA - COLOR ARTIST
VC'S CLAYTON COWLES - LETTERER
!
THE END

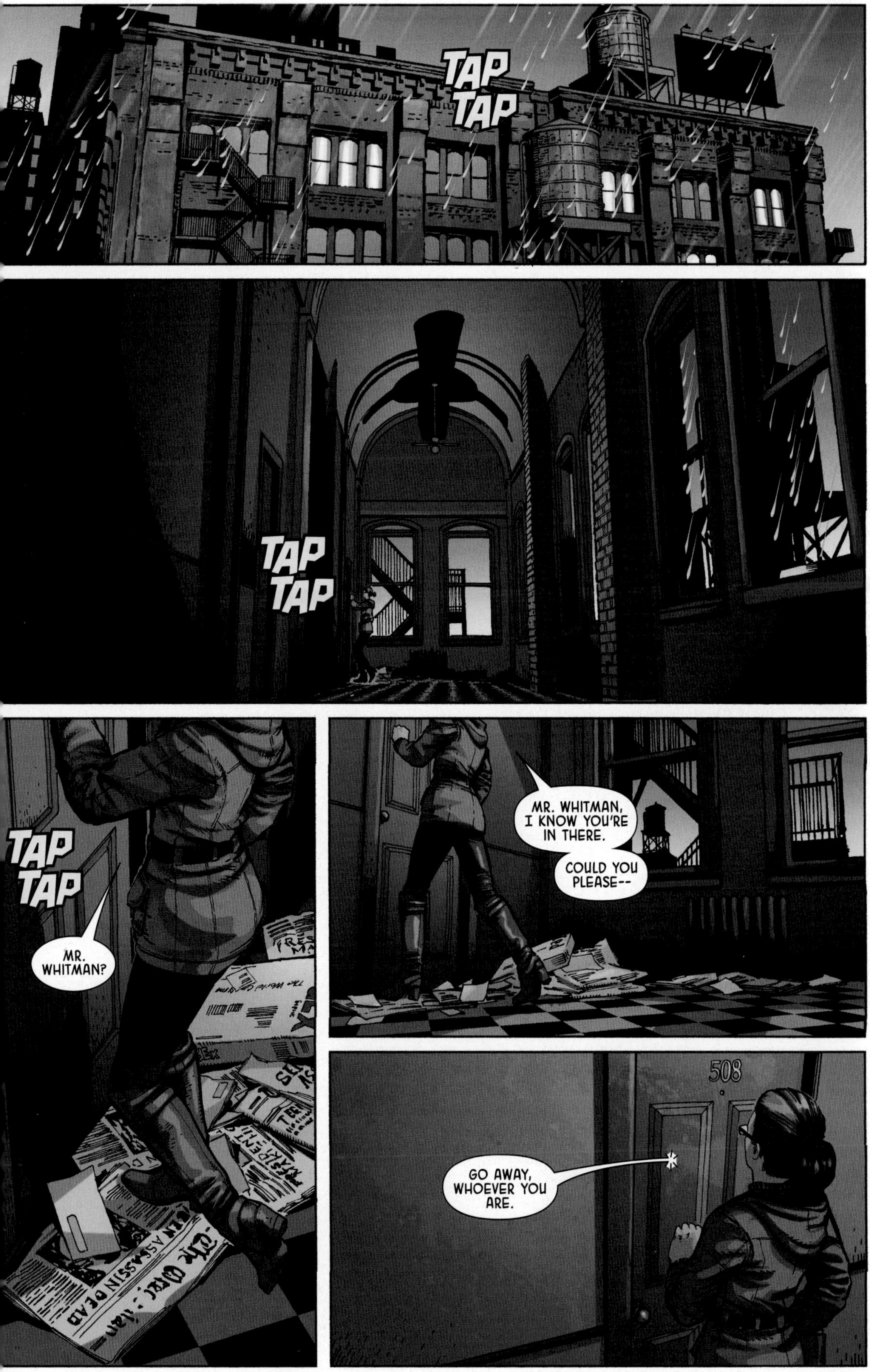
TAP TAP
TAP TAP
TAP TAP
MR. WHITMAN?
MR. WHITMAN, I KNOW YOU'RE IN THERE.
COULD YOU PLEASE--
508
GO AWAY, WHOEVER YOU ARE.

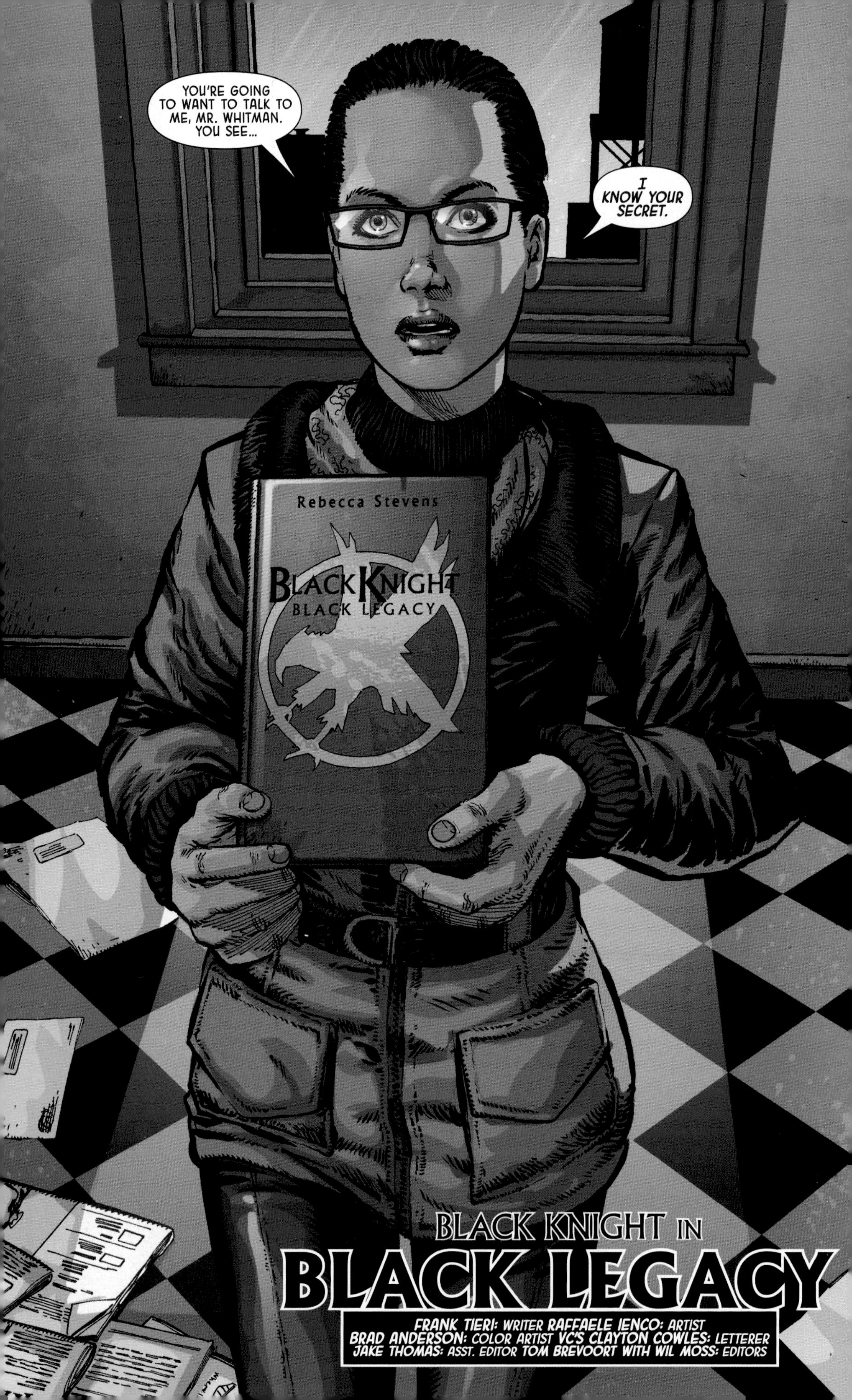

YOU'RE GOING TO WANT TO TALK TO ME, MR. WHITMAN. YOU SEE...
I KNOW YOUR SECRET.
Rebecca Stevens
BLACK KNIGHT
BLACK LEGACY
BLACK KNIGHT IN
BLACK LEGACY
FRANK TIERI: WRITER RAFFAELE IENCO: ARTIST
BRAD ANDERSON: COLOR ARTIST VC'S CLAYTON COWLES: LETTERER
JAKE THOMAS: ASST. EDITOR TOM BREVOORT WITH WIL MOSS: EDITORS

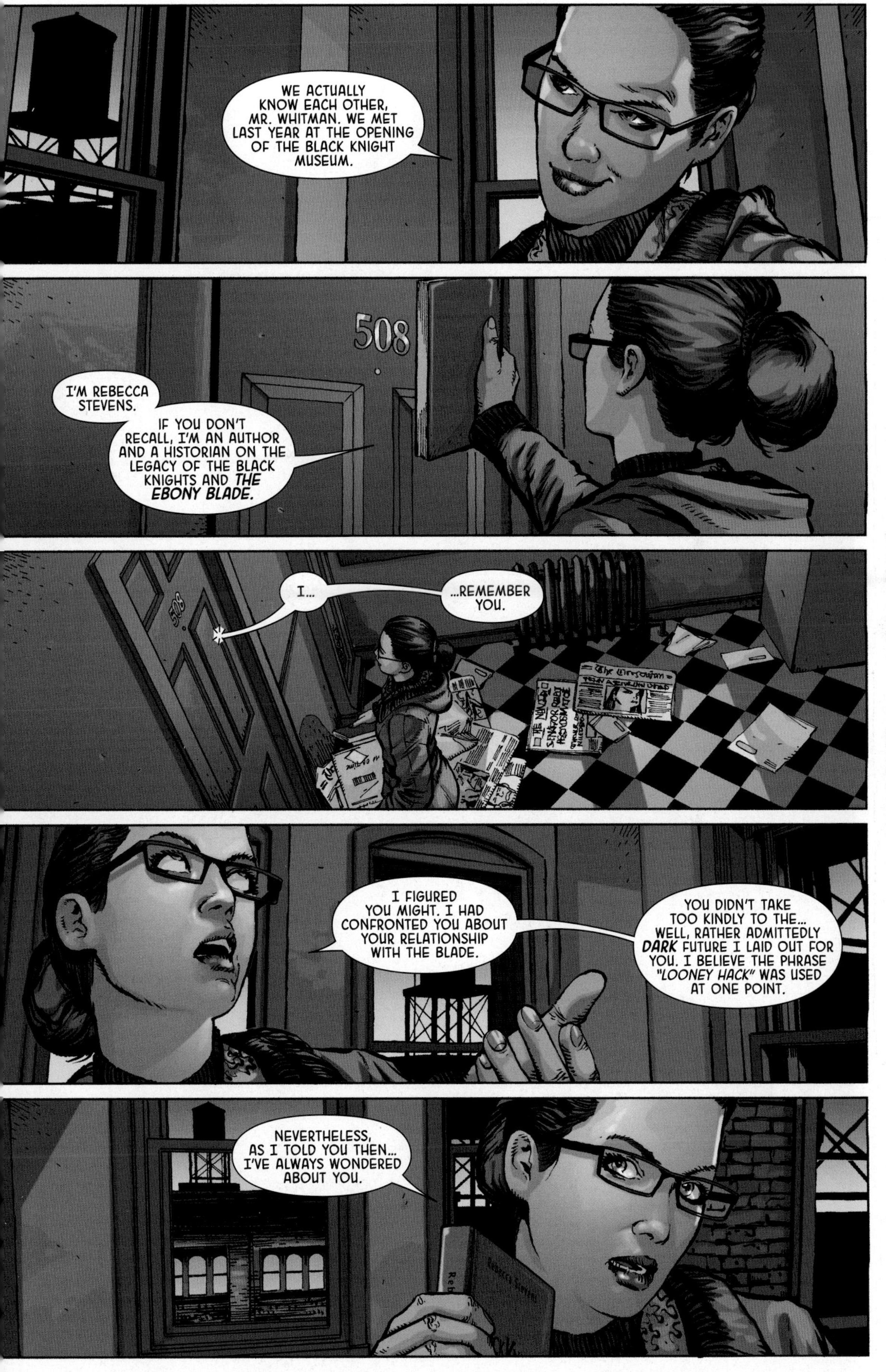
WE ACTUALLY KNOW EACH OTHER, MR. WHITMAN. WE MET LAST YEAR AT THE OPENING OF THE BLACK KNIGHT MUSEUM.
508
I'M REBECCA STEVENS.
IF YOU DON'T RECALL, I'M AN AUTHOR AND A HISTORIAN ON THE LEGACY OF THE BLACK KNIGHTS AND *THE EBONY BLADE.*
I...
...REMEMBER YOU.
I FIGURED YOU MIGHT. I HAD CONFRONTED YOU ABOUT YOUR RELATIONSHIP WITH THE BLADE.
YOU DIDN'T TAKE TOO KINDLY TO THE... WELL, RATHER ADMITTEDLY *DARK* FUTURE I LAID OUT FOR YOU. I BELIEVE THE PHRASE *"LOONEY HACK"* WAS USED AT ONE POINT.
NEVERTHELESS, AS I TOLD YOU THEN... I'VE ALWAYS WONDERED ABOUT YOU.

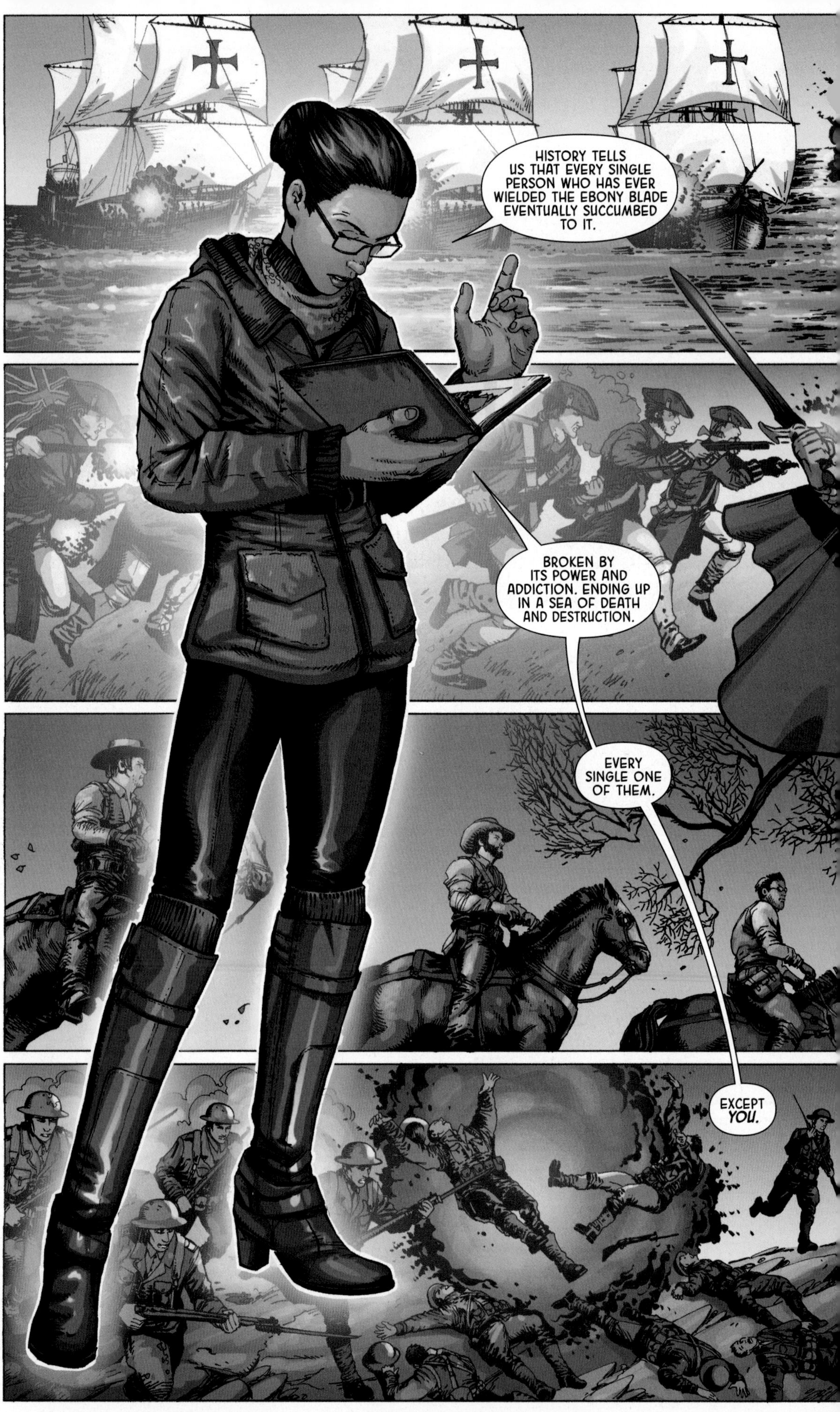
HISTORY TELLS US THAT EVERY SINGLE PERSON WHO HAS EVER WIELDED THE EBONY BLADE EVENTUALLY SUCCUMBED TO IT.
BROKEN BY ITS POWER AND ADDICTION. ENDING UP IN A SEA OF DEATH AND DESTRUCTION.
EVERY SINGLE ONE OF THEM.
EXCEPT *YOU.*

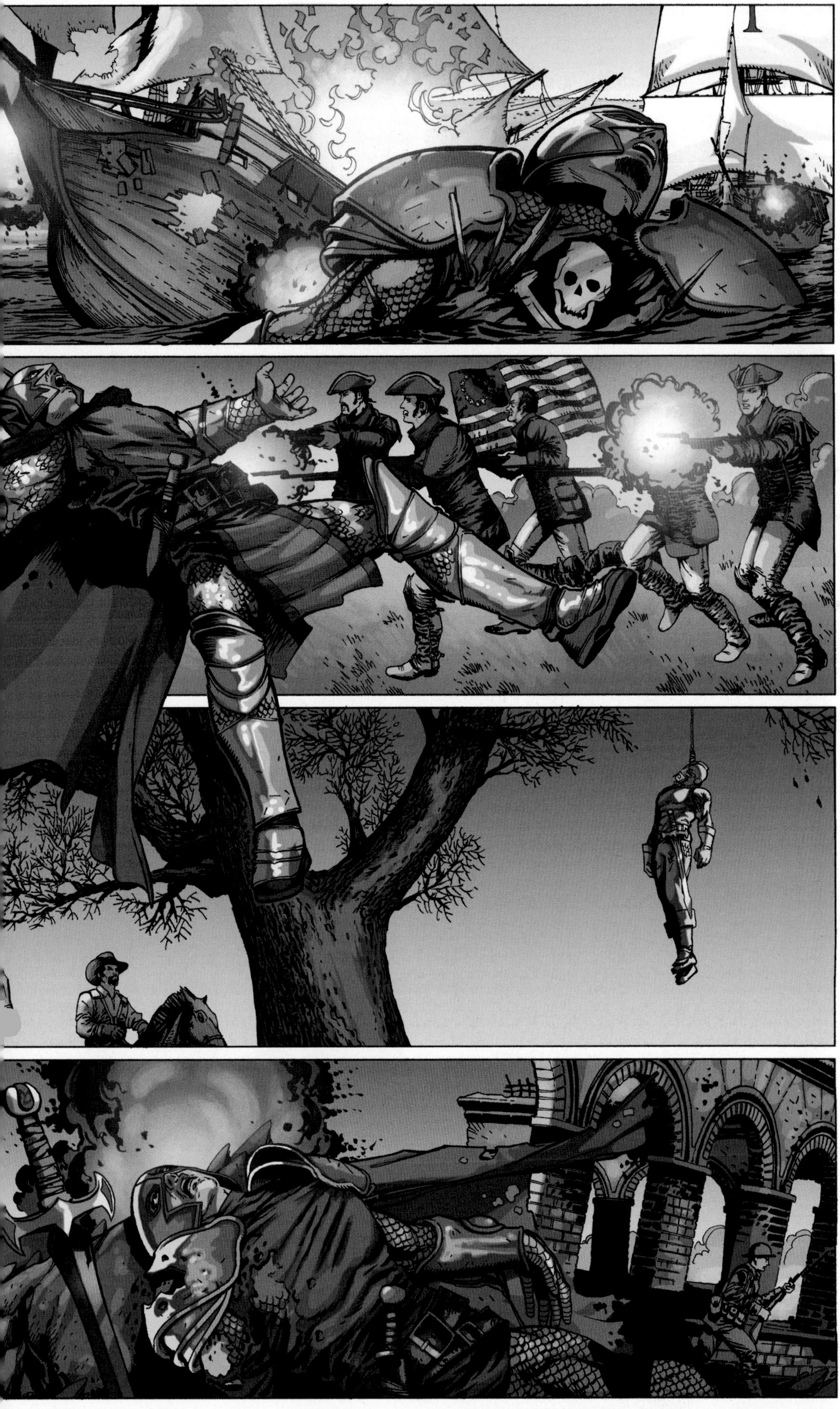

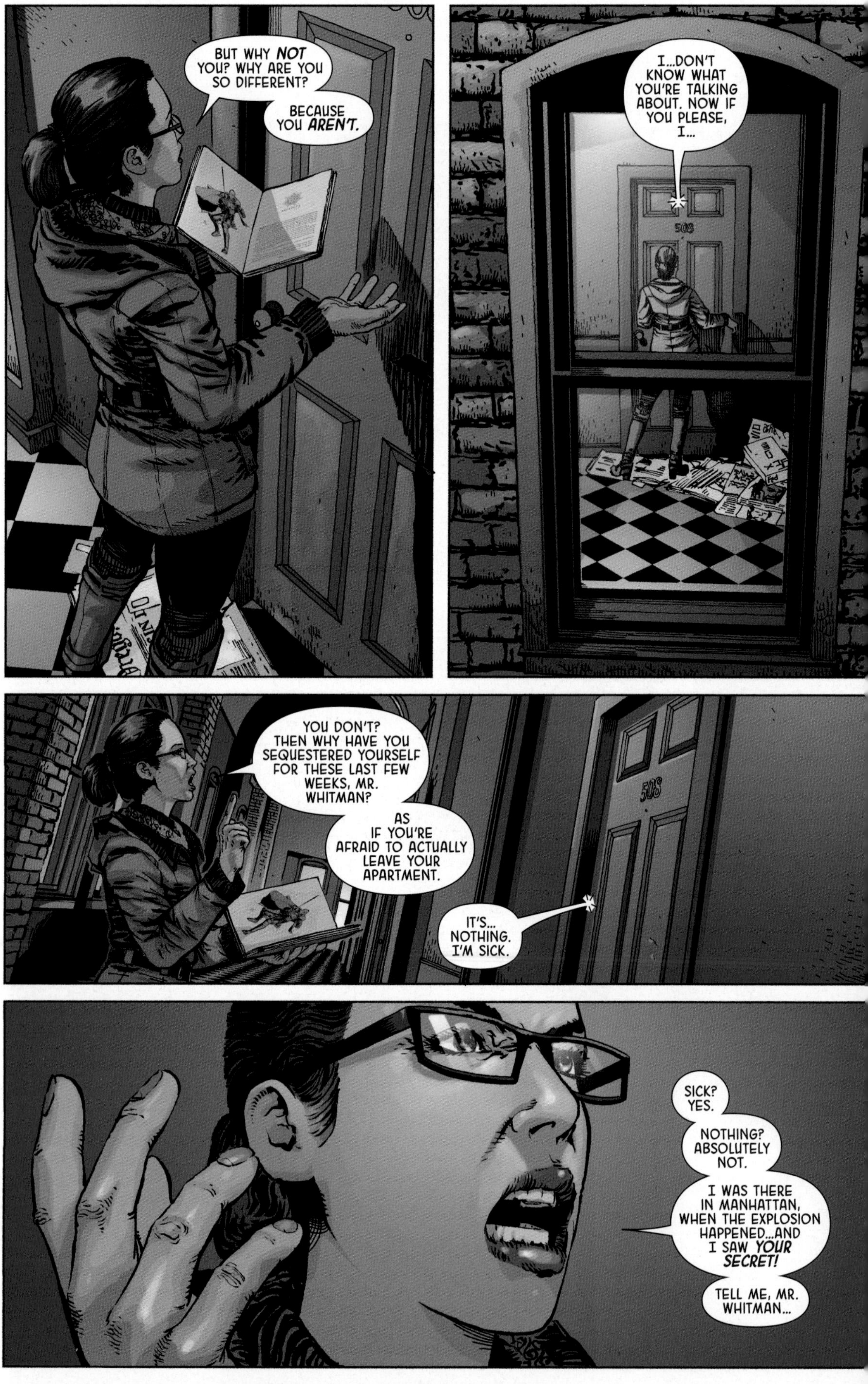

BUT WHY NOT YOU? WHY ARE YOU SO DIFFERENT?
BECAUSE YOU AREN'T.
I...DON'T KNOW WHAT YOU'RE TALKING ABOUT. NOW IF YOU PLEASE, I...
YOU DON'T? THEN WHY HAVE YOU SEQUESTERED YOURSELF FOR THESE LAST FEW WEEKS, MR. WHITMAN?
AS IF YOU'RE AFRAID TO ACTUALLY LEAVE YOUR APARTMENT.
IT'S... NOTHING. I'M SICK.
SICK? YES.
NOTHING? ABSOLUTELY NOT.
I WAS THERE IN MANHATTAN, WHEN THE EXPLOSION HAPPENED...AND I SAW YOUR SECRET!
TELL ME, MR. WHITMAN...

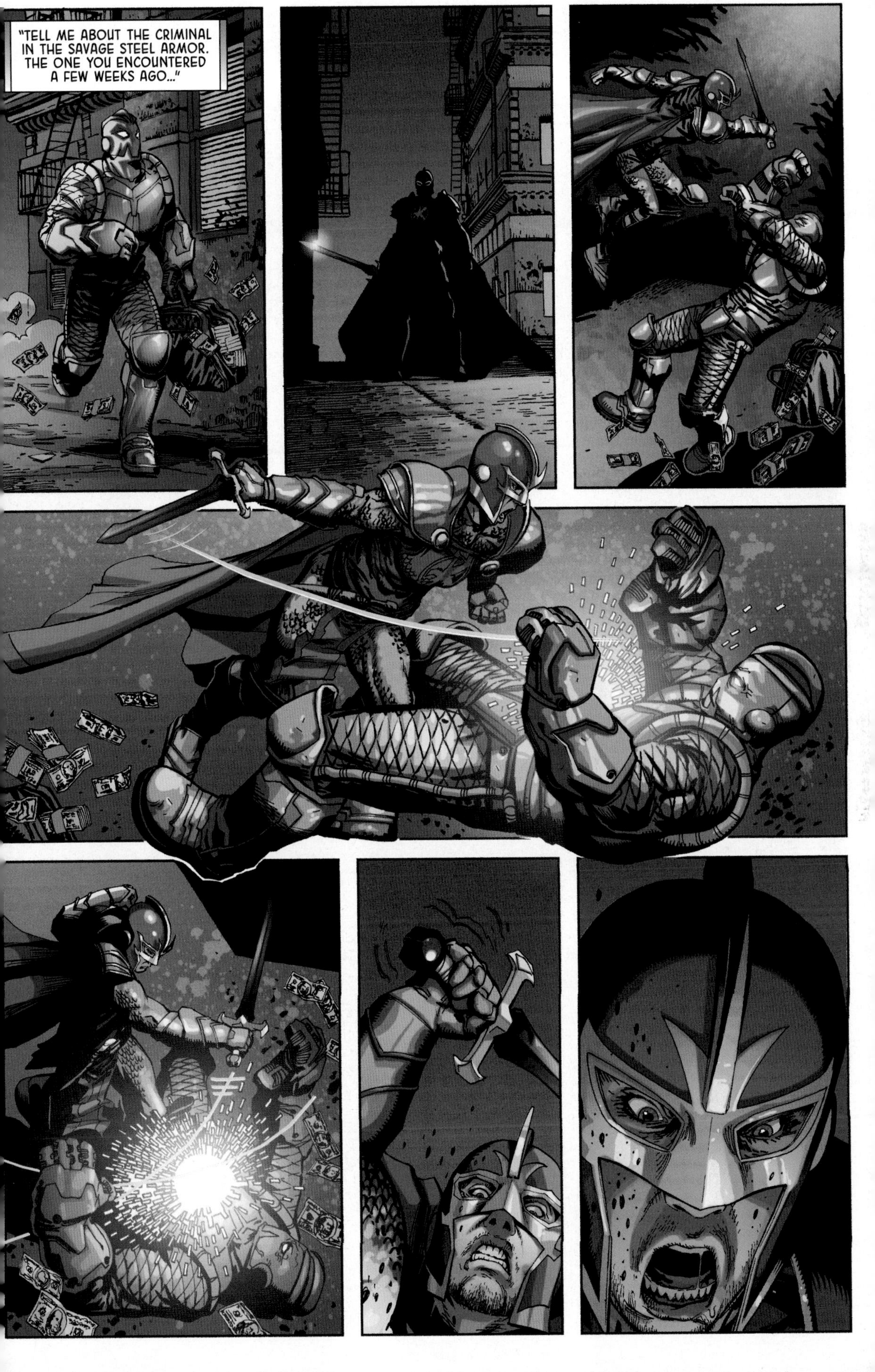
"TELL ME ABOUT THE CRIMINAL IN THE SAVAGE STEEL ARMOR. THE ONE YOU ENCOUNTERED A FEW WEEKS AGO..."

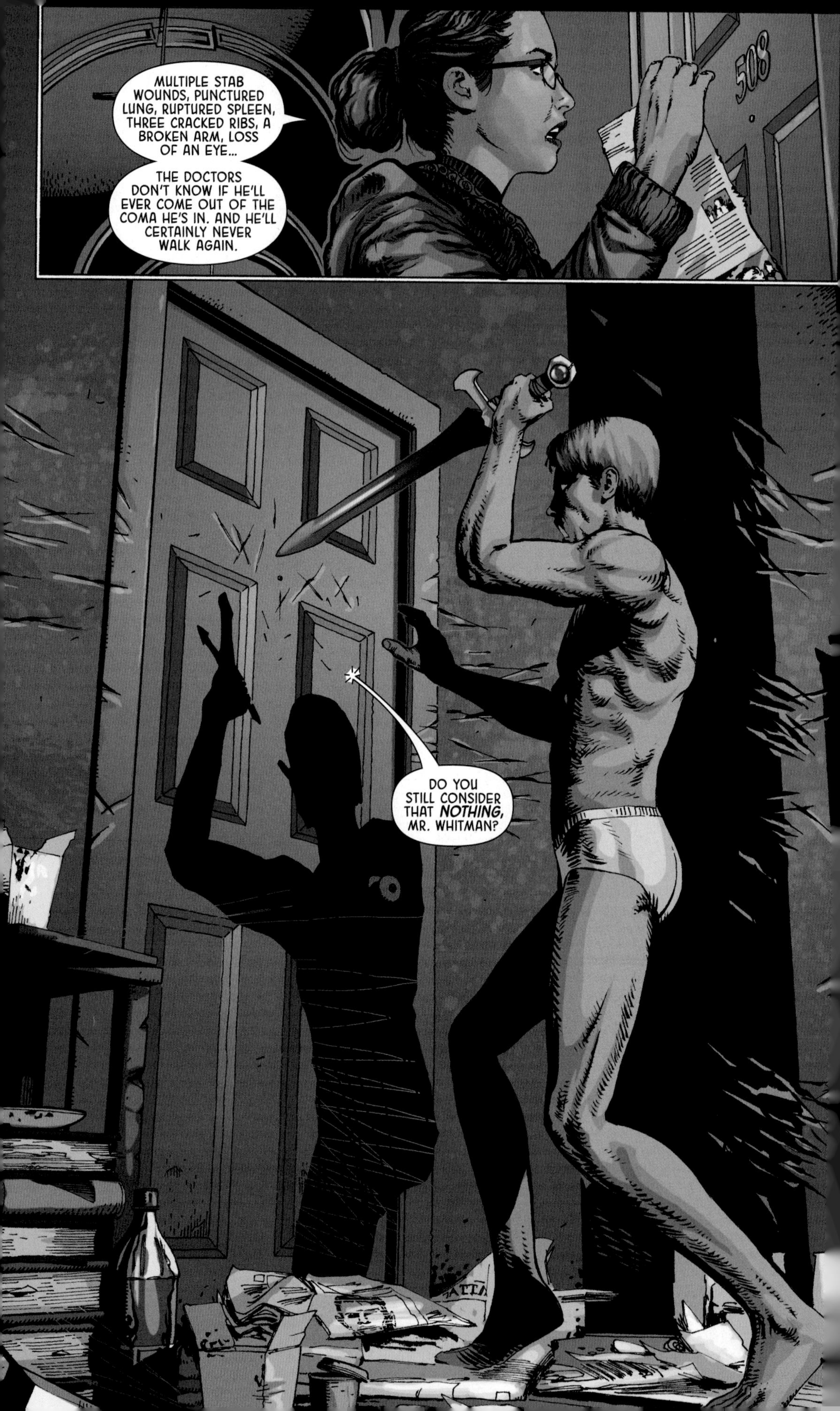
MULTIPLE STAB WOUNDS, PUNCTURED LUNG, RUPTURED SPLEEN, THREE CRACKED RIBS, A BROKEN ARM, LOSS OF AN EYE...
THE DOCTORS DON'T KNOW IF HE'LL EVER COME OUT OF THE COMA HE'S IN. AND HE'LL CERTAINLY NEVER WALK AGAIN.
508
DO YOU STILL CONSIDER THAT ***NOTHING***, MR. WHITMAN?

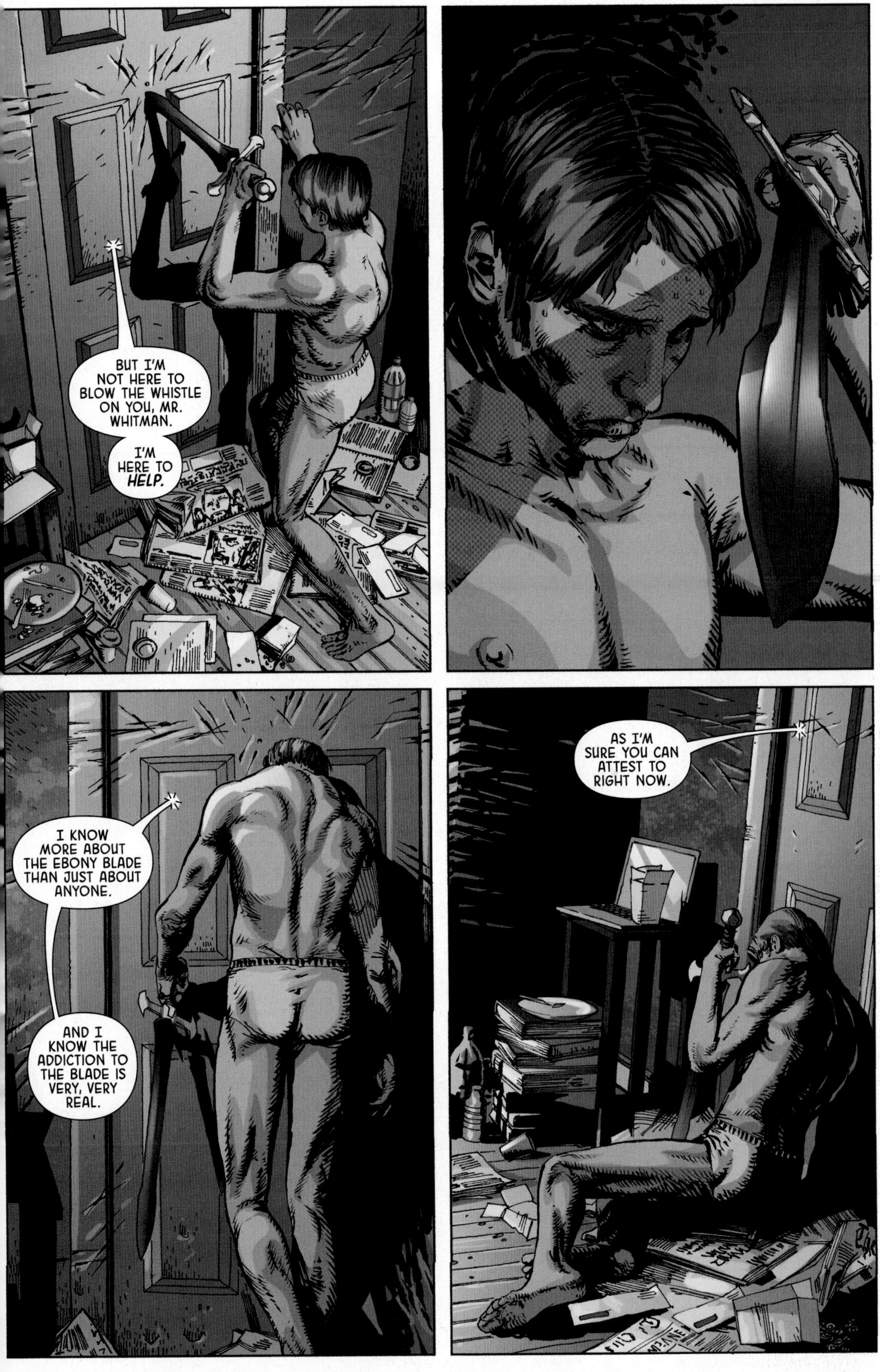
BUT I'M NOT HERE TO BLOW THE WHISTLE ON YOU, MR. WHITMAN.
I'M HERE TO HELP.
I KNOW MORE ABOUT THE EBONY BLADE THAN JUST ABOUT ANYONE.
AND I KNOW THE ADDICTION TO THE BLADE IS VERY, VERY REAL.
AS I'M SURE YOU CAN ATTEST TO RIGHT NOW.

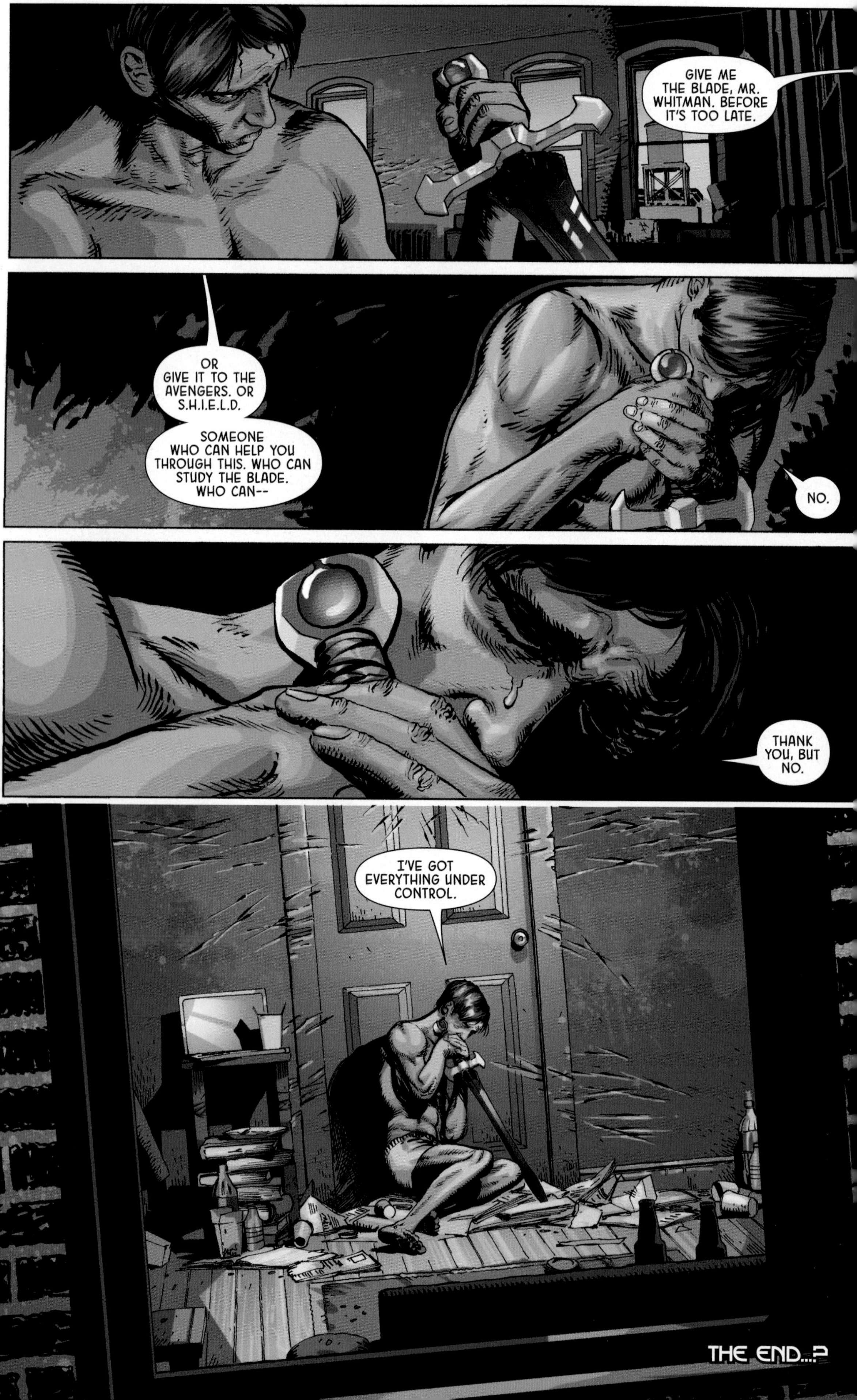
GIVE ME THE BLADE, MR. WHITMAN. BEFORE IT'S TOO LATE.
OR GIVE IT TO THE AVENGERS. OR S.H.I.E.L.D.
SOMEONE WHO CAN HELP YOU THROUGH THIS. WHO CAN STUDY THE BLADE. WHO CAN--
NO.
THANK YOU, BUT NO.
I'VE GOT EVERYTHING UNDER CONTROL.
THE END...?

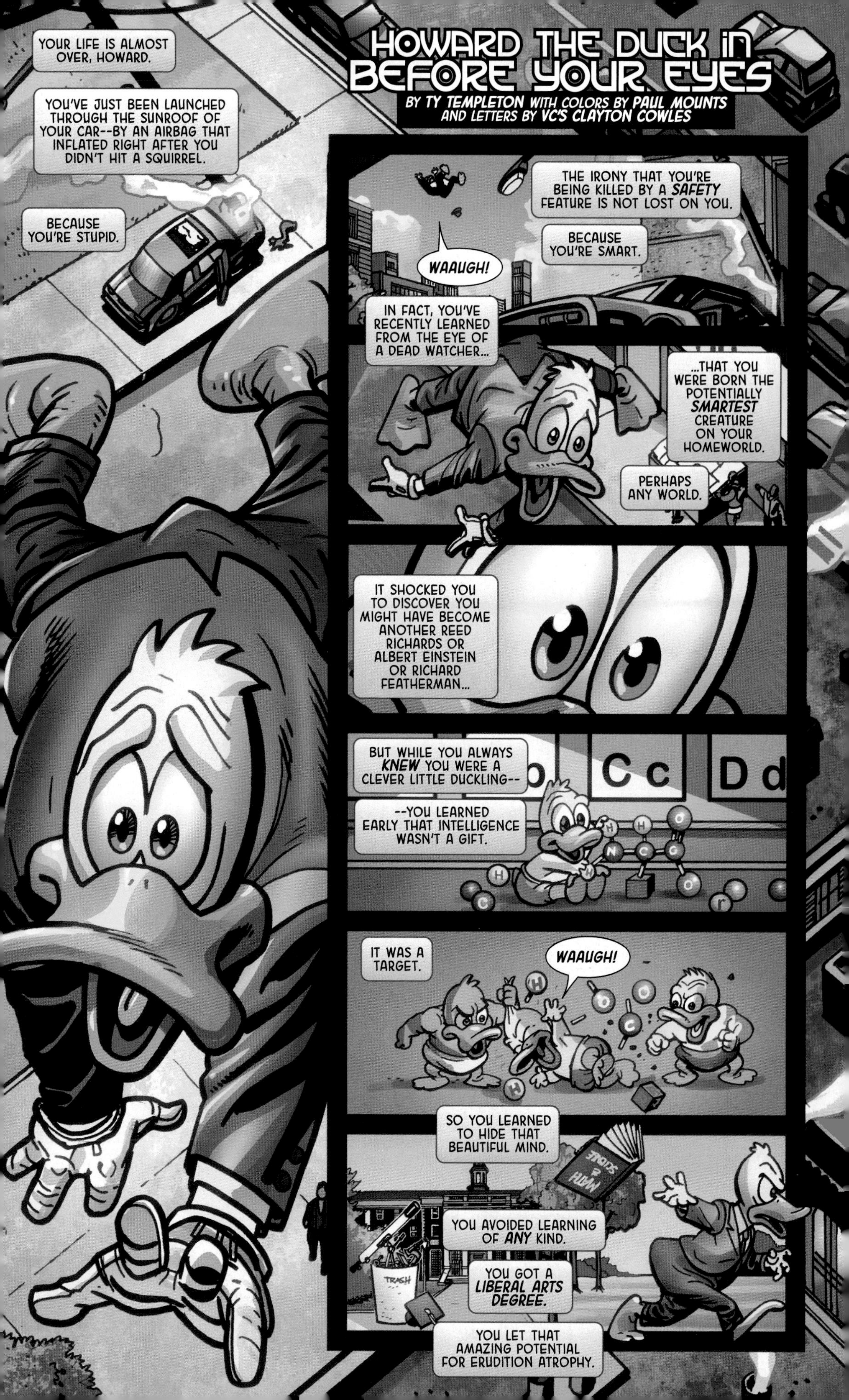

YOUR LIFE IS ALMOST OVER, HOWARD.
HOWARD THE DUCK IN BEFORE YOUR EYES
BY TY TEMPLETON WITH COLORS BY PAUL MOUNTS AND LETTERS BY VC'S CLAYTON COWLES
YOU'VE JUST BEEN LAUNCHED THROUGH THE SUNROOF OF YOUR CAR--BY AN AIRBAG THAT INFLATED RIGHT AFTER YOU DIDN'T HIT A SQUIRREL.
BECAUSE YOU'RE STUPID.
THE IRONY THAT YOU'RE BEING KILLED BY A SAFETY FEATURE IS NOT LOST ON YOU.
BECAUSE YOU'RE SMART.
WAAUGH!
IN FACT, YOU'VE RECENTLY LEARNED FROM THE EYE OF A DEAD WATCHER...
...THAT YOU WERE BORN THE POTENTIALLY SMARTEST CREATURE ON YOUR HOMEWORLD.
PERHAPS ANY WORLD.
IT SHOCKED YOU TO DISCOVER YOU MIGHT HAVE BECOME ANOTHER REED RICHARDS OR ALBERT EINSTEIN OR RICHARD FEATHERMAN...
BUT WHILE YOU ALWAYS KNEW YOU WERE A CLEVER LITTLE DUCKLING--
--YOU LEARNED EARLY THAT INTELLIGENCE WASN'T A GIFT.
IT WAS A TARGET.
WAAUGH!
SO YOU LEARNED TO HIDE THAT BEAUTIFUL MIND.
YOU AVOIDED LEARNING OF ANY KIND.
YOU GOT A LIBERAL ARTS DEGREE.
YOU LET THAT AMAZING POTENTIAL FOR ERUDITION ATROPHY.

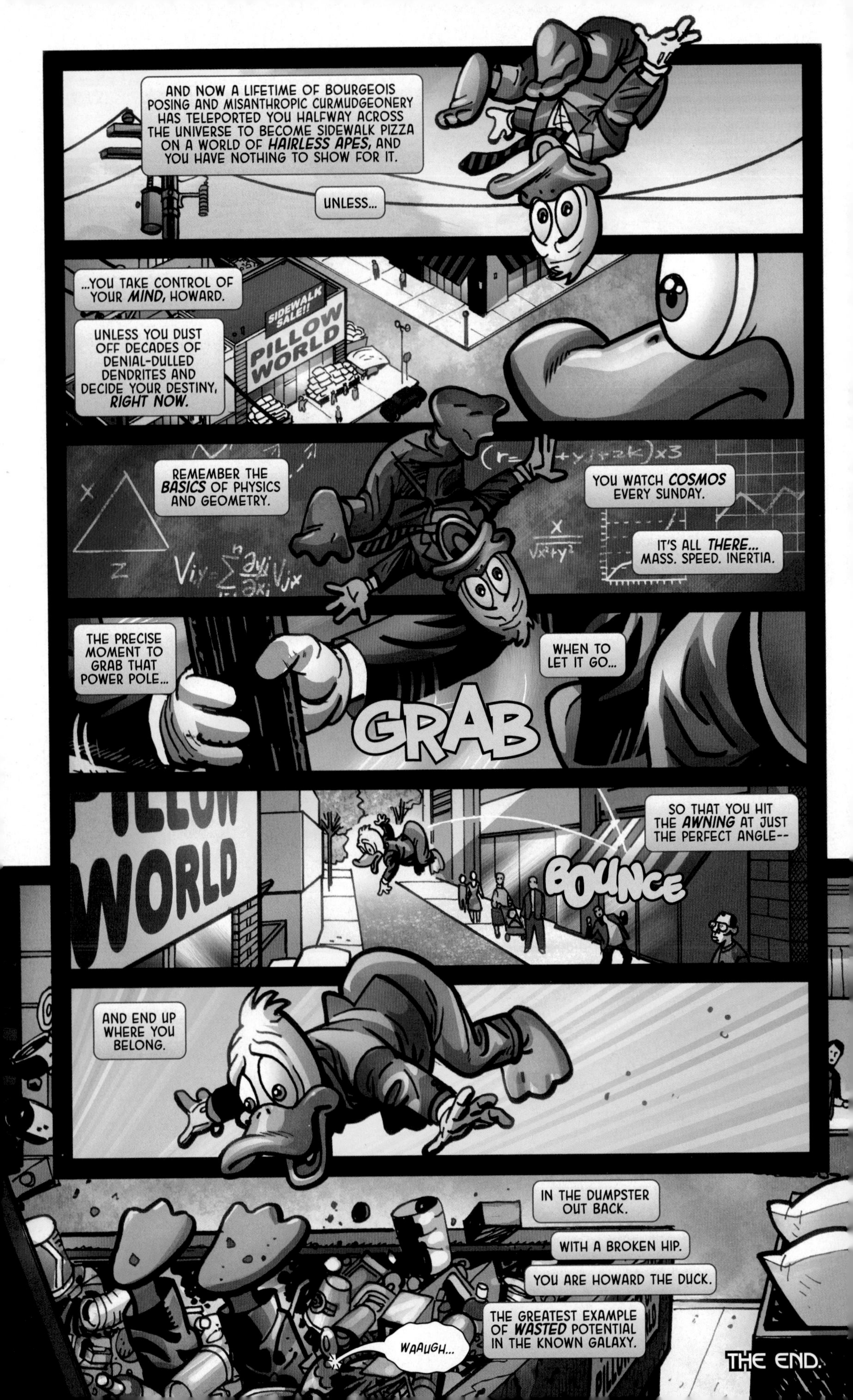
AND NOW A LIFETIME OF BOURGEOIS POSING AND MISANTHROPIC CURMUDGEONERY HAS TELEPORTED YOU HALFWAY ACROSS THE UNIVERSE TO BECOME SIDEWALK PIZZA ON A WORLD OF *HAIRLESS APES,* AND YOU HAVE NOTHING TO SHOW FOR IT.
UNLESS...
...YOU TAKE CONTROL OF YOUR *MIND,* HOWARD.
SIDEWALK SALE!!
PILLOW WORLD
UNLESS YOU DUST OFF DECADES OF DENIAL-DULLED DENDRITES AND DECIDE YOUR DESTINY, ***RIGHT NOW.***
REMEMBER THE *BASICS* OF PHYSICS AND GEOMETRY.
YOU WATCH *COSMOS* EVERY SUNDAY.
IT'S ALL *THERE...* MASS. SPEED. INERTIA.
THE PRECISE MOMENT TO GRAB THAT POWER POLE...
WHEN TO LET IT GO...
GRAB
WORLD
SO THAT YOU HIT THE *AWNING* AT JUST THE PERFECT ANGLE--
BOUNCE
AND END UP WHERE YOU BELONG.
IN THE DUMPSTER OUT BACK.
WITH A BROKEN HIP.
YOU ARE HOWARD THE DUCK.
THE GREATEST EXAMPLE OF *WASTED* POTENTIAL IN THE KNOWN GALAXY.
WAAUGH...
THE END.

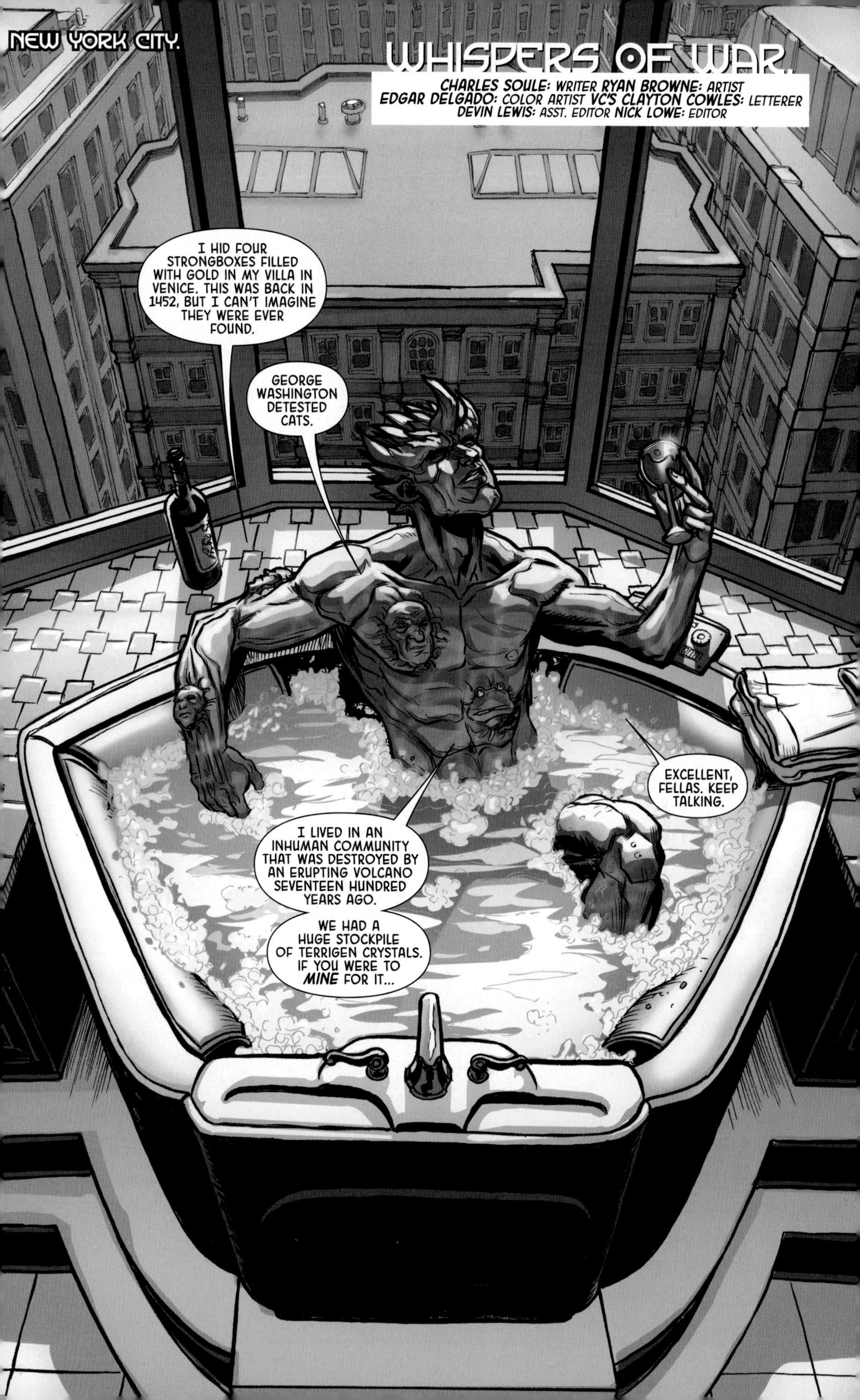
NEW YORK CITY.
WHISPERS OF WAR.
CHARLES SOULE: WRITER RYAN BROWNE: ARTIST
EDGAR DELGADO: COLOR ARTIST VC'S CLAYTON COWLES: LETTERER
DEVIN LEWIS: ASST. EDITOR NICK LOWE: EDITOR
I HID FOUR STRONGBOXES FILLED WITH GOLD IN MY VILLA IN VENICE. THIS WAS BACK IN 1452, BUT I CAN'T IMAGINE THEY WERE EVER FOUND.
GEORGE WASHINGTON DETESTED CATS.
I LIVED IN AN INHUMAN COMMUNITY THAT WAS DESTROYED BY AN ERUPTING VOLCANO SEVENTEEN HUNDRED YEARS AGO.
WE HAD A HUGE STOCKPILE OF TERRIGEN CRYSTALS. IF YOU WERE TO *MINE* FOR IT...
EXCELLENT, FELLAS. KEEP TALKING.

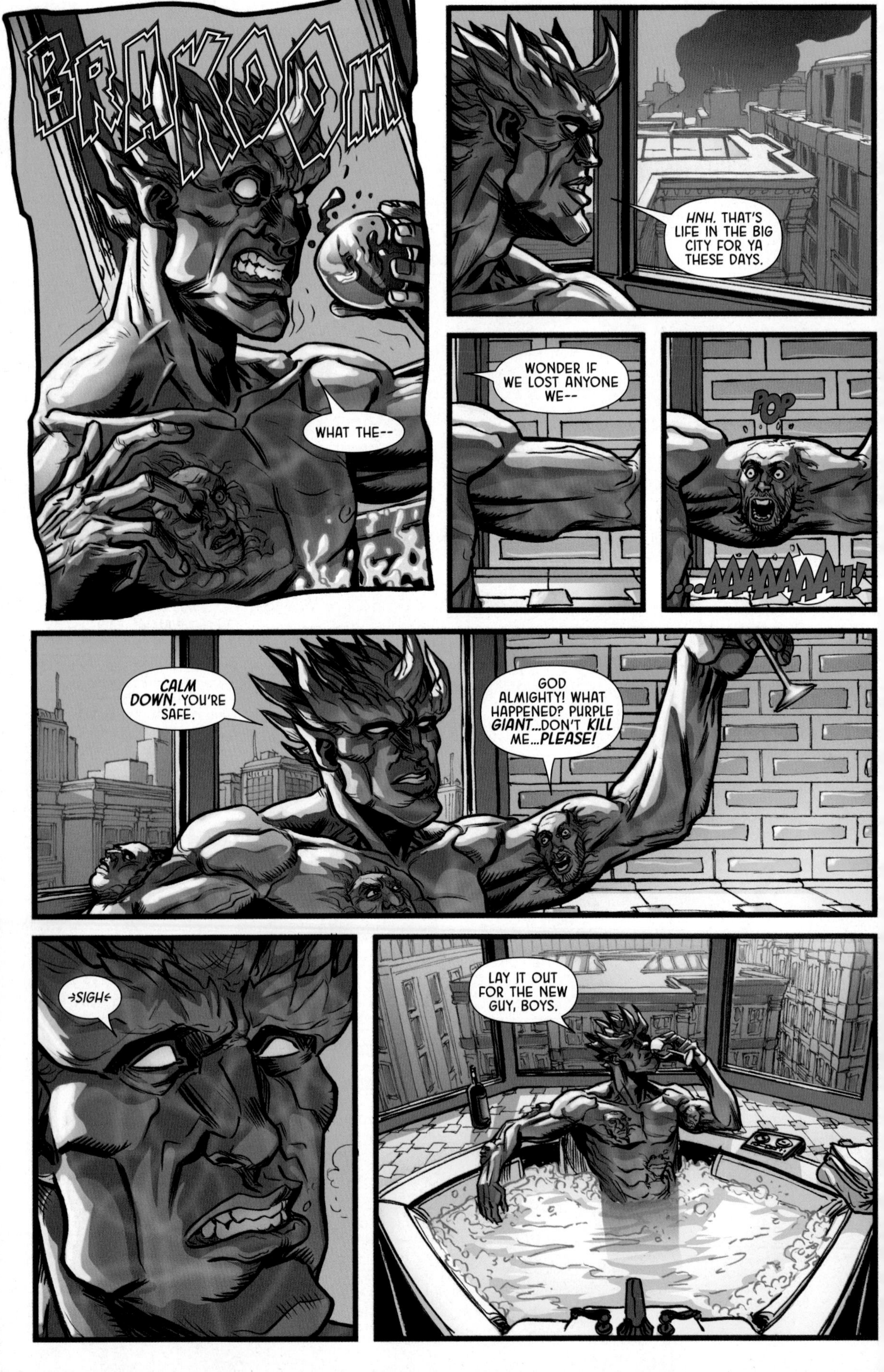
BRAKOOM
WHAT THE--
HNH. THAT'S LIFE IN THE BIG CITY FOR YA THESE DAYS.
WONDER IF WE LOST ANYONE WE--
POP
...AAAAAAAH!
CALM DOWN. YOU'RE SAFE.
GOD ALMIGHTY! WHAT HAPPENED? PURPLE GIANT...DON'T KILL ME...PLEASE!
SIGH
LAY IT OUT FOR THE NEW GUY, BOYS.

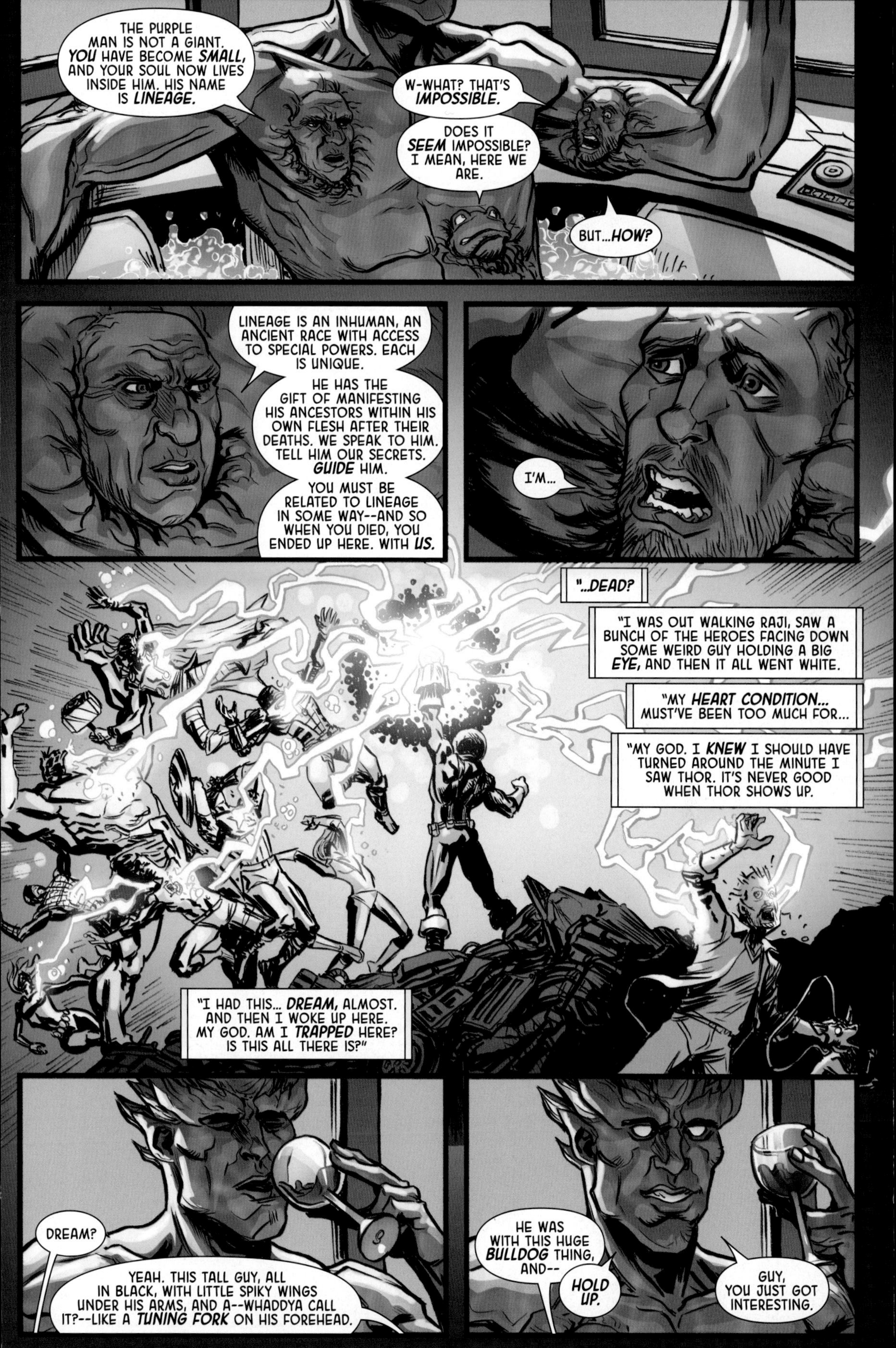
THE PURPLE MAN IS NOT A GIANT. YOU HAVE BECOME SMALL, AND YOUR SOUL NOW LIVES INSIDE HIM. HIS NAME IS LINEAGE.
W-WHAT? THAT'S IMPOSSIBLE.
DOES IT SEEM IMPOSSIBLE? I MEAN, HERE WE ARE.
BUT...HOW?
LINEAGE IS AN INHUMAN, AN ANCIENT RACE WITH ACCESS TO SPECIAL POWERS. EACH IS UNIQUE.
HE HAS THE GIFT OF MANIFESTING HIS ANCESTORS WITHIN HIS OWN FLESH AFTER THEIR DEATHS. WE SPEAK TO HIM. TELL HIM OUR SECRETS. GUIDE HIM.
YOU MUST BE RELATED TO LINEAGE IN SOME WAY--AND SO WHEN YOU DIED, YOU ENDED UP HERE. WITH US.
I'M...
"...DEAD?
"I WAS OUT WALKING RAJI, SAW A BUNCH OF THE HEROES FACING DOWN SOME WEIRD GUY HOLDING A BIG EYE, AND THEN IT ALL WENT WHITE.
"MY HEART CONDITION... MUST'VE BEEN TOO MUCH FOR...
"MY GOD. I KNEW I SHOULD HAVE TURNED AROUND THE MINUTE I SAW THOR. IT'S NEVER GOOD WHEN THOR SHOWS UP.
"I HAD THIS... DREAM, ALMOST. AND THEN I WOKE UP HERE. MY GOD. AM I TRAPPED HERE? IS THIS ALL THERE IS?"
DREAM?
YEAH. THIS TALL GUY, ALL IN BLACK, WITH LITTLE SPIKY WINGS UNDER HIS ARMS, AND A--WHADDYA CALL IT?--LIKE A TUNING FORK ON HIS FOREHEAD.
HE WAS WITH THIS HUGE BULLDOG THING, AND--
HOLD UP.
GUY, YOU JUST GOT INTERESTING.

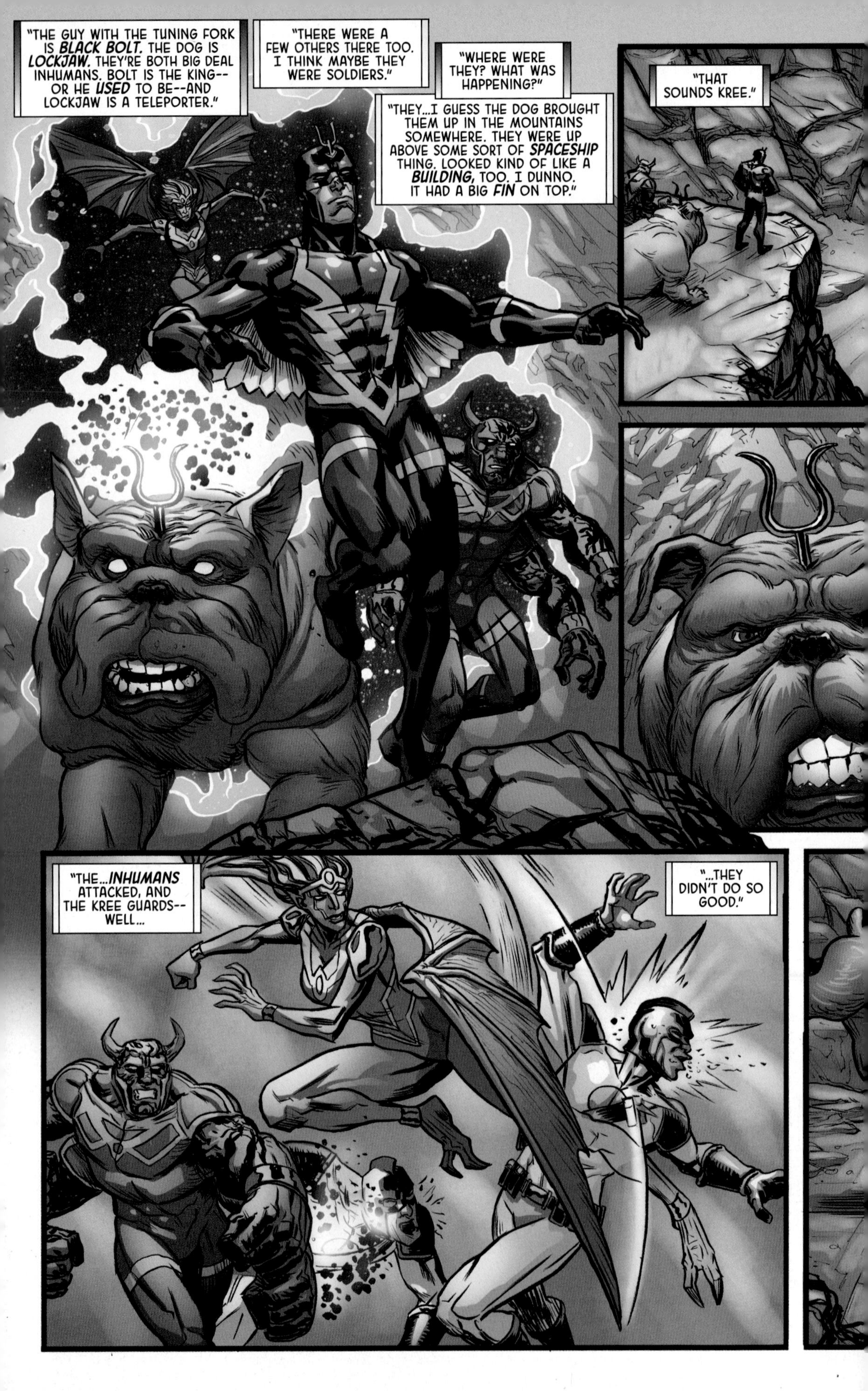
"THE GUY WITH THE TUNING FORK IS BLACK BOLT. THE DOG IS LOCKJAW. THEY'RE BOTH BIG DEAL INHUMANS. BOLT IS THE KING-- OR HE USED TO BE--AND LOCKJAW IS A TELEPORTER."
"THERE WERE A FEW OTHERS THERE TOO. I THINK MAYBE THEY WERE SOLDIERS."
"WHERE WERE THEY? WHAT WAS HAPPENING?"
"THEY...I GUESS THE DOG BROUGHT THEM UP IN THE MOUNTAINS SOMEWHERE. THEY WERE UP ABOVE SOME SORT OF SPACESHIP THING. LOOKED KIND OF LIKE A BUILDING, TOO. I DUNNO. IT HAD A BIG FIN ON TOP."
"THAT SOUNDS KREE."
"THE...INHUMANS ATTACKED, AND THE KREE GUARDS-- WELL...
"...THEY DIDN'T DO SO GOOD."

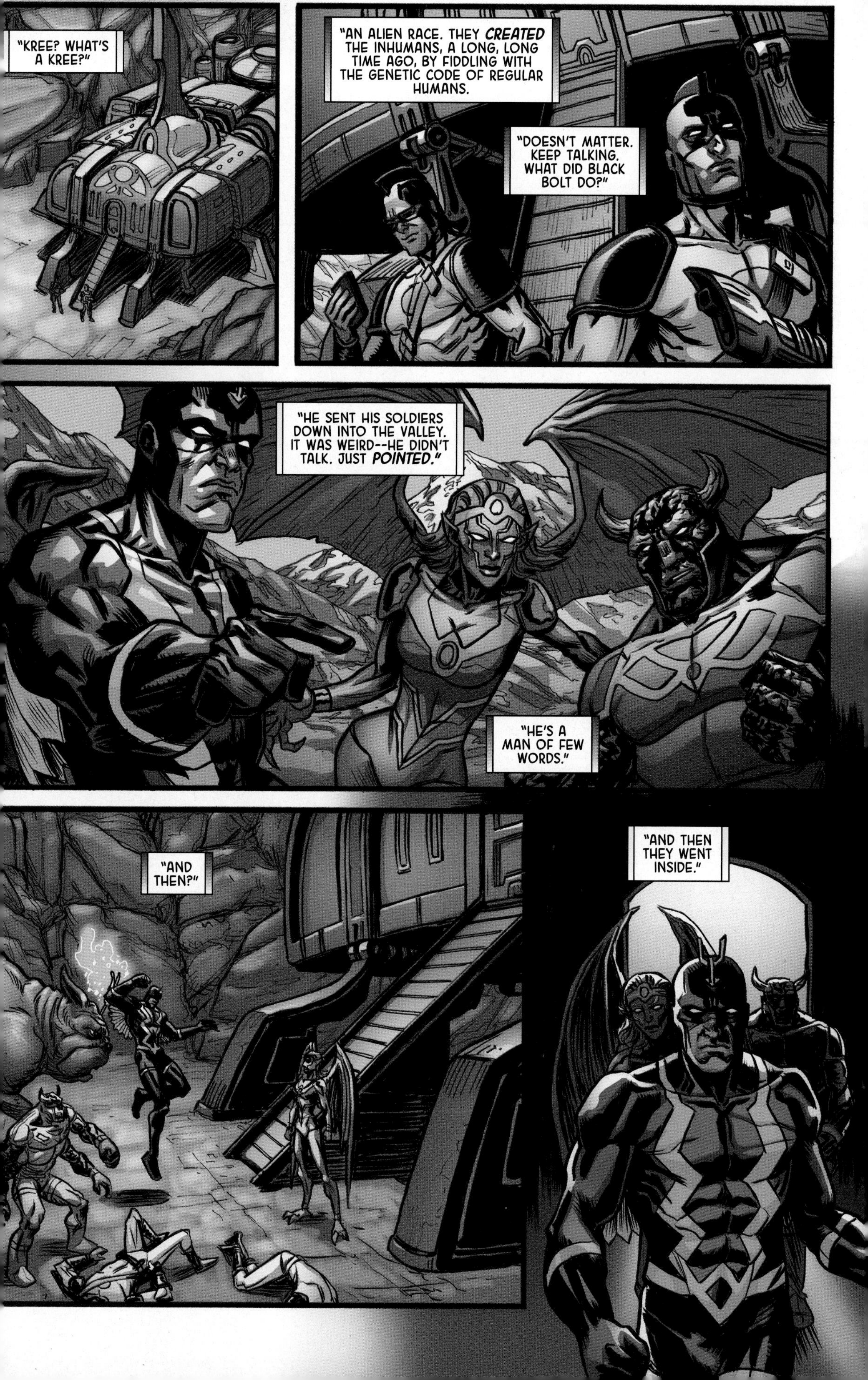
"KREE? WHAT'S A KREE?"
"AN ALIEN RACE. THEY *CREATED* THE INHUMANS, A LONG, LONG TIME AGO, BY FIDDLING WITH THE GENETIC CODE OF REGULAR HUMANS.
"DOESN'T MATTER. KEEP TALKING. WHAT DID BLACK BOLT DO?"
"HE SENT HIS SOLDIERS DOWN INTO THE VALLEY. IT WAS WEIRD--HE DIDN'T TALK. JUST *POINTED.*"
"HE'S A MAN OF FEW WORDS."
"AND THEN?"
"AND THEN THEY WENT INSIDE."

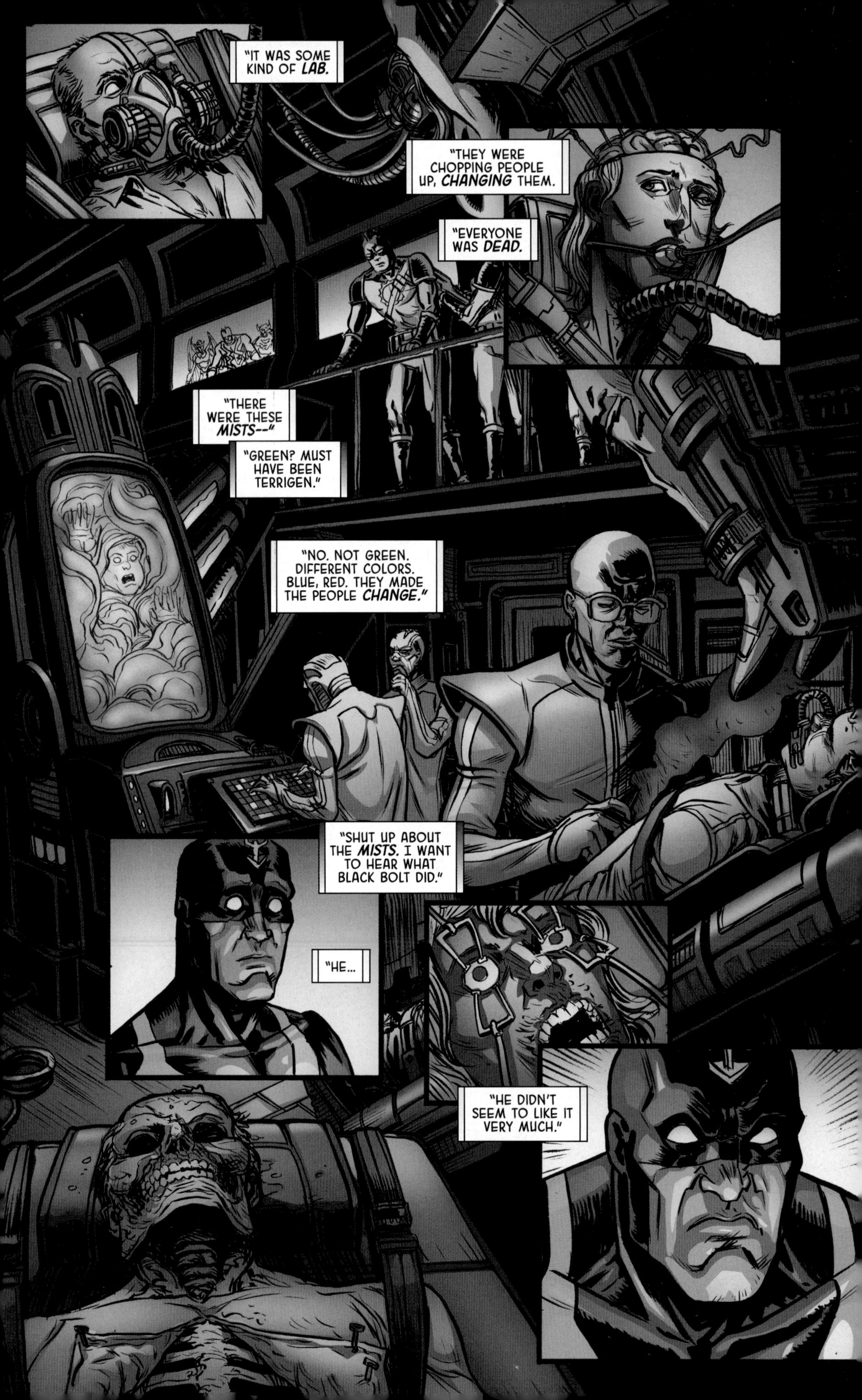
"IT WAS SOME KIND OF LAB.
"THEY WERE CHOPPING PEOPLE UP, CHANGING THEM.
"EVERYONE WAS DEAD.
"THERE WERE THESE MISTS--"
"GREEN? MUST HAVE BEEN TERRIGEN."
"NO. NOT GREEN. DIFFERENT COLORS. BLUE, RED. THEY MADE THE PEOPLE CHANGE."
"SHUT UP ABOUT THE MISTS. I WANT TO HEAR WHAT BLACK BOLT DID."
"HE...
"HE DIDN'T SEEM TO LIKE IT VERY MUCH."

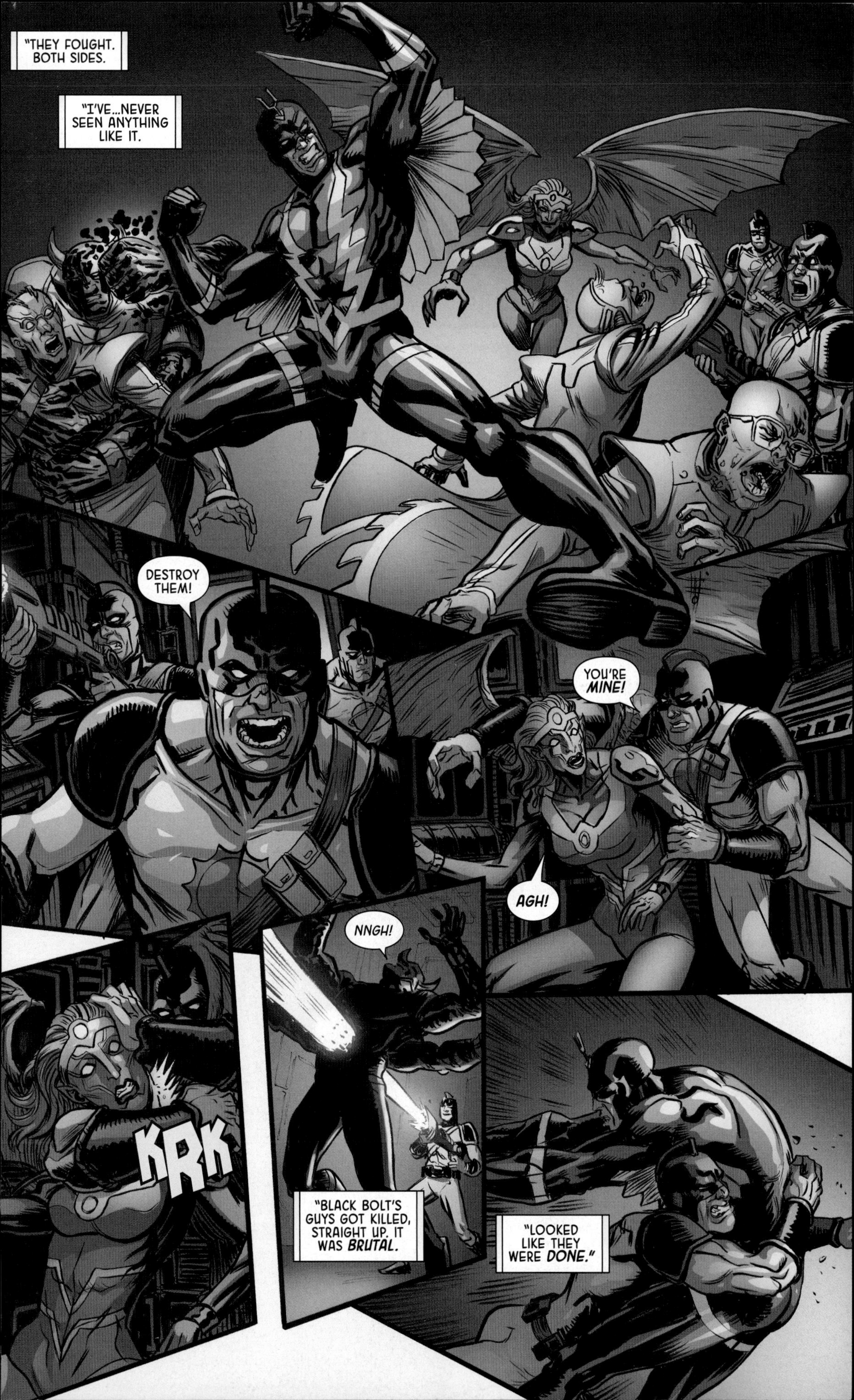
"THEY FOUGHT. BOTH SIDES.
"I'VE...NEVER SEEN ANYTHING LIKE IT.
DESTROY THEM!
YOU'RE *MINE!*
AGH!
NNGH!
KRK
"BLACK BOLT'S GUYS GOT KILLED, STRAIGHT UP. IT WAS *BRUTAL.*
"LOOKED LIKE THEY WERE *DONE.*"

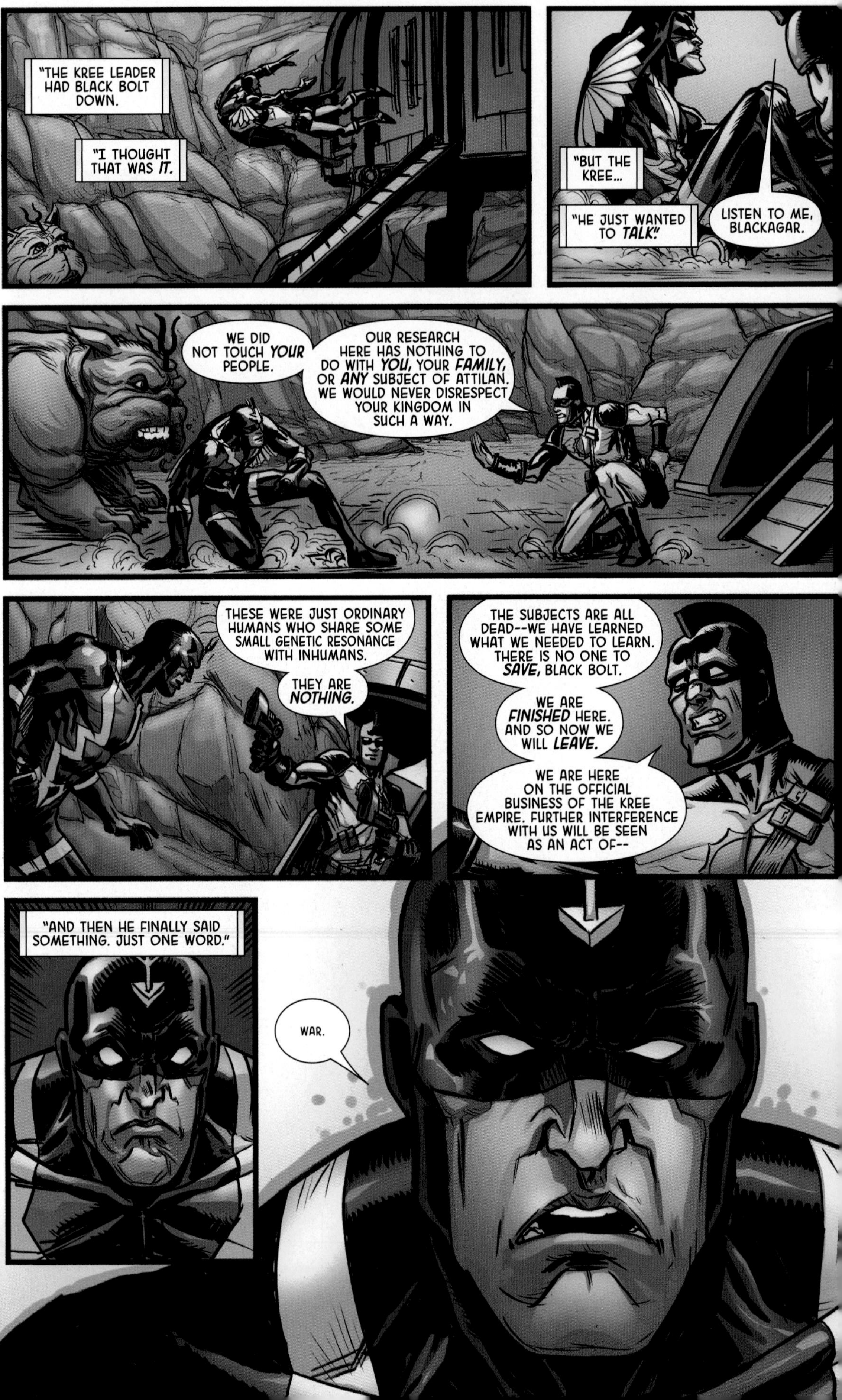
"THE KREE LEADER HAD BLACK BOLT DOWN.
"I THOUGHT THAT WAS *IT*.
"BUT THE KREE...
"HE JUST WANTED TO *TALK*."
LISTEN TO ME, BLACKAGAR.
WE DID NOT TOUCH *YOUR* PEOPLE.
OUR RESEARCH HERE HAS NOTHING TO DO WITH *YOU*, YOUR *FAMILY*, OR *ANY* SUBJECT OF ATTILAN. WE WOULD NEVER DISRESPECT YOUR KINGDOM IN SUCH A WAY.
THESE WERE JUST ORDINARY HUMANS WHO SHARE SOME SMALL GENETIC RESONANCE WITH INHUMANS.
THEY ARE *NOTHING*.
THE SUBJECTS ARE ALL DEAD--WE HAVE LEARNED WHAT WE NEEDED TO LEARN. THERE IS NO ONE TO *SAVE*, BLACK BOLT.
WE ARE *FINISHED* HERE. AND SO NOW WE WILL *LEAVE*.
WE ARE HERE ON THE OFFICIAL BUSINESS OF THE KREE EMPIRE. FURTHER INTERFERENCE WITH US WILL BE SEEN AS AN ACT OF--
"AND THEN HE FINALLY SAID SOMETHING. JUST ONE WORD."
WAR.

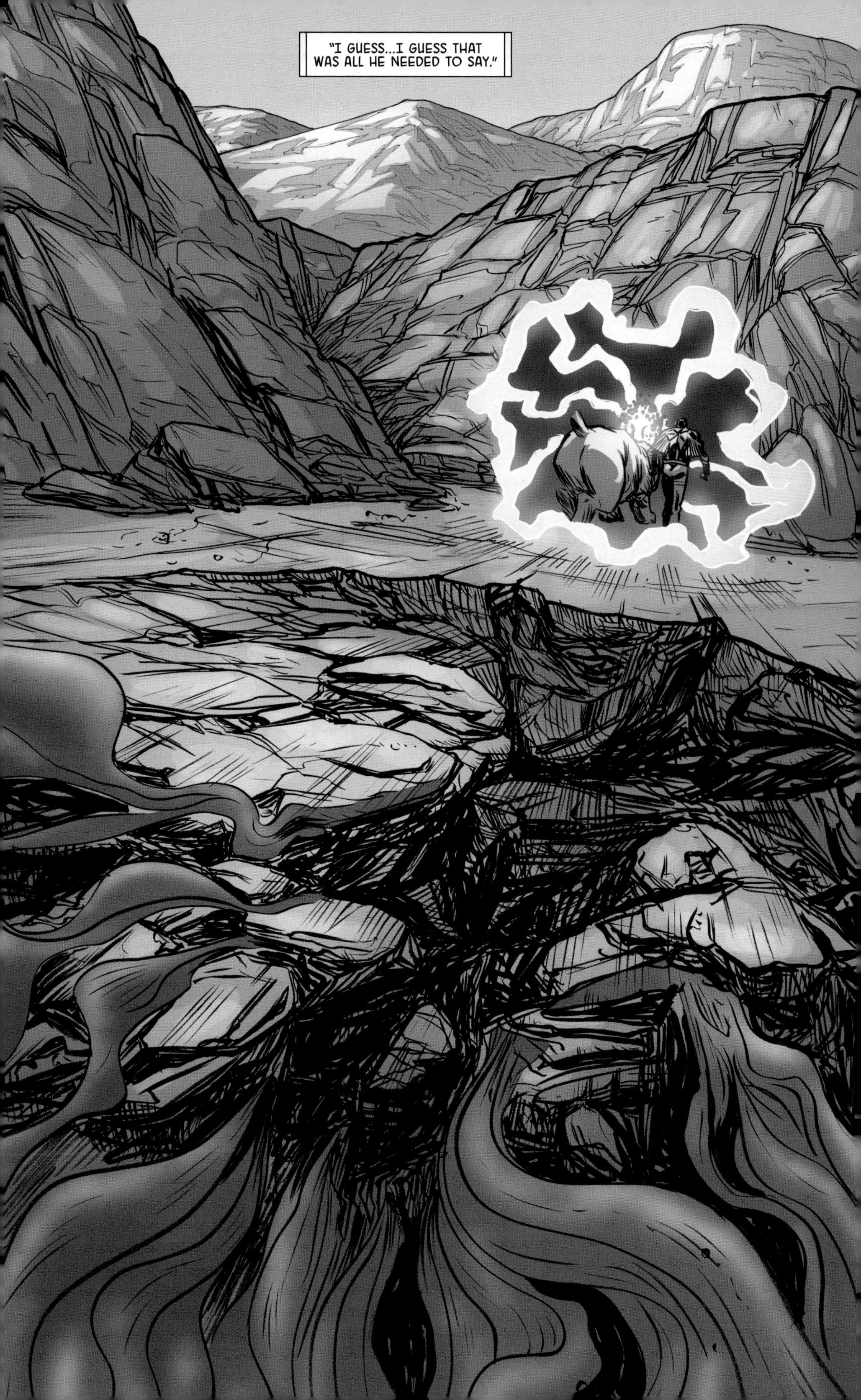
"I GUESS...I GUESS THAT WAS ALL HE NEEDED TO SAY."

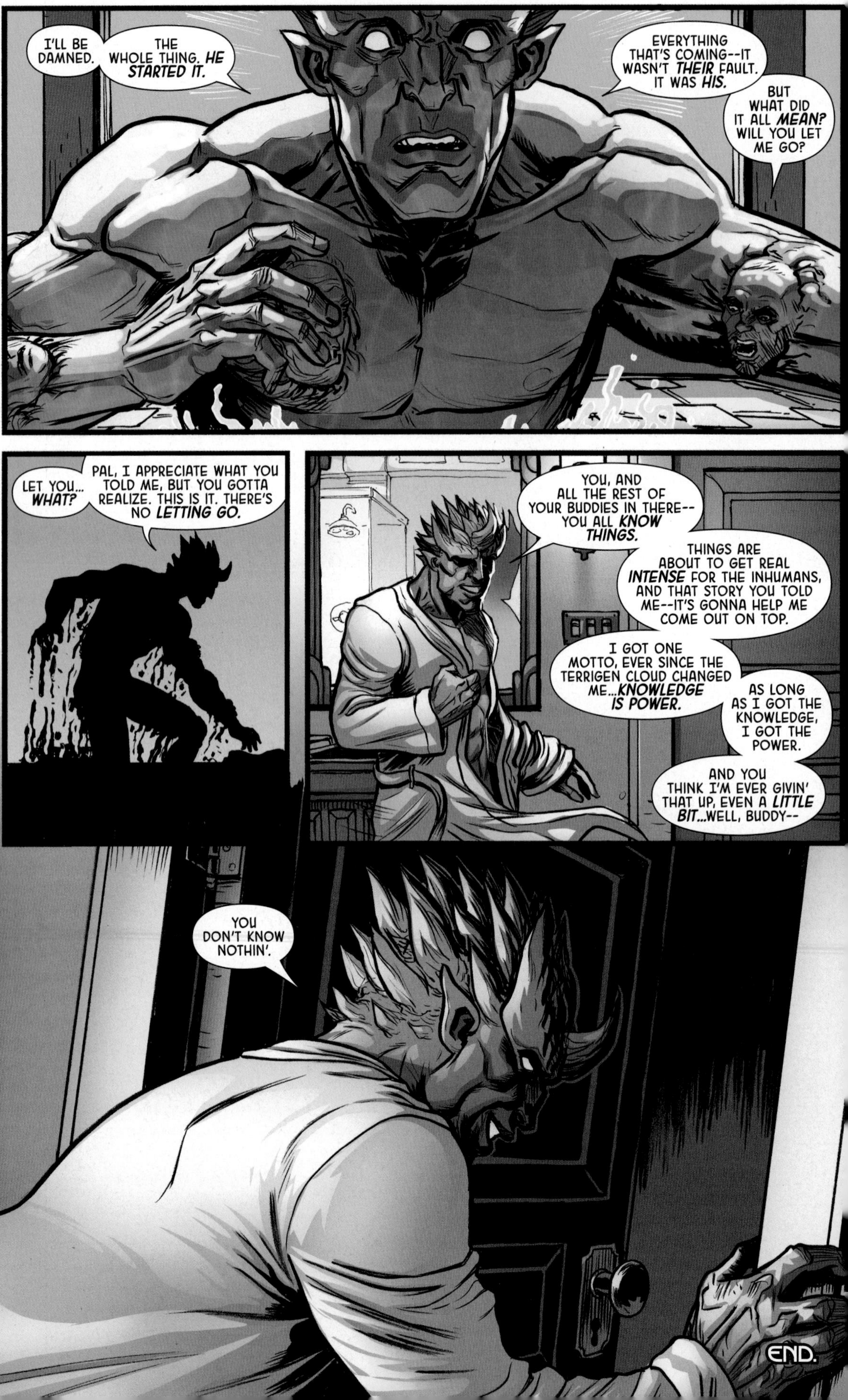

I'LL BE DAMNED.
THE WHOLE THING. HE STARTED IT.
EVERYTHING THAT'S COMING--IT WASN'T THEIR FAULT. IT WAS HIS.
BUT WHAT DID IT ALL MEAN? WILL YOU LET ME GO?
LET YOU... WHAT?
PAL, I APPRECIATE WHAT YOU TOLD ME, BUT YOU GOTTA REALIZE. THIS IS IT. THERE'S NO LETTING GO.
YOU, AND ALL THE REST OF YOUR BUDDIES IN THERE--YOU ALL KNOW THINGS.
THINGS ARE ABOUT TO GET REAL INTENSE FOR THE INHUMANS, AND THAT STORY YOU TOLD ME--IT'S GONNA HELP ME COME OUT ON TOP.
I GOT ONE MOTTO, EVER SINCE THE TERRIGEN CLOUD CHANGED ME...KNOWLEDGE IS POWER.
AS LONG AS I GOT THE KNOWLEDGE, I GOT THE POWER.
AND YOU THINK I'M EVER GIVIN' THAT UP, EVEN A LITTLE BIT...WELL, BUDDY--
YOU DON'T KNOW NOTHIN'.
END.

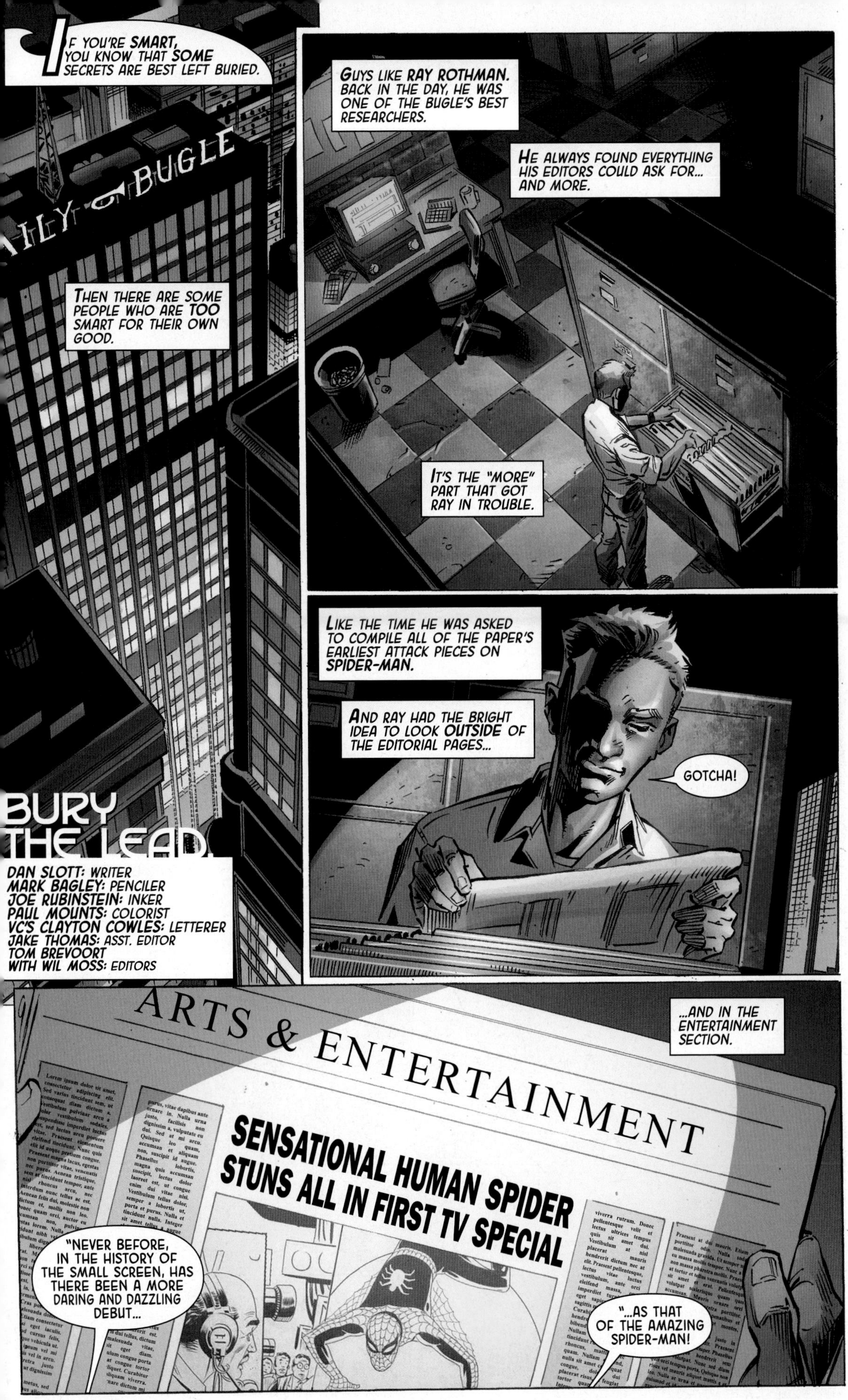

IF YOU'RE SMART, YOU KNOW THAT SOME SECRETS ARE BEST LEFT BURIED.
GUYS LIKE RAY ROTHMAN. BACK IN THE DAY, HE WAS ONE OF THE BUGLE'S BEST RESEARCHERS.
HE ALWAYS FOUND EVERYTHING HIS EDITORS COULD ASK FOR... AND MORE.
THEN THERE ARE SOME PEOPLE WHO ARE TOO SMART FOR THEIR OWN GOOD.
IT'S THE "MORE" PART THAT GOT RAY IN TROUBLE.
LIKE THE TIME HE WAS ASKED TO COMPILE ALL OF THE PAPER'S EARLIEST ATTACK PIECES ON SPIDER-MAN.
AND RAY HAD THE BRIGHT IDEA TO LOOK OUTSIDE OF THE EDITORIAL PAGES...
GOTCHA!
BURY THE LEAD
DAN SLOTT: WRITER
MARK BAGLEY: PENCILER
JOE RUBINSTEIN: INKER
PAUL MOUNTS: COLORIST
VC'S CLAYTON COWLES: LETTERER
JAKE THOMAS: ASST. EDITOR
TOM BREVOORT
WITH WIL MOSS: EDITORS
ARTS & ENTERTAINMENT
...AND IN THE ENTERTAINMENT SECTION.
SENSATIONAL HUMAN SPIDER STUNS ALL IN FIRST TV SPECIAL
"NEVER BEFORE, IN THE HISTORY OF THE SMALL SCREEN, HAS THERE BEEN A MORE DARING AND DAZZLING DEBUT...
"...AS THAT OF THE AMAZING SPIDER-MAN!

"'FOR ONE SOLID HOUR I WAS HELD MESMERIZED BY HIS AWESOME, INSECT-LIKE ACROBATICS...

"'...HIS WONDROUS WEB-'SPINNING, AND HIS HILARIOUS ONE-LINERS AND NONSTOP ANTICS."

"MARK MY WORDS, TRUE BELIEVERS...

"...OR MY NAME ISN'T...

"...J. JONAH JAMESON"?!

Never before, in the history of the small screen, has there been a more daring and dazzling debut as that of the Amazing Spider-Man! For one solid hour I was held mesmerized by his

awesome, insect-like acrobatics, his wondrous web-spinning, and his hilarious one-liners and non-stop antics. Mark my words, true-believers, I see nothing but sold out shows for this costumed cut-up or my name isn't J. Jameson.

"I SEE NOTHING BUT SOLD OUT SHOWS FOR THIS COSTUMED CUT-UP...

ROTHMAN, YOU'RE FIRED!

WHA--?! MR. JAMESON? I HAD NO IDEA YOU WROTE--

NOTHING! THAT NEVER HAPPENED! IT DOESN'T EXIST!

BUT I--

AND NEITHER DO YOU! GOT THAT?!

I'LL SEE TO IT YOU NEVER WORK IN THIS TOWN AGAIN!

AND HE NEVER DID.

WHAT A SHAME.

THAT WAS A FINE PIECE OF WRITING.

END.

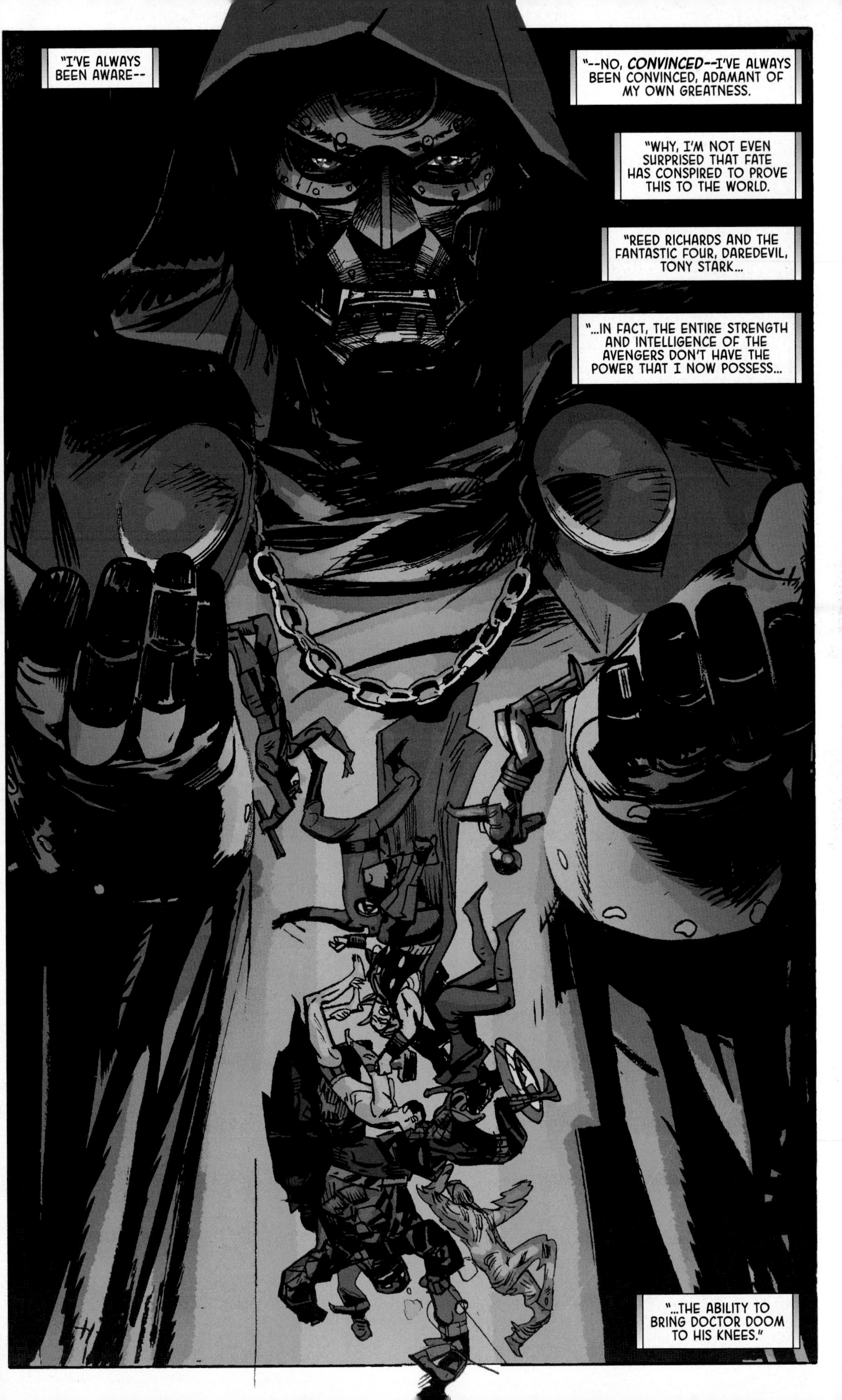
"I'VE ALWAYS BEEN AWARE--
"--NO, CONVINCED--I'VE ALWAYS BEEN CONVINCED, ADAMANT OF MY OWN GREATNESS.
"WHY, I'M NOT EVEN SURPRISED THAT FATE HAS CONSPIRED TO PROVE THIS TO THE WORLD.
"REED RICHARDS AND THE FANTASTIC FOUR, DAREDEVIL, TONY STARK...
"...IN FACT, THE ENTIRE STRENGTH AND INTELLIGENCE OF THE AVENGERS DON'T HAVE THE POWER THAT I NOW POSSESS...
"...THE ABILITY TO BRING DOCTOR DOOM TO HIS KNEES."

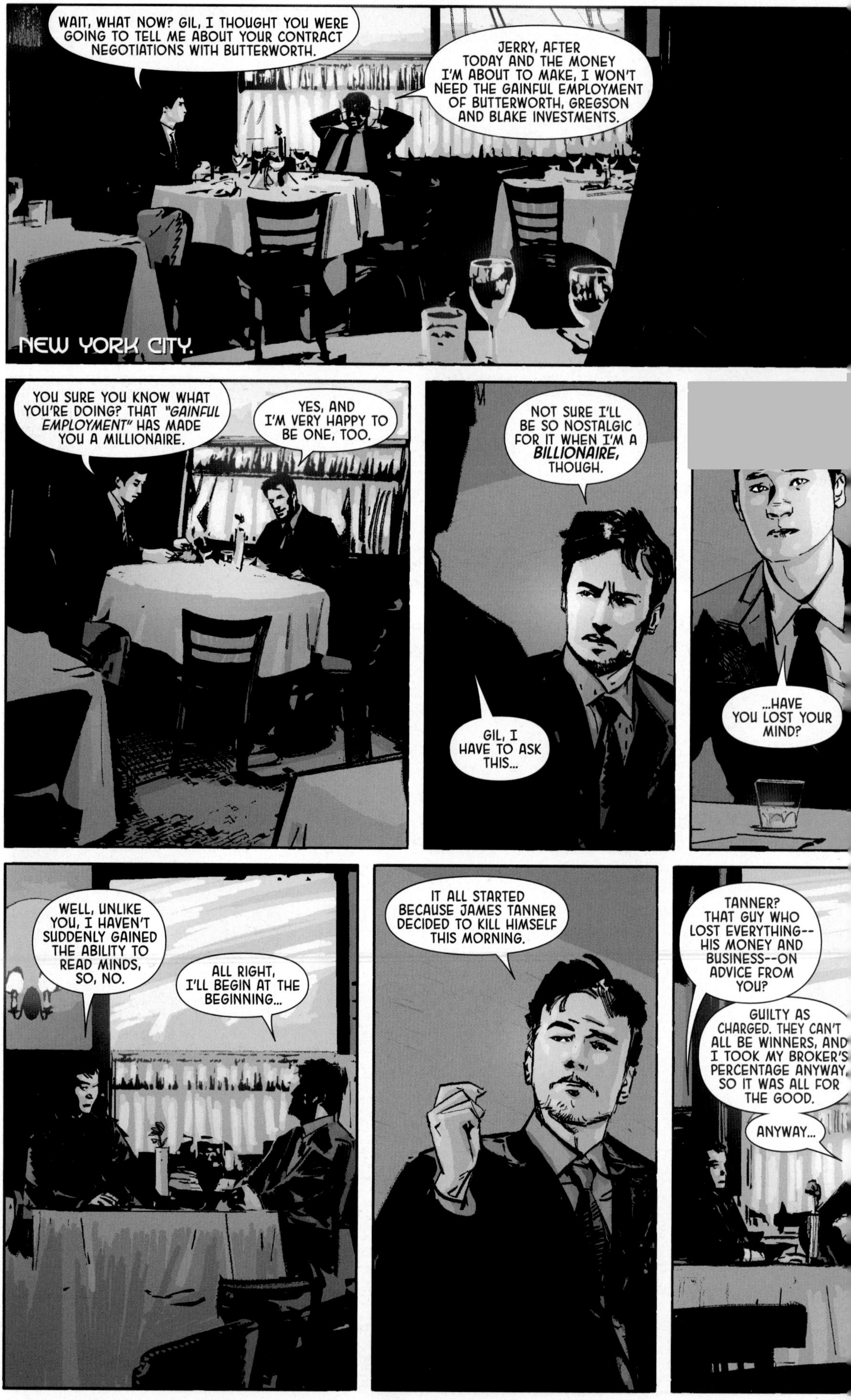
WAIT, WHAT NOW? GIL, I THOUGHT YOU WERE GOING TO TELL ME ABOUT YOUR CONTRACT NEGOTIATIONS WITH BUTTERWORTH.
JERRY, AFTER TODAY AND THE MONEY I'M ABOUT TO MAKE, I WON'T NEED THE GAINFUL EMPLOYMENT OF BUTTERWORTH, GREGSON AND BLAKE INVESTMENTS.
NEW YORK CITY.
YOU SURE YOU KNOW WHAT YOU'RE DOING? THAT "GAINFUL EMPLOYMENT" HAS MADE YOU A MILLIONAIRE.
YES, AND I'M VERY HAPPY TO BE ONE, TOO.
NOT SURE I'LL BE SO NOSTALGIC FOR IT WHEN I'M A BILLIONAIRE, THOUGH.
GIL, I HAVE TO ASK THIS...
...HAVE YOU LOST YOUR MIND?
WELL, UNLIKE YOU, I HAVEN'T SUDDENLY GAINED THE ABILITY TO READ MINDS, SO, NO.
ALL RIGHT, I'LL BEGIN AT THE BEGINNING...
IT ALL STARTED BECAUSE JAMES TANNER DECIDED TO KILL HIMSELF THIS MORNING.
TANNER? THAT GUY WHO LOST EVERYTHING--HIS MONEY AND BUSINESS--ON ADVICE FROM YOU?
GUILTY AS CHARGED. THEY CAN'T ALL BE WINNERS, AND I TOOK MY BROKER'S PERCENTAGE ANYWAY, SO IT WAS ALL FOR THE GOOD.
ANYWAY...

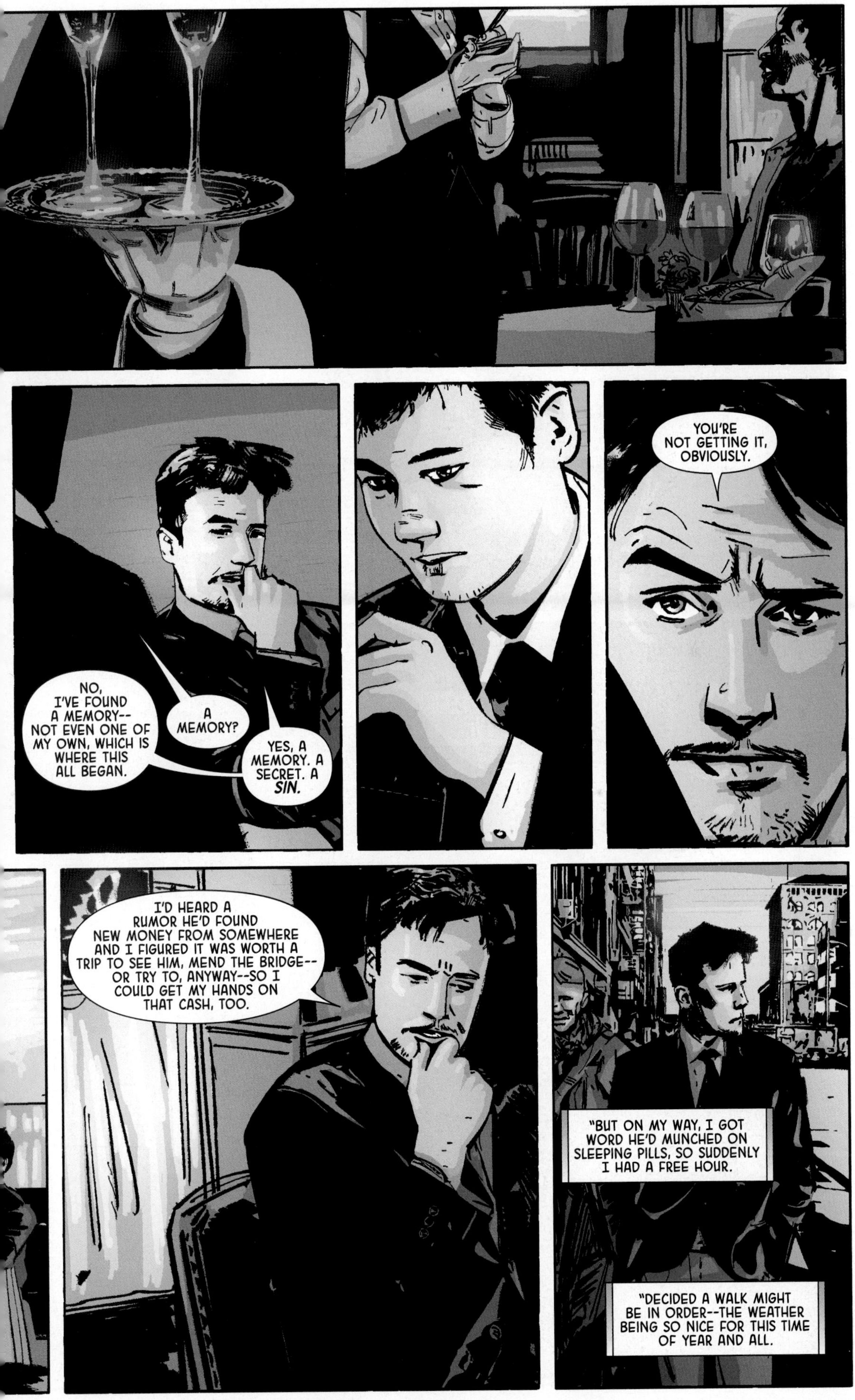

NO, I'VE FOUND A MEMORY-- NOT EVEN ONE OF MY OWN, WHICH IS WHERE THIS ALL BEGAN.
A MEMORY?
YES, A MEMORY. A SECRET. A *SIN.*
YOU'RE NOT GETTING IT, OBVIOUSLY.
I'D HEARD A RUMOR HE'D FOUND NEW MONEY FROM SOMEWHERE AND I FIGURED IT WAS WORTH A TRIP TO SEE HIM, MEND THE BRIDGE-- OR TRY TO, ANYWAY--SO I COULD GET MY HANDS ON THAT CASH, TOO.
"BUT ON MY WAY, I GOT WORD HE'D MUNCHED ON SLEEPING PILLS, SO SUDDENLY I HAD A FREE HOUR.
"DECIDED A WALK MIGHT BE IN ORDER--THE WEATHER BEING SO NICE FOR THIS TIME OF YEAR AND ALL.

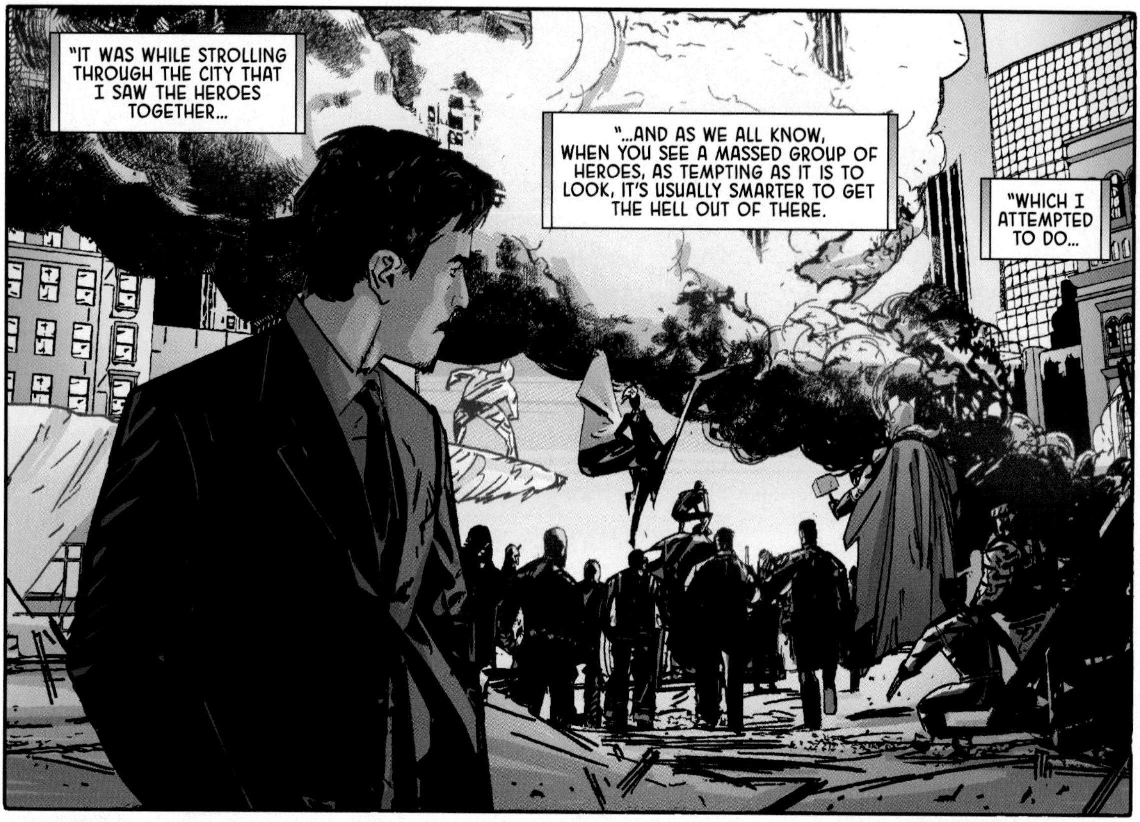
"IT WAS WHILE STROLLING THROUGH THE CITY THAT I SAW THE HEROES TOGETHER...
"...AND AS WE ALL KNOW, WHEN YOU SEE A MASSED GROUP OF HEROES, AS TEMPTING AS IT IS TO LOOK, IT'S USUALLY SMARTER TO GET THE HELL OUT OF THERE.
"WHICH I ATTEMPTED TO DO...

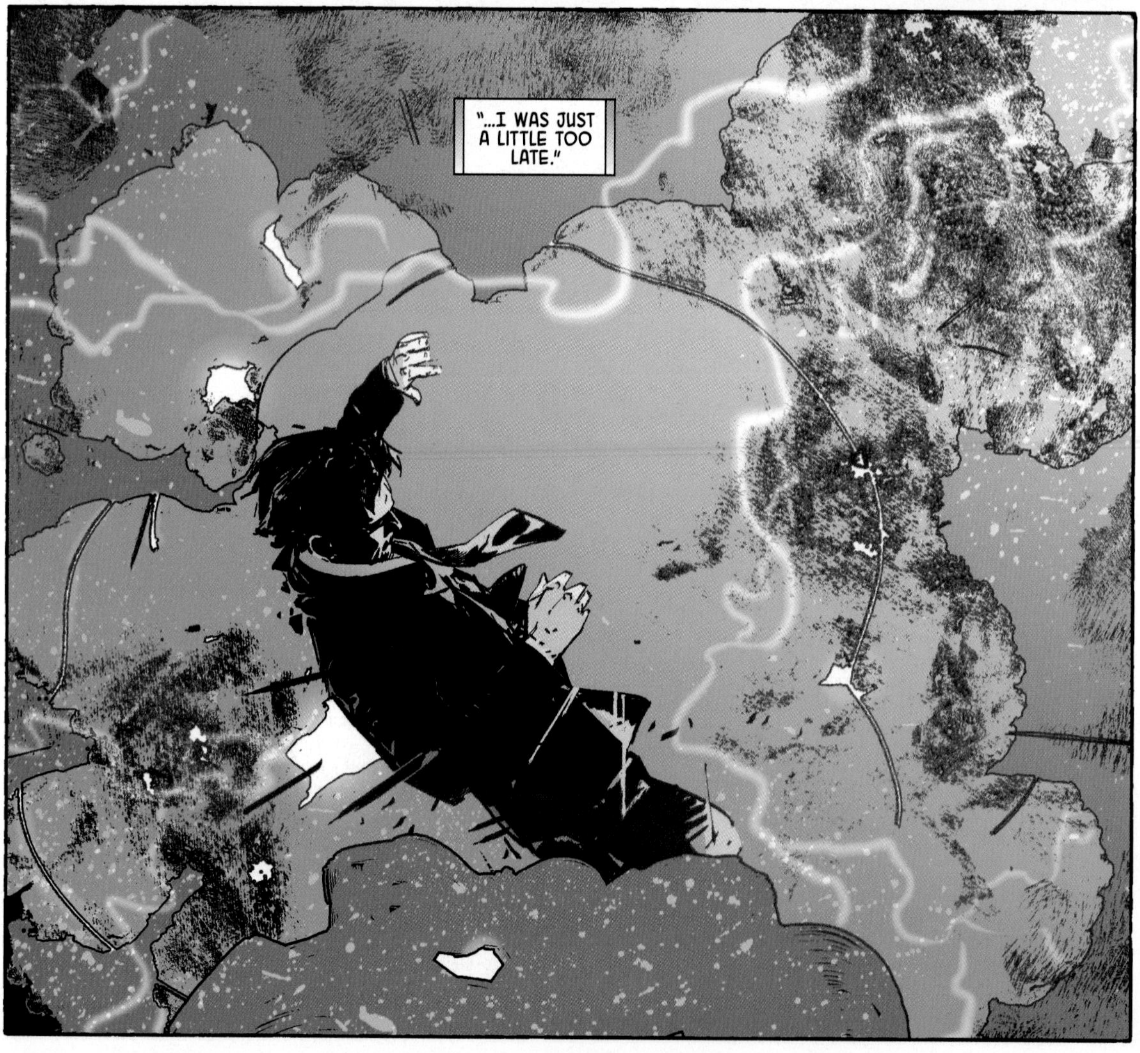
"...I WAS JUST A LITTLE TOO LATE."

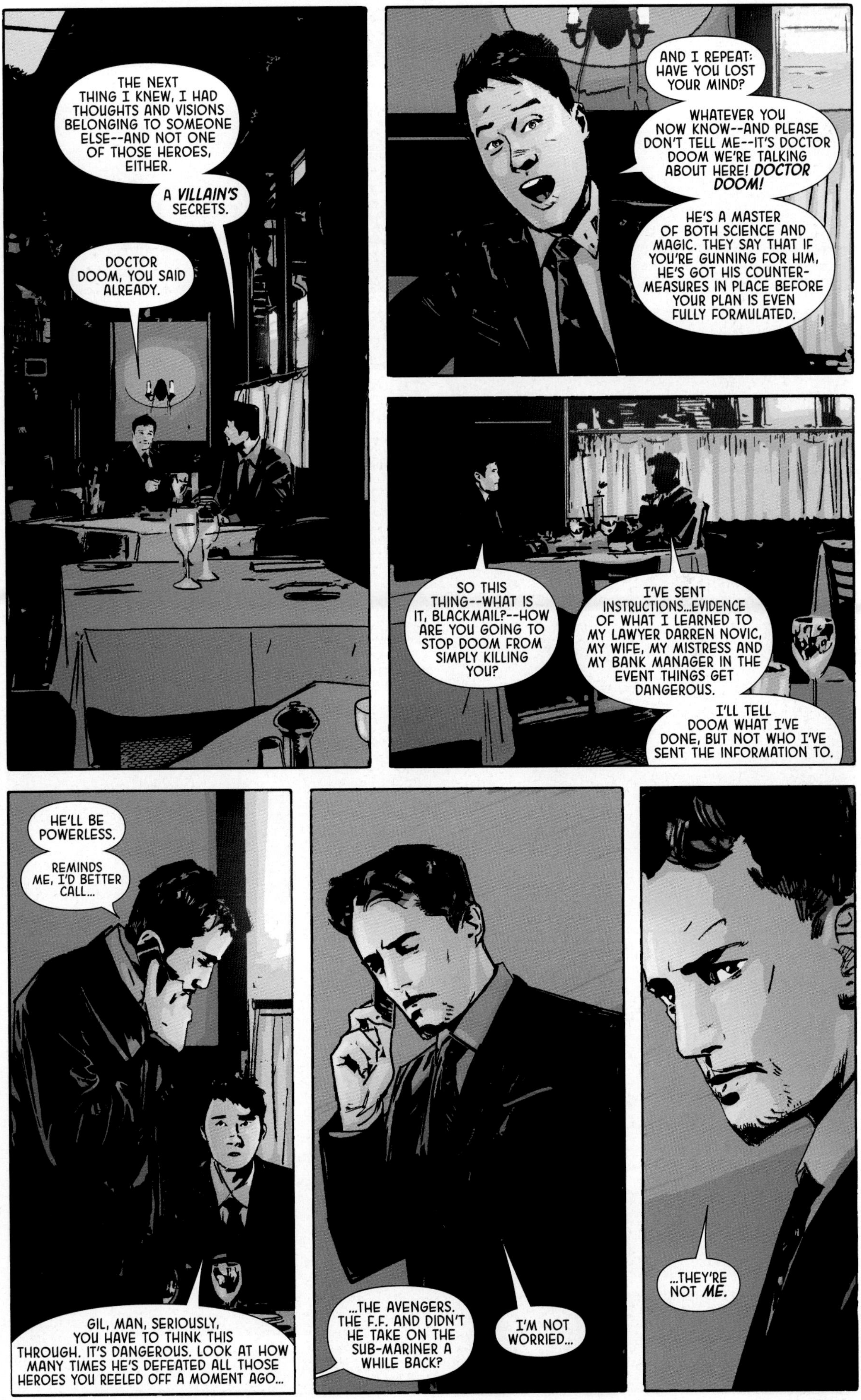
THE NEXT THING I KNEW, I HAD THOUGHTS AND VISIONS BELONGING TO SOMEONE ELSE--AND NOT ONE OF THOSE HEROES, EITHER.
A *VILLAIN'S* SECRETS.
DOCTOR DOOM, YOU SAID ALREADY.
AND I REPEAT: HAVE YOU LOST YOUR MIND?
WHATEVER YOU NOW KNOW--AND PLEASE DON'T TELL ME--IT'S DOCTOR DOOM WE'RE TALKING ABOUT HERE! *DOCTOR DOOM!*
HE'S A MASTER OF BOTH SCIENCE AND MAGIC. THEY SAY THAT IF YOU'RE GUNNING FOR HIM, HE'S GOT HIS COUNTER-MEASURES IN PLACE BEFORE YOUR PLAN IS EVEN FULLY FORMULATED.
SO THIS THING--WHAT IS IT, BLACKMAIL?--HOW ARE YOU GOING TO STOP DOOM FROM SIMPLY KILLING YOU?
I'VE SENT INSTRUCTIONS...EVIDENCE OF WHAT I LEARNED TO MY LAWYER DARREN NOVIC, MY WIFE, MY MISTRESS AND MY BANK MANAGER IN THE EVENT THINGS GET DANGEROUS.
I'LL TELL DOOM WHAT I'VE DONE, BUT NOT WHO I'VE SENT THE INFORMATION TO.
HE'LL BE POWERLESS.
REMINDS ME, I'D BETTER CALL...
GIL, MAN, SERIOUSLY, YOU HAVE TO THINK THIS THROUGH. IT'S DANGEROUS. LOOK AT HOW MANY TIMES HE'S DEFEATED ALL THOSE HEROES YOU REELED OFF A MOMENT AGO...
...THE AVENGERS. THE F.F. AND DIDN'T HE TAKE ON THE SUB-MARINER A WHILE BACK?
I'M NOT WORRIED...
...THEY'RE NOT *ME.*

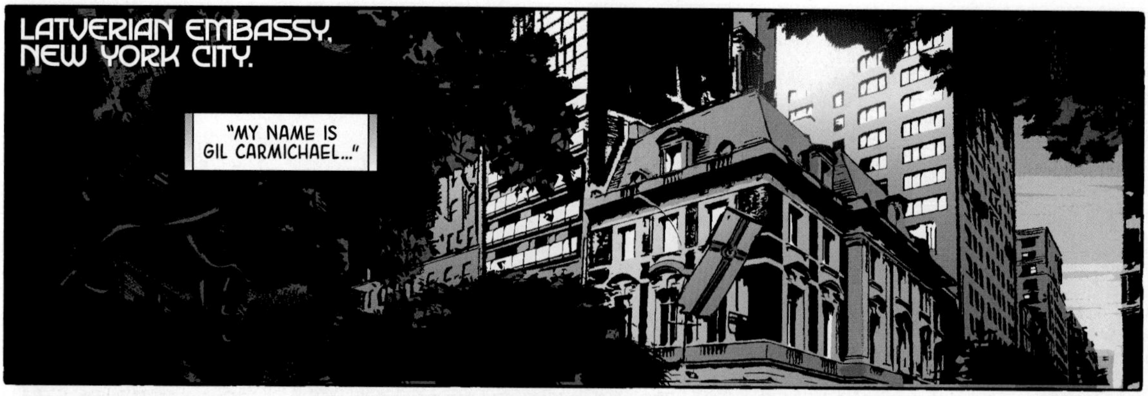
LATVERIAN EMBASSY, NEW YORK CITY.
"MY NAME IS GIL CARMICHAEL..."

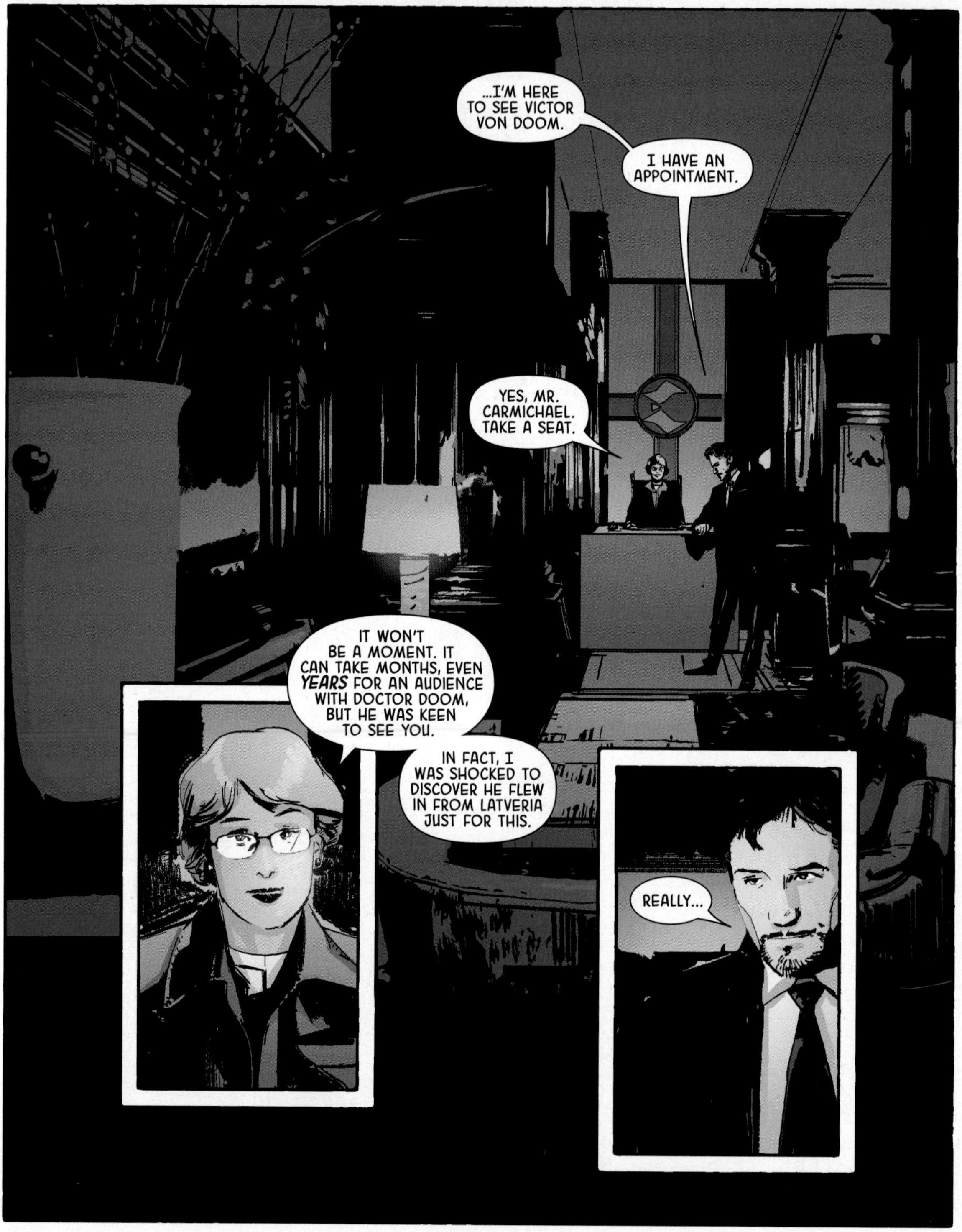
...I'M HERE TO SEE VICTOR VON DOOM.
I HAVE AN APPOINTMENT.
YES, MR. CARMICHAEL. TAKE A SEAT.
IT WON'T BE A MOMENT. IT CAN TAKE MONTHS, EVEN *YEARS* FOR AN AUDIENCE WITH DOCTOR DOOM, BUT HE WAS KEEN TO SEE YOU.
IN FACT, I WAS SHOCKED TO DISCOVER HE FLEW IN FROM LATVERIA JUST FOR THIS.
REALLY...

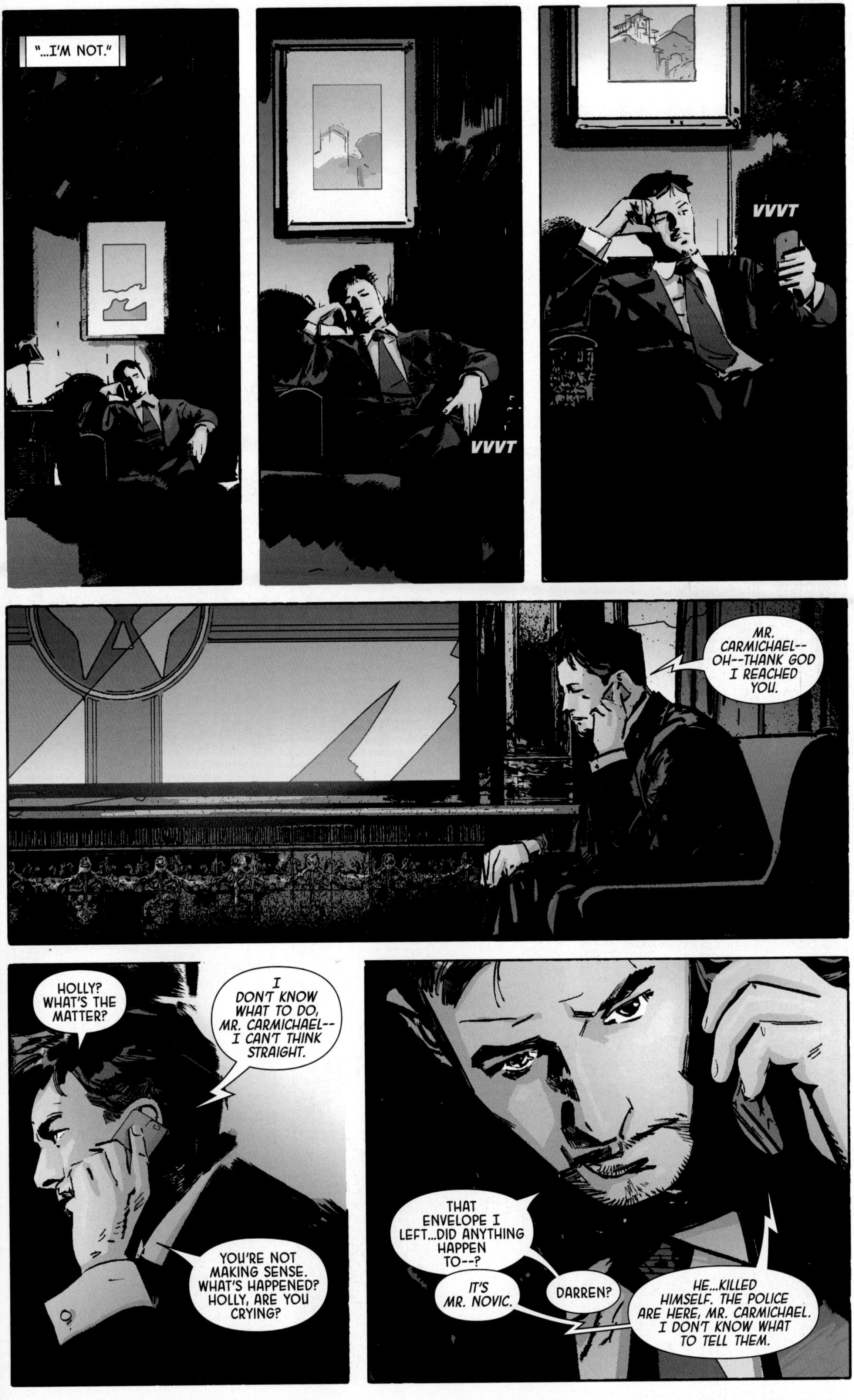
"...I'M NOT."
VVVT
VVVT
MR. CARMICHAEL-- OH--THANK GOD I REACHED YOU.
HOLLY? WHAT'S THE MATTER?
I DON'T KNOW WHAT TO DO, MR. CARMICHAEL-- I CAN'T THINK STRAIGHT.
YOU'RE NOT MAKING SENSE. WHAT'S HAPPENED? HOLLY, ARE YOU CRYING?
THAT ENVELOPE I LEFT...DID ANYTHING HAPPEN TO--?
DARREN?
IT'S MR. NOVIC.
HE...KILLED HIMSELF. THE POLICE ARE HERE, MR. CARMICHAEL. I DON'T KNOW WHAT TO TELL THEM.

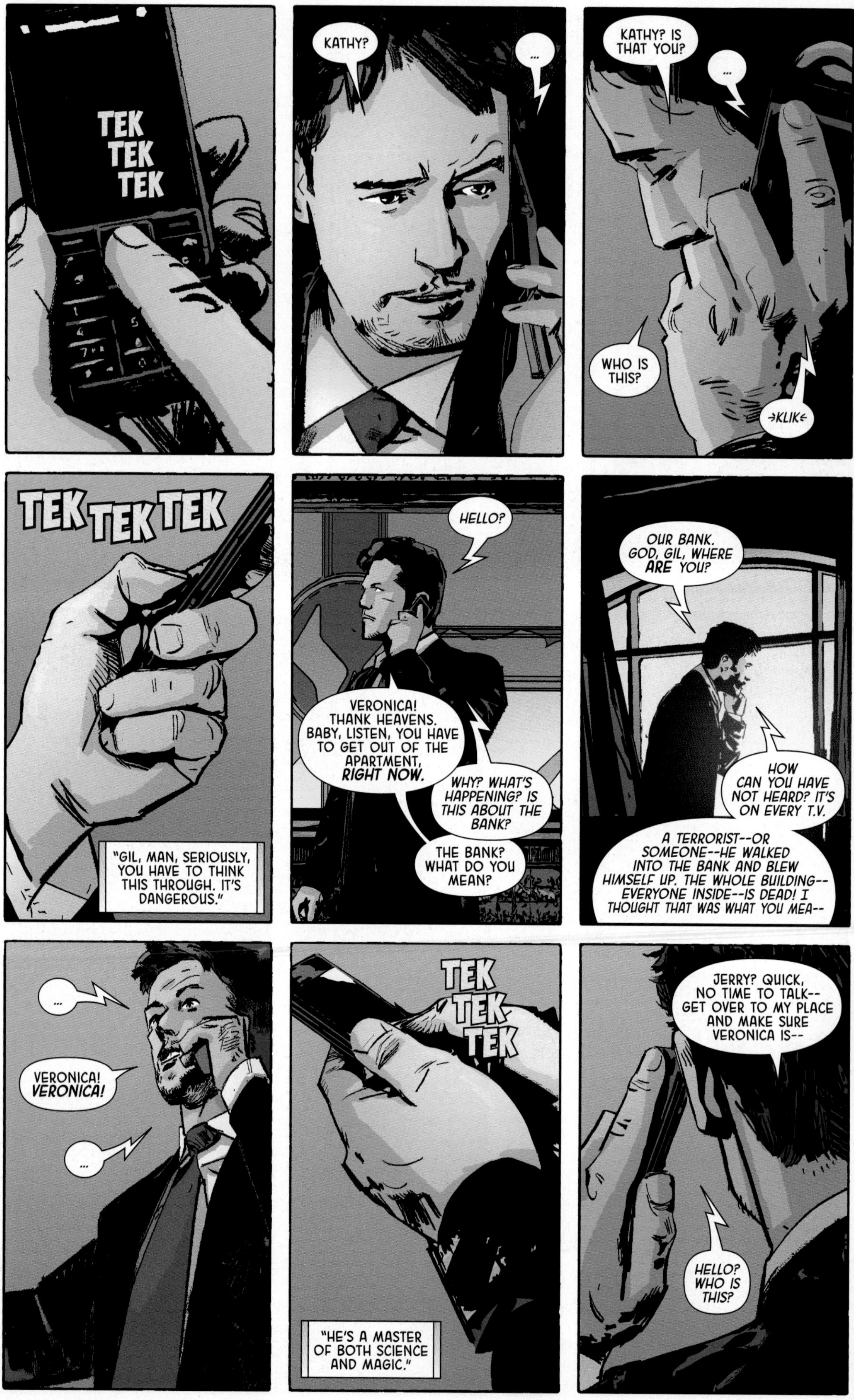
TEK
TEK
TEK
KATHY?
...
KATHY? IS THAT YOU?
...
WHO IS THIS?
→KLIK←
TEK TEK TEK
"GIL, MAN, SERIOUSLY, YOU HAVE TO THINK THIS THROUGH. IT'S DANGEROUS."
HELLO?
VERONICA! THANK HEAVENS. BABY, LISTEN, YOU HAVE TO GET OUT OF THE APARTMENT, RIGHT NOW.
WHY? WHAT'S HAPPENING? IS THIS ABOUT THE BANK?
THE BANK? WHAT DO YOU MEAN?
OUR BANK. GOD, GIL, WHERE ARE YOU?
HOW CAN YOU HAVE NOT HEARD? IT'S ON EVERY T.V.
A TERRORIST--OR SOMEONE--HE WALKED INTO THE BANK AND BLEW HIMSELF UP. THE WHOLE BUILDING--EVERYONE INSIDE--IS DEAD! I THOUGHT THAT WAS WHAT YOU MEA--
...
VERONICA! VERONICA!
...
TEK
TEK
TEK
"HE'S A MASTER OF BOTH SCIENCE AND MAGIC."
JERRY? QUICK, NO TIME TO TALK--GET OVER TO MY PLACE AND MAKE SURE VERONICA IS--
HELLO? WHO IS THIS?

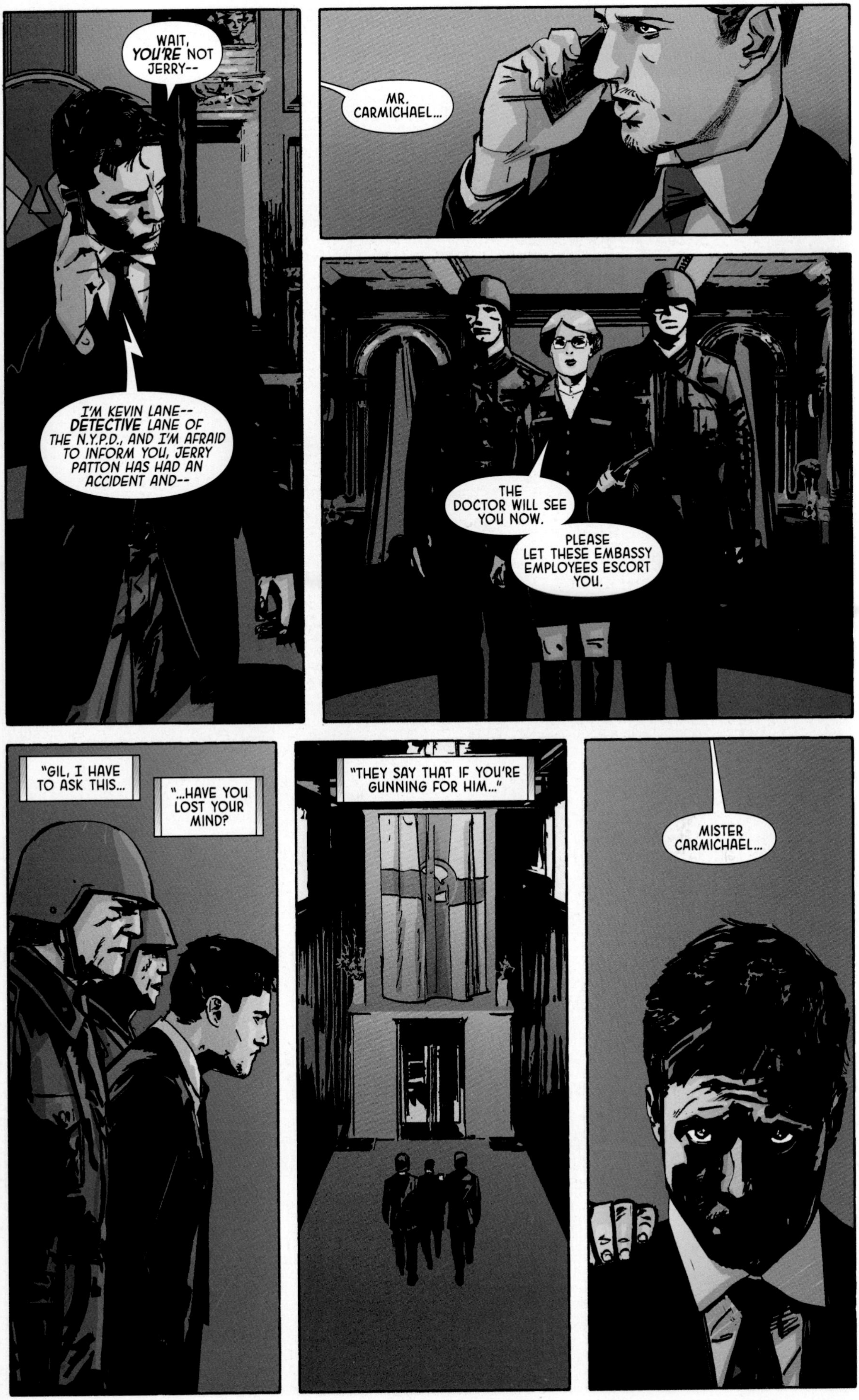
WAIT, YOU'RE NOT JERRY--
MR. CARMICHAEL...
I'M KEVIN LANE-- DETECTIVE LANE OF THE N.Y.P.D., AND I'M AFRAID TO INFORM YOU, JERRY PATTON HAS HAD AN ACCIDENT AND--
THE DOCTOR WILL SEE YOU NOW.
PLEASE LET THESE EMBASSY EMPLOYEES ESCORT YOU.
"GIL, I HAVE TO ASK THIS...
"...HAVE YOU LOST YOUR MIND?
"THEY SAY THAT IF YOU'RE GUNNING FOR HIM..."
MISTER CARMICHAEL...

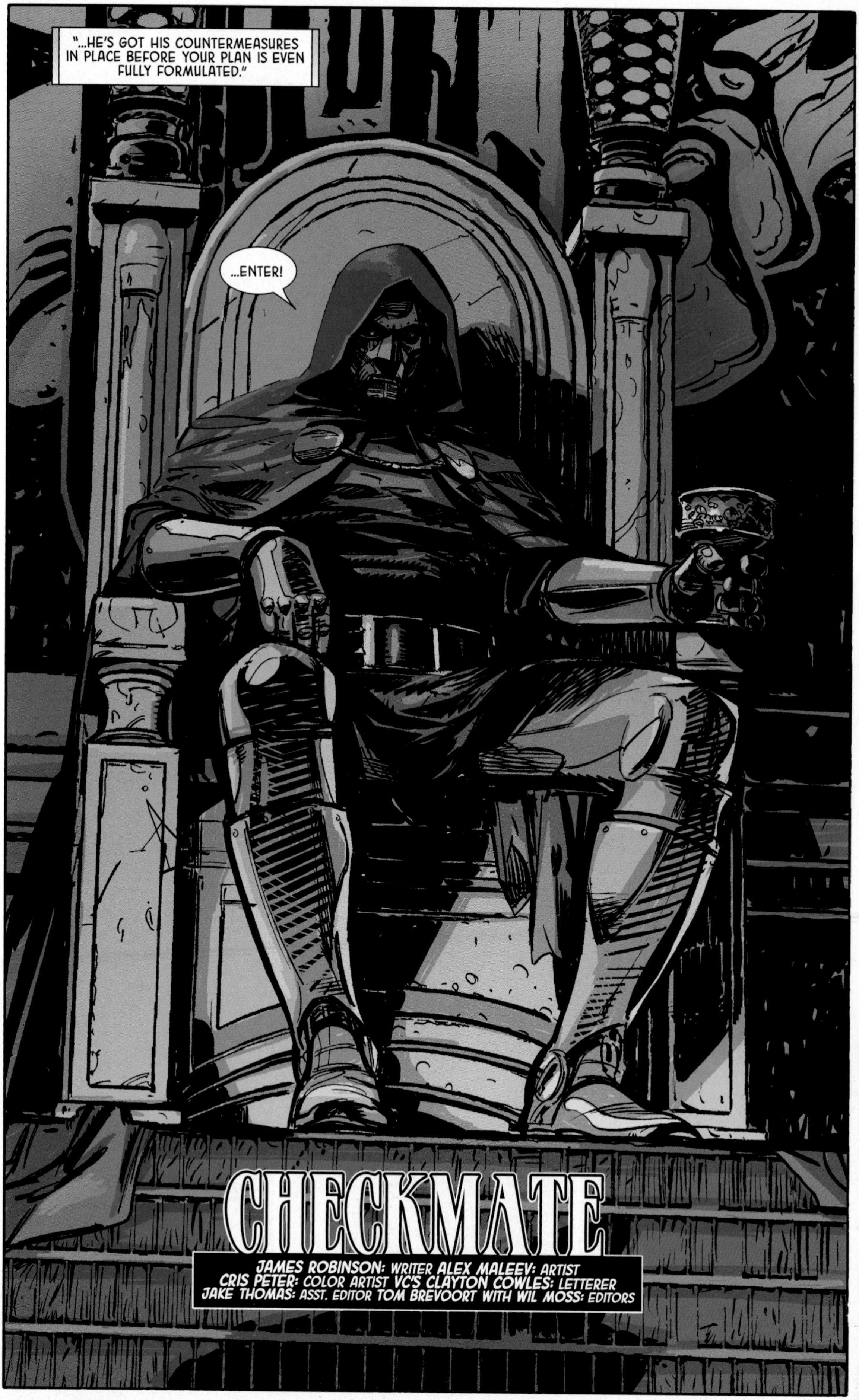
"...HE'S GOT HIS COUNTERMEASURES IN PLACE BEFORE YOUR PLAN IS EVEN FULLY FORMULATED."
...ENTER!
CHECKMATE
JAMES ROBINSON: WRITER ALEX MALEEV: ARTIST
CRIS PETER: COLOR ARTIST VC'S CLAYTON COWLES: LETTERER
JAKE THOMAS: ASST. EDITOR TOM BREVOORT WITH WIL MOSS: EDITORS

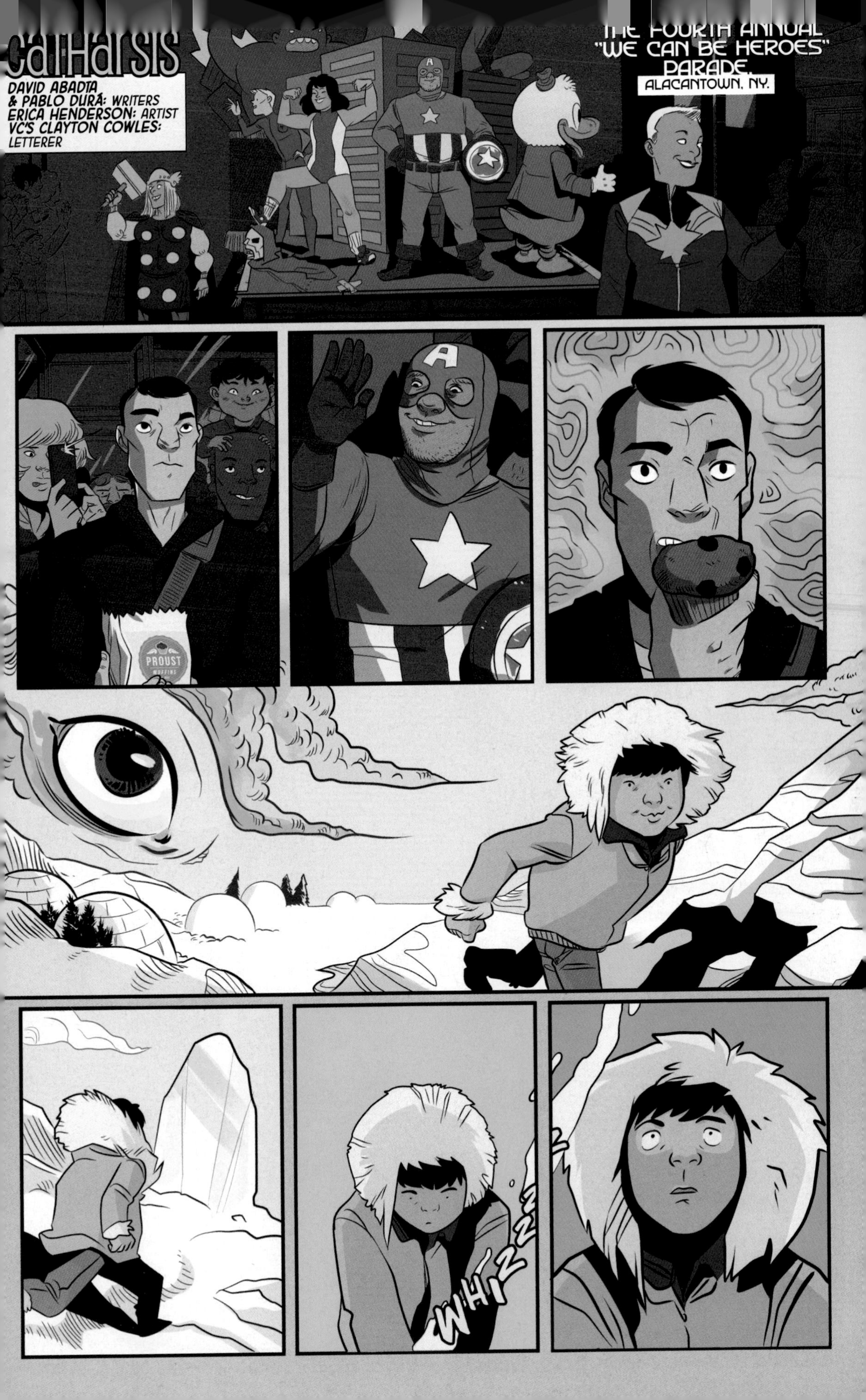
CATHARSIS
DAVID ABADÍA & PABLO DURÁ: WRITERS
ERICA HENDERSON: ARTIST
VC'S CLAYTON COWLES: LETTERER
THE FOURTH ANNUAL "WE CAN BE HEROES" PARADE.
ALACANTOWN, NY.
PROUST MUFFINS
WHIZZZ

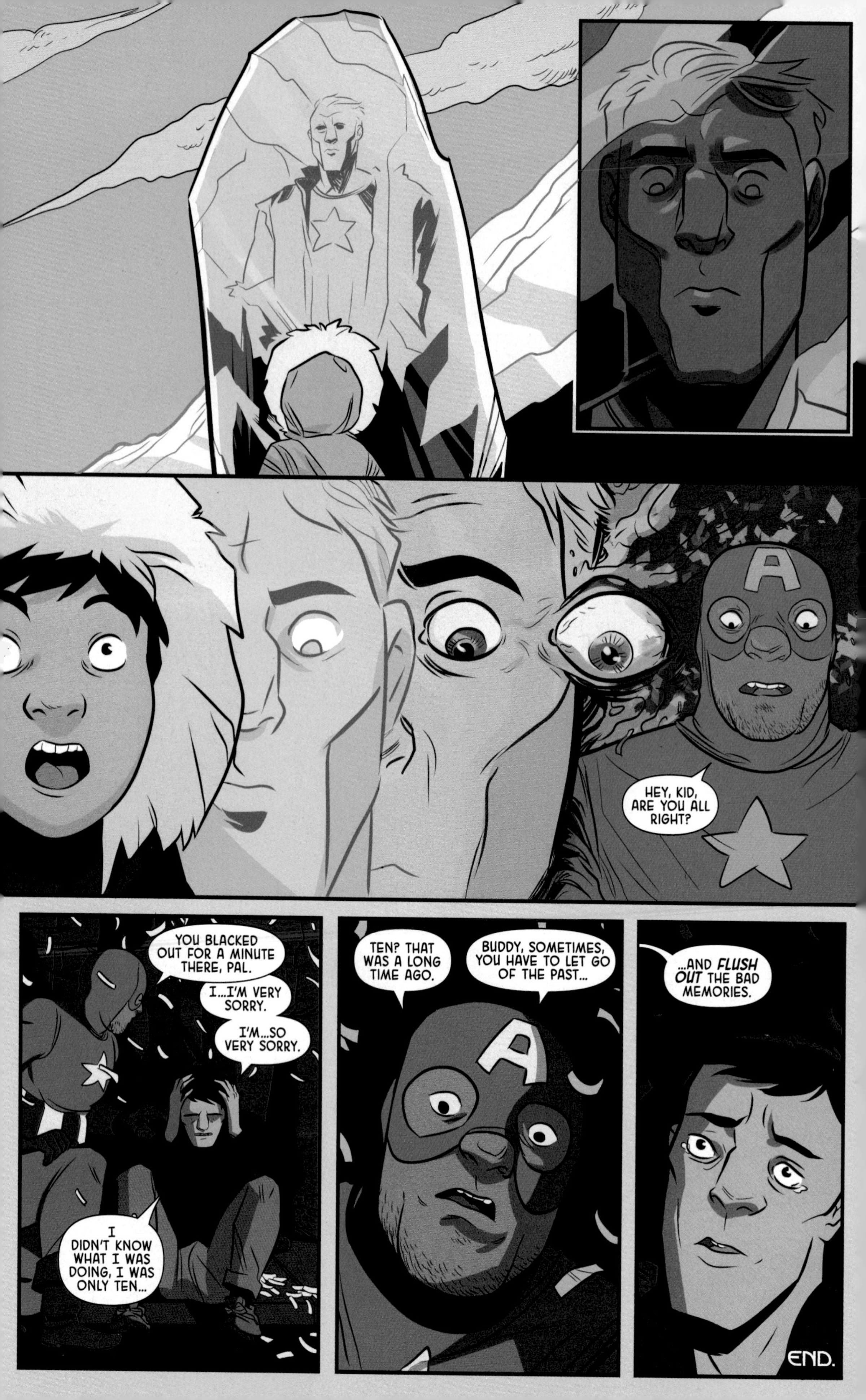
HEY, KID, ARE YOU ALL RIGHT?
YOU BLACKED OUT FOR A MINUTE THERE, PAL.
I...I'M VERY SORRY.
I'M...SO VERY SORRY.
I DIDN'T KNOW WHAT I WAS DOING, I WAS ONLY TEN...
TEN? THAT WAS A LONG TIME AGO.
BUDDY, SOMETIMES, YOU HAVE TO LET GO OF THE PAST...
...AND FLUSH OUT THE BAD MEMORIES.
END.

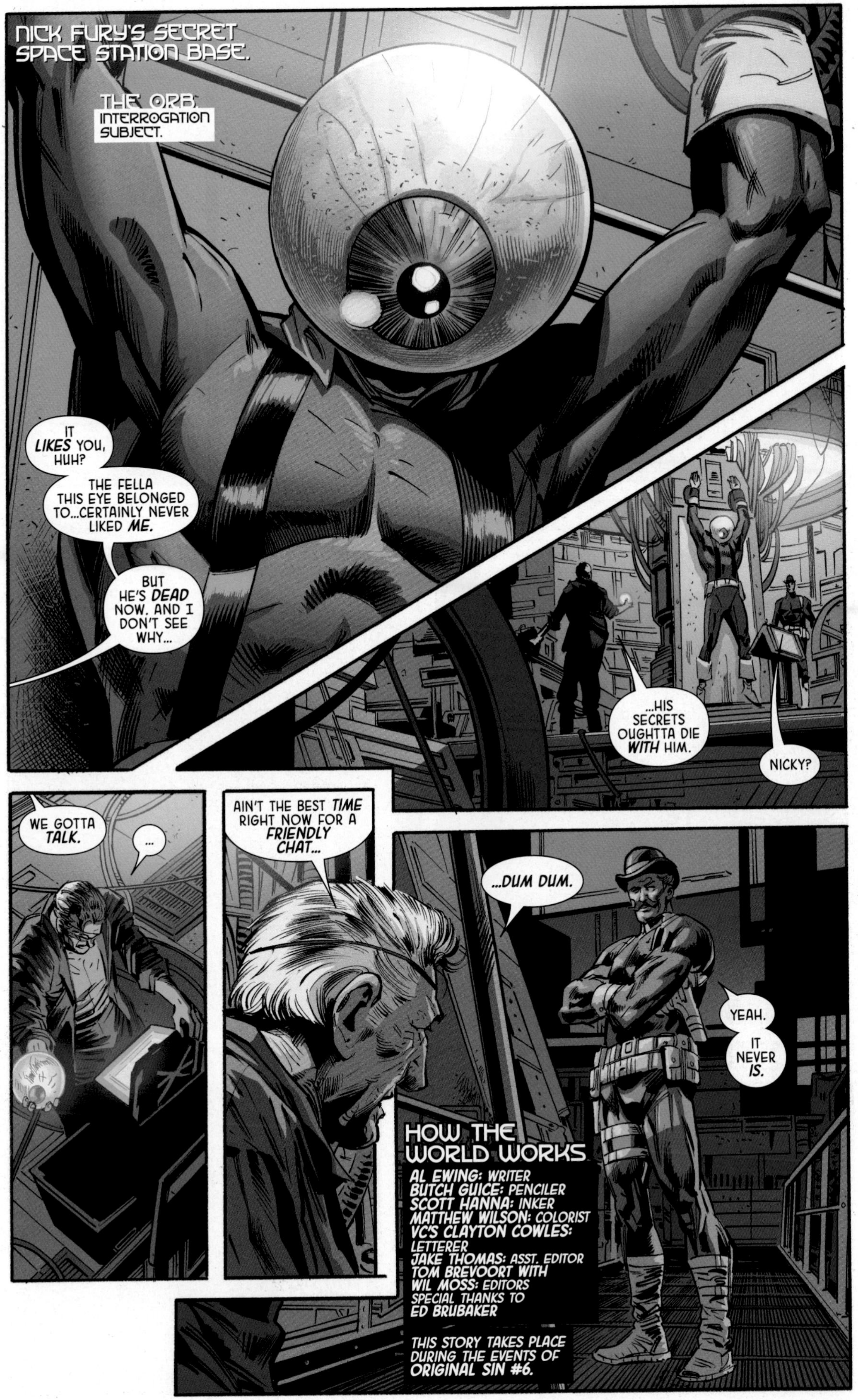

NICK FURY'S SECRET SPACE STATION BASE.
THE ORB: INTERROGATION SUBJECT.
IT LIKES YOU, HUH?
THE FELLA THIS EYE BELONGED TO...CERTAINLY NEVER LIKED ME.
BUT HE'S DEAD NOW. AND I DON'T SEE WHY...
...HIS SECRETS OUGHTTA DIE WITH HIM.
NICKY?
WE GOTTA TALK.
...
AIN'T THE BEST TIME RIGHT NOW FOR A FRIENDLY CHAT...
...DUM DUM.
YEAH.
IT NEVER IS.
HOW THE WORLD WORKS
AL EWING: WRITER
BUTCH GUICE: PENCILER
SCOTT HANNA: INKER
MATTHEW WILSON: COLORIST
VC'S CLAYTON COWLES: LETTERER
JAKE THOMAS: ASST. EDITOR
TOM BREVOORT WITH WIL MOSS: EDITORS
SPECIAL THANKS TO ED BRUBAKER
THIS STORY TAKES PLACE DURING THE EVENTS OF ORIGINAL SIN #6.

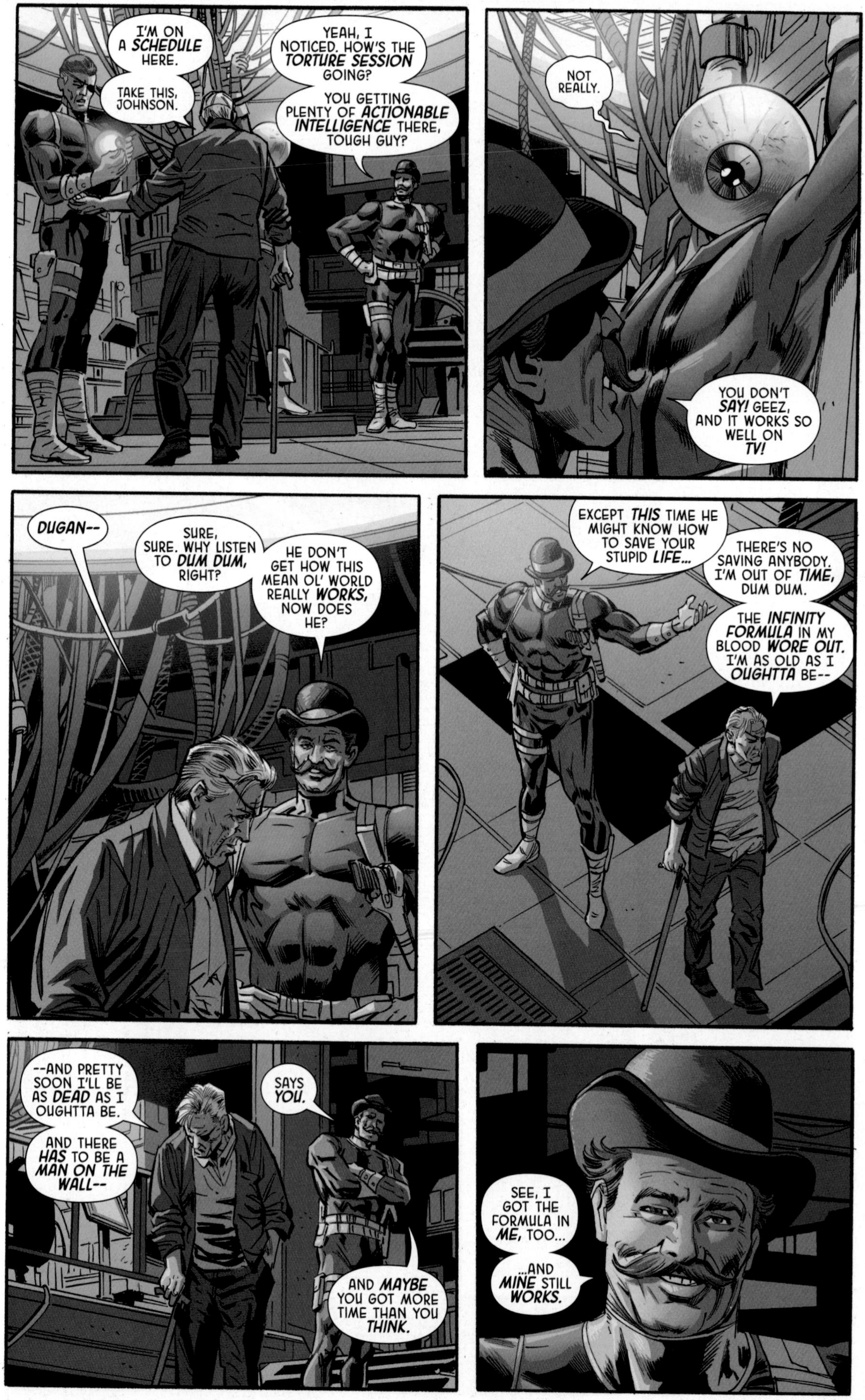
I'M ON A SCHEDULE HERE.
TAKE THIS, JOHNSON.
YEAH, I NOTICED. HOW'S THE TORTURE SESSION GOING?
YOU GETTING PLENTY OF ACTIONABLE INTELLIGENCE THERE, TOUGH GUY?
NOT REALLY.
YOU DON'T SAY! GEEZ, AND IT WORKS SO WELL ON TV!
DUGAN--
SURE, SURE. WHY LISTEN TO DUM DUM, RIGHT?
HE DON'T GET HOW THIS MEAN OL' WORLD REALLY WORKS, NOW DOES HE?
EXCEPT THIS TIME HE MIGHT KNOW HOW TO SAVE YOUR STUPID LIFE...
THERE'S NO SAVING ANYBODY. I'M OUT OF TIME, DUM DUM.
THE INFINITY FORMULA IN MY BLOOD WORE OUT. I'M AS OLD AS I OUGHTTA BE--
--AND PRETTY SOON I'LL BE AS DEAD AS I OUGHTTA BE.
AND THERE HAS TO BE A MAN ON THE WALL--
SAYS YOU.
AND MAYBE YOU GOT MORE TIME THAN YOU THINK.
SEE, I GOT THE FORMULA IN ME, TOO...
...AND MINE STILL WORKS.

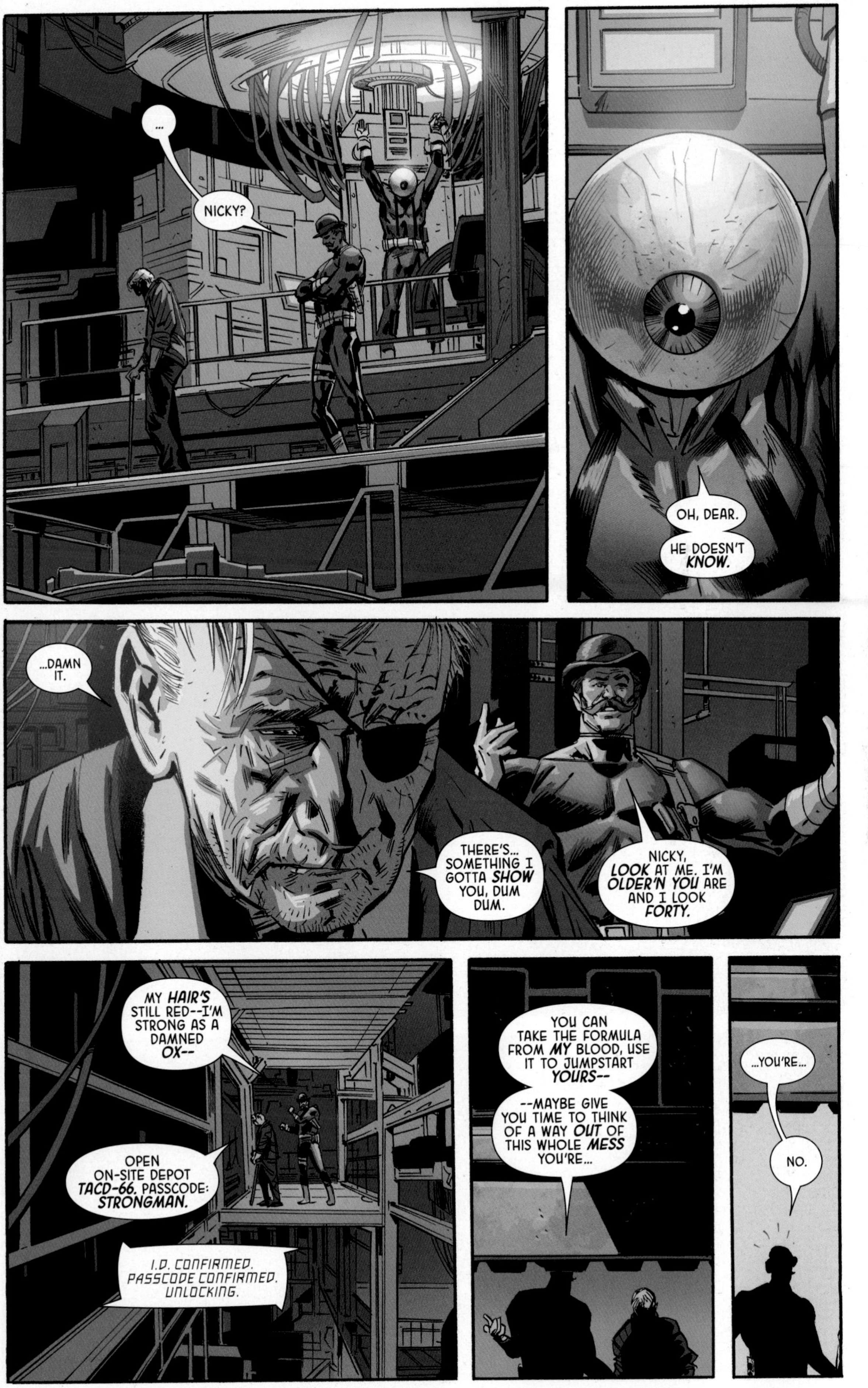
...
NICKY?
OH, DEAR.
HE DOESN'T KNOW.
...DAMN IT.
THERE'S... SOMETHING I GOTTA SHOW YOU, DUM DUM.
NICKY, LOOK AT ME. I'M OLDER'N YOU ARE AND I LOOK FORTY.
MY HAIR'S STILL RED--I'M STRONG AS A DAMNED OX--
OPEN ON-SITE DEPOT TACD-66. PASSCODE: STRONGMAN.
I.D. CONFIRMED. PASSCODE CONFIRMED. UNLOCKING.
YOU CAN TAKE THE FORMULA FROM MY BLOOD, USE IT TO JUMPSTART YOURS--
--MAYBE GIVE YOU TIME TO THINK OF A WAY OUT OF THIS WHOLE MESS YOU'RE...
...YOU'RE...
NO.

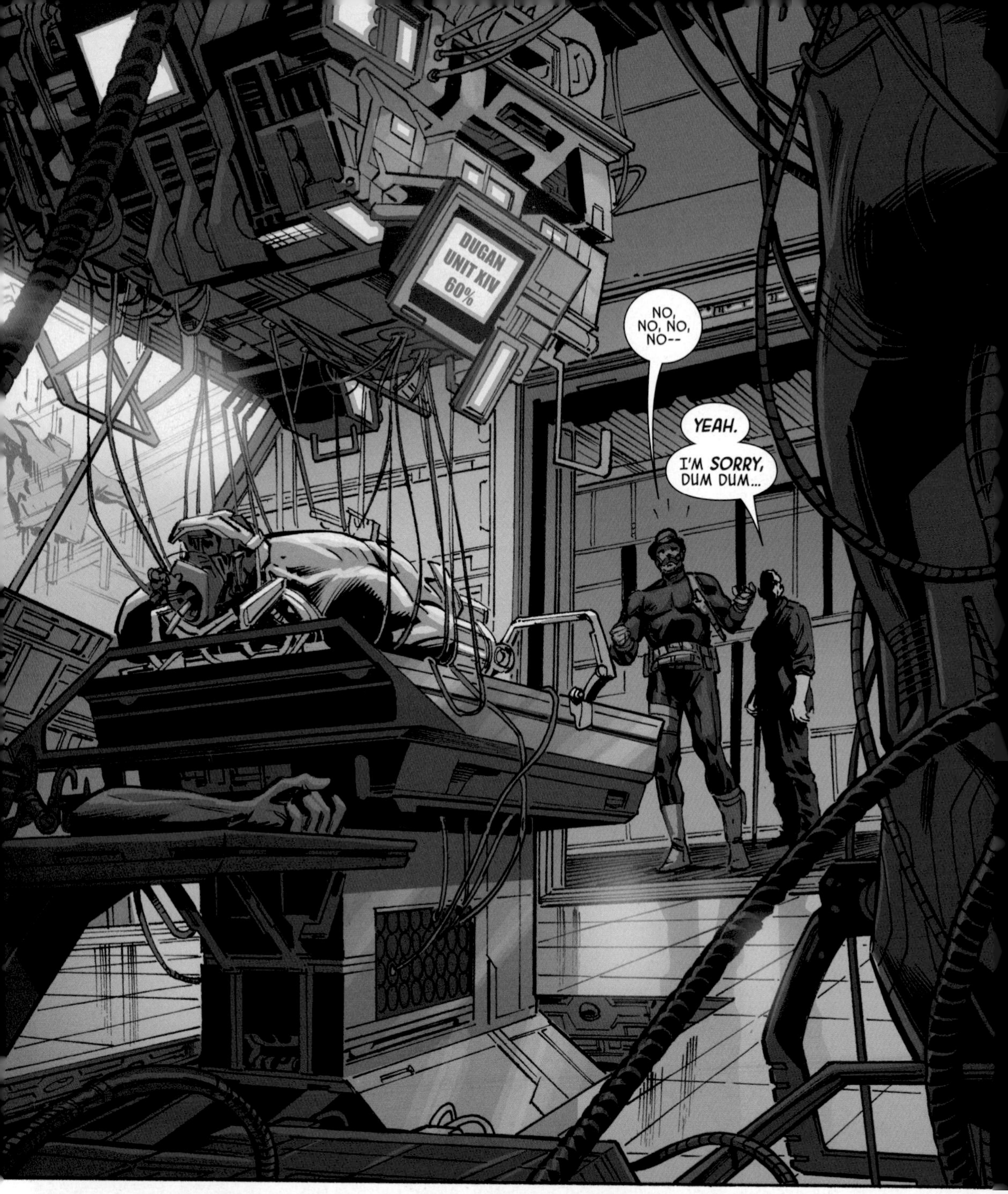
DUGAN
UNIT XIV
60%
NO, NO, NO, NO--
YEAH.
I'M SORRY, DUM DUM...

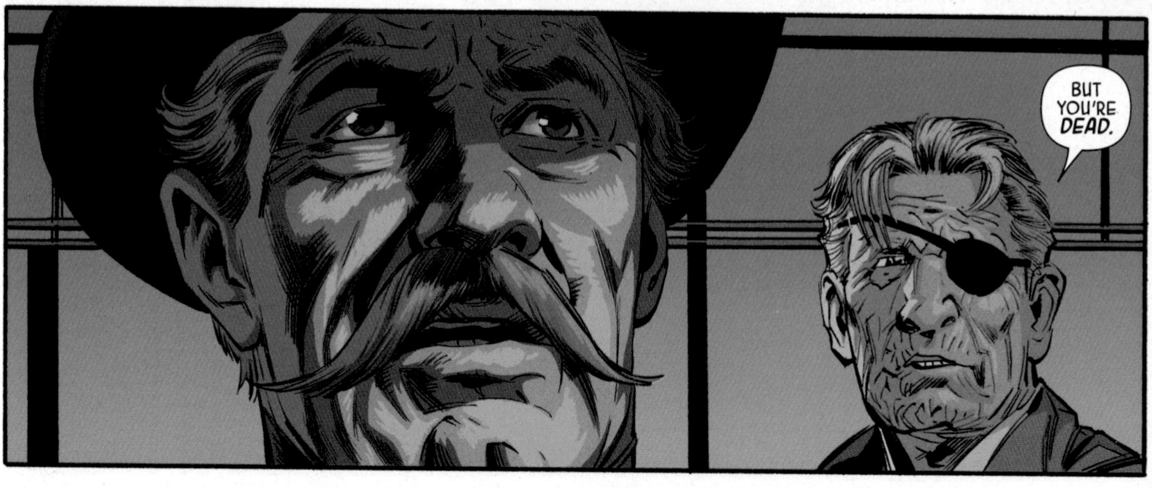
BUT YOU'RE DEAD.

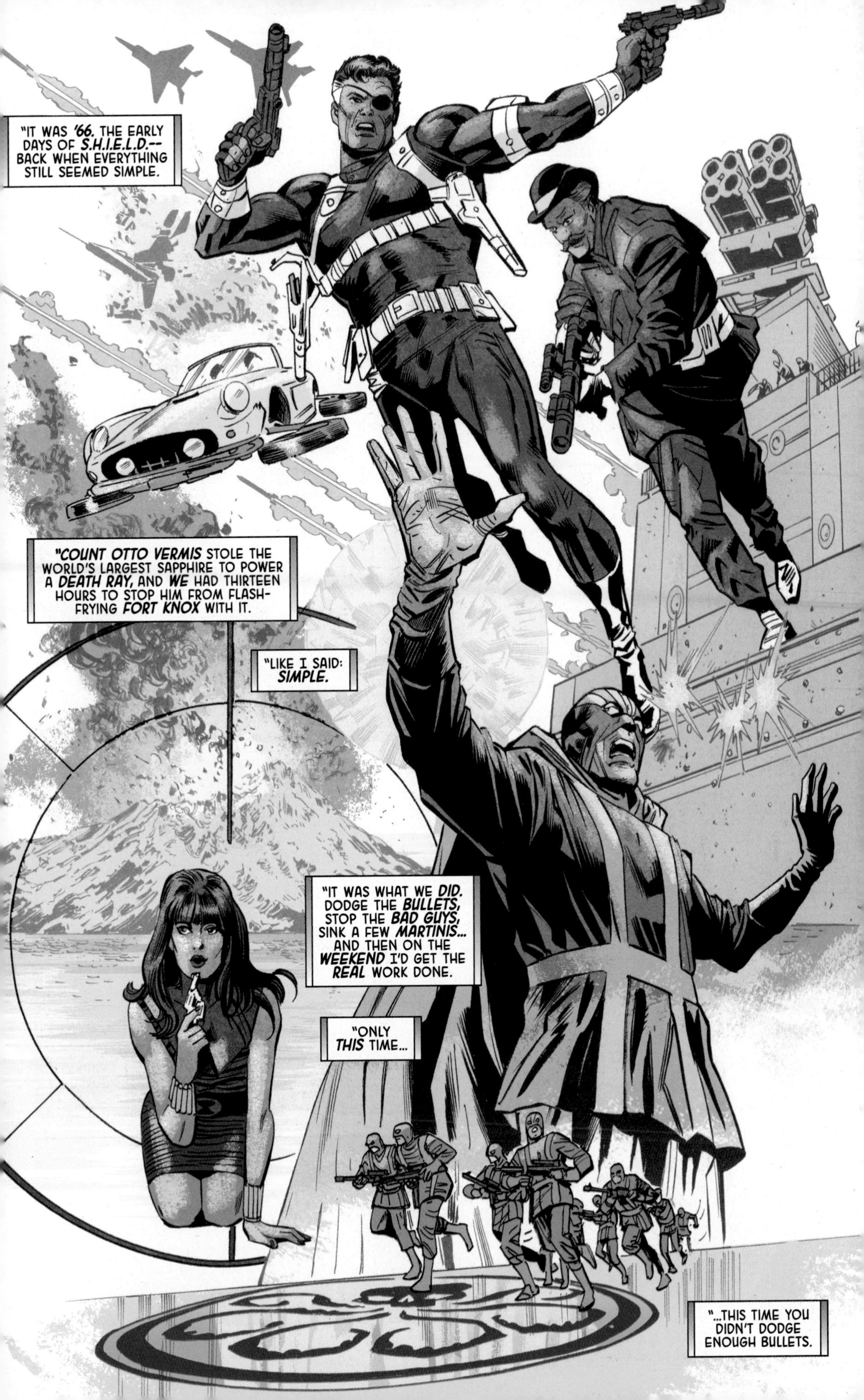
"IT WAS '66. THE EARLY DAYS OF S.H.I.E.L.D.-- BACK WHEN EVERYTHING STILL SEEMED SIMPLE.
"COUNT OTTO VERMIS STOLE THE WORLD'S LARGEST SAPPHIRE TO POWER A DEATH RAY, AND WE HAD THIRTEEN HOURS TO STOP HIM FROM FLASH-FRYING FORT KNOX WITH IT.
"LIKE I SAID: SIMPLE.
"IT WAS WHAT WE DID. DODGE THE BULLETS, STOP THE BAD GUYS, SINK A FEW MARTINIS... AND THEN ON THE WEEKEND I'D GET THE REAL WORK DONE.
"ONLY THIS TIME...
"...THIS TIME YOU DIDN'T DODGE ENOUGH BULLETS.

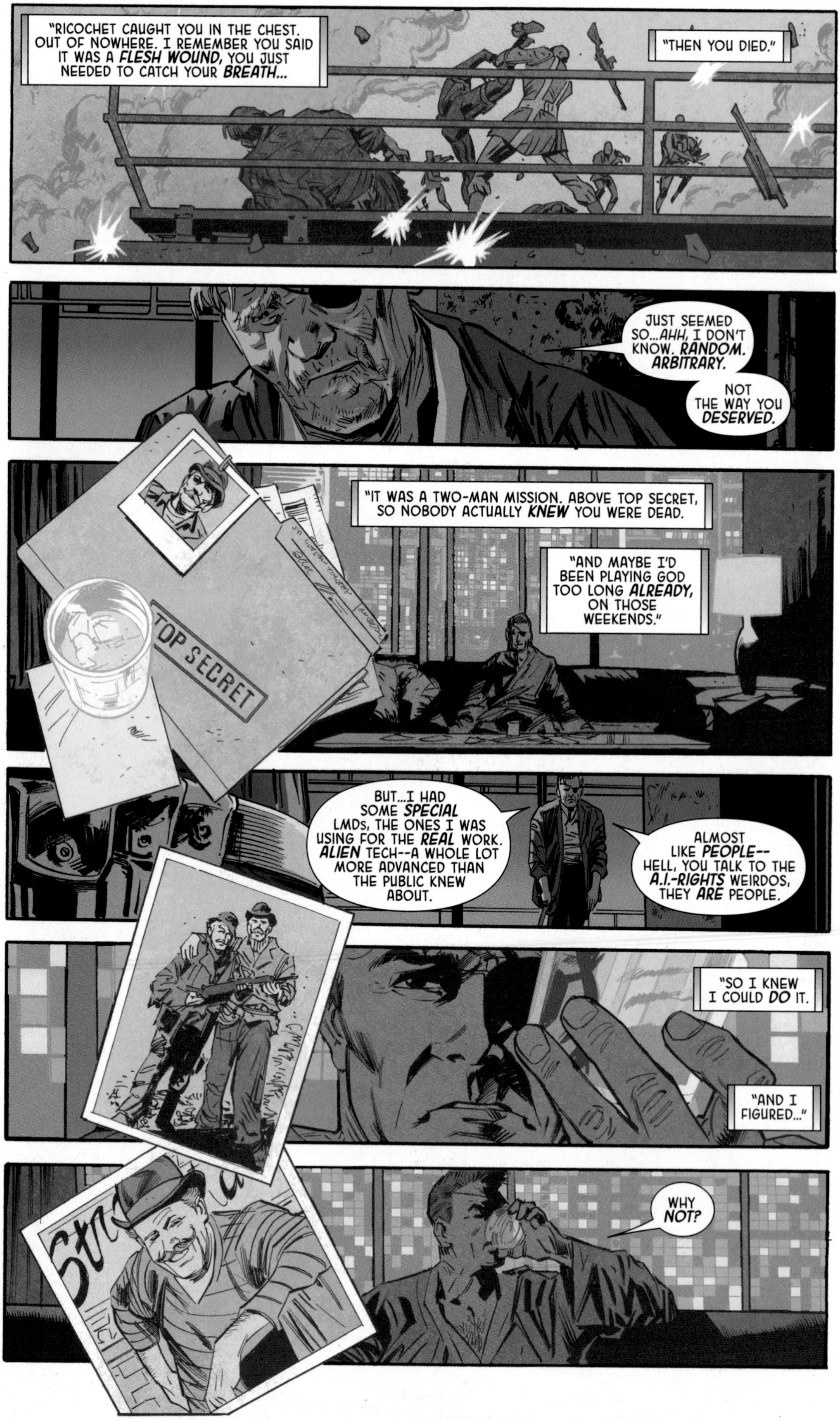
"RICOCHET CAUGHT YOU IN THE CHEST. OUT OF NOWHERE. I REMEMBER YOU SAID IT WAS A FLESH WOUND, YOU JUST NEEDED TO CATCH YOUR BREATH...
"THEN YOU DIED."
JUST SEEMED SO...AHH, I DON'T KNOW. RANDOM. ARBITRARY.
NOT THE WAY YOU DESERVED.
TOP SECRET
"IT WAS A TWO-MAN MISSION. ABOVE TOP SECRET, SO NOBODY ACTUALLY KNEW YOU WERE DEAD.
"AND MAYBE I'D BEEN PLAYING GOD TOO LONG ALREADY, ON THOSE WEEKENDS."
BUT...I HAD SOME SPECIAL LMDs, THE ONES I WAS USING FOR THE REAL WORK. ALIEN TECH--A WHOLE LOT MORE ADVANCED THAN THE PUBLIC KNEW ABOUT.
ALMOST LIKE PEOPLE-- HELL, YOU TALK TO THE A.I.-RIGHTS WEIRDOS, THEY ARE PEOPLE.
"SO I KNEW I COULD DO IT.
"AND I FIGURED..."
WHY NOT?

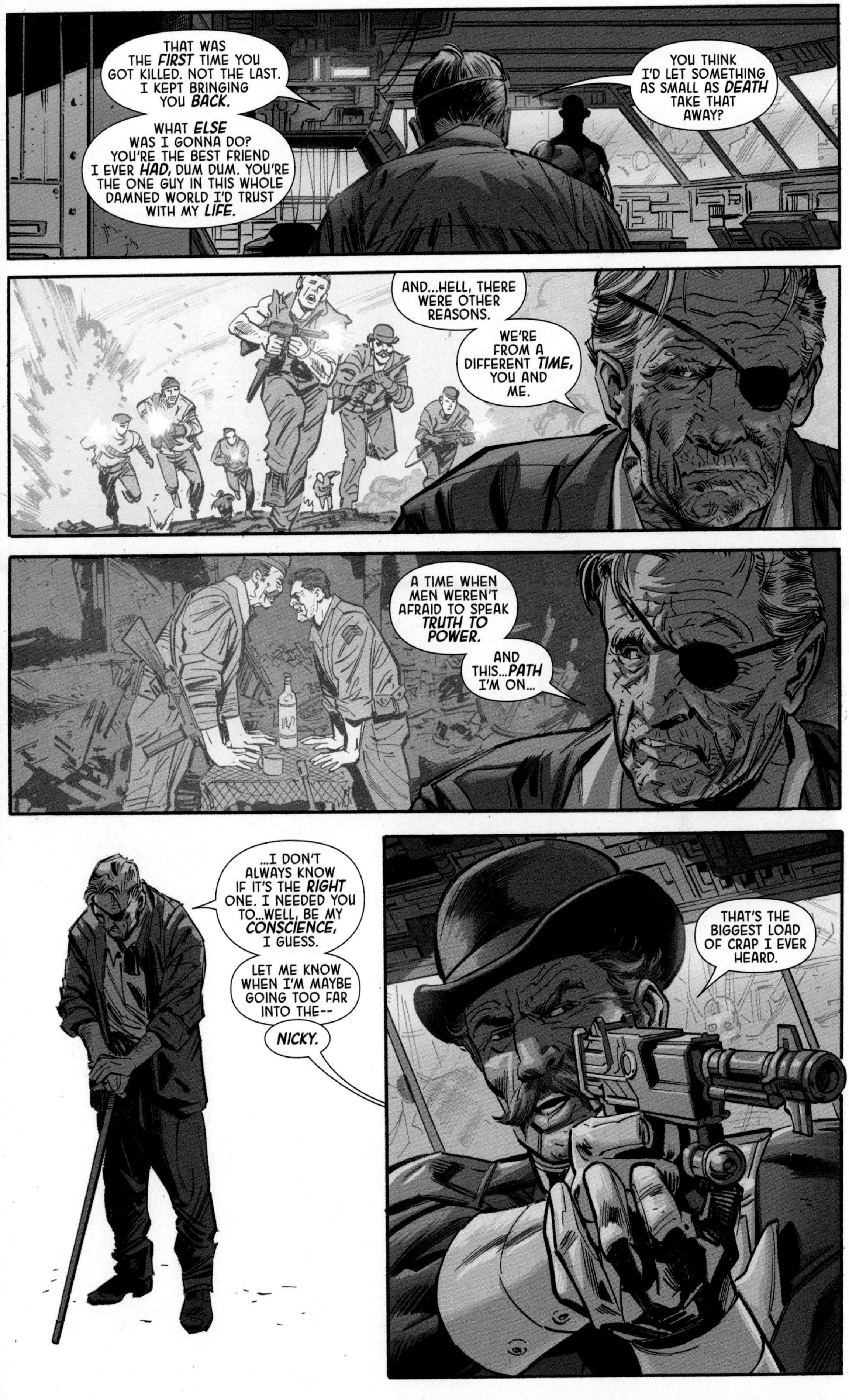
THAT WAS THE FIRST TIME YOU GOT KILLED. NOT THE LAST. I KEPT BRINGING YOU BACK.
WHAT ELSE WAS I GONNA DO? YOU'RE THE BEST FRIEND I EVER HAD, DUM DUM. YOU'RE THE ONE GUY IN THIS WHOLE DAMNED WORLD I'D TRUST WITH MY LIFE.
YOU THINK I'D LET SOMETHING AS SMALL AS DEATH TAKE THAT AWAY?
AND...HELL, THERE WERE OTHER REASONS.
WE'RE FROM A DIFFERENT TIME, YOU AND ME.
A TIME WHEN MEN WEREN'T AFRAID TO SPEAK TRUTH TO POWER.
AND THIS...PATH I'M ON...
...I DON'T ALWAYS KNOW IF IT'S THE RIGHT ONE. I NEEDED YOU TO...WELL, BE MY CONSCIENCE, I GUESS.
LET ME KNOW WHEN I'M MAYBE GOING TOO FAR INTO THE--
NICKY.
THAT'S THE BIGGEST LOAD OF CRAP I EVER HEARD.

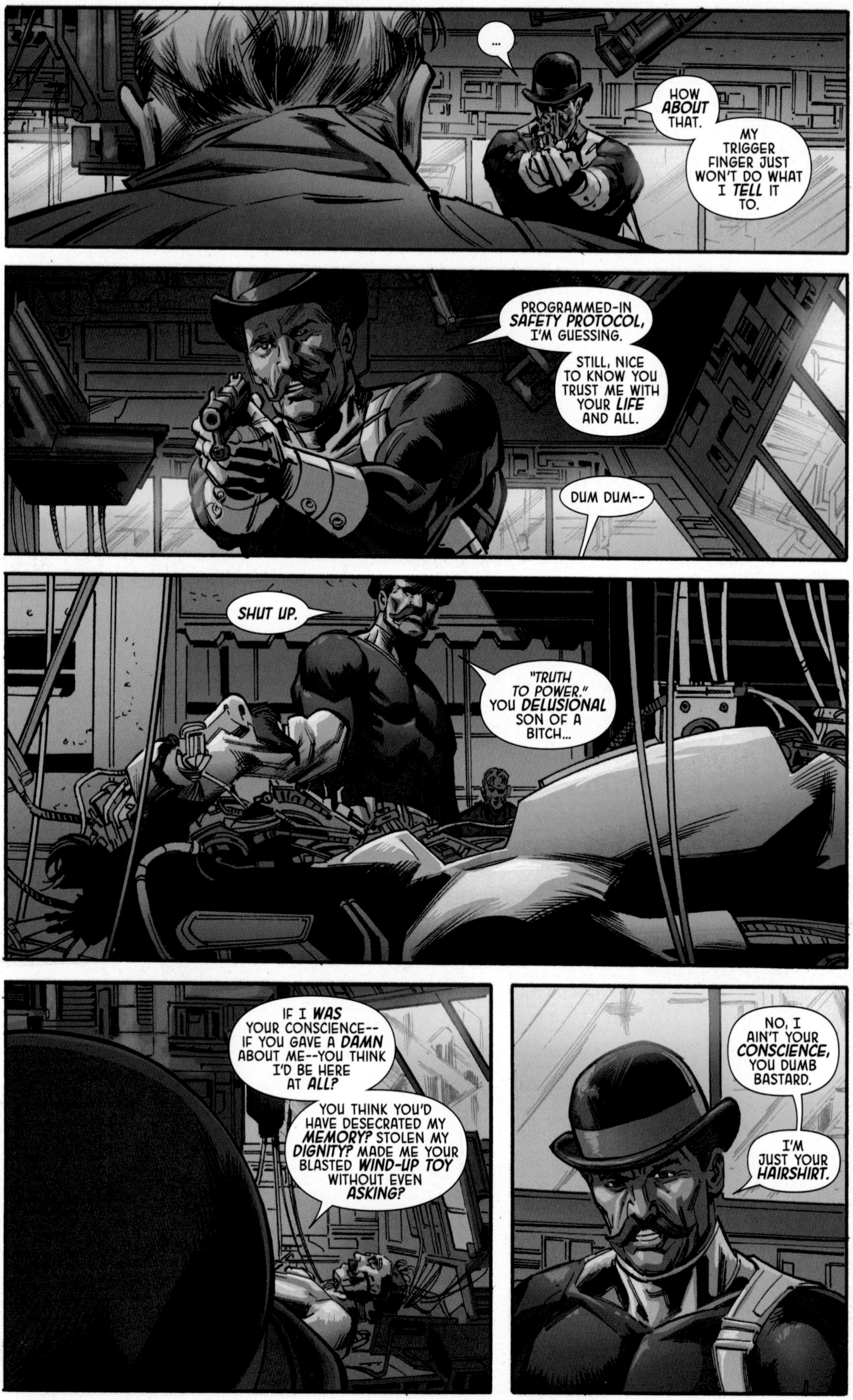
...
HOW ABOUT THAT.
MY TRIGGER FINGER JUST WON'T DO WHAT I TELL IT TO.
PROGRAMMED-IN SAFETY PROTOCOL, I'M GUESSING.
STILL, NICE TO KNOW YOU TRUST ME WITH YOUR LIFE AND ALL.
DUM DUM--
SHUT UP.
"TRUTH TO POWER." YOU DELUSIONAL SON OF A BITCH...
IF I WAS YOUR CONSCIENCE-- IF YOU GAVE A DAMN ABOUT ME--YOU THINK I'D BE HERE AT ALL?
YOU THINK YOU'D HAVE DESECRATED MY MEMORY? STOLEN MY DIGNITY? MADE ME YOUR BLASTED WIND-UP TOY WITHOUT EVEN ASKING?
NO, I AIN'T YOUR CONSCIENCE, YOU DUMB BASTARD.
I'M JUST YOUR HAIRSHIRT.

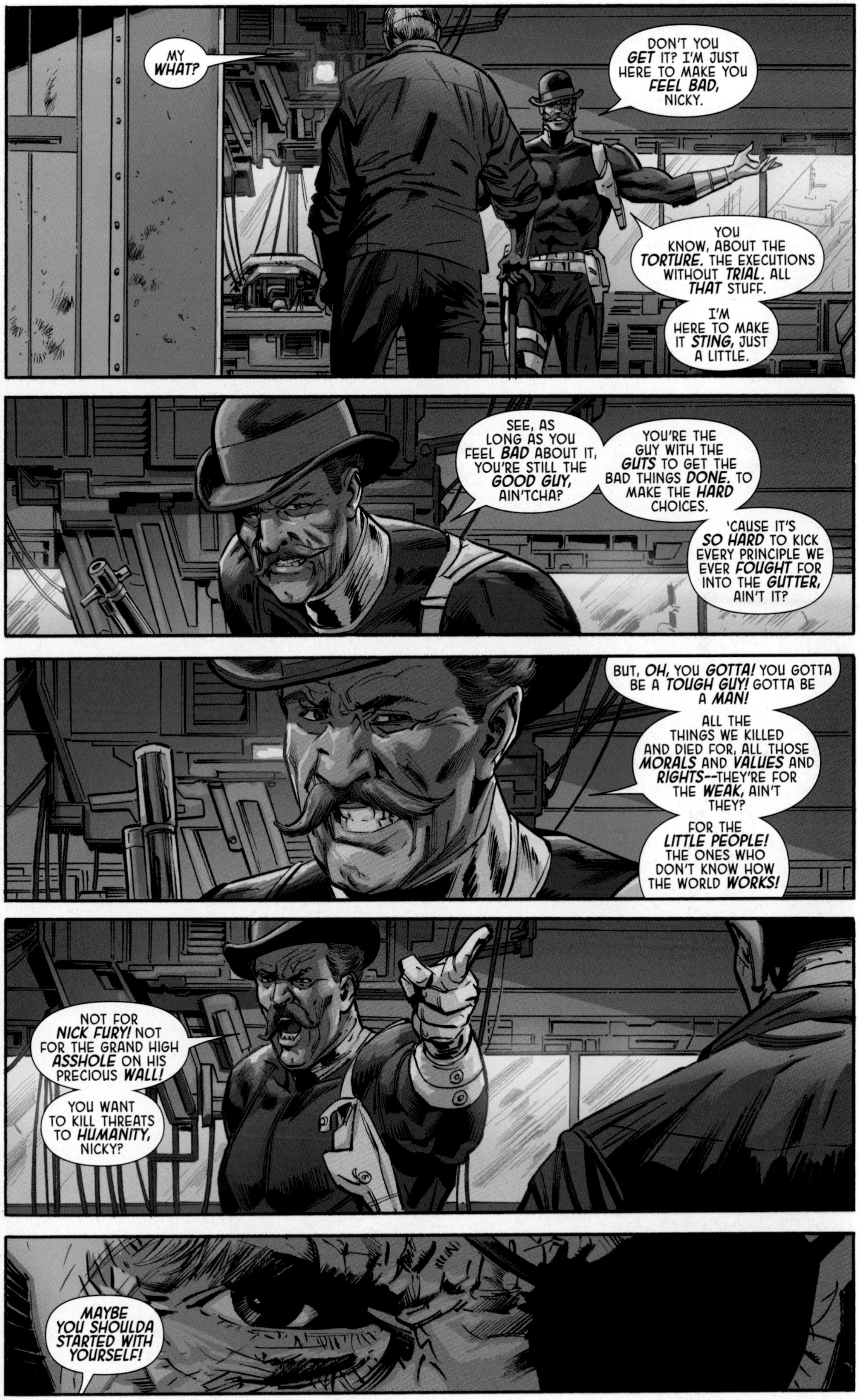
MY WHAT?
DON'T YOU GET IT? I'M JUST HERE TO MAKE YOU FEEL BAD, NICKY.
YOU KNOW, ABOUT THE TORTURE. THE EXECUTIONS WITHOUT TRIAL. ALL THAT STUFF.
I'M HERE TO MAKE IT STING, JUST A LITTLE.
SEE, AS LONG AS YOU FEEL BAD ABOUT IT, YOU'RE STILL THE GOOD GUY, AIN'TCHA?
YOU'RE THE GUY WITH THE GUTS TO GET THE BAD THINGS DONE. TO MAKE THE HARD CHOICES.
'CAUSE IT'S SO HARD TO KICK EVERY PRINCIPLE WE EVER FOUGHT FOR INTO THE GUTTER, AIN'T IT?
BUT, OH, YOU GOTTA! YOU GOTTA BE A TOUGH GUY! GOTTA BE A MAN!
ALL THE THINGS WE KILLED AND DIED FOR, ALL THOSE MORALS AND VALUES AND RIGHTS--THEY'RE FOR THE WEAK, AIN'T THEY?
FOR THE LITTLE PEOPLE! THE ONES WHO DON'T KNOW HOW THE WORLD WORKS!
NOT FOR NICK FURY! NOT FOR THE GRAND HIGH ASSHOLE ON HIS PRECIOUS WALL!
YOU WANT TO KILL THREATS TO HUMANITY, NICKY?
MAYBE YOU SHOULDA STARTED WITH YOURSELF!

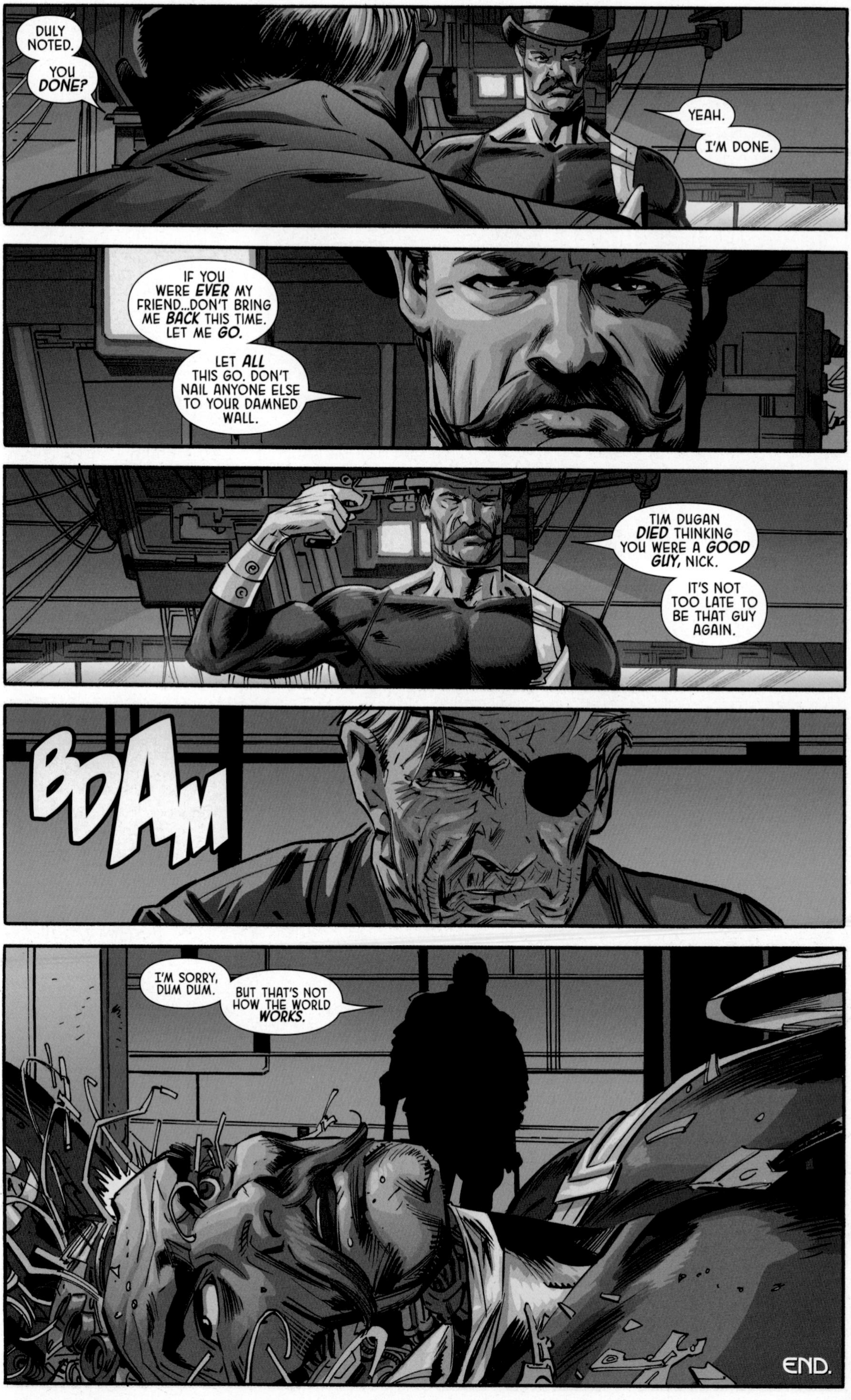
DULY NOTED.
YOU DONE?
YEAH.
I'M DONE.
IF YOU WERE EVER MY FRIEND...DON'T BRING ME BACK THIS TIME. LET ME GO.
LET ALL THIS GO. DON'T NAIL ANYONE ELSE TO YOUR DAMNED WALL.
TIM DUGAN DIED THINKING YOU WERE A GOOD GUY, NICK.
IT'S NOT TOO LATE TO BE THAT GUY AGAIN.
BDAM
I'M SORRY, DUM DUM.
BUT THAT'S NOT HOW THE WORLD WORKS.
END.

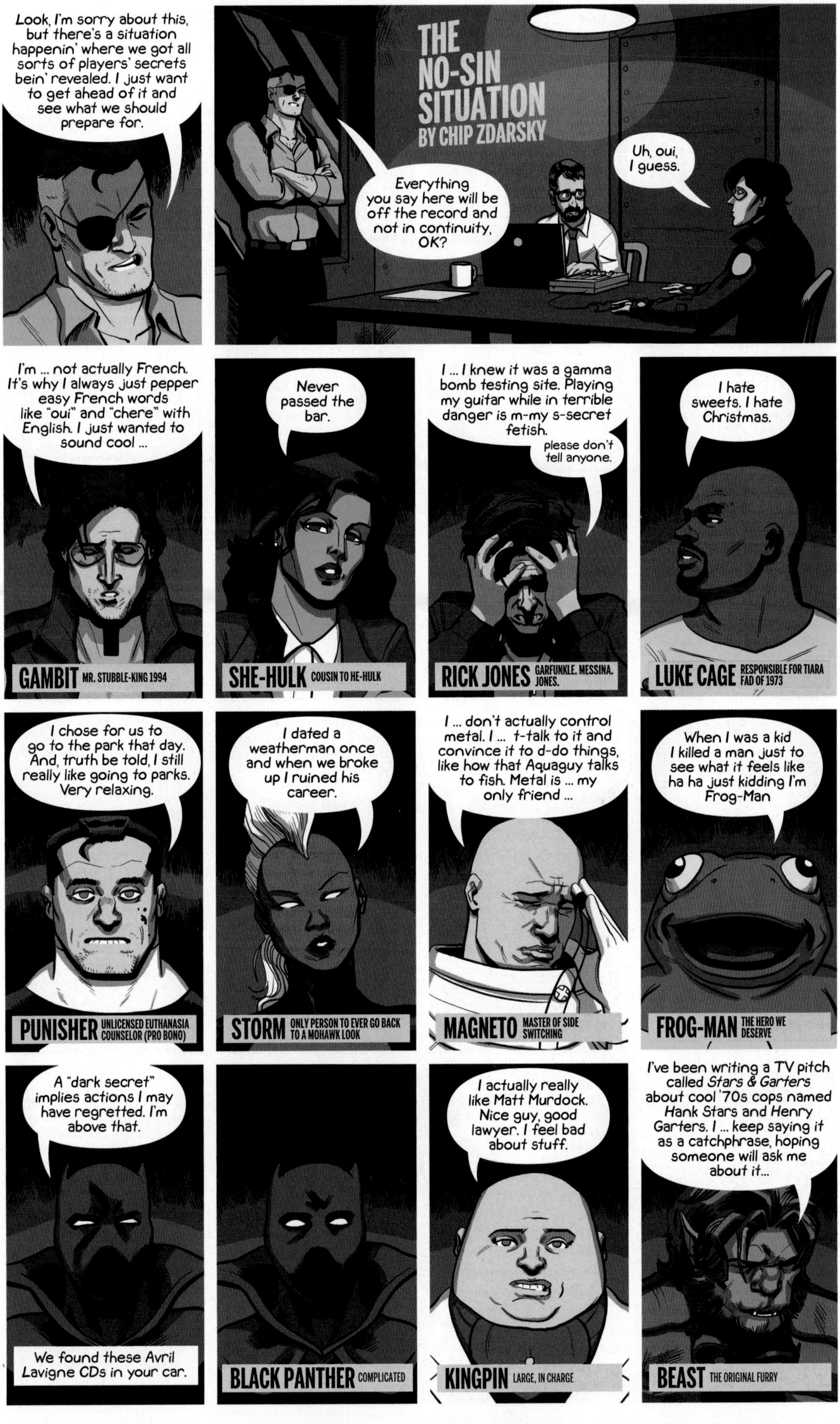
Look, I'm sorry about this, but there's a situation happenin' where we got all sorts of players' secrets bein' revealed. I just want to get ahead of it and see what we should prepare for.
THE NO-SIN SITUATION
BY CHIP ZDARSKY
Everything you say here will be off the record and not in continuity, OK?
Uh, oui, I guess.
I'm ... not actually French. It's why I always just pepper easy French words like "oui" and "chere" with English. I just wanted to sound cool ...
GAMBIT MR. STUBBLE-KING 1994
Never passed the bar.
SHE-HULK COUSIN TO HE-HULK
I ... I knew it was a gamma bomb testing site. Playing my guitar while in terrible danger is m-my s-secret fetish.
please don't tell anyone.
RICK JONES GARFUNKLE. MESSINA. JONES.
I hate sweets. I hate Christmas.
LUKE CAGE RESPONSIBLE FOR TIARA FAD OF 1973
I chose for us to go to the park that day. And, truth be told, I still really like going to parks. Very relaxing.
PUNISHER UNLICENSED EUTHANASIA COUNSELOR (PRO BONO)
I dated a weatherman once and when we broke up I ruined his career.
STORM ONLY PERSON TO EVER GO BACK TO A MOHAWK LOOK
I ... don't actually control metal. I ... t-talk to it and convince it to d-do things, like how that Aquaguy talks to fish. Metal is ... my only friend ...
MAGNETO MASTER OF SIDE SWITCHING
When I was a kid I killed a man just to see what it feels like ha ha just kidding I'm Frog-Man
FROG-MAN THE HERO WE DESERVE
A "dark secret" implies actions I may have regretted. I'm above that.
We found these Avril Lavigne CDs in your car.
BLACK PANTHER COMPLICATED
I actually really like Matt Murdock. Nice guy, good lawyer. I feel bad about stuff.
KINGPIN LARGE, IN CHARGE
I've been writing a TV pitch called *Stars & Garters* about cool '70s cops named Hank Stars and Henry Garters. I ... keep saying it as a catchphrase, hoping someone will ask me about it...
BEAST THE ORIGINAL FURRY

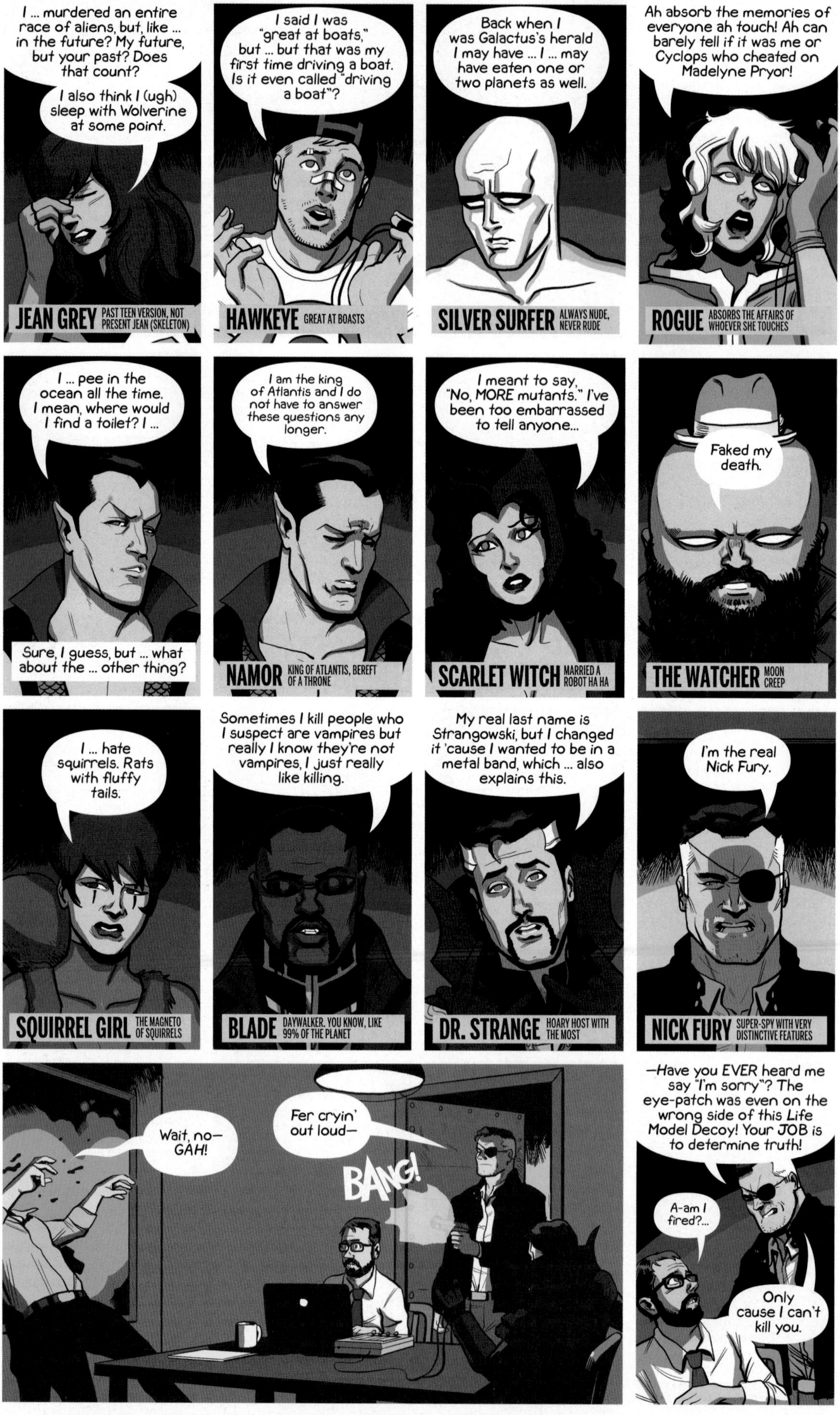
I ... murdered an entire race of aliens, but, like ... in the future? My future, but your past? Does that count?
I also think I (ugh) sleep with Wolverine at some point.
JEAN GREY PAST TEEN VERSION, NOT PRESENT JEAN (SKELETON)
I said I was "great at boats," but ... but that was my first time driving a boat. Is it even called "driving a boat"?
HAWKEYE GREAT AT BOASTS
Back when I was Galactus's herald I may have ... I ... may have eaten one or two planets as well.
SILVER SURFER ALWAYS NUDE, NEVER RUDE
Ah absorb the memories of everyone ah touch! Ah can barely tell if it was me or Cyclops who cheated on Madelyne Pryor!
ROGUE ABSORBS THE AFFAIRS OF WHOEVER SHE TOUCHES
I ... pee in the ocean all the time. I mean, where would I find a toilet? I ...
Sure, I guess, but ... what about the ... other thing?
I am the king of Atlantis and I do not have to answer these questions any longer.
NAMOR KING OF ATLANTIS, BEREFT OF A THRONE
I meant to say, "No, MORE mutants." I've been too embarrassed to tell anyone...
SCARLET WITCH MARRIED A ROBOT HA HA
Faked my death.
THE WATCHER MOON CREEP
I ... hate squirrels. Rats with fluffy tails.
SQUIRREL GIRL THE MAGNETO OF SQUIRRELS
Sometimes I kill people who I suspect are vampires but really I know they're not vampires, I just really like killing.
BLADE DAYWALKER. YOU KNOW, LIKE 99% OF THE PLANET
My real last name is Strangowski, but I changed it 'cause I wanted to be in a metal band, which ... also explains this.
DR. STRANGE HOARY HOST WITH THE MOST
I'm the real Nick Fury.
NICK FURY SUPER-SPY WITH VERY DISTINCTIVE FEATURES
Wait, no— GAH!
Fer cryin' out loud—
BANG!
—Have you EVER heard me say "I'm sorry"? The eye-patch was even on the wrong side of this Life Model Decoy! Your JOB is to determine truth!
A-am I fired?...
Only cause I can't kill you.

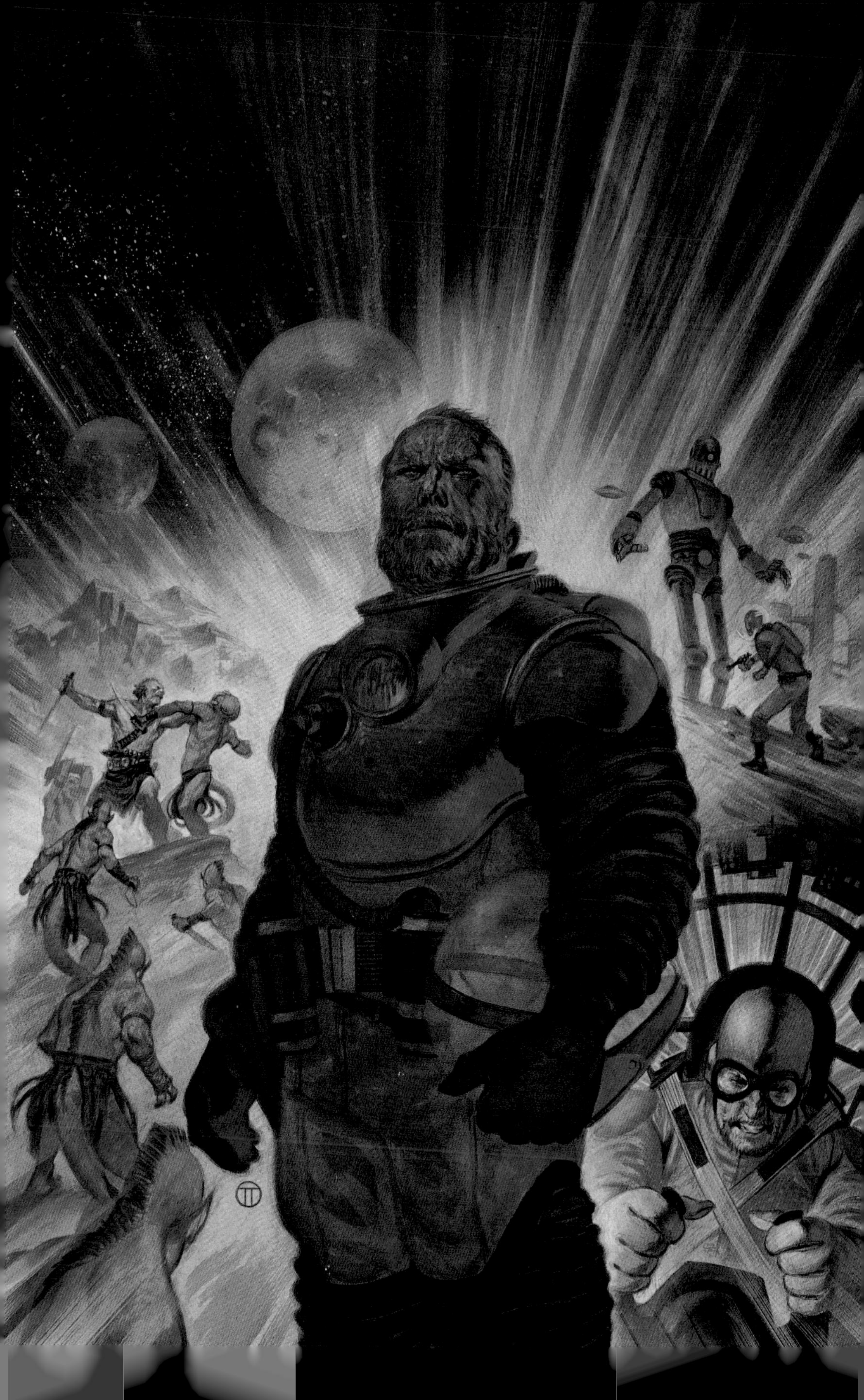

NICK FURY HAS LONG BEEN THE "MAN ON THE WALL," OUR LAST LINE OF DEFENSE AGAINST THE COSMIC FORCES WHO WOULD PREY ON THE EARTH. BUT HE WAS FAR FROM THE FIRST.

BEFORE FURY THERE WAS WOODROW MCCORD, A MAN WITH ALLEGIANCE TO NO GOVERNMENT, BROTHERHOOD OR AGENCY. A SOLITARY MAN BURDENED WITH THE SAFETY OF AN ENTIRE PLANET.

OUR STORY BEGINS IN 1958. KANSAS. THE TRIBELLIAN INVASION OF EARTH HAS BEEN THWARTED, BUT WOODROW MCCORD IS DEAD.

NICK FURY, THEN AN OFFICER IN ARMY INTELLIGENCE, AND HOWARD STARK, NOTED INVENTOR AND FATHER OF TONY STARK, ARE ON HAND TO BEAR WITNESS TO THE DEATH OF THE EARTH'S PROTECTOR…BUT WHAT OF HIS LIFE?

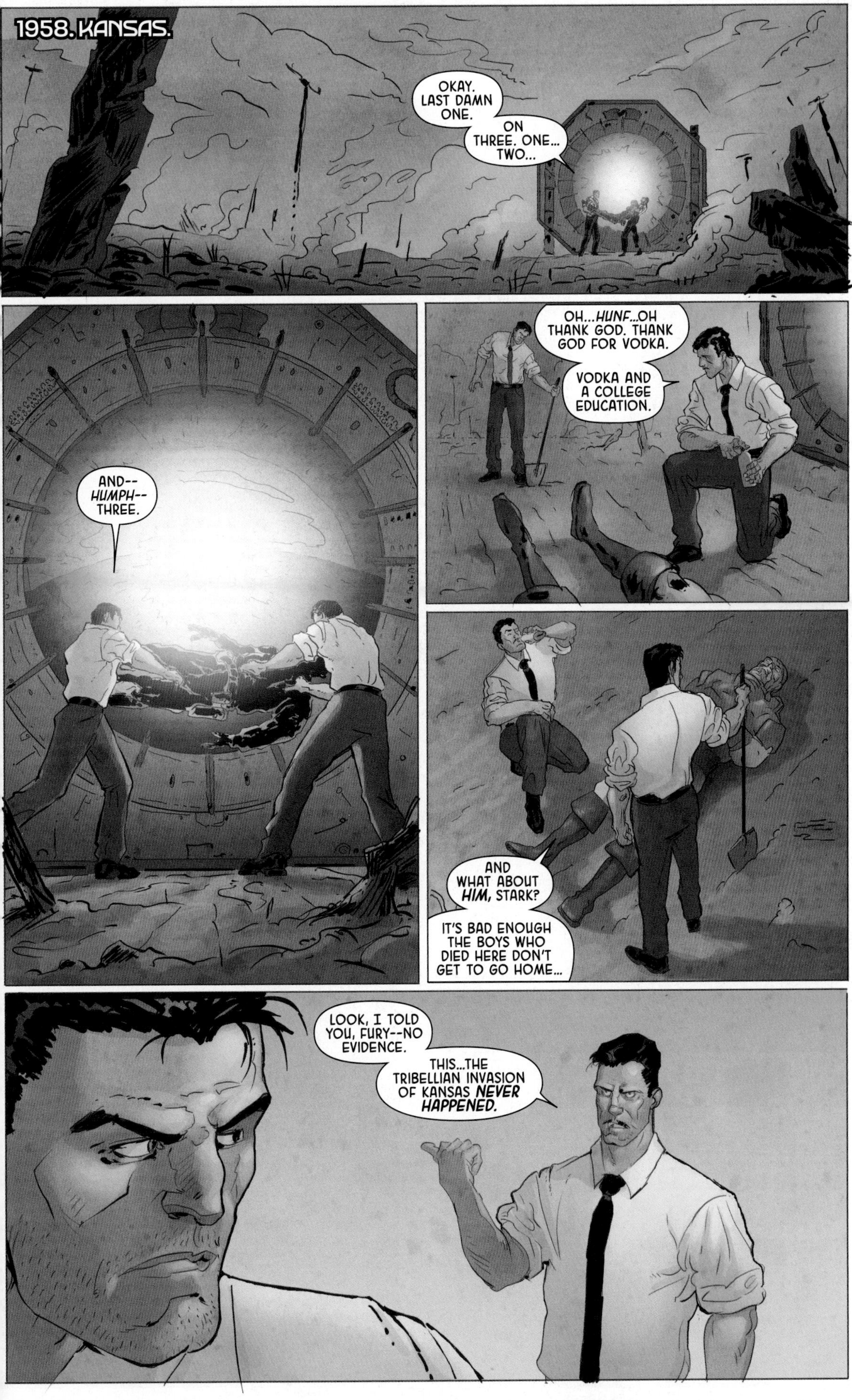
1958. KANSAS.
OKAY. LAST DAMN ONE.
ON THREE. ONE... TWO...
AND-- *HUMPH*-- THREE.
OH... *HUNF*...OH THANK GOD. THANK GOD FOR VODKA.
VODKA AND A COLLEGE EDUCATION.
AND WHAT ABOUT *HIM*, STARK?
IT'S BAD ENOUGH THE BOYS WHO DIED HERE DON'T GET TO GO HOME...
LOOK, I TOLD YOU, FURY--NO EVIDENCE.
THIS...THE TRIBELLIAN INVASION OF KANSAS *NEVER HAPPENED.*

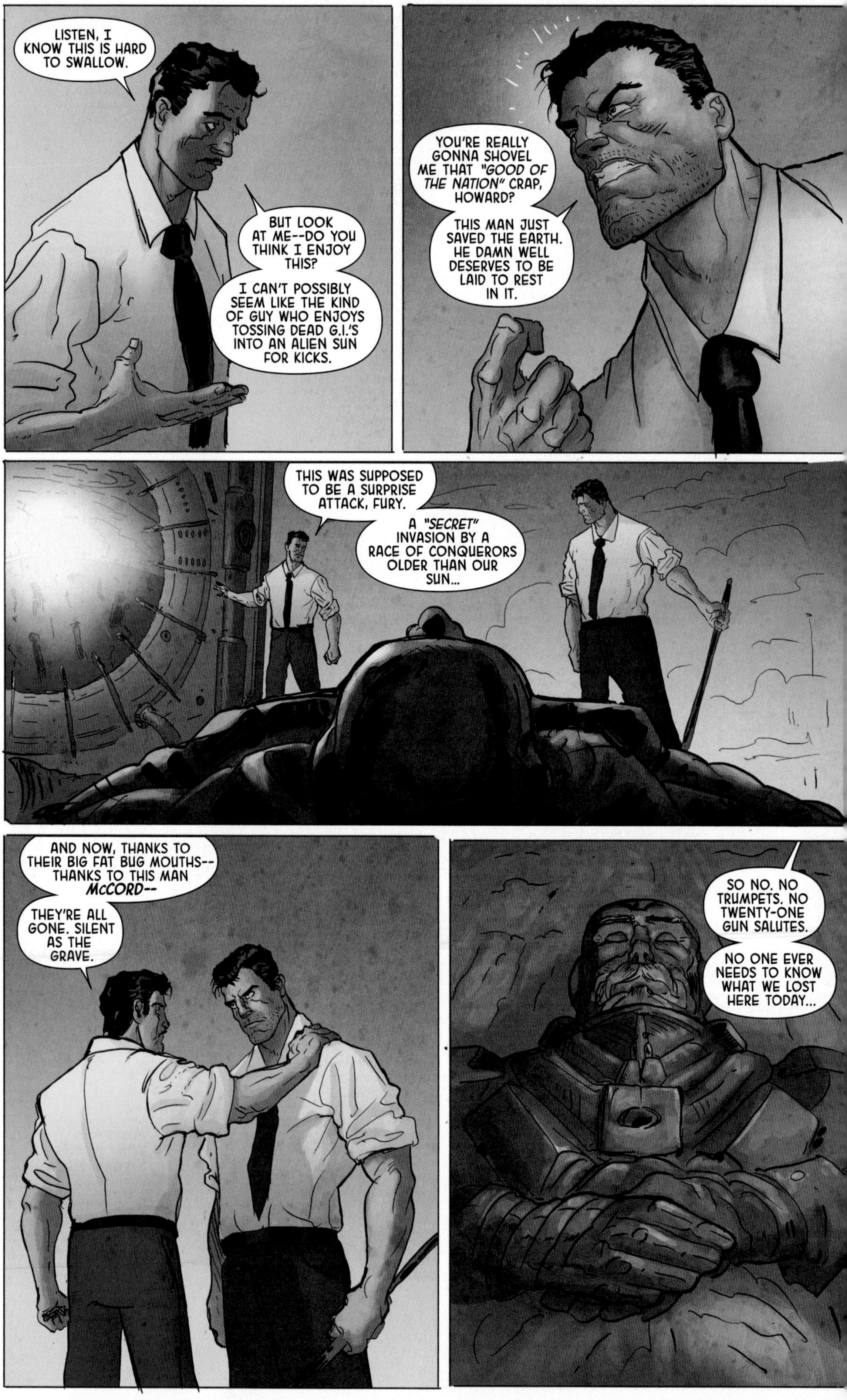
LISTEN, I KNOW THIS IS HARD TO SWALLOW.
BUT LOOK AT ME--DO YOU THINK I ENJOY THIS?
I CAN'T POSSIBLY SEEM LIKE THE KIND OF GUY WHO ENJOYS TOSSING DEAD G.I.'S INTO AN ALIEN SUN FOR KICKS.
YOU'RE REALLY GONNA SHOVEL ME THAT "GOOD OF THE NATION" CRAP, HOWARD?
THIS MAN JUST SAVED THE EARTH. HE DAMN WELL DESERVES TO BE LAID TO REST IN IT.
THIS WAS SUPPOSED TO BE A SURPRISE ATTACK, FURY.
A "SECRET" INVASION BY A RACE OF CONQUERORS OLDER THAN OUR SUN...
AND NOW, THANKS TO THEIR BIG FAT BUG MOUTHS--THANKS TO THIS MAN McCORD--
THEY'RE ALL GONE. SILENT AS THE GRAVE.
SO NO. NO TRUMPETS. NO TWENTY-ONE GUN SALUTES.
NO ONE EVER NEEDS TO KNOW WHAT WE LOST HERE TODAY...

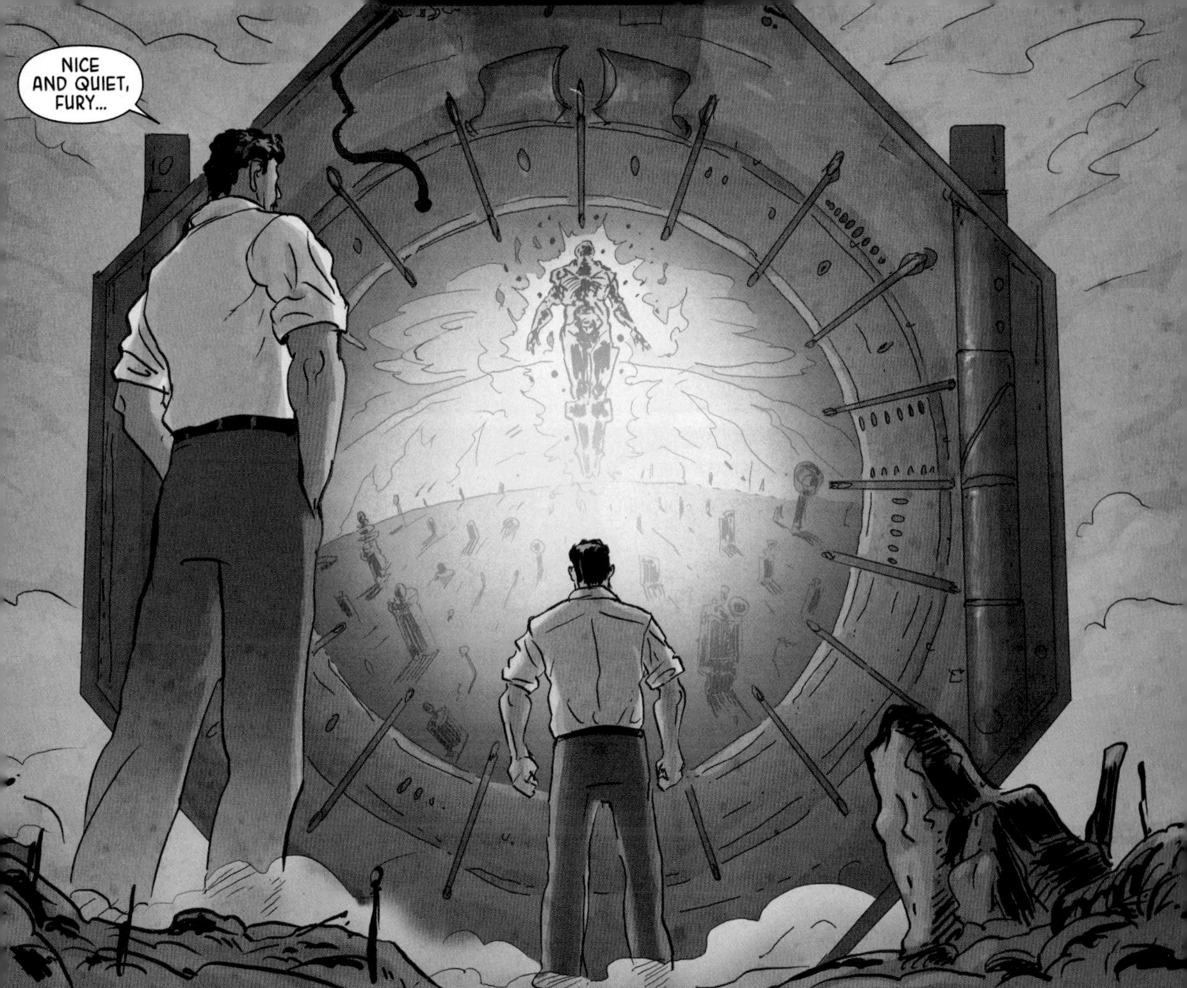
NICE AND QUIET, FURY...

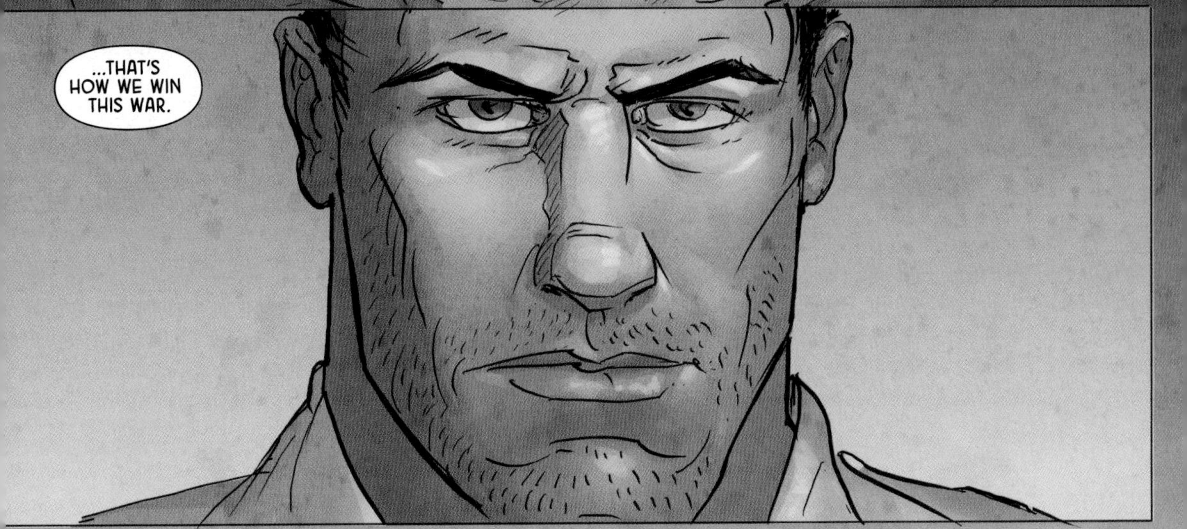
...THAT'S HOW WE WIN THIS WAR.

THE SILENT WAR OF WOODROW McCORD

JASON LATOUR — WRITER
ENIS CISIC — ARTIST
CHRIS CHUCKRY — COLOR ARTIST
CHRIS ELIOPOULOS AND CLAYTON COWLES — LETTERERS
JAKE THOMAS — ASSISTANT EDITOR
TOM BREVOORT WITH WIL MOSS — EDITORS
AXEL ALONSO — EDITOR IN CHIEF
JOE QUESADA — CHIEF CREATIVE OFFICER
DAN BUCKLEY — PUBLISHER
ALAN FINE — EXECUTIVE PRODUCER
JULIAN TOTINO TEDESCO — COVER
FRANCESCO FRANCAVILLA AND CHRISTIAN WARD — VARIANT COVERS

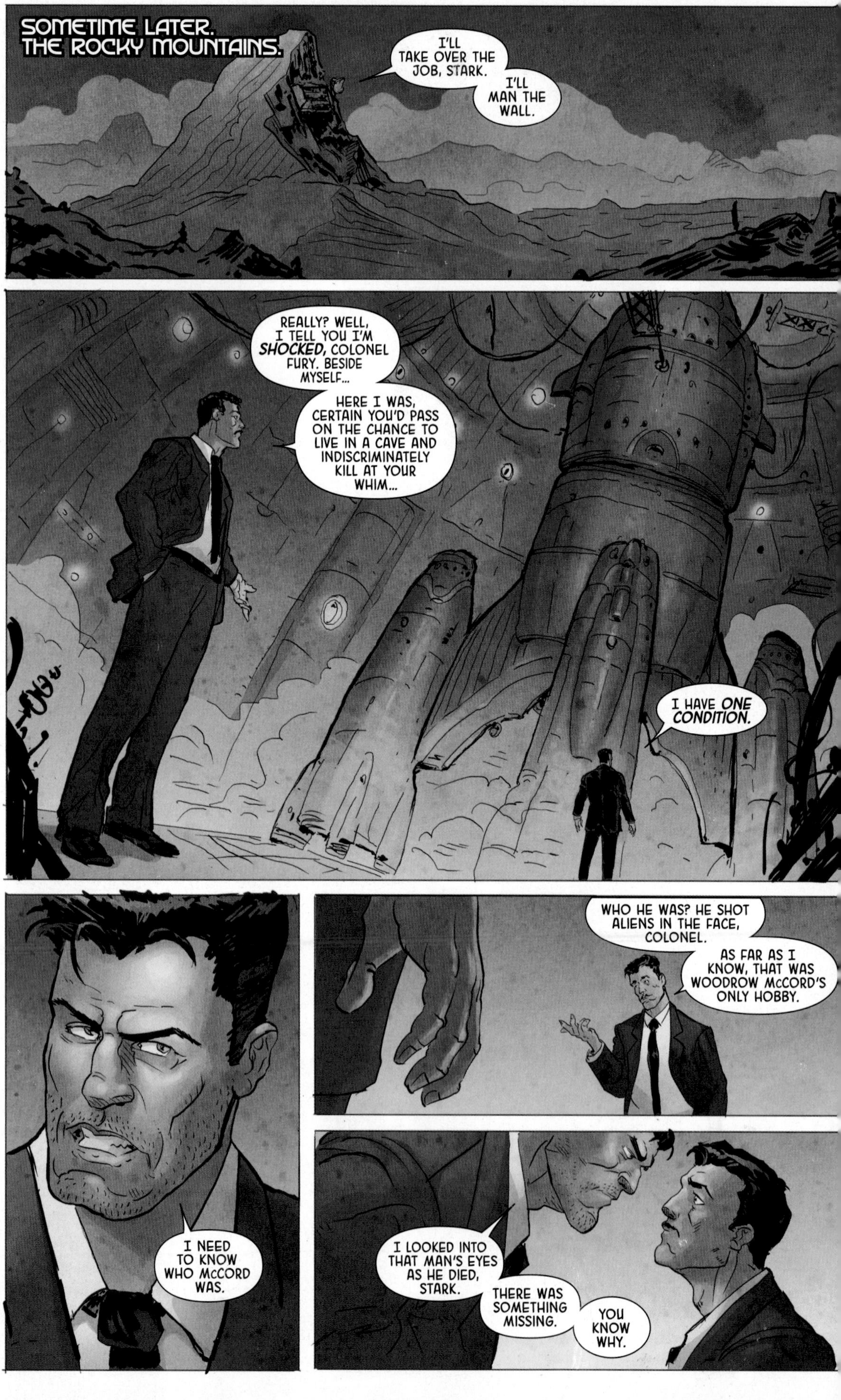
SOMETIME LATER.
THE ROCKY MOUNTAINS.
I'LL TAKE OVER THE JOB, STARK.
I'LL MAN THE WALL.
REALLY? WELL, I TELL YOU I'M SHOCKED, COLONEL FURY. BESIDE MYSELF...
HERE I WAS, CERTAIN YOU'D PASS ON THE CHANCE TO LIVE IN A CAVE AND INDISCRIMINATELY KILL AT YOUR WHIM...
I HAVE ONE CONDITION.
I NEED TO KNOW WHO McCORD WAS.
WHO HE WAS? HE SHOT ALIENS IN THE FACE, COLONEL.
AS FAR AS I KNOW, THAT WAS WOODROW McCORD'S ONLY HOBBY.
I LOOKED INTO THAT MAN'S EYES AS HE DIED, STARK.
THERE WAS SOMETHING MISSING.
YOU KNOW WHY.

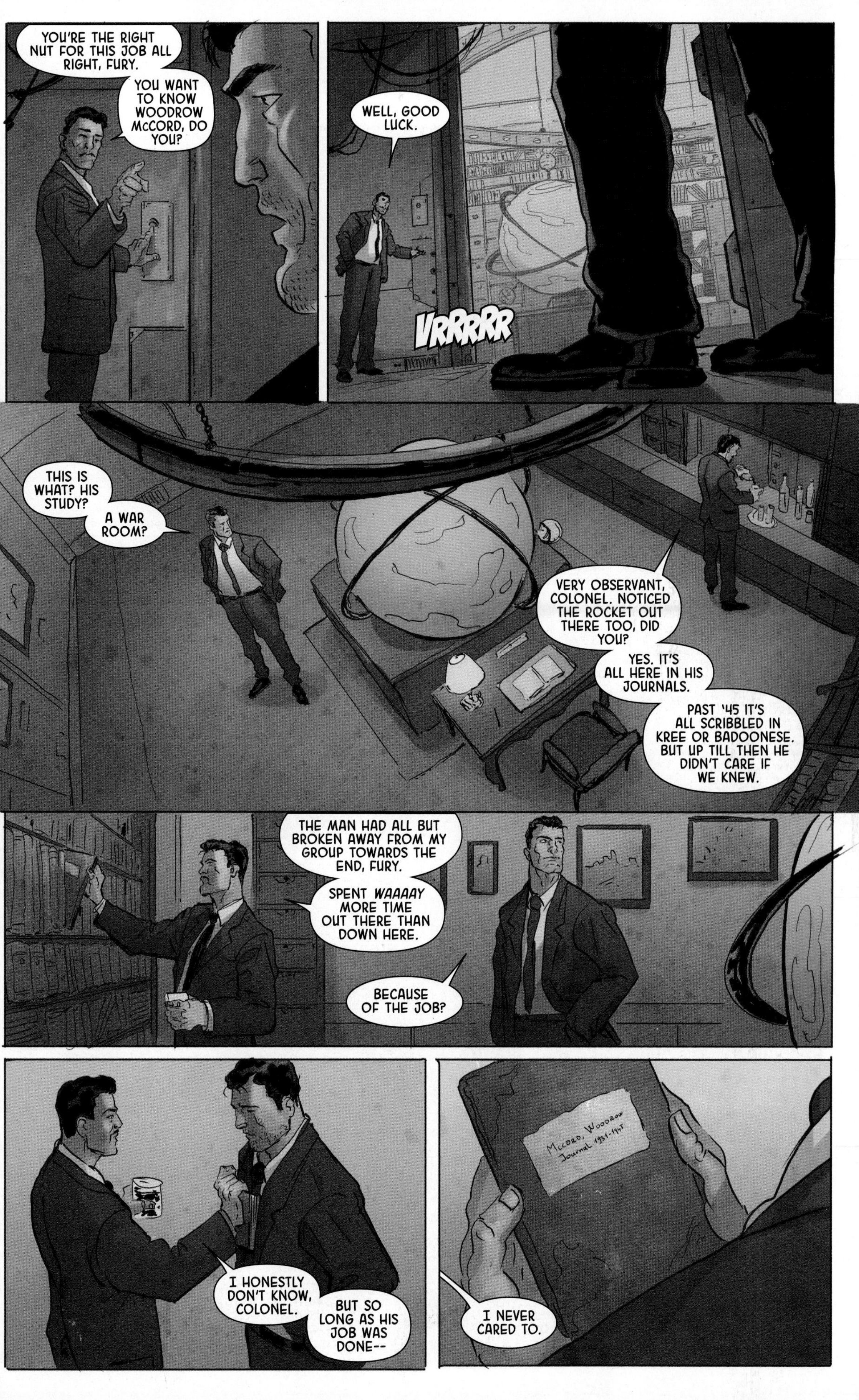
YOU'RE THE RIGHT NUT FOR THIS JOB ALL RIGHT, FURY.
YOU WANT TO KNOW WOODROW McCORD, DO YOU?
WELL, GOOD LUCK.
VRRRRR
THIS IS WHAT? HIS STUDY?
A WAR ROOM?
VERY OBSERVANT, COLONEL. NOTICED THE ROCKET OUT THERE TOO, DID YOU?
YES. IT'S ALL HERE IN HIS JOURNALS.
PAST '45 IT'S ALL SCRIBBLED IN KREE OR BADOONESE. BUT UP TILL THEN HE DIDN'T CARE IF WE KNEW.
THE MAN HAD ALL BUT BROKEN AWAY FROM MY GROUP TOWARDS THE END, FURY.
SPENT *WAAAAY* MORE TIME OUT THERE THAN DOWN HERE.
BECAUSE OF THE JOB?
I HONESTLY DON'T KNOW, COLONEL.
BUT SO LONG AS HIS JOB WAS DONE--
McCORD, WOODROW
Journal 1931-1945
I NEVER CARED TO.

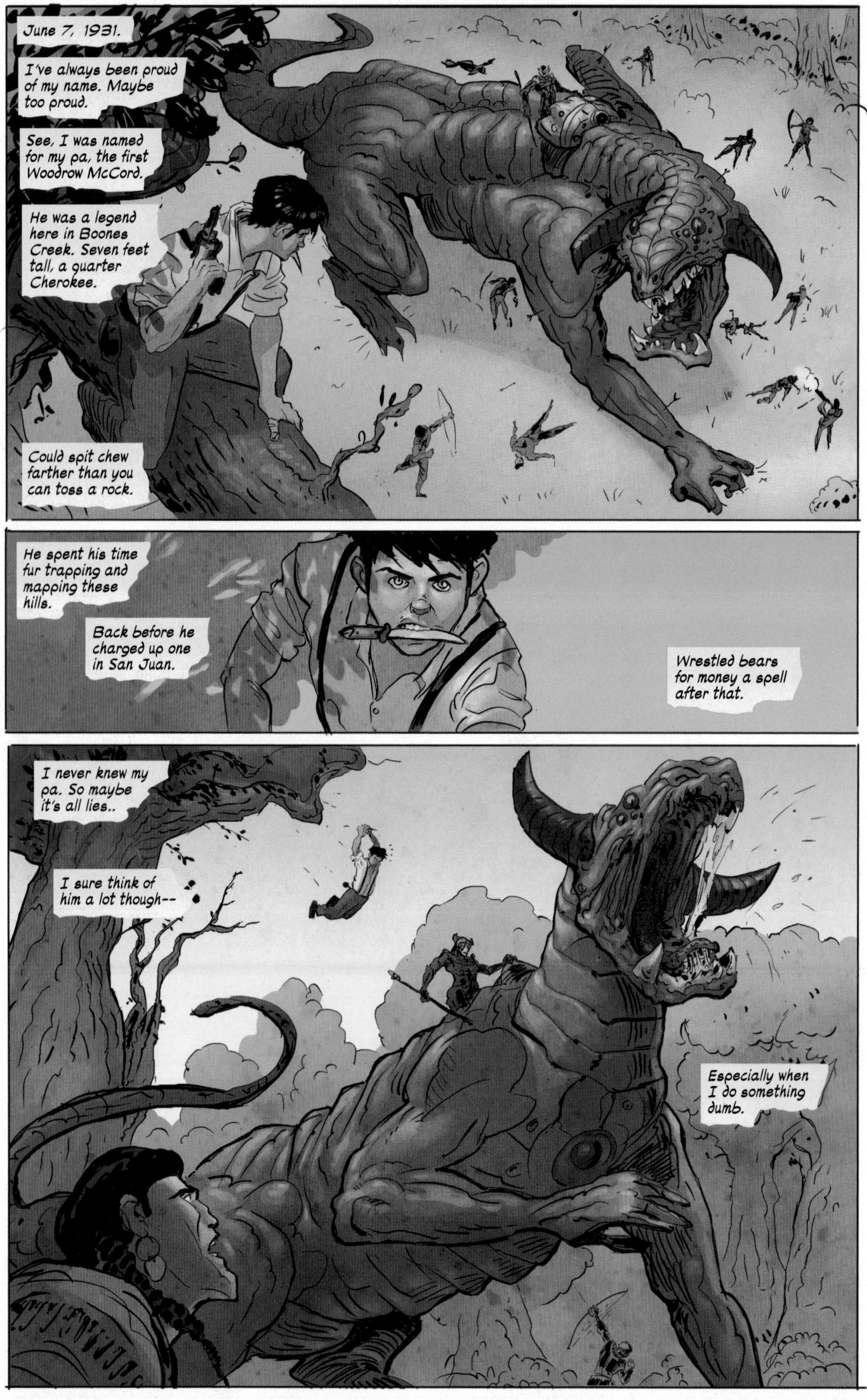
June 7, 1931.
I've always been proud of my name. Maybe too proud.
See, I was named for my pa, the first Woodrow McCord.
He was a legend here in Boones Creek. Seven feet tall, a quarter Cherokee.
Could spit chew farther than you can toss a rock.
He spent his time fur trapping and mapping these hills.
Back before he charged up one in San Juan.
Wrestled bears for money a spell after that.
I never knew my pa. So maybe it's all lies..
I sure think of him a lot though--
Especially when I do something dumb.

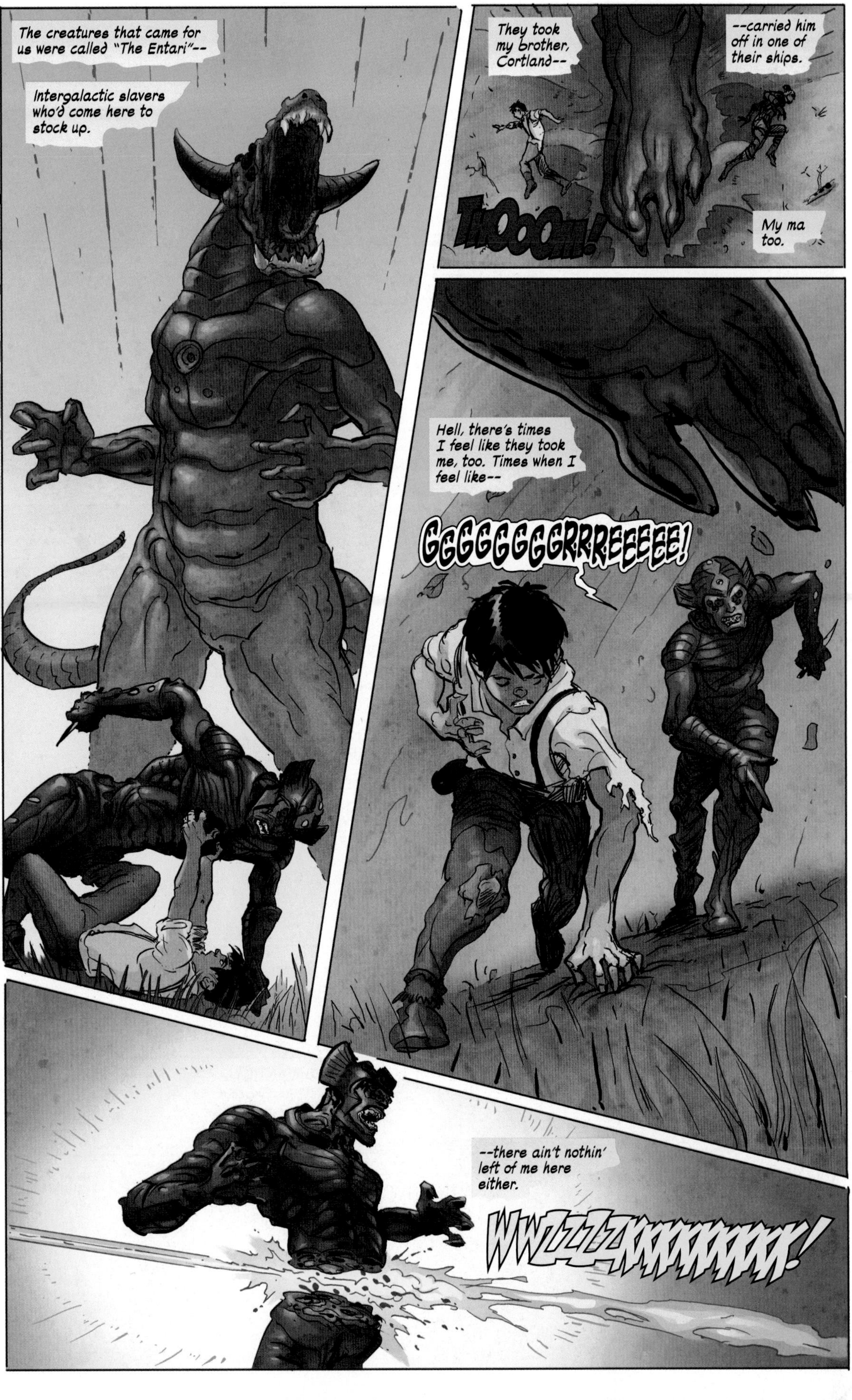
The creatures that came for us were called "The Entari"--
Intergalactic slavers who'd come here to stock up.
They took my brother, Cortland--
--carried him off in one of their ships.
THOOOM!
My ma too.
Hell, there's times I feel like they took me, too. Times when I feel like--
GGGGGGGGRRREEEEE!
--there ain't nothin' left of me here either.
WWZZZZKKKKKKKKK!

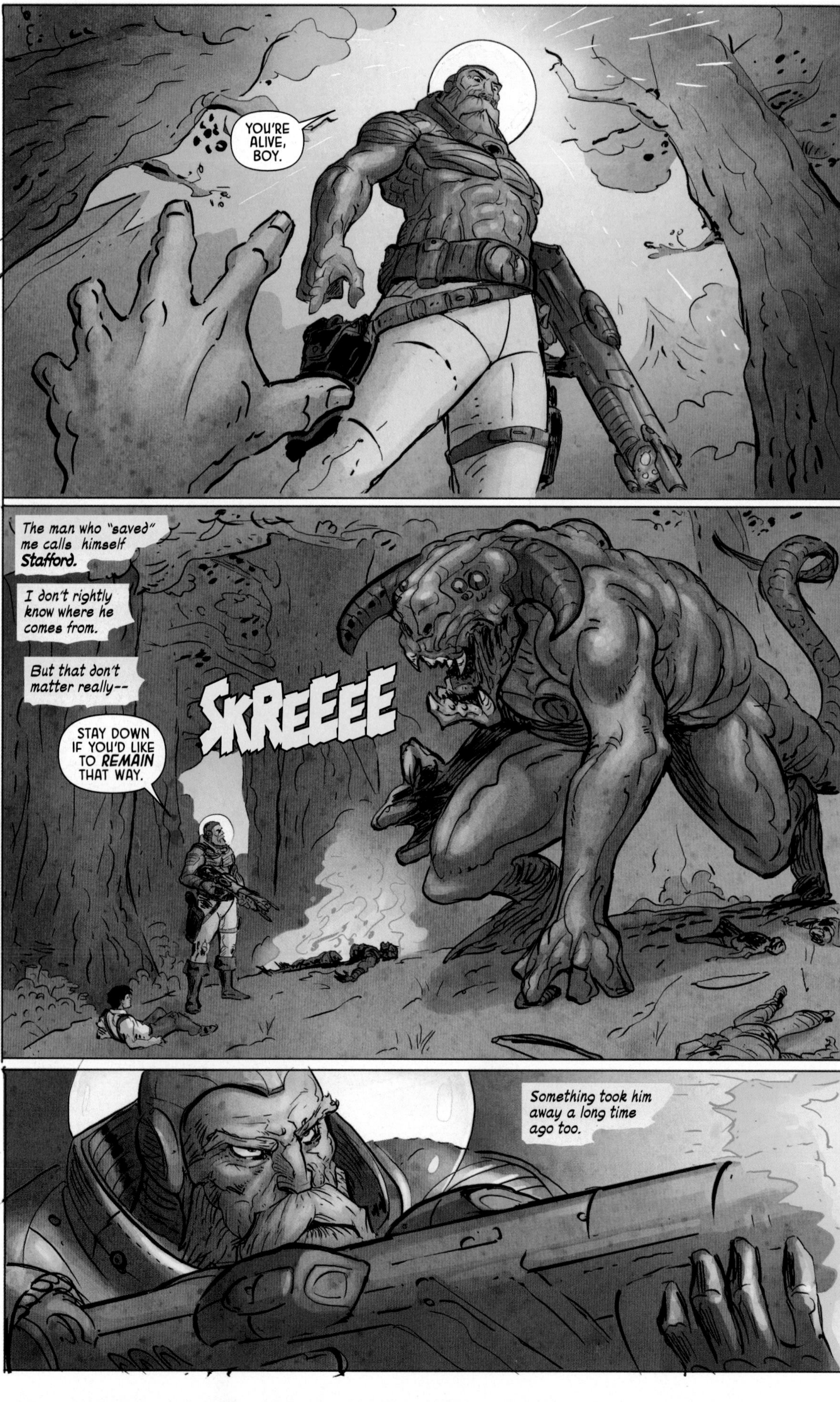

YOU'RE ALIVE, BOY.
The man who "saved" me calls himself Stafford.
I don't rightly know where he comes from.
But that don't matter really--
SKREEEE
STAY DOWN IF YOU'D LIKE TO REMAIN THAT WAY.
Something took him away a long time ago too.

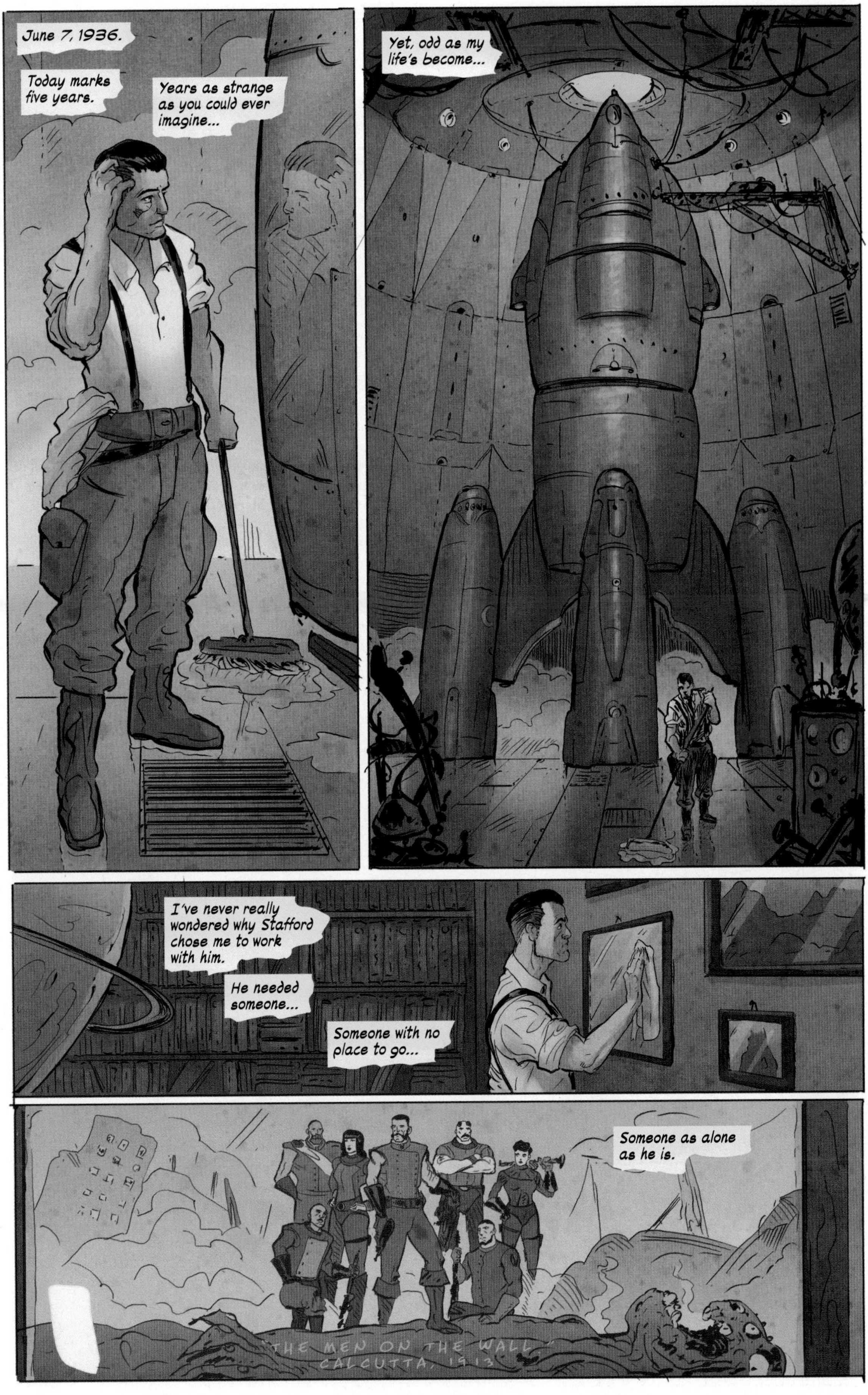
June 7, 1936.
Today marks five years.
Years as strange as you could ever imagine...
Yet, odd as my life's become...
I've never really wondered why Stafford chose me to work with him.
He needed someone...
Someone with no place to go...
Someone as alone as he is.
"THE MEN ON THE WALL"
CALCUTTA, 1913

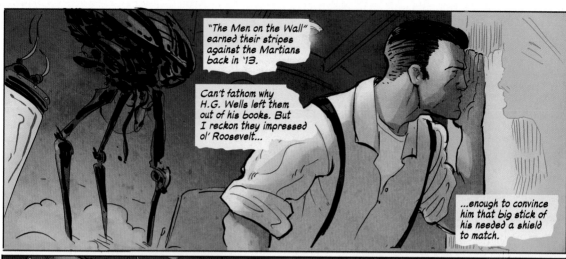

"The Men on the Wall" earned their stripes against the Martians back in '13.

Can't fathom why H.G. Wells left them out of his books. But I reckon they impressed ol' Roosevelt...

...enough to convince him that big stick of his needed a shield to match.

They'd operated alone. With complete autonomy.

'Cause some things are bigger than the rules, after all.

For decades, they manned an impenetrable wall.

Until the Entari arrived and took it apart brick by brick.

After that, Stafford vowed never to sit on his hands again.

He threw down his shield...

And took up a sword.

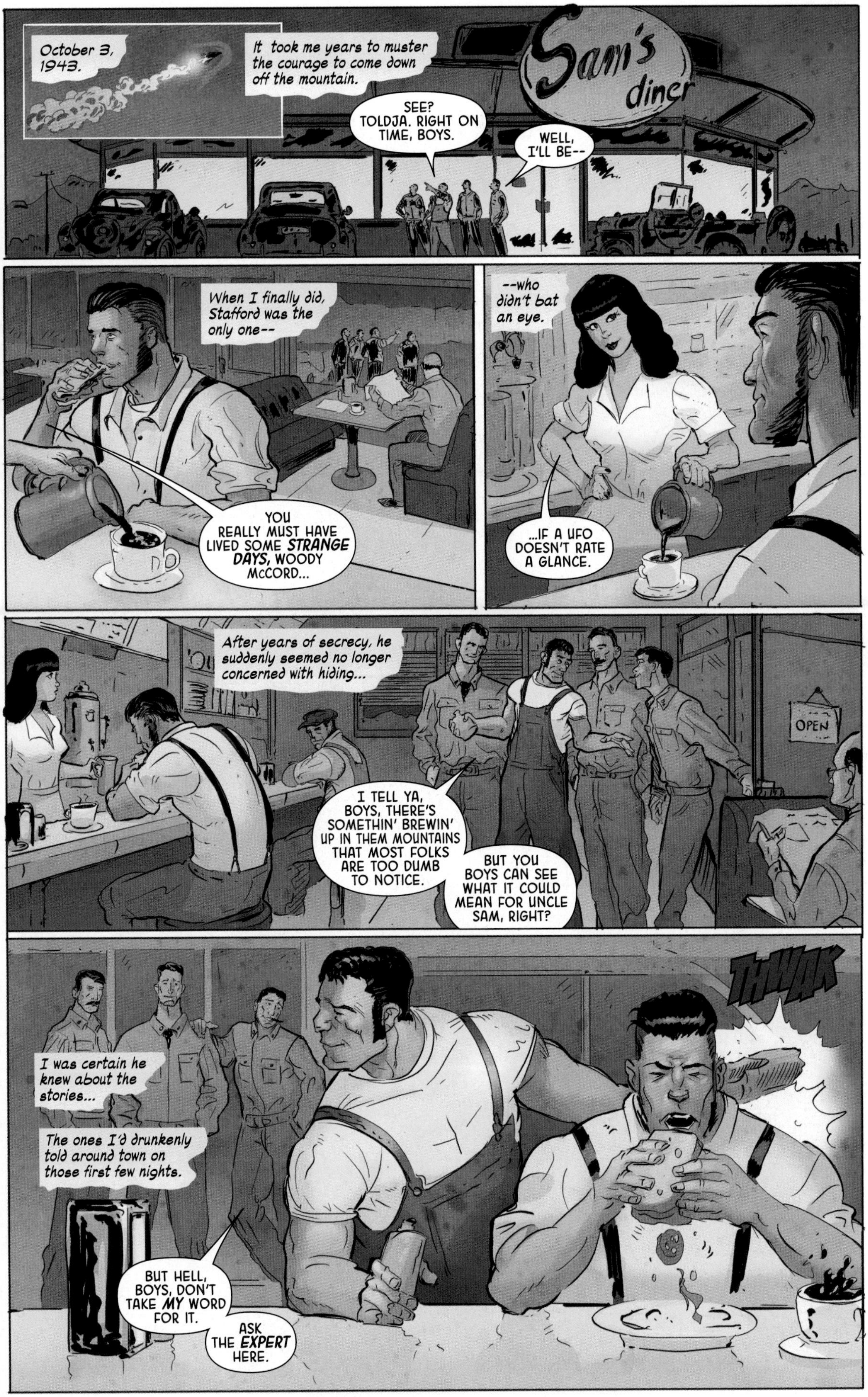

October 3, 1943.
It took me years to muster the courage to come down off the mountain.
Sam's diner
SEE? TOLDJA. RIGHT ON TIME, BOYS.
WELL, I'LL BE--
When I finally did, Stafford was the only one--
YOU REALLY MUST HAVE LIVED SOME STRANGE DAYS, WOODY McCORD...
--who didn't bat an eye.
...IF A UFO DOESN'T RATE A GLANCE.
After years of secrecy, he suddenly seemed no longer concerned with hiding...
OPEN
I TELL YA, BOYS, THERE'S SOMETHIN' BREWIN' UP IN THEM MOUNTAINS THAT MOST FOLKS ARE TOO DUMB TO NOTICE.
BUT YOU BOYS CAN SEE WHAT IT COULD MEAN FOR UNCLE SAM, RIGHT?
THWAK
I was certain he knew about the stories...
The ones I'd drunkenly told around town on those first few nights.
BUT HELL, BOYS, DON'T TAKE MY WORD FOR IT.
ASK THE EXPERT HERE.

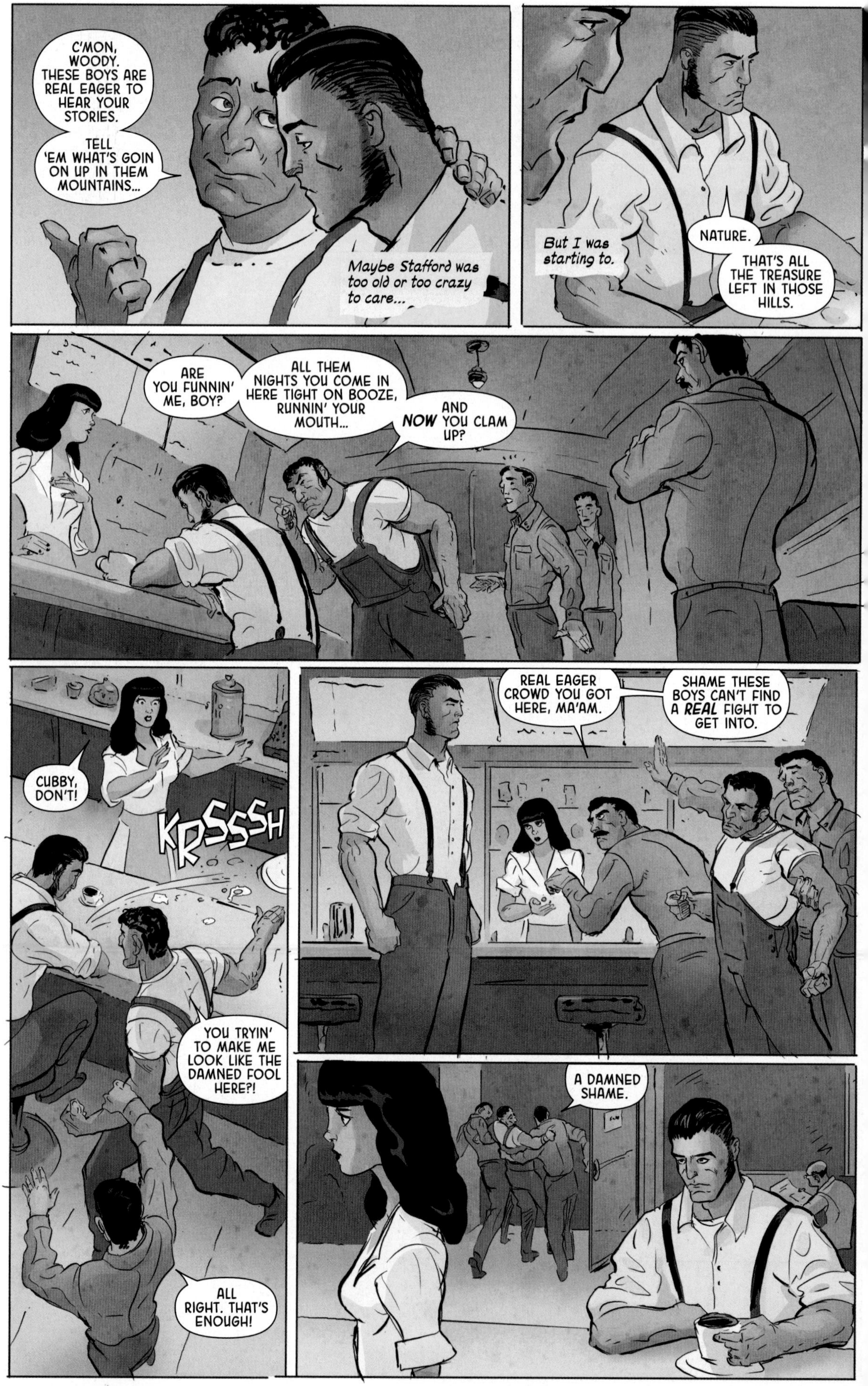
C'MON, WOODY. THESE BOYS ARE REAL EAGER TO HEAR YOUR STORIES.
TELL 'EM WHAT'S GOIN ON UP IN THEM MOUNTAINS...
Maybe Stafford was too old or too crazy to care...
But I was starting to.
NATURE.
THAT'S ALL THE TREASURE LEFT IN THOSE HILLS.
ARE YOU FUNNIN' ME, BOY?
ALL THEM NIGHTS YOU COME IN HERE TIGHT ON BOOZE, RUNNIN' YOUR MOUTH...
AND NOW YOU CLAM UP?
CUBBY, DON'T!
KRSSSH
YOU TRYIN' TO MAKE ME LOOK LIKE THE DAMNED FOOL HERE?!
ALL RIGHT. THAT'S ENOUGH!
REAL EAGER CROWD YOU GOT HERE, MA'AM.
SHAME THESE BOYS CAN'T FIND A REAL FIGHT TO GET INTO.
A DAMNED SHAME.

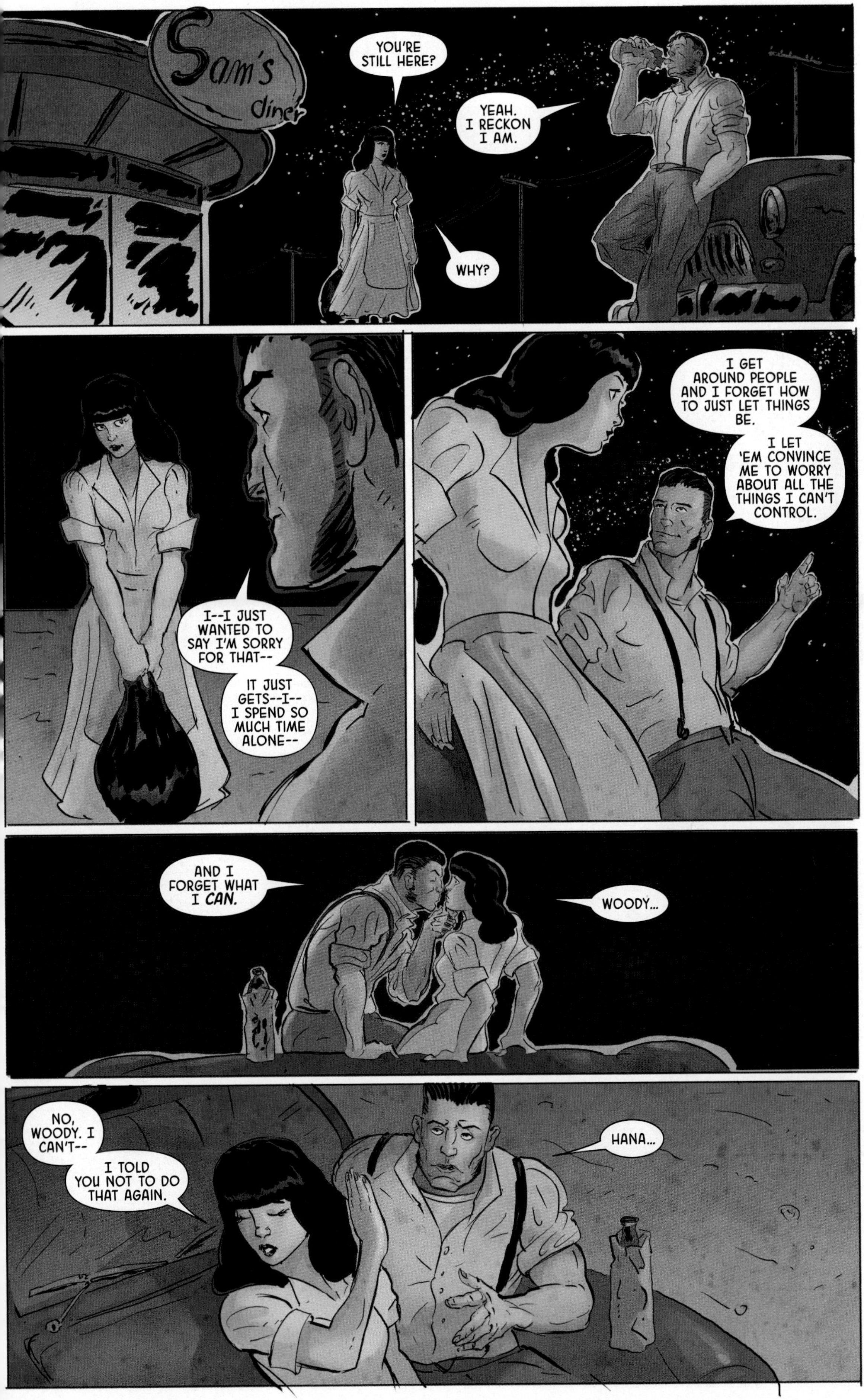
Sam's
diner
YOU'RE STILL HERE?
YEAH. I RECKON I AM.
WHY?
I--I JUST WANTED TO SAY I'M SORRY FOR THAT--
IT JUST GETS--I-- I SPEND SO MUCH TIME ALONE--
I GET AROUND PEOPLE AND I FORGET HOW TO JUST LET THINGS BE.
I LET 'EM CONVINCE ME TO WORRY ABOUT ALL THE THINGS I CAN'T CONTROL.
AND I FORGET WHAT I *CAN.*
WOODY...
NO, WOODY. I CAN'T--
I TOLD YOU NOT TO DO THAT AGAIN.
HANA...

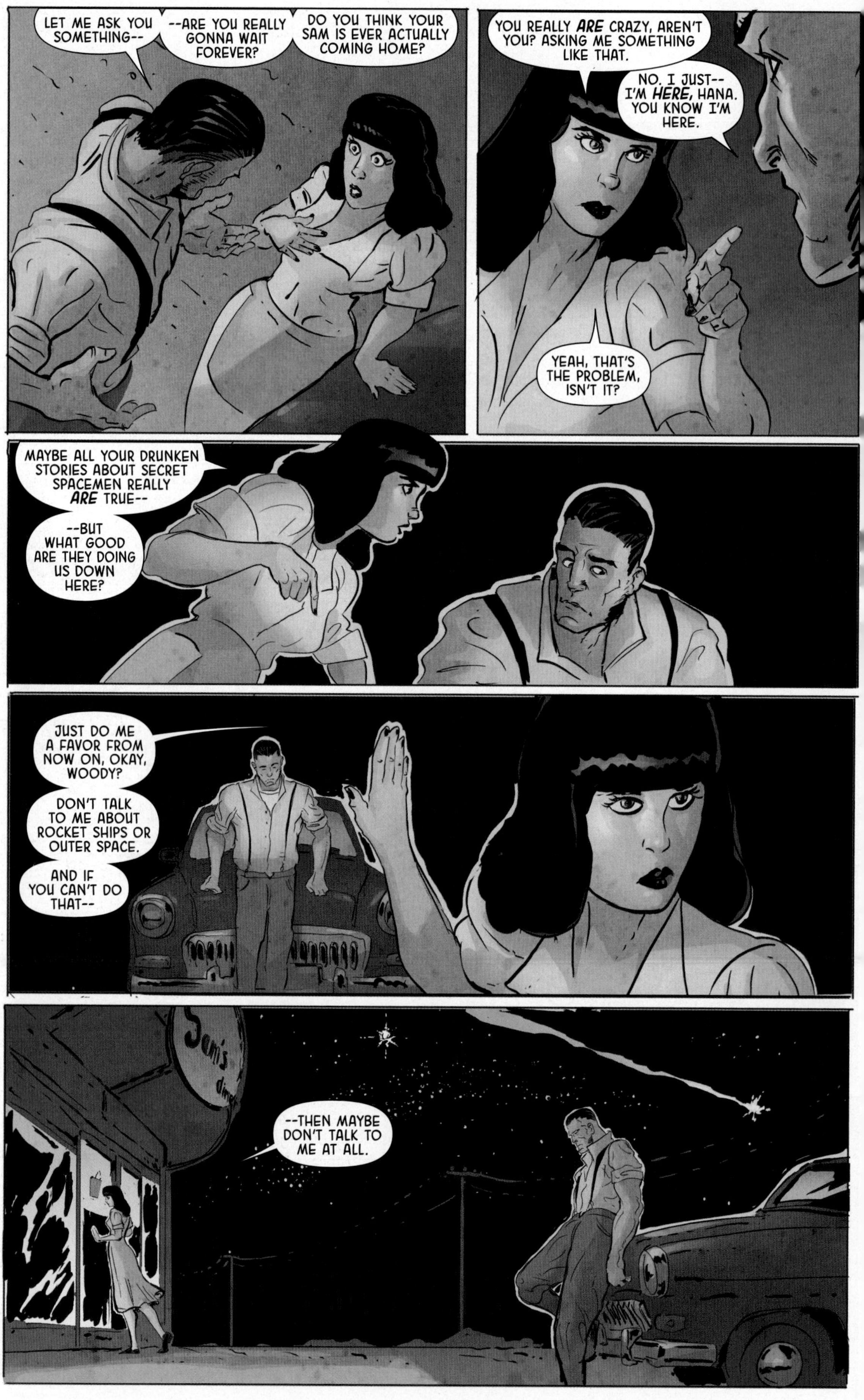
LET ME ASK YOU SOMETHING--
--ARE YOU REALLY GONNA WAIT FOREVER?
DO YOU THINK YOUR SAM IS EVER ACTUALLY COMING HOME?
YOU REALLY *ARE* CRAZY, AREN'T YOU? ASKING ME SOMETHING LIKE THAT.
NO. I JUST-- I'M *HERE,* HANA. YOU KNOW I'M HERE.
YEAH, THAT'S THE PROBLEM, ISN'T IT?
MAYBE ALL YOUR DRUNKEN STORIES ABOUT SECRET SPACEMEN REALLY *ARE* TRUE--
--BUT WHAT GOOD ARE THEY DOING US DOWN HERE?
JUST DO ME A FAVOR FROM NOW ON, OKAY, WOODY?
DON'T TALK TO ME ABOUT ROCKET SHIPS OR OUTER SPACE.
AND IF YOU CAN'T DO THAT--
Sam's
--THEN MAYBE DON'T TALK TO ME AT ALL.

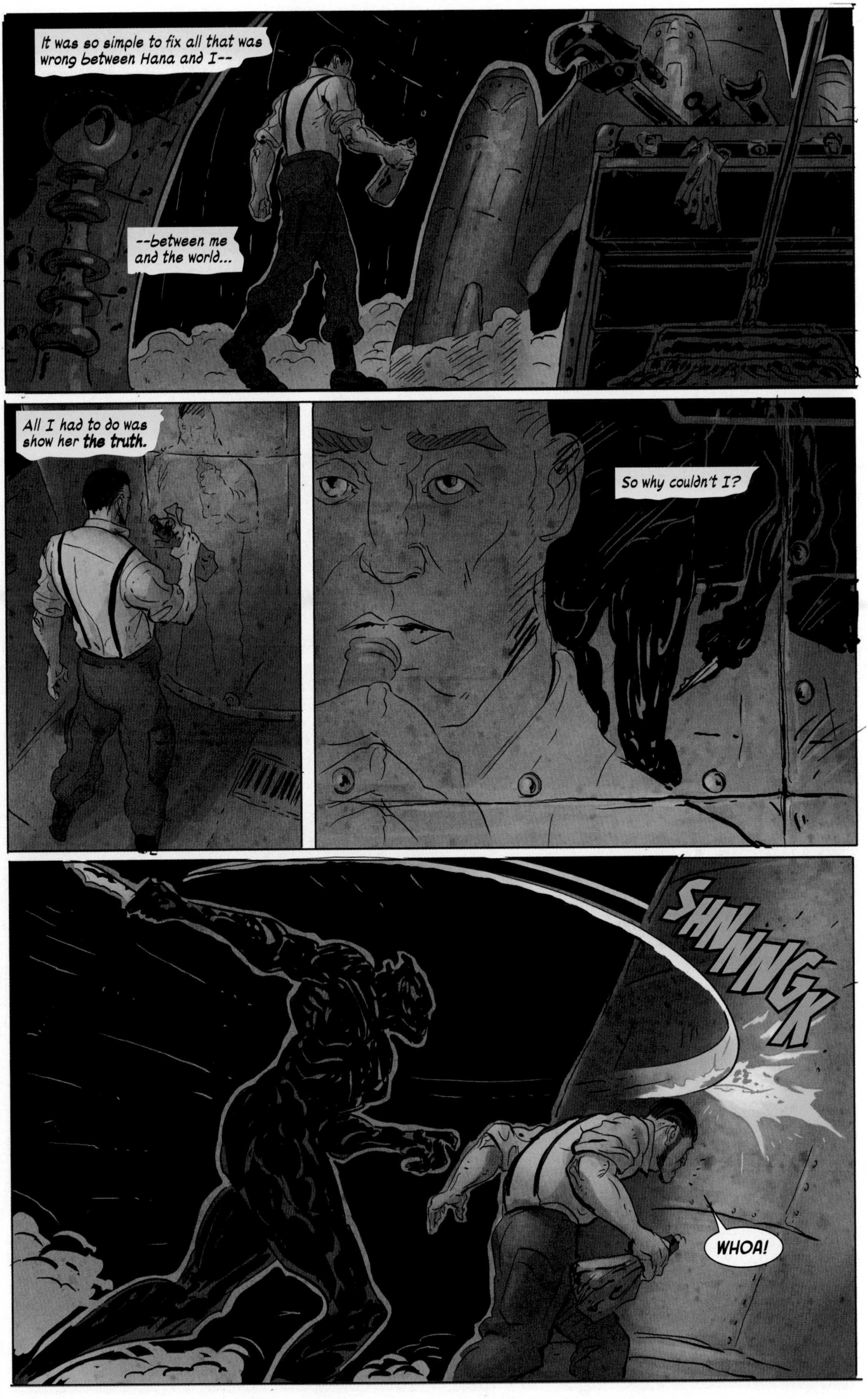
It was so simple to fix all that was wrong between Hana and I--
--between me and the world...
All I had to do was show her **the truth.**
So why couldn't I?
SHNNNGK
WHOA!

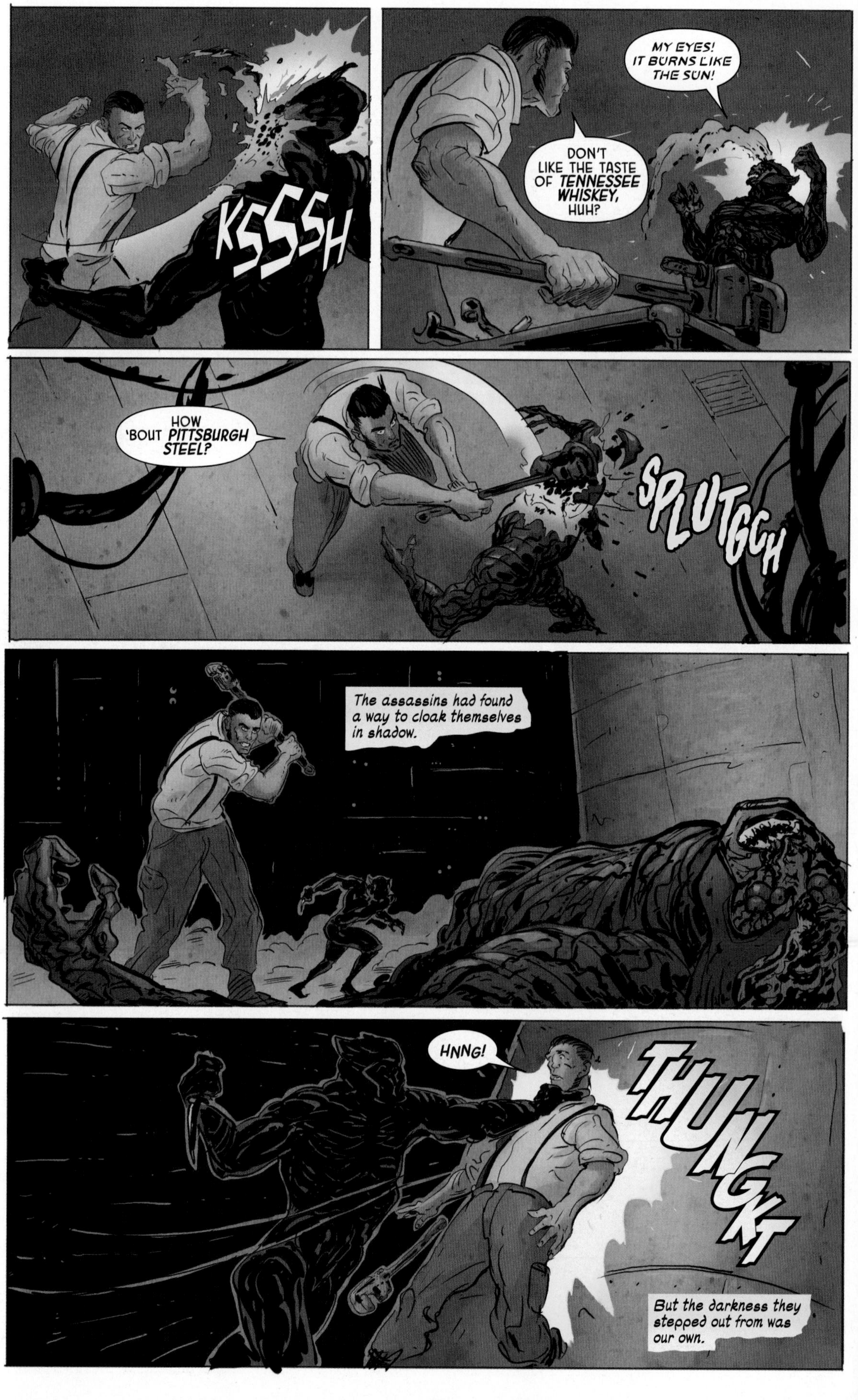

KSSSH
MY EYES! IT BURNS LIKE THE SUN!
DON'T LIKE THE TASTE OF TENNESSEE WHISKEY, HUH?
HOW 'BOUT PITTSBURGH STEEL?
SPLUTGCH
The assassins had found a way to cloak themselves in shadow.
HNNG!
THUNGKT
But the darkness they stepped out from was our own.

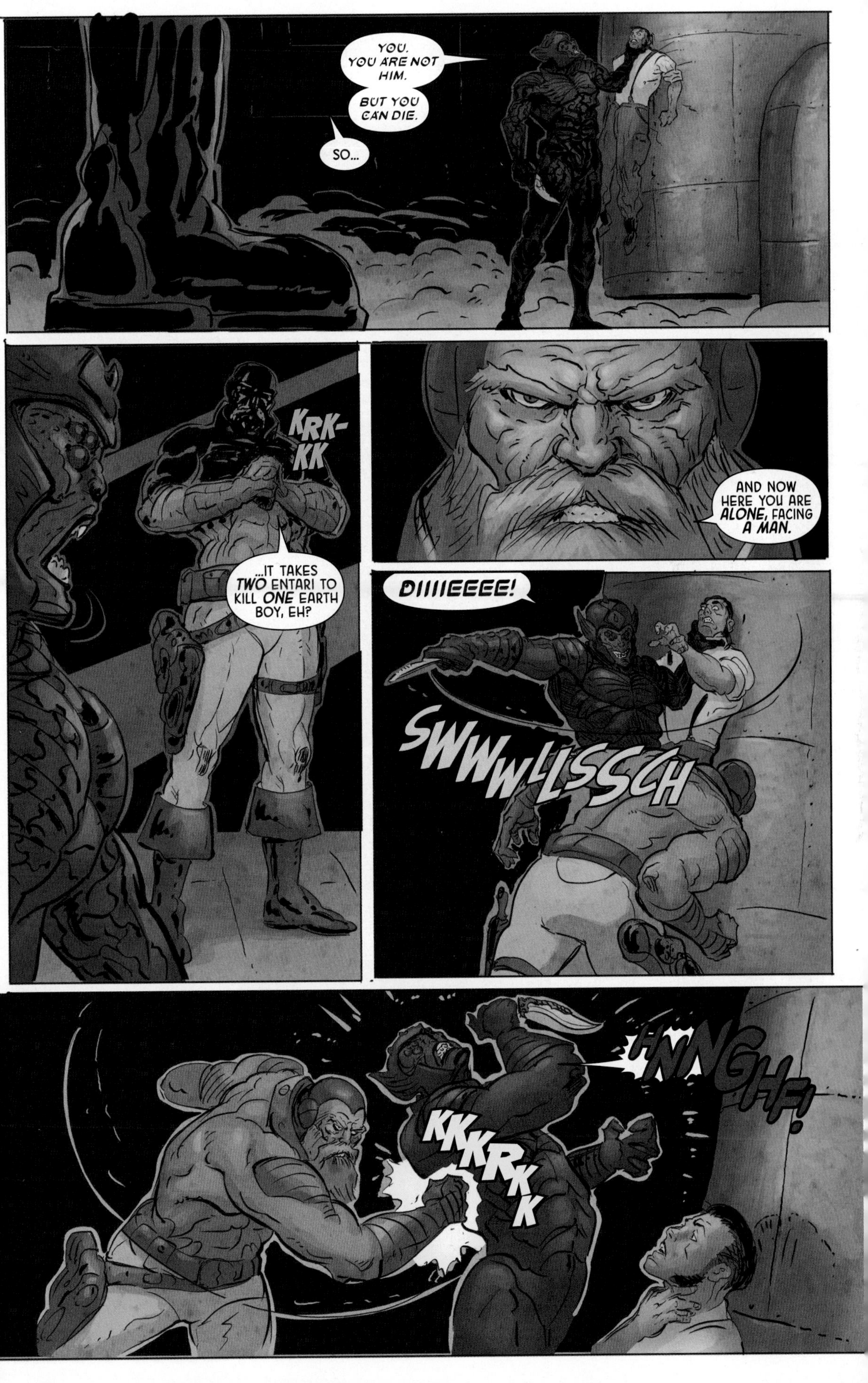
YOU. YOU ARE NOT HIM.
BUT YOU CAN DIE.
SO...
KRK-KK
...IT TAKES TWO ENTARI TO KILL ONE EARTH BOY, EH?
AND NOW HERE YOU ARE ALONE, FACING A MAN.
DIIIIEEEE!
SWWWLLSSCH
HNNGHF!
KKKRKKK

RÄÄRRGGH!

I...MAKE... THE SOUP...FROM YOU BONESES...

SKRAKRRRK

RRRGGH!

The intruders were Entari Commandos. Stone killers.

Thanks to Stafford's newfound bluster, they'd finally found him.

NO! NO!

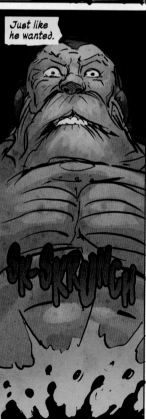

Just like he wanted.

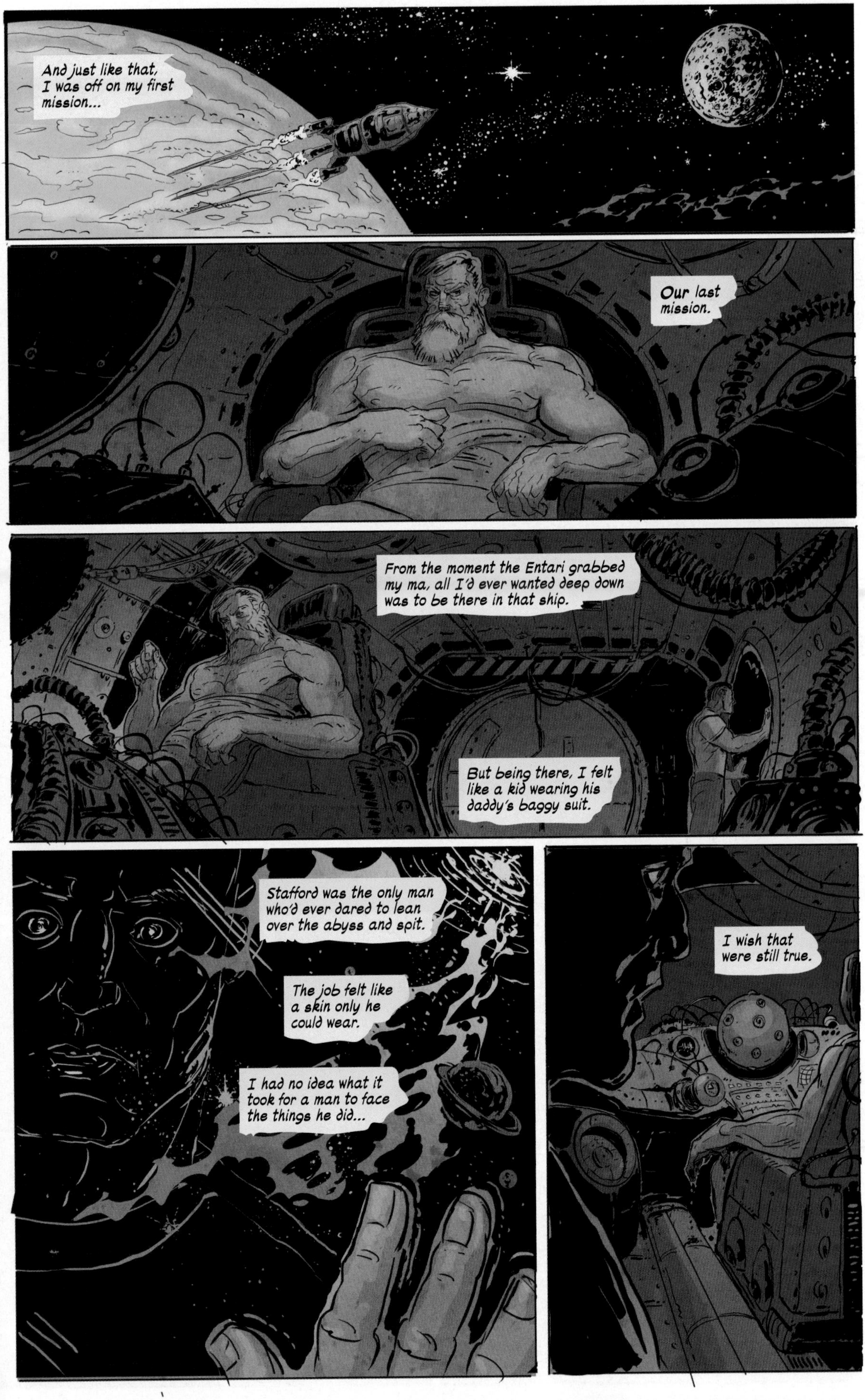
And just like that, I was off on my first mission...
Our last mission.
From the moment the Entari grabbed my ma, all I'd ever wanted deep down was to be there in that ship.
But being there, I felt like a kid wearing his daddy's baggy suit.
Stafford was the only man who'd ever dared to lean over the abyss and spit.
The job felt like a skin only he could wear.
I had no idea what it took for a man to face the things he did...
I wish that were still true.

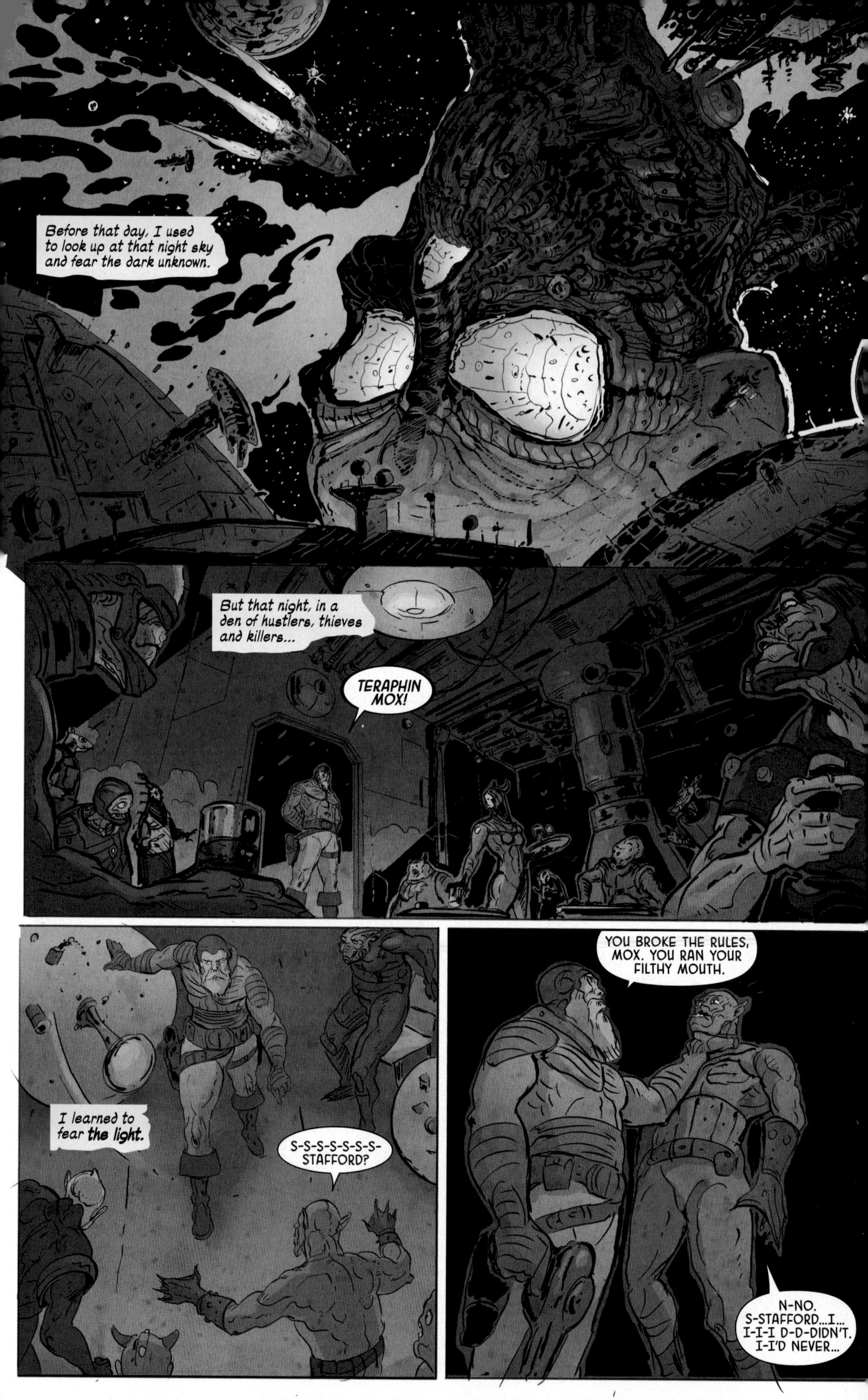
Before that day, I used to look up at that night sky and fear the dark unknown.
But that night, in a den of hustlers, thieves and killers...
TERAPHIN MOX!
I learned to fear the light.
S-S-S-S-S-S-S-STAFFORD?
YOU BROKE THE RULES, MOX. YOU RAN YOUR FILTHY MOUTH.
N-NO. S-STAFFORD...I... I-I-I D-D-DIDN'T. I-I'D NEVER...

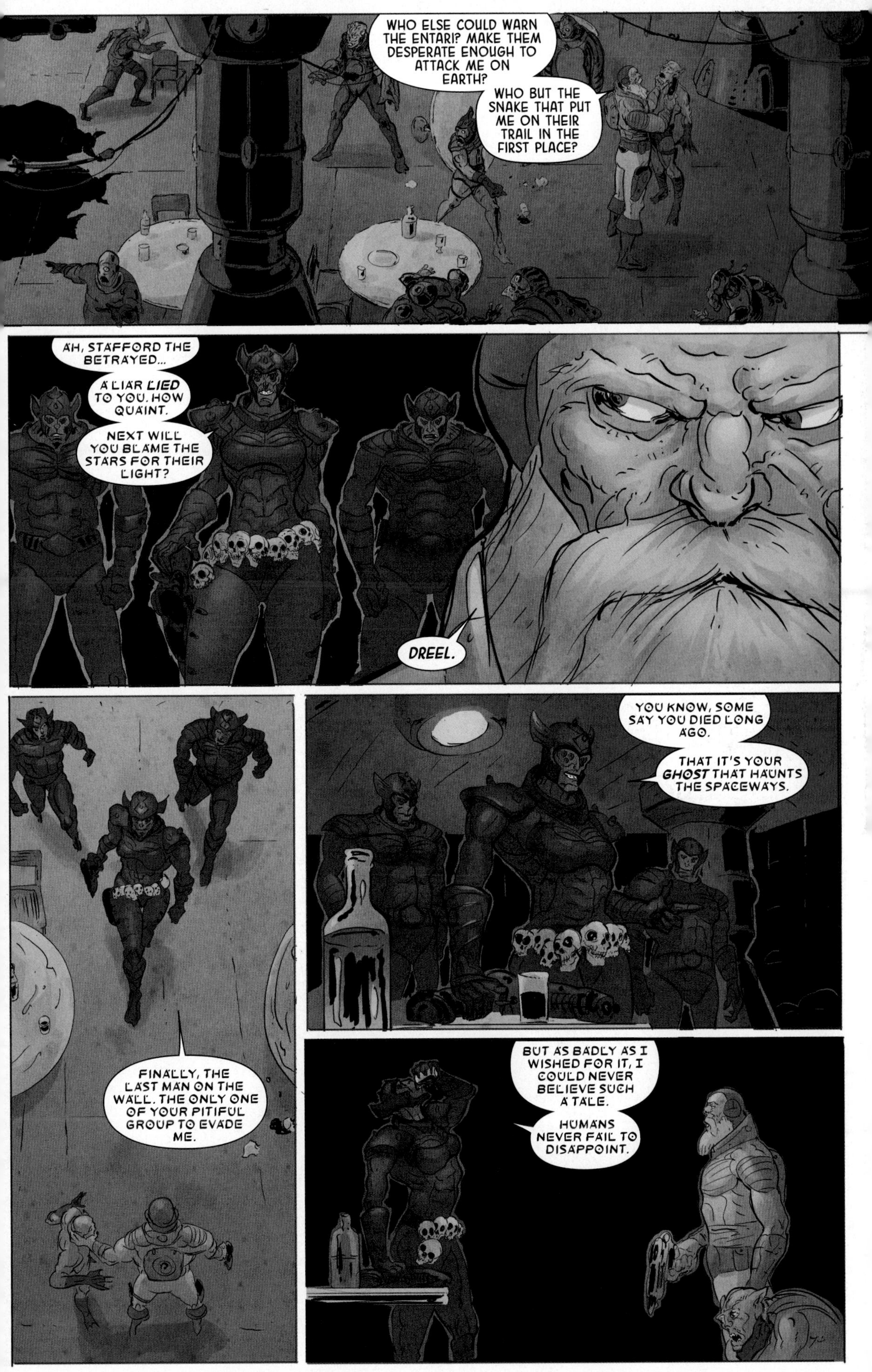
WHO ELSE COULD WARN THE ENTARI? MAKE THEM DESPERATE ENOUGH TO ATTACK ME ON EARTH?
WHO BUT THE SNAKE THAT PUT ME ON THEIR TRAIL IN THE FIRST PLACE?
AH, STAFFORD THE BETRAYED...
A LIAR *LIED* TO YOU. HOW QUAINT.
NEXT WILL YOU BLAME THE STARS FOR THEIR LIGHT?
DREEL.
FINALLY, THE LAST MAN ON THE WALL. THE ONLY ONE OF YOUR PITIFUL GROUP TO EVADE ME.
YOU KNOW, SOME SAY YOU DIED LONG AGO.
THAT IT'S YOUR *GHOST* THAT HAUNTS THE SPACEWAYS.
BUT AS BADLY AS I WISHED FOR IT, I COULD NEVER BELIEVE SUCH A TALE.
HUMANS NEVER FAIL TO DISAPPOINT.

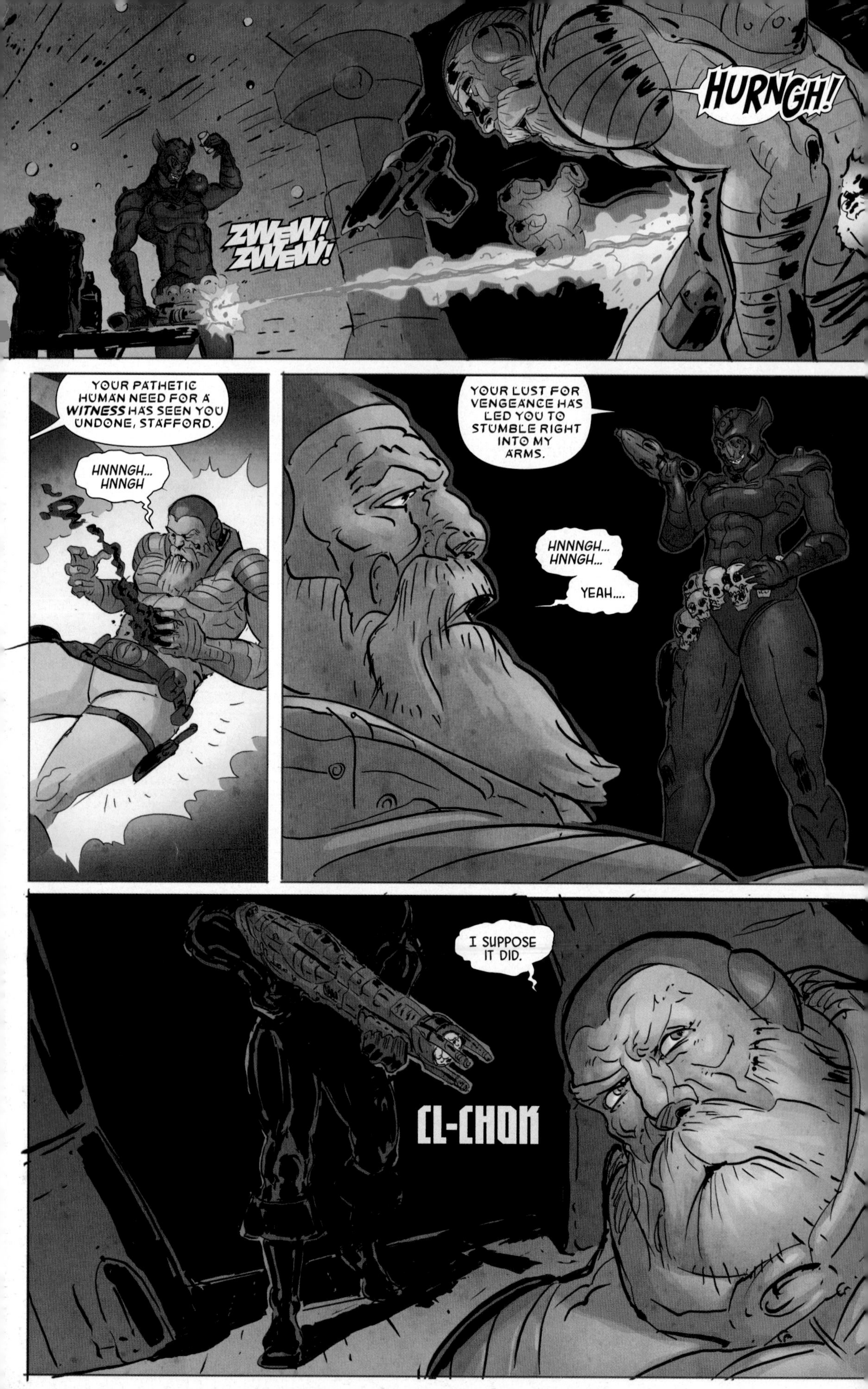
HURNGH!
ZWEW! ZWEW!
YOUR PATHETIC HUMAN NEED FOR A WITNESS HAS SEEN YOU UNDONE, STAFFORD.
HNNNGH... HNNGH
YOUR LUST FOR VENGEANCE HAS LED YOU TO STUMBLE RIGHT INTO MY ARMS.
HNNNGH... HNNGH...
YEAH....
I SUPPOSE IT DID.
CL-CHOK

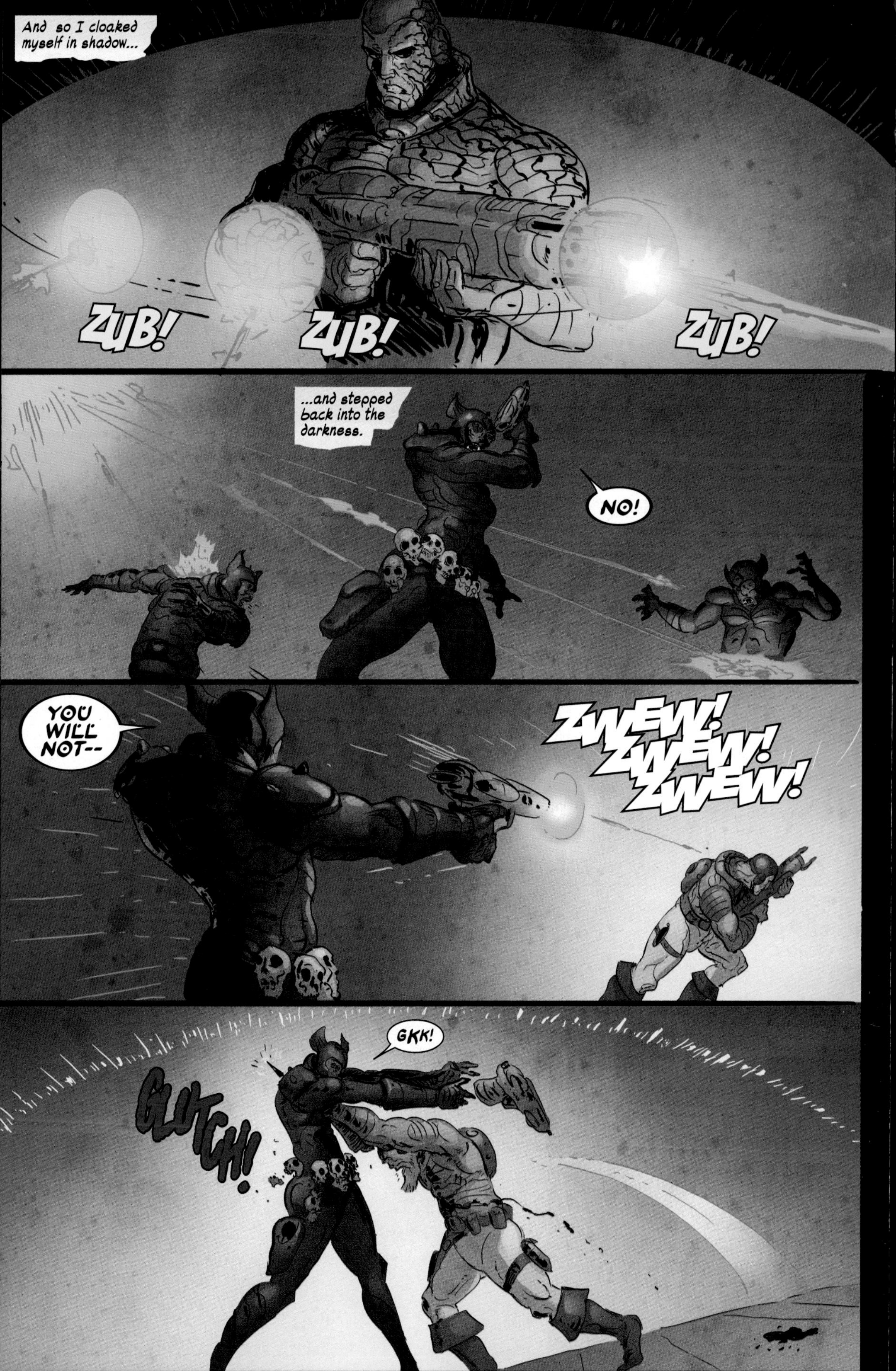
And so I cloaked myself in shadow...
ZUB!
ZUB!
ZUB!
...and stepped back into the darkness.
NO!
YOU WILL NOT--
ZWEW! ZWEW! ZWEW!
GKK!
GLITCH!

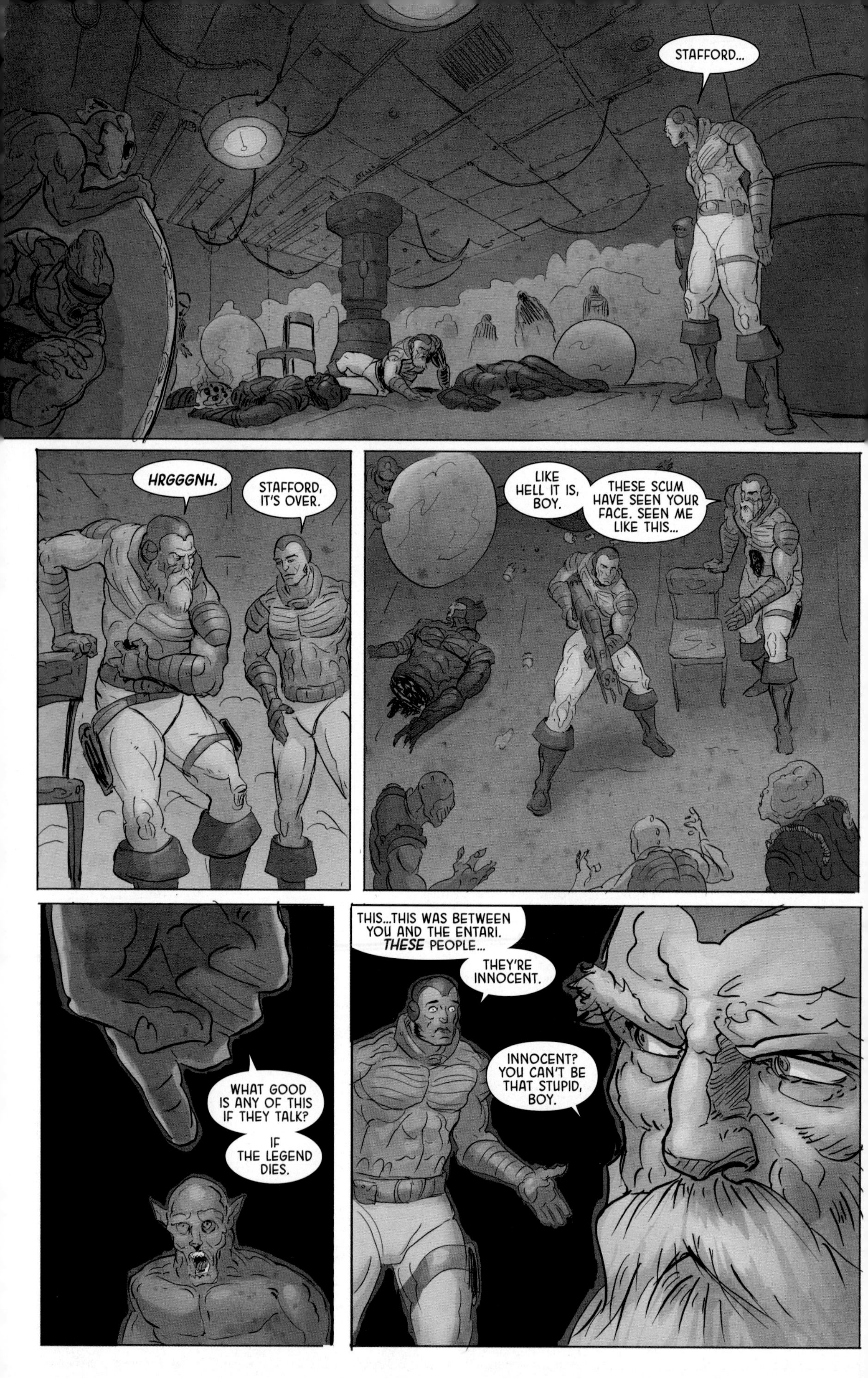
STAFFORD...
HRGGGNH.
STAFFORD, IT'S OVER.
LIKE HELL IT IS, BOY.
THESE SCUM HAVE SEEN YOUR FACE. SEEN ME LIKE THIS...
WHAT GOOD IS ANY OF THIS IF THEY TALK?
IF THE LEGEND DIES.
THIS...THIS WAS BETWEEN YOU AND THE ENTARI. *THESE* PEOPLE...
THEY'RE INNOCENT.
INNOCENT? YOU CAN'T BE THAT STUPID, BOY.

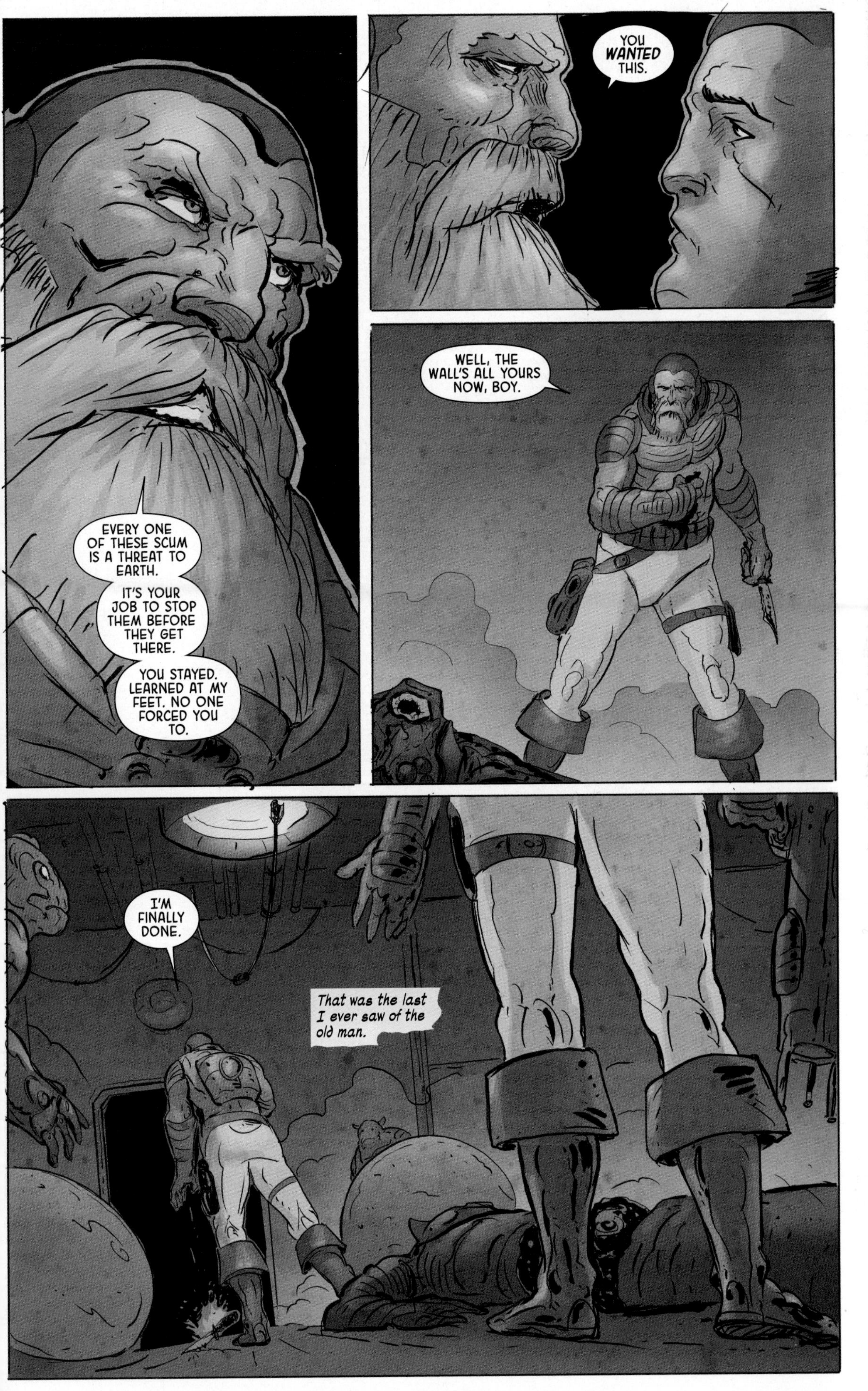
EVERY ONE OF THESE SCUM IS A THREAT TO EARTH.
IT'S YOUR JOB TO STOP THEM BEFORE THEY GET THERE.
YOU STAYED. LEARNED AT MY FEET. NO ONE FORCED YOU TO.
YOU *WANTED* THIS.
WELL, THE WALL'S ALL YOURS NOW, BOY.
I'M FINALLY DONE.
That was the last I ever saw of the old man.

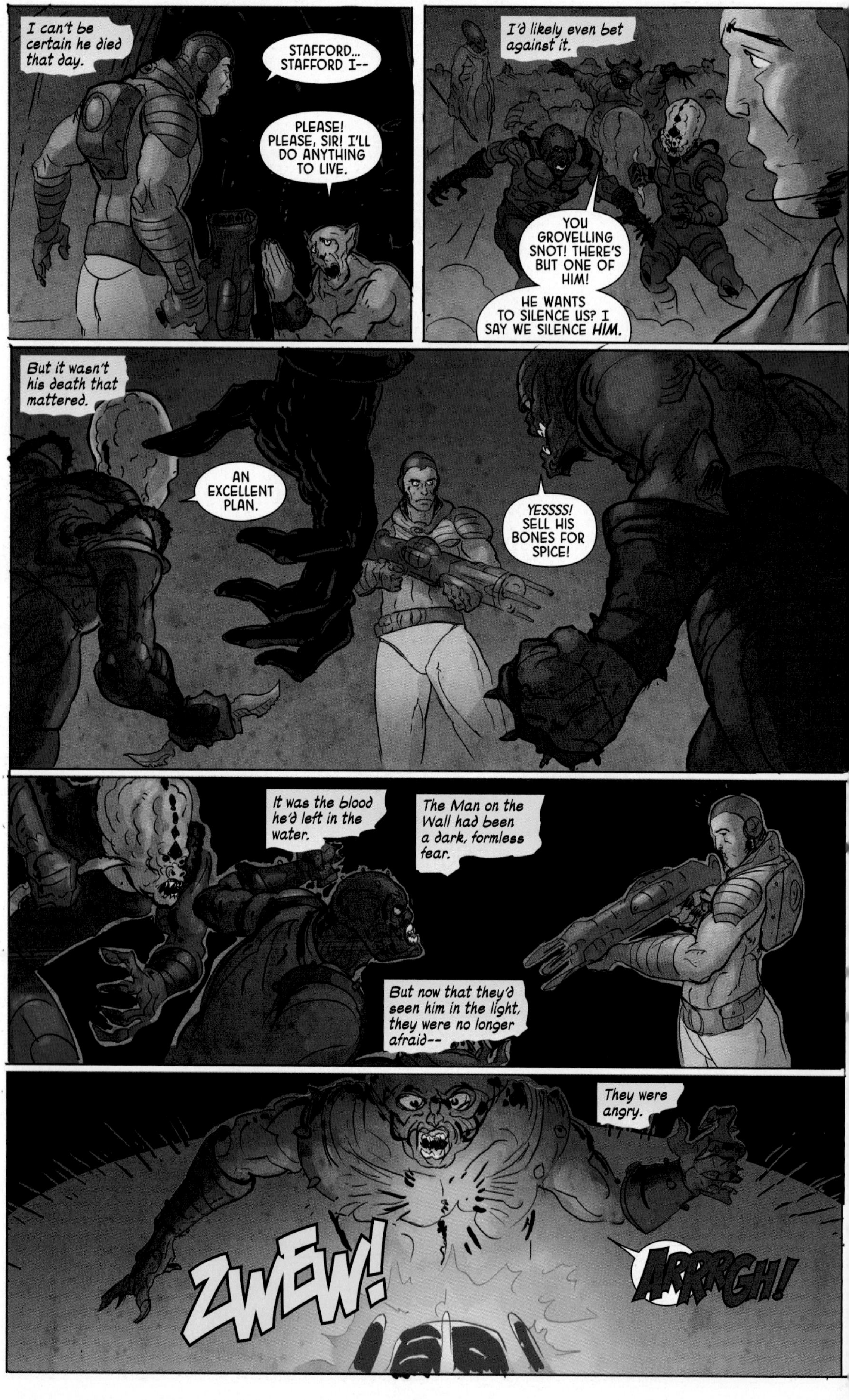

I can't be certain he died that day.
STAFFORD... STAFFORD I--
PLEASE! PLEASE, SIR! I'LL DO ANYTHING TO LIVE.
I'd likely even bet against it.
YOU GROVELLING SNOT! THERE'S BUT ONE OF HIM!
HE WANTS TO SILENCE US? I SAY WE SILENCE HIM.
But it wasn't his death that mattered.
AN EXCELLENT PLAN.
YESSSS! SELL HIS BONES FOR SPICE!
It was the blood he'd left in the water.
The Man on the Wall had been a dark, formless fear.
But now that they'd seen him in the light, they were no longer afraid--
They were angry.
ZWEW!
ARRRGH!

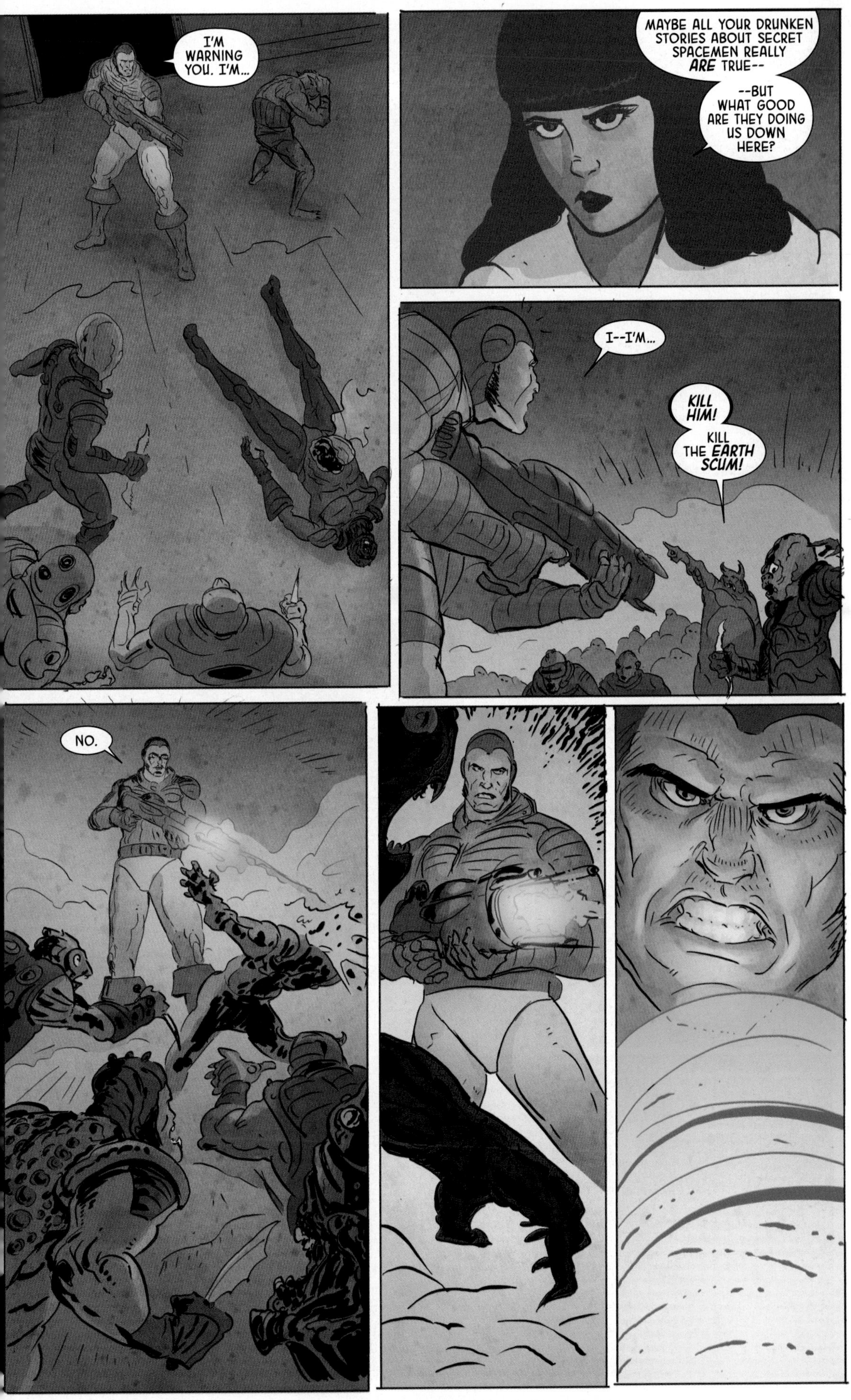
I'M WARNING YOU. I'M...
MAYBE ALL YOUR DRUNKEN STORIES ABOUT SECRET SPACEMEN REALLY ARE TRUE--
--BUT WHAT GOOD ARE THEY DOING US DOWN HERE?
I--I'M...
KILL HIM!
KILL THE EARTH SCUM!
NO.

I--I--I'M ALIVE?

SP-SP-SPARED?

OH. OH, *THANK YOU,* SIR. M-M-MOX... MOX IS GOOD FOR HIS WORD!

NO--NO ONE WILL KNOW, NO ONE WILL EVER, EVER...

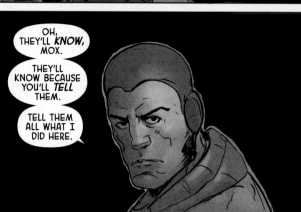

OH, THEY'LL *KNOW,* MOX.

THEY'LL KNOW BECAUSE YOU'LL *TELL* THEM.

TELL THEM ALL WHAT I DID HERE.

"TELL THEM THAT I'M OUT HERE. AMONG THEM.

"A WHISPER. A SHADOW. A GHOST THAT HAUNTS THEM.

"YOU'LL TELL THEM IF THEY EVEN *THINK* OF COMING FOR EARTH--

"THE MAN ON THE WALL WILL COME FOR *THEM.*"

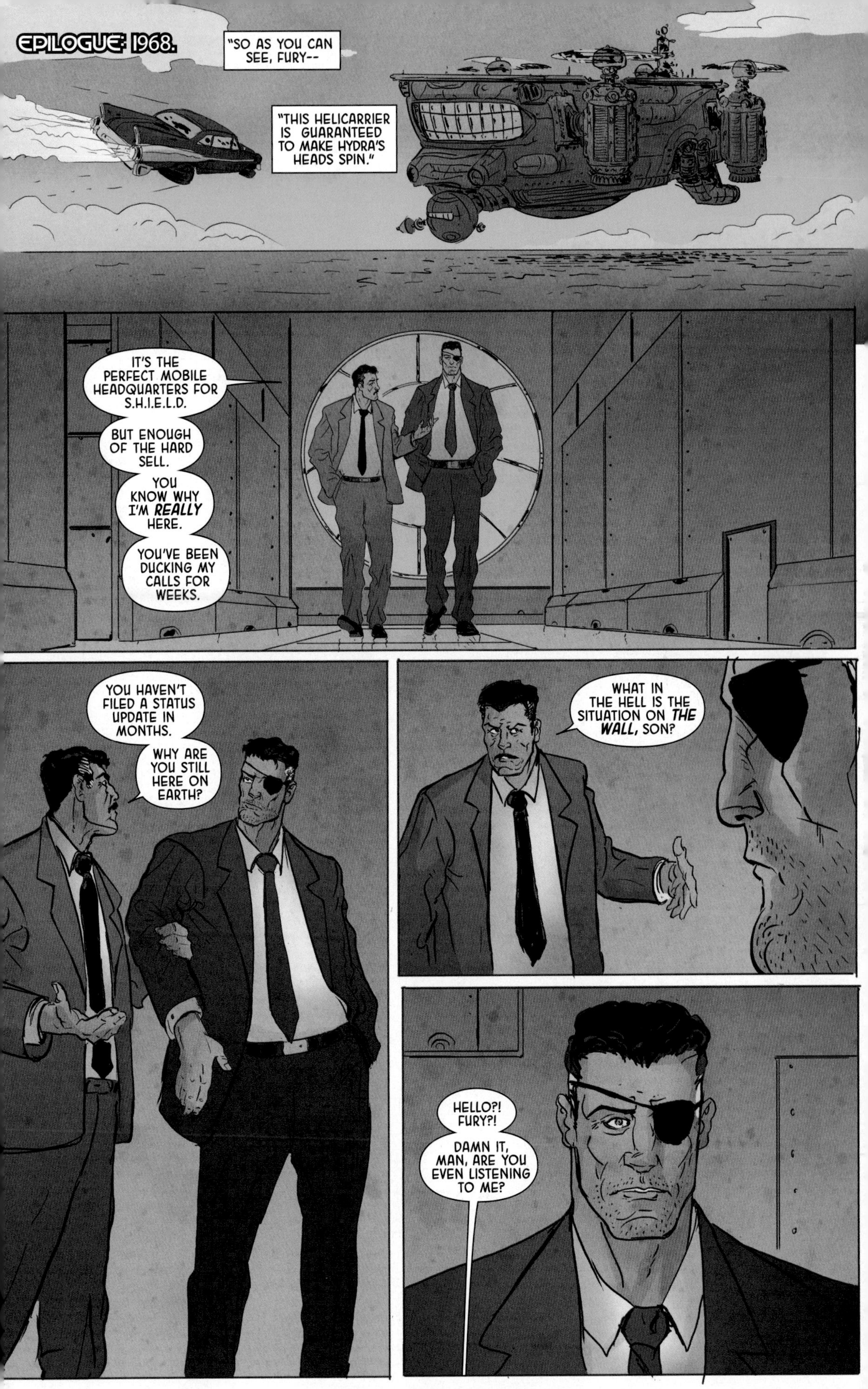
EPILOGUE: 1968.
"SO AS YOU CAN SEE, FURY--
"THIS HELICARRIER IS GUARANTEED TO MAKE HYDRA'S HEADS SPIN."
IT'S THE PERFECT MOBILE HEADQUARTERS FOR S.H.I.E.L.D.
BUT ENOUGH OF THE HARD SELL.
YOU KNOW WHY I'M *REALLY* HERE.
YOU'VE BEEN DUCKING MY CALLS FOR WEEKS.
YOU HAVEN'T FILED A STATUS UPDATE IN MONTHS.
WHY ARE YOU STILL HERE ON EARTH?
WHAT IN THE HELL IS THE SITUATION ON *THE WALL,* SON?
HELLO?! FURY?!
DAMN IT, MAN, ARE YOU EVEN LISTENING TO ME?

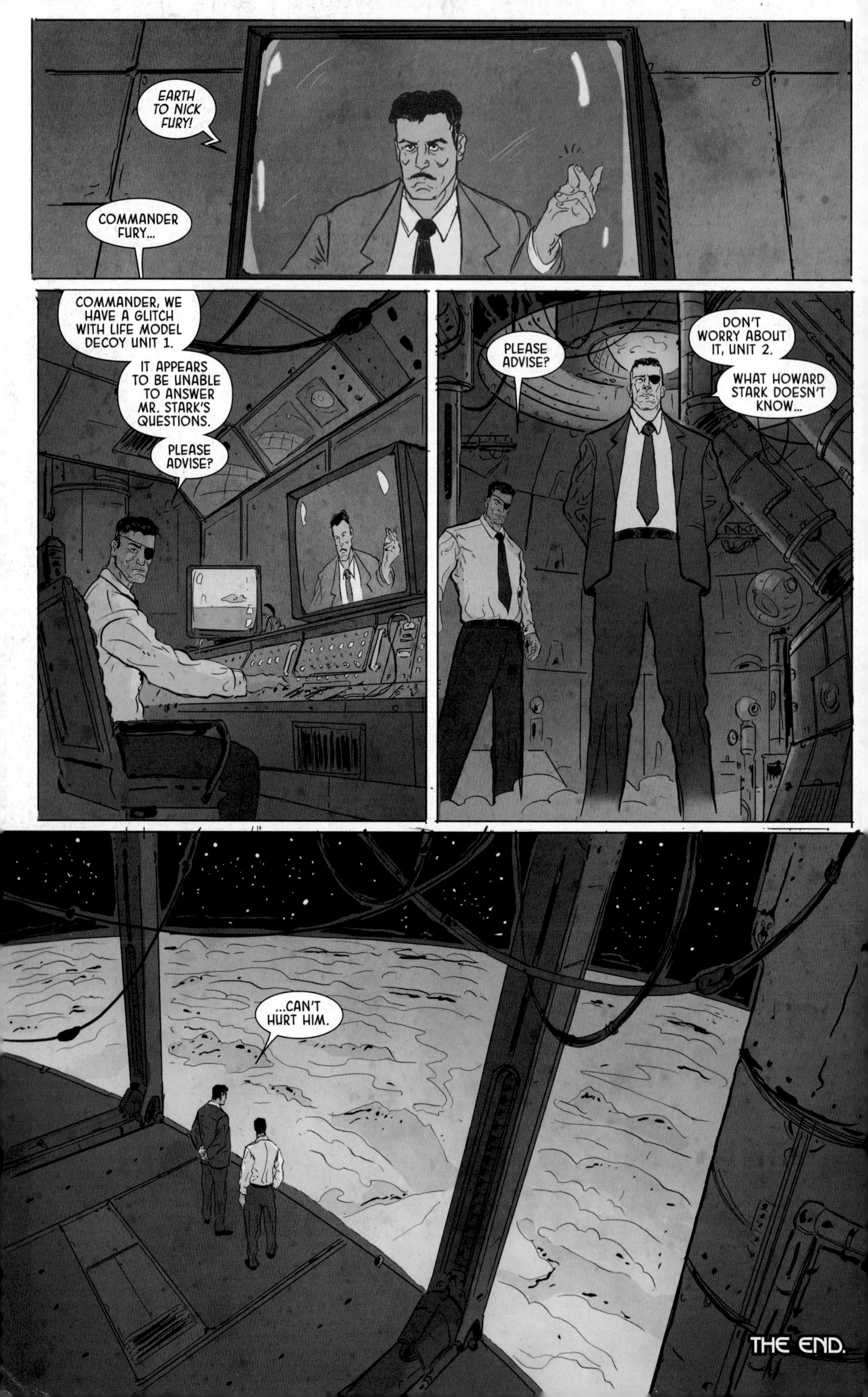
EARTH TO NICK FURY!
COMMANDER FURY...
COMMANDER, WE HAVE A GLITCH WITH LIFE MODEL DECOY UNIT 1.
IT APPEARS TO BE UNABLE TO ANSWER MR. STARK'S QUESTIONS.
PLEASE ADVISE?
PLEASE ADVISE?
DON'T WORRY ABOUT IT, UNIT 2.
WHAT HOWARD STARK DOESN'T KNOW...
...CAN'T HURT HIM.
THE END.

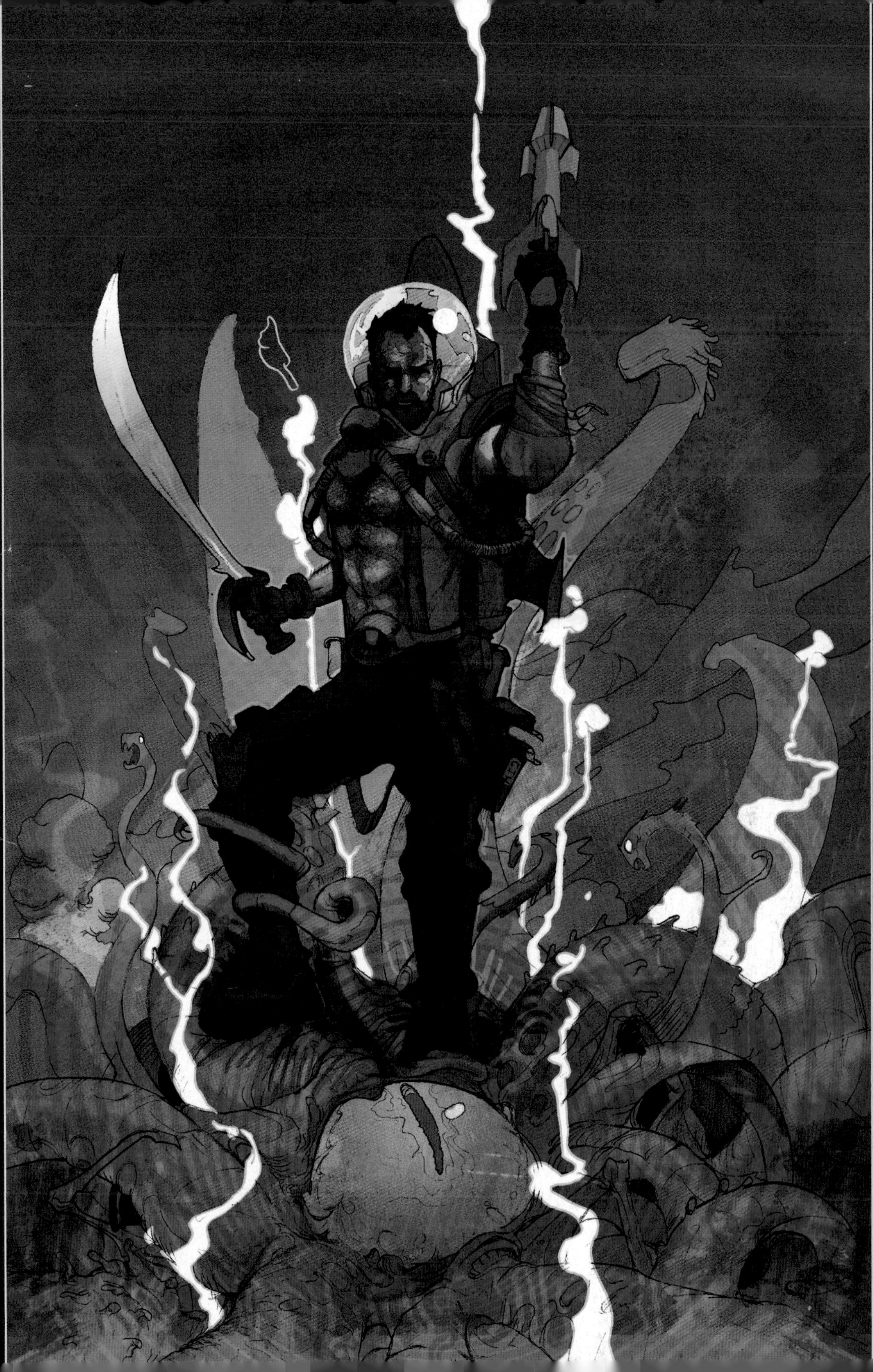

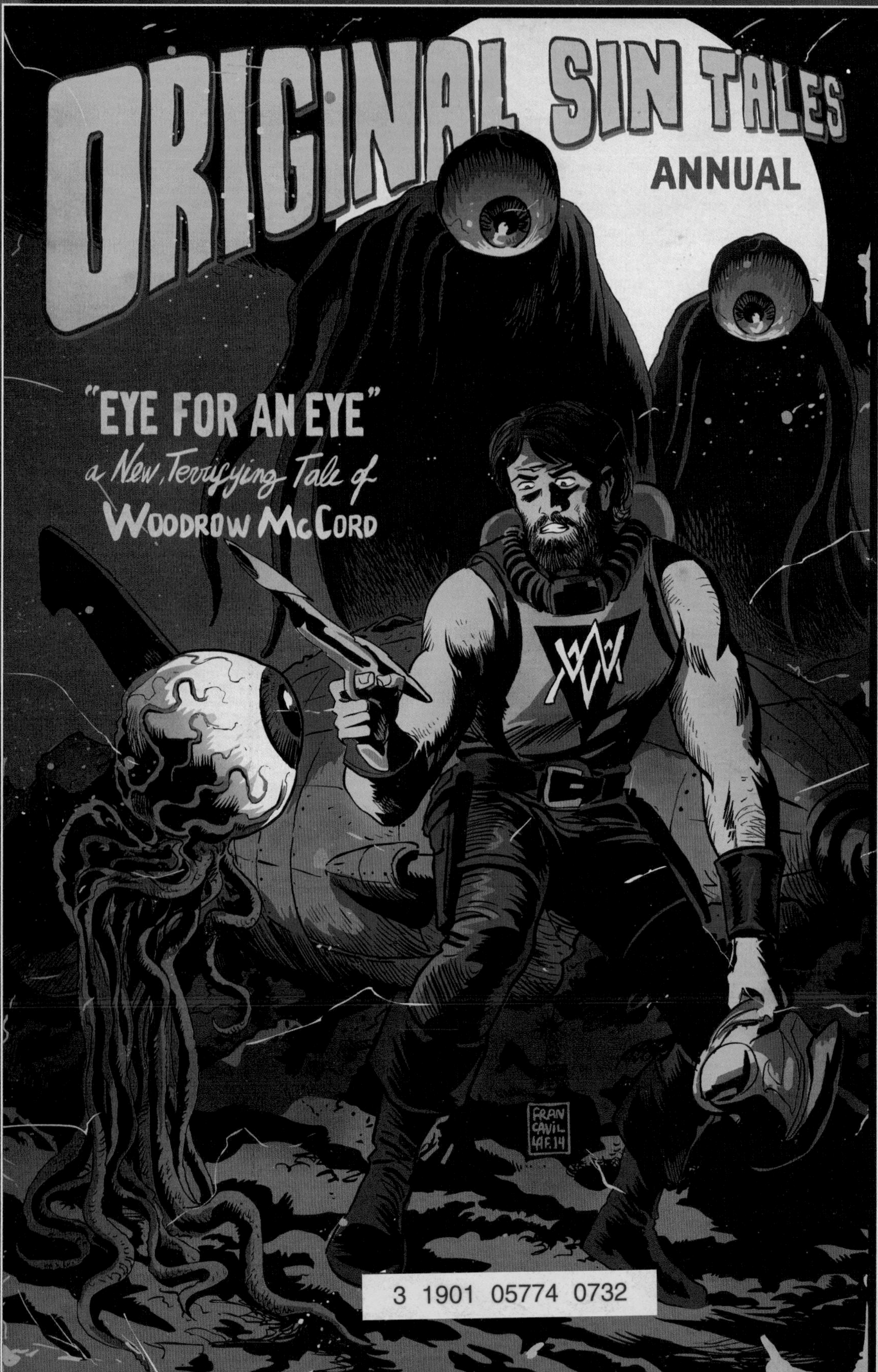
ORIGINAL SIN TALES
ANNUAL
"EYE FOR AN EYE"
a New, Terrifying Tale of
WOODROW McCORD